Student Manual

Theories of Psychotherapy and Counseling
Concepts and Cases
FIFTH EDITION

Richard S. Sharf
University of Delaware

Prepared by

Richard S. Sharf
University of Delaware

BROOKS/COLE
CENGAGE Learning

Australia • Brazil • Japan • Korea • Mexico • Singapore • Spain • United Kingdom • United States

ISBN-13: 978-0-8400-3474-8
ISBN-10: 0-8400-3474-1

Brooks/Cole
20 Davis Drive
Belmont, CA 94002-3098
USA

Cengage Learning is a leading provider of customized learning solutions with office locations around the globe, including Singapore, the United Kingdom, Australia, Mexico, Brazil, and Japan. Locate your local office at:
www.cengage.com/global

Cengage Learning products are represented in Canada by Nelson Education, Ltd.

To learn more about Brooks/Cole, visit
www.cengage.com/brookscole

Purchase any of our products at your local college store or at our preferred online store
www.cengagebrain.com

Printed in the United States of America
1 2 3 4 5 6 7 15 14 13 12 11

TABLE OF CONTENTS

PREFACE

This Student Manual is designed to help students use the text, Theories of Psychotherapy and Counseling: Concepts and Cases, Fifth Edition. Like the text book, this manual focuses on cases. The core of the manual is the opportunity for the student to take the role of a therapist using one theory and try to apply concepts and techniques to a "client." The student can then apply techniques that he or she learns in the chapter by answering multiple-choice and (less frequently) open-ended questions.

There are several sections of the manual that help students understand the theories and learn significant concepts. The self-inventory assists students in seeing how similar their views of therapy are to theorists'. The self-inventory also helps students get a brief overview of the theorists' approaches to helping clients. Background information about the theory is presented in outline form to give students an overview of factors that led to the development of the theory. Concepts that are defined in the glossary are also defined in the personality theory and techniques sections. Case studies illustrate the personality theory and techniques. Students then answer questions about the cases. For difficult questions, immediate feedback is given to students about the correctness of their responses. For other questions, answers are provided at the end of each chapter. In the special topics section, students answer open-ended questions about current trends, using a theory with other theories, gender issues, and multicultural issues. To help students think critically about theories, another section asks them to list the strengths and limitations of each theory. The final section of most chapters includes 10 true-false and 15 multiple-choice questions.

There are several different ways to use the Student Manual. Taking the self-inventory before reading the chapter will help provide an overview of the chapter. Students can read the entire chapter and then skim the concepts in the manual and answer questions about them and about the cases. Another approach is to read each major section in the text and then review the corresponding section in the manual. Some instructors may wish to discuss the cases described in the manual in class. The quizzes at the end of the chapter can be used when students have finished the chapter or they can be saved for review for exams.

ACKNOWLEDGMENTS

In writing this manual, I received the help of several experts who reviewed the manuscript for accuracy and relevance. I would like to thank the following individuals who read the entire Student Manual: Kris Bronson, private practice; Christopher Faiver, John Carroll University; Jodie Janisak, University of Delaware; Beverly Palmer, California State University—Dominquez.

I am very appreciative of the helpfulness of the following individuals who critiqued specific chapters.

Chapter 2: Psychoanalysis—Michele Downie, University of Delaware
Chapter 4: Adlerian Therapy—Michael Maniacci, Adler School of Professional Psychology
Chapter 6: Person-Centered Therapy—Douglas Bower, private practice
Chapter 7: Gestalt Therapy—Gary Yontef, private practice
Chapter 9: Rational Emotive Behavior Therapy—Albert Ellis, The Albert Ellis Institute
Chapter 10: Cognitive Therapy—Christine Reilly, University of Delaware
Chapter 11: Reality Therapy—Robert Wubbolding, Center for Reality Therapy

I would also like to thank Lisa Sweder for typing earlier versions of this manuscript. Additionally, I wish to thank Mia Dreyer of Cengage Learning who provided assistance with this manuscript. Finally, I would like to thank my wife Jane for her proofreading and editorial comments.

Richard S. Sharf

October 31, 2010

CHAPTER 1

INTRODUCTION

STUDENT MANUAL OUTLINE

The purpose of this manual is to help you learn concepts basic to theories of personality and techniques of change used in a variety of theories of psychotherapy. There are seven major sections in each chapter:

1. A self-inventory to compare your views of counseling and psychotherapy to those of the theorist or theorists is at the beginning of most of the chapters.

2. A chart that summarizes influences on the theorist(s) and important contributions by the theorist or theorists.

3. Basic information about the personality theory is summarized and important concepts are defined. Using multiple-choice questions, and occasionally open-ended questions, you are presented with a case study and asked to assess or identify aspects of the client's personality as well as goals of treatment from one theoretical perspective. When multiple-choice questions are difficult and require an explanation, answers are given following the question; otherwise, they are placed at the end of each chapter.

4. Techniques or methods of change are summarized and defined. You are asked to be the client's therapist and choose the appropriate response that you would make to the client from the point of view of the theory. Sometimes you will be asked to decide on a technique to use or a general therapeutic direction. This exercise should help you to acquire a clearer understanding of the theory.

5. Open-ended questions are asked so that you can summarize and clarify special topics that are discussed in each chapter. Page numbers from the text that contain the answers are given at the end of each question.

6. You will be asked to summarize what you believe are the strengths and limitations of each theory. If you want hints, see the Critique section on page 653 of Chapter 16.

7. In the final section of each chapter, there is a quiz consisting (usually) of 10 true and false questions and 15 multiple-choice questions. The quiz is followed by an answer key that includes answers to questions given in case examples and other parts of each chapter as well as to the quiz.

ABBREVIATIONS THAT ARE USED IN THE STUDENT MANUAL

Q = Quiz question, answers at the end of each chapter

OE = Open ended question

*OE = Open ended question with answers at the end of each chapter

HOW TO USE THIS STUDENT MANUAL

You may choose to use the Student Manual in the same way for each chapter or you may alter your approach. I will give you my suggestions about how to use this guide as you read the text.

1. Before you read each chapter in the text, complete the self inventory at the beginning of each chapter in this guide. The questions will give you a broad idea of what to expect in the chapter and how different the theorist's views are from your own.

2. Skim the definitions of concepts in the Student Manual. This will help you learn the essence of the theory.

3. Read the chapter in the text.

4. Complete the rest of the material in the Student Manual for that chapter. You may want to delay taking the quiz at the end of each chapter until you start to prepare for an exam.

CHAPTER ONE: INTRODUCTION

This chapter explains important concepts such as the meanings of theory, counseling, and psychotherapy. A very brief summary of each chapter is given. Then, I describe the important chapter segments and how the Student Manual will help with each segment. Definitions of concepts that are used throughout the text, such as terms for psychological disorders, are presented here. A 25 item quiz on Chapter 1 of the text concludes the chapter.

THEORY

Theories are a group of related laws or relationships that are used to provide explanations within a discipline. In counseling and psychotherapy, theories provide an understanding of personality and methods that help individuals change behaviors, thoughts, or feelings, as well as gain insights into each of these. The criteria that are used to evaluate theories are defined here.

clarity Rules must be clear and specific. Operational definitions are used to define procedures used in theories.

operational definition An empirical definition that seeks to specify procedures that are used to measure a variable or to distinguish it from others.

2

comprehensiveness Theories differ in the types of events they make predictions about. Some theories predict many related events; others have a more limited goal.

testability A theory must be able to be verified or confirmed through research.

usefulness A theory should provide methods or concepts that can be applied to problems in the field of study.

PSYCHOTHERAPY AND COUNSELING

There are many different views on how psychotherapy and counseling are similar. Increasingly, most therapists see a broad overlap between the two. Many of the theorists discussed in this text do not make a distinction between counseling and psychotherapy as it applies to their theories. When there is a distinction, I will describe what the distinction is. Generally, I will use psychotherapy and counseling interchangeably to describe the process of helping others with emotional or psychological problems.

The terms patient and client are also used interchangeably in this text. Theories that are derived by psychiatrists and are used in a medical setting tend to use patient. Those people seen in a non-medical setting are usually called clients. Often, I will use the term that the theorist and practitioners of the theory use.

THEORIES OF PSYCHOTHERAPY AND COUNSELING

Estimates of the number of theories of counseling and psychotherapy suggest that there may be over 400. About 30 of these theories are included in this text. Surveys such as those on page 5 of the text indicate the popularity of various theories. Many therapists use more than one theory. Those who apply techniques from a variety of theories are called integrative therapists. Integration of theories is discussed in Chapter 17.

Only those theories that have been used by a number of practitioners and have published information about them are included here. These theories represent a very wide range of approaches. To provide a sense of the wide range of theories, I will summarize each in a sentence. This should give you a broad, though partial, overview of the different approaches.

Chapter 2. Psychoanalysis. Psychoanalytic approaches emphasize the importance of unconscious processes and the impact of childhood experiences (prior to the age of 6) on the development of personality.

Chapter 3. Jungian Analysis. Universal patterns that are reflected in the unconscious processes of all people as they affect the patient are brought into consciousness.

Chapter 4. Adlerian Therapy. Early relationships in the family can lead to dysfunctional beliefs which become the focus of therapy.

Chapter 5. Existential Therapy. A philosophy for understanding human existence becomes the basis for helping clients deal with life themes such as death, freedom, responsibility, and meaninglessness.

Chapter 6. Person-Centered Therapy. Client change comes about from understanding the client and communicating that understanding to the client so that an atmosphere of trust can develop which fosters client growth.

Chapter 7. Gestalt Therapy. Therapists emphasize psychological and bodily awareness that leads to greater client self-responsibility and self-awareness.

3

Chapter 8. Behavior Therapy. Scientific principles of behavior, such as reinforcement and modeling, are used to bring about changes in clients' behaviors or actions.

Chapter 9. Rational Emotive Behavior Therapy. Challenging irrational beliefs through disputing techniques and teaching rational ways of acting and thinking is the focus of this therapy.

Chapter 10. Cognitive Therapy. Clients are taught to recognize a variety of distorted thoughts and replace them with more accurate thoughts.

Chapter 11. Reality Therapy. Individuals learn to be responsible for their lives and to take control of what they do, think, and feel.

Chapter 12. Constructivist Approaches. Therapists try to understand clients' constructs or ways of viewing the problem. Solution-focused therapists ask questions to get at ways to solve the problem. Narrative therapists view client problems as stories. They try to develop positive endings (or solutions) to the stories.

Chapter 13. Feminist Therapy. Emphasis is placed on dealing with problems that society creates for clients (especially women and minorities) and empowering them to deal effectively with these problems.

Chapter 14. Family Systems Therapy. Viewing the family as a single unit, assessing interactions within the family, and making suggestions for change are the focus of four therapies discussed in this chapter.

Chapter 15. Other Therapies. Five different therapies are explained. Asian therapies emphasize quiet reflection and personal responsibility to others. Body psychotherapies assess and manipulate the body to bring about psychological change. Interpersonal therapy is used with depression and focuses on changes in four areas of problems. In psychodrama, clients and audience or group members play roles to enact their problems, and the therapist directs and facilitates this process. Creative arts therapies include art, dance movement, drama, and music to encourage expressive action and therapeutic change.

Chapter 16. Comparison and Critique. This chapter summarizes the theories in this text and critiques them. The chapter should provide help for you when preparing for exams for this course.

Chapter 17. Integrative Theories. Integrative theorists combine two or more theories to help their clients. Three different integrative approaches are explained, as well as methods to make your own integrative theory.

ORGANIZATION OF THE CHAPTERS

To help you use this Student Manual in conjunction with the text, I will briefly describe the contents of each major section. In this way you can see how the Student Manual will help you learn the content of each section of the text.

HISTORY OR BACKGROUND

Text. To understand each theory, I describe its development. Usually this includes information about the lives of the theorists and important personal and intellectual influences on the development of their theories as well as their own writings. The theorists' use of specific psychological and philosophical ideas that were available at the time the theorists were developing their theories are explained.

> *Student Manual.* Using tables, I list people who influenced the theorists as well as their significant writings or contributions.

PERSONALITY THEORY

Text. How theorists understand personality is the basis for making therapeutic change. I describe and illustrate each concept that the theorists use to understand individuals' personalities.

> *Student Manual.* The personality theory is briefly described. Most concepts that the theorists use in their theory are defined. In most chapters, I use a case example in which you become the therapist. Using a multiple choice format, you select the personality concept that best fits the client.

THEORY OF PSYCHOTHERAPY

Text. This is the most important section of each chapter. The goals of the theory show the theorists' approach to bringing about change. Assessment methods indicate how theorists plan to assess personality and decide which therapeutic approaches to take. The techniques or methods used by the theorists are described here. Several case illustrations help to explain the techniques and methods.

> *Student Manual.* Goals and approaches to assessment are briefly summarized. For almost all of the techniques, a definition is given. Using the same case that illustrates personality concepts, you pick the therapeutic response or statement that you would use to help the client and that is most consistent with the theory. In this way, you can try to put the theory into practice or try it out.

PSYCHOLOGICAL DISORDERS

Text. For each theory, I give between three and five case examples to illustrate the theory. Each example represents a different diagnostic category or problem type. The purpose of these examples is to show how therapists use techniques and methods to bring about positive changes in their clients' lives. You can also compare theories across problem type. For example, you can compare how Adlerian therapists and cognitive therapists help individuals who are depressed.

> *Student Manual.* This Student Manual does not focus on specific psychological disorders but rather on becoming familiar with theories of psychotherapy and counseling. However, throughout the text, reference is made to disorders such as depression, anxiety, phobias, borderline disorders and many others. Chapter 1 explains these terms, giving examples. A textbook on abnormal psychology would give much more detailed explanation. During your course, you may have a need to find a brief definition of one or more of these terms. For that reason, I am listing their definitions in alphabetical order to use as a reference. Like almost all terms defined in this Student Manual, they may also be found in the glossary of the text.

anorexia A disorder in which individuals are unable to eat food, may have a severe decrease in appetite, and have an intense fear of becoming obese even when emaciated. Anorexia is diagnosed when individuals lose at least 25 percent of their normal weight.

anxiety An unpleasant feeling of fear and/or apprehension accompanied by physiological changes such as fast pulse, quick breathing, sweating, flushing, muscle aches, or stomach tension.

borderline personality disorder Characteristics include unstable interpersonal relationships and rapid mood changes in a short period of time. Behavior is often erratic, unpredictable, and impulsive in areas such as spending, eating, sex, or gambling. Emotional relationships tend to be intense, with individuals becoming easily angry or disappointed in the relationship.

bulimia Binge eating and inappropriate methods of preventing weight gain, such as vomiting and use of laxatives, characterize bulimia.

compulsion An irresistible impulse to repeat behaviors continually.

5

conversion disorder A disorder in which a psychological disturbance takes a physical form, such as when arms or legs are paralyzed and there is no physiological explanation.

delusions Beliefs that are contrary to reality and are firmly held despite evidence that they are inaccurate.

depression An emotional state characterized by deep sadness, feelings of worthlessness, guilt, and withdrawal from others. Other symptoms include difficulty in sleeping, loss of appetite or sexual desire, and loss of interest in normal activities. When not accompanied by manic episodes, it is usually referred to as major depression or unipolar depression.

drug abuse Using a drug to the extent that individuals have difficulty meeting social and occupational obligations.

generalized anxiety disorder One of a group of anxiety disorders, it is characterized by a persistent pervasive state of tension. Physical symptoms may include a pounding heart, fast pulse and breathing, sweating, muscle aches, and stomach upset. Individuals may be easily distractible and fearful that something bad is going to happen.

hallucinations Perceiving (seeing, hearing, feeling, tasting, or smelling) things that are not there.

hysteria A disorder occurring when psychological disturbances take a physical form and there is no physiological explanation, such as an unexplained paralysis of the arms or legs. This term has been replaced by conversion reaction in common usage.

mania (manic episodes) Individuals may demonstrate unfounded elation as indicated by making grandiose plans, being extremely talkative, easily distracted, and engaging in purposeless activity.

narcissistic personality disorder A pattern of self-importance; a need for admiration from others, and a lack of empathy for others are common characteristics of individuals with this disorder. Boasting or being pretentious and feeling that one is superior to others and deserves recognition are also prominent characteristics.

neurosis A large group of disorders characterized by unrealistic anxiety, fears, or obsessions. They are contrasted with more severe psychotic disorders.

obsessions Pervasive and uncontrollable recurring thoughts that interfere with day-to-day functioning.

obsessive-compulsive disorder Persistent and uncontrollable thoughts or feelings in which individuals feel compelled to repeat behaviors again and again.

personality disorders These are characterized by being inflexible, lasting many years or a lifetime, and include traits that make social or occupational functioning difficult.

phobia Fear of a situation or object out of proportion to the danger of the situation or the threatening qualities of the object. Examples include fear of heights, rats, or spiders.

posttraumatic stress disorder (PTSD) Extreme reactions to a highly stressful or traumatic event such as being raped, robbed, or assaulted define PTSD. Resulting behaviors may include being easily startled, having recurrent dreams or nightmares, or feeling estranged from or afraid of others.

psychosis A broad term used for severe mental disorders in which thinking and emotion are so impaired that individuals have lost contact with reality.

schizophrenia Severe disturbances of thought, emotions, or behaviors may be evident by observing disorganized speech and obtaining reports of delusions or hallucinations.

sociopathy Also called antisocial personality or psychopathic, this term refers to behavior which shows no regard for others, an inability to form meaningful relationships, and a lack of responsibility for one's own actions.

somatoform disorders Physical symptoms are known and present, but there is no physiological cause, and a psychological cause is suspected. Reporting headaches or stomachaches when no physiological cause can be found constitutes an example of somatoform disorders.

BRIEF THERAPY

Text. Sometimes called short-term therapy, brief therapy refers to limiting therapy to a certain number of sessions. Time-limited therapy is a term that refers to a theoretical approach that is designed to be completed in a certain number of sessions. Often several aspects of therapy are to be completed in sessions one through three, and other aspects in sessions four through seven, and so forth. Many therapeutic approaches are brief in their general therapeutic plans. The theory that has developed many different methods of brief or time-limited therapy is psychoanalysis.

>*Student Manual.* Brief therapy is addressed directly in Chapter 2 of this guide and in a few other chapters where there is specific reference to time limits or brief therapy such as Chapters 12, 13, and 14. The Special Topics section of the guide often includes a question about the duration of therapy.

CURRENT TRENDS

Text. Theories are often growing and changing. Depending on research or other factors, theories may be modified or changed. Sometimes they are applied to new client populations. These trends are described in the book. Three specific trends that are addressed for almost all of the theories in the book are treatment manuals, evidence-based psychotherapy, and postmodernism. Within postmodernism two important philosophical areas that address psychotherapy are constructivism and social constructionism.

treatment manuals Written guidelines for therapists on how to treat patients with a particular disorder. They describe skills to be used and the specific sequencing of these skills.

research supported psychological treatments (RSPT) Therapies that have been tested to be effective are said to be research supported psychological treatments. Strict criteria for thorough research procedures are used to determine whether or not therapy is effective.

postmodernism A philosophical position that does not assume that there is a fixed truth, but rather that individuals have their own perception of reality or the truth.

modernism Modernists take a rationalist view, believing that there is scientific truth which can be achieved through advances in technology and science.

constructivism Believing that individuals create their own views or constructs of events or relationships in their own lives.

social constructionism A constructivist point of view that focuses on the shared meanings that people in a culture or society develop.

>*Student Manual.* In a section called Special Topics, you will be asked to summarize some specific current trends.

7

USING A THEORY WITH OTHER THEORIES

Text. Theories vary as to how open they are to using methods and techniques of other theories. Also, some theories are more easily incorporated into the methods of other theories. This section describes one theory as it relates to other theories, especially those that are similar to it.

> *Student Manual*. Usually, I will include a question about using one theory with another in the Special Topics section.

RESEARCH

Text. Theories vary widely as to the amount of research that has been done on testing specific concepts or in studying the effectiveness of therapy. I describe recent typical investigations for many of the theories. Also, there have been meta-analyses to examine the results of many studies. Because research is a complex topic, only some of the most basic concepts are discussed in Chapter 1. These concepts are defined here.

factorial design A research method that can study more than one variable at a time.

meta-analysis A method of statistically summarizing the results of a large number of studies.

methodology A systematic application of procedures used in research investigations.

pretest-posttest control group design Comparing a group given one treatment to another group given another treatment or no treatment by testing individuals before and after therapy.

patient focused research Monitors the progress of clients and then uses this information to develop treatment methods.

> *Student Manual*. Because I concentrate on helping you understand personality theory concepts and techniques of change, I do not address research in this guide except briefly in Chapter 16. Also, to further summarize summaries of research tends to give a simplified overview of therapy research. Despite my reservations, I have done this on pages 645 to 647 of the text in Chapter 16.

GENDER ISSUES

Text. Many people have asked whether or not a theory can be applied fairly to both men and women. Chapter 13, Feminist Therapy, addresses the question most thoroughly. However, gender issues have been addressed by therapists who follow each theoretical orientation described in the text. Using these writings, I have described issues as they affect gender for each of the major theories in the text.

> *Student Manual*. In the Special Topics part of each chapter of this guide, I ask a question about how information in this section in the text applies to gender issues in the theory.

MULTICULTURAL ISSUES

Text. The consideration of the application of theory to people with diverse cultural backgrounds has been relatively recent (since the 1960s and 1970s). The relationship between culture and therapy has been of particular interest in the 1990s. Psychoanalysis, the theory that was developed first, has been particularly subject to criticism in part due to its origins in 19th century Vienna. Some early theorists such as Carl Jung and Erik Erikson were interested in issues that relate to people living in cultures that were very different from traditional Western culture. Chapter 13, Feminist Therapy, uses a multicultural model and provides some techniques that can be used with individuals from different cultures as well as genders. Each chapter describes how multicultural issues have been addressed within the theory.

Student Manual. In the Special Topics part of each chapter of this guide, I ask a question about how information in this section in the text applies to multicultural issues in the theory.

GROUP THERAPY

Text. All theories that have been applied to individual therapy have also been adapted for group therapy. Therapists as well as theorists differ in terms of the importance that they place on group therapy. This section shows how concepts and methods from the theory can be applied to group therapy.

> *Student Manual*. In the Special Topics section of this guide, I have summarized how each theory can be applied to group therapy. This information can also be found on pages 650 to 652 of the text.

ETHICS

Regardless of their theories of psychotherapy or counseling, all practitioners must adhere to a code of ethics. All therapists, psychiatrists, psychologists, counselors, social workers, psychiatric nurses, pastoral counselors, marriage counselors, and sex therapists must follow their own code of professional ethics. Theories do not have their own code of ethics; rather their principles, concepts, and techniques must be consistent with professional ethical guidelines. Although there are minor differences between ethical guidelines that various mental health professionals adhere to, there are many more similarities.

Many graduate training programs have entire courses that deal with ethical principles. I have chosen not to go into detail about ethics because this subject is handled better elsewhere. Furthermore, theories of psychotherapy follow ethical guidelines; they do not make them. Unethical behavior would not be sanctioned by any theory of therapy discussed in this book.

THE INTRODUCTION: A QUIZ

True or false items. Decide if the following items are more "true" or more "false" as they apply to concepts discussed in the first chapter.

T F   Q1. For a theory to be applied to psychotherapy, it should be tested through research.

T F   Q2. Operational definitions only apply to medicine, not to psychology or counseling.

T F   Q3. Definitions of psychotherapy and counseling overlap so much that they are used interchangeably in the text.

T F   Q4. Psychodynamic or psychoanalytic therapies are derived from the work of Sigmund Freud.

T F   Q5. Two types of depression are unipolar and bipolar depression.

T F   Q6. Compulsions are thoughts that cannot be controlled.

T F   Q7. Neuroses are more severe in their effects than psychoses.

T F   Q8. If a psychological cause is suspected for a physiological problem, then that individual may have a somatoform disorder.

T F   Q9. Each theory of psychotherapy has its own ethical code.

T F   Q10. Each theory of psychotherapy has its own techniques of research which it applies to testing the effectiveness of its procedures.

9

Multiple choice items. Select the best answer from the alternatives given.

_____ Q11. Which of the following is the LEAST important characteristic of a theory?

    a. precision
    b. comprehensiveness
    c. simplicity
    d. testability
    e. usefulness

_____ Q12. Operational definitions are useful to a theory because they help establish

    a. clarity.
    b. comprehensiveness.
    c. simplicity.
    d. usefulness.

_____ Q13. An integrative therapist is one who

    a. is a counselor.
    b. is a psychologist.
    c. draws from more than one theory of therapy or counseling.
    d. appreciates the uniqueness of each client.

_____ Q14. The number of theories of therapy is likely to be more than

    a. 4.
    b. 40.
    c. 400.
    d. 4000.

_____ Q15. The major difference between "patients" and "clients" is that

    a. patients are more deeply disturbed than clients.
    b. patients pay higher fees than clients.
    c. patients are covered by health maintenance organizations and clients are not.
    d. none of the above.

_____ Q16. Muscle tension and restlessness are symptoms associated with

    a. depression.
    b. generalized anxiety disorder.
    c. borderline disorder.
    d. obsessive-compulsive disorder.
    e. somatoform disorder.

_____ Q17. Becoming extremely talkative and "hyper" are sometimes symptoms found in a type of

    a. depression.
    b. phobia.
    c. borderline disorder.
    d. obsessive-compulsive disorder.
    e. somatoform disorder.

_____ Q18. A pattern of unstable relationships is a characteristic of

    a.   depression.
    b.   generalized anxiety disorder.
    c.   borderline disorder.
    d.   posttraumatic stress disorder.
    e.   a phobia.

_____ Q19. A reaction to being robbed in your home at gunpoint may lead to a variety of reactions, but the most common is likely to be

    a.   depression.
    b.   generalized anxiety disorder.
    c.   a borderline disorder.
    d.   posttraumatic stress disorder.
    e.   a phobia.

_____ Q20. A fear of heights is characteristic of

    a.   depression.
    b.   generalized anxiety disorder.
    c.   a borderline disorder.
    d.   posttraumatic stress disorder.
    e.   a phobia.

_____ Q21. "Black flack runs in packs, blue, blue" is a statement that is most likely to be made by someone with symptoms of

    a.   hysteria.
    b.   borderline disorder.
    c.   narcissistic personality disorder.
    d.   schizophrenia.

_____ Q22. Hearing a voice in one's head that is screaming loudly is an example of

    a.   a delusion.
    b.   an hallucination.
    c.   a conversion reaction.
    d.   psychological dependency

_____ Q23. Going back to check to see if you locked your front door 12 times in a row is called

    a.   a delusion.
    b.   an hallucination.
    c.   a compulsion.
    d.   an obsession.
    e.   being thorough.

_____ Q24. The philosophical view that individuals create their own reality as opposed to the existence of a fixed truth is called

    a.   existentialism.
    b.   modernism.
    c.   postmodernism.
    d.   rationalism.

_____ Q25. A professional group's code of ethics can be applied to the practice of

    a.   no theories of psychotherapy and counseling.
    b.   one theory of psychotherapy and counseling.
    c.   some theories of psychotherapy and counseling.
    d.   all theories of psychotherapy and counseling.

ANSWER KEY

Q1.	T	Q11.	c	Q21.	d
Q2.	F	Q12.	a	Q22.	b
Q3.	T	Q13.	c	Q23.	c
Q4.	T	Q14.	c	Q24.	c
Q5.	T	Q15.	d	Q25.	d
Q6.	F	Q16.	b		
Q7.	F	Q17.	a		
Q8.	T	Q18.	c		
Q9.	F	Q19.	d		
Q10.	F	Q20.	e		

12

CHAPTER 2

PSYCHOANALYSIS

A SPECIAL NOTE ABOUT PSYCHOANALYSIS

WHY IS PSYCHOANALYSIS SO IMPORTANT?

Psychoanalysis was the first approach to therapy. Almost all other psychotherapy theorists have been trained as psychoanalysts. Sometimes their theories are somewhat similar to psychoanalysis; more often they are in reaction to psychoanalysis and very different. Behavior therapy is one of the few therapies not directly influenced by psychoanalysis.

WHY IS THIS CHAPTER SO LONG?

First, psychoanalysis contains many more concepts than any other theory. Second, there are five sub-theories that are described, each with specific concepts. Third, besides Freud, there have been many contributors to psychoanalysis, only some of whom are described in this chapter.

WHY DOES SOME OF THE MATERIAL SEEM DIFFICULT TO GRASP?

Psychoanalysis is concerned with unconscious forces, those aspects of our lives that we are not aware of. It is easier to understand those theories that deal with conscious processes, those parts of our lives that we can directly experience.

PSYCHOANALYSIS SELF-INVENTORY

Directions: By comparing your beliefs about personality to those of psychoanalysis, you should have a clearer idea of how much you will need to suspend your beliefs or change your attitudes to understand the psychoanalytic approaches to personality. You may find it helpful to complete this section before and after you read the chapter. In this way you can see if your views have changed. There are no correct answers, only an opportunity to express your views.

Put an "X" on the line so that it indicates how much you agree or disagree with the statement: A = Agree, D = Disagree.

D   A

1. The purpose of therapy is to make the unconscious conscious.

2. To understand human behavior, therapists need to understand the unconscious.

3. Most psychological conflicts have been repressed and contain elements that we are not aware of.

4. Those aspects of our experience that we are not aware of have a great influence on our behavior.

5. It is the first six years of life that have the greatest influence on determining adult personality.

6. Client problems reflect a failure to resolve issues related to childhood psychosexual development.

7. Trust is developed in early childhood through interactions with one's mother.

8. Clients' struggles to control sexual and aggressive impulses are an important aspect of therapy.

9. Children's early parental relationships form the basis of their later adult development.

10. Separating from parents and becoming an independent adult is one of the most important developmental tasks that individuals face.

11. Mothering must be adequate for healthy psychological development to take place.

12. Being too self-absorbed can be an appropriate therapeutic issue.

13. Developing insight and understanding repressed material is an important part of therapy.

14. The type of therapeutic relationship can have an influence on the outcome of therapy.

15. Therapy that meets three or four times a week for five or more years is the best way to resolve problems.

16. Interpretation of dreams is a critical aspect of therapy.

14

_____ X____ 17. Interpretation of the client's resistance to therapeutic change is an important aspect of therapy.

_____ X____ 18. Understanding the underlying unconscious motivations that are at the root of a client's problem is essential in bringing about therapeutic change.

_____ X____ 19. Therapists should be aware of their own reactions to their patients.

_____ Λ____ 20. Insight into problems will bring about changes in feelings and behaviors.

HISTORY OF PSYCHOANALYSIS

Which influences do you think were most important in the development of psychoanalysis?

INFLUENCES ON SIGMUND FREUD

PERSONAL LIFE	PROFESSIONAL LIFE
Born on May 6, 1856 Austrian parents Near Vienna Oldest of 7 children Father had 2 children from a previous marriage Encouraged by mother Very bright student Graduated high school summa cum laude 1873 - started study of medicine at University of Vienna 1879 - one year of military service 1883 - studied neurology and physiology at Viennese General Hospital 1885 - studied in Paris with Jean Charcot 1886 - married Martha Bernays - 6 children slowly built a private practice 1938 - emigrated to England 1939 - died of throat cancer	Influenced by his knowledge of physics, chemistry, biology, philosophy, psychology, literature, ideas about the unconscious Nietzsche and Spinoza - philosophers Wilhelm Wundt and Gustave Fechner - psychologists Ludwig Borne - free association - writer Darwin - evolution Brucke - physiological research Pierre Janet and Hippolyte Bernheim - psychiatrists *Studies on Hysteria* - 1895 *The Interpretation of Dreams* - 1900 1902 - Wednesday Psychological Society *The Psychopathology of Everyday Life* - 1901 *Three Essays on Sexuality* - 1905 *Jokes and Their Relations to the Unconscious* - 1905 *On Narcissism: An Introduction* - 1914 *Introductory Lectures on Psychoanalysis* - 1917 *The Ego and Id* - 1923 1909 - G. Stanley Hall Lecture at Clark University in Worcester, Massachusetts

FREUD'S DRIVE THEORY OF PERSONALITY

Freud developed many different concepts that cover a wide range of aspects of his theory of personality. Some concepts deal with the importance that he placed on drives or instincts. Other concepts explain terms related to the unconscious. Freud's concepts of id, ego, and superego, and related ideas explain how individuals deal with their basic drives and instincts. In order to cope with unconscious instincts, individuals learn a variety of defense mechanisms. Several are explained in the text and described here. The psychosexual stages (oral, anal, phallic, latency, and genital) describe the part of the body and the developmental sequence in which drives are dealt with in early childhood. Knowing the meaning of the concepts in each of theses areas provides a way of understanding the language of psychoanalysis. Because terms like ego, anal retentive, rationalization, and repression have made their way into normal vocabulary and are sometimes used by other theorists, it is helpful to understand their roots and the theory on which they are based.

CONCEPTS BASIC TO DRIVE THEORY AND INSTINCTS

The following terms describe the basic ideas that Freud uses in explaining his drive theory.

drive   A physiological state of tension such as hunger, sex, or elimination, that motivates an individual to perform actions to reduce the tension.

instinct Basic drives such as hunger, thirst, sex, and aggression that must be fulfilled in order to maintain physical or psychological equilibrium.

libido   The basic driving force of personality which includes sexual energy but is not limited to it.

eros   The life instinct, derived from libidinal energy, in opposition to the death instinct (thanatos).

thanatos An instinct toward self-destruction and death in opposition to the life instinct (eros).

CONCEPTS RELATED TO THE UNCONSCIOUS

Freud believed that many psychological problems that individuals develop occur outside of their own awareness. He was particularly interested in unconscious forces.

conscious or consciousness That portion of the mind or mental functioning that individuals are aware of, including sensations and experiences.

preconscious Memories of events and experiences that can be retrieved with relatively little effort, such as remembering what one said to a friend yesterday. Information is available to awareness but not immediately.

unconscious The part of the mind that people have no knowledge of. It includes memories and emotions that are threatening to the conscious mind and are pushed away.

CONCEPTS THAT DESCRIBE DRIVE THEORY

The concepts of id, ego, and superego help to explain how Freud believed individuals deal with instinctual drives. Most of these concepts are related to regulating id forces or to the way individuals must cope with id forces in order to deal with their external world.

id   The biological instincts, including sexual and aggressive impulses, that seek pleasure. At birth, the id represents the total personality.

pleasure principle The tendency to avoid pain and seek pleasure; the principle by which the id operates. It is particularly important in infancy.

16

cathect Investing psychic energy in a mental representation of a person, behavior, or idea. Infants cathect in objects that gratify their needs.

object cathexis The investment of psychic energy or libido in objects outside the self, such as a person or activity. Such investment is designed to reduce needs.

primary process An action of the id that satisfies a need, thus reducing drive tension, by producing a mental image of an object.

ego A means of mediating between one's instincts or drives and the external world. The ego mediates between the id and the superego.

reality principle A guiding principle of the ego. It allows postponement of gratification so that environmental demands can be met or so that greater pleasure can be obtained at a later time.

secondary process A process of the ego that reduces intrapsychic tension by dealing with external reality. Logic and problem solving skills may be used. It is in contrast with the primary process of the id.

anticathexes The control or restraint exercised by the ego over the id to keep id impulses out of consciousness.

superego That portion of the personality that represents parental values, and more broadly, society's standards. It develops from the ego and is a reflection of early moral training and parental injunctions.

ego ideal A representation in the child of values that are approved by the parents. It is present in the superego as a concern with movement toward perfectionist goals.

DEFENSE MECHANISMS

Freud viewed defense mechanisms as a means that the ego uses to fight off instinctual outbursts of the id or to deal with injunctions by the superego. Ego defense mechanisms are unconscious. They deny or distort reality to reduce stress to the individual. They only become pathological when they are used too frequently. Although Freud and his followers developed a number of defense mechanisms, ten are described in Chapter 2 and are defined here.

repression Threatening or painful thoughts or feelings are excluded from awareness.

denial Individuals may distort or not acknowledge what they think, feel, or see. For example, not believing that a relative has been killed in an auto accident is an illustration of denial.

reaction formation Unacceptable impulses can be avoided by acting in an opposite way. Claiming that you like your occupational choice when you do not can help you avoid dealing with problems that result from not liking your work.

projection People can attribute their own unacceptable desires to others and not deal with their own strong sexual or destructive drives.

displacement Individuals can place their negative feelings about a dangerous object or person, not on that person, but on one who may be safe. For example, it may be safer to express anger at a friend than at a boss who has been angry with you.

sublimation Sexual or aggressive drives can be modified into acceptable social behaviors. For example, anger at others can be sublimated by expressing anger or frustration while being an active spectator at a sports event.

rationalization Individuals can provide a plausible but inaccurate explanation for their failures. An individual who blames her roommate for her own poor performance on an examination may be making excuses for her lack of study and thus rationalizing.

regression When an individual retreats to an earlier stage of development that was both more secure and pleasant, this is referred to as regression. A child hurt by a reprimand of the teacher may suck his thumb and cry, returning to a more secure and less mature time.

identification When individuals take on characteristics of another, often a parent, to reduce their own anxieties and internal conflicts, they are identifying with that person. By identifying with the successful parent, an individual can feel successful even though she has done little that might make her feel productive.

intellectualization Emotional issues are not dealt with directly but rather are handled indirectly by abstract thought.

DEVELOPMENTAL STAGES AND RELATED CONCEPTS

According to Freud, the id, ego, and superego, as well as defense mechanisms, developed over time. Their development could be understood by knowledge of the psychosexual stages. Each psychosexual stage represents a specific area of the body. These stages, along with the Oedipus complex, are defined here.

oral stage The initial stage of psychosexual development lasts about eighteen months. Focus is on gratification through eating and sucking that involves the lips, mouth, and throat.

anal stage The second stage of psychosexual development occurs between the ages of about eighteen months and 3 years. The anal area becomes the main source of pleasure.

phallic stage The third stage of psychosexual development lasts from about the age of three until five or six. The major source of sexual gratification shifts from the anal to the genital region.

latency Following the phallic stage, there is a relatively calm period before adolescence. When Oedipal issues are resolved, the child enters the latency period.

genital stage The final stage of psychosexual development usually starts about the age of twelve and continues throughout life. The focus of sexual energy is toward members of the other sex rather than toward oneself.

Oedipus complex The unconscious sexual desire of the male child for his mother, along with feelings of hostility or fear toward the father. This conflict occurs in the phallic stage.

CASE EXAMPLE:
JUNE AS SEEN FROM A FREUDIAN DRIVE PERSPECTIVE

June is a 30-year-old marketing executive living in Albuquerque, New Mexico. She is married and has one seven-year-old daughter. June has complained of bouts of depression before, but now they seem to stay longer and to become deeper. She complains of having difficulty getting up in the morning. Her interest in spending time with her daughter has also decreased. This is particularly bothering her as June is very concerned about being a good mother. June finds it an effort to help her daughter, Erin, get ready for school. More and more she relies on her husband to take over the child raising functions, which previously she had enjoyed.

18

At work, June had been known for her enthusiasm and eagerness to take on new projects. Now she is rather quiet in marketing meetings and presents fewer creative ideas. Because of her changing level of interest in work, she worries that her bosses will be critical of her performance. To this point, they have not.

June and her husband, Rob, have been married for ten years and knew each other for a year before that. Since they got married at an early age, June had had relatively little experience with other men. She had come to depend on Rob's protectiveness and his ability to make decisions. Sometimes she found it amusing that she would defer to him so often in questions about home but took on such an independent role at work. Recently, she and Rob have been talking less, and their sexual relationship has been very sporadic.

When June was four, her father, an alcoholic, left the family. He moved from Albuquerque to Los Angeles, and June rarely spoke to him or saw him. When he was employed, which was about half the time, he would send some child support. However, June rarely saw him. When her father visited his brother in a nearby town, he might visit June. However, these visits occurred once or twice a year.

When June's mother was left on her own to deal with June and her sister, two years younger, she managed to care for them, but with some difficulty. At first, she was extremely depressed and flustered. She became very irritable and upset. After about a year, she became more involved in a local church. As the years went by, her involvement increased, and June and her sister were very involved with church activities and were influenced by their mother's strict religious upbringing. The bitterness that June's mother felt toward her ex-husband was not lost on June. June learned to distrust men and to be careful of outsiders. It took Rob about two years to really convince June that he was to be trusted. Even when they were first married, June was cautious in her relationship with him. She found that one part of her was trusting and caring of Rob, while the other was worried that somehow he might disappoint or leave.

QUESTIONS ABOUT JUNE FROM A FREUDIAN DRIVE PERSPECTIVE

1. One aspect of June's problems is her diminished

    a. id.
    b. libido.
    c. superego.
    d. unconscious.

2. June's concern about her lack of interest in caring for her daughter is an example of

    a. conscious thoughts.
    b. the preconscious.
    c. the unconscious.
    d. thanatos.

3. When June does care for her daughter, without thinking of herself, this would be an example of

    a. anticathexis.
    b. drive impulse.
    c. object cathexes.
    d. primary process.

4. When June was a young girl and learned from her mother about men and religious values, her mother influenced her about what she should and should not do. Her _____ was developing.

    a. ego
    b. id
    c. superego
    d. all of the above

19

5. When June was a child, she very much wanted to do well at school. She did not want to be like her father and was concerned about disappointing her mother. In this process June was developing her

   a. ego ideal.
   b. preconscious.
   c. pleasure principle.
   d. primary process.

6. According to Freud, June's basic motivational forces come from her

   a. drives.
   b. ego.
   c. pleasure principle.
   d. reality principle.

7. Although June is spending less time with her daughter, she does not believe that this is true and does not acknowledge this. Which defense mechanism is being used?

   a. denial
   b. displacement
   c. projection
   d. rationalization

8. Sometimes when June is depressed, she starts to sing hymns that she sang in church when she was a little girl. This reminds her of the security she felt being close to her mother and sister. This is an example of

   a. projection.
   b. regression.
   c. repression.
   d. sublimation.

9. Sometimes June blames her problems on the commute to work and the fact that she has a cubicle rather than a private office. This is an example of

   a. intellectualization.
   b. repression.
   c. rationalization.
   d. sublimation.

10. When June was 6, her father took her to a carnival, and then got drunk. On the way home, he shouted and yelled at her, blaming her for the divorce. Although June started to behave differently towards him because of this, she doesn't remember the incident. This is an example of

    a. intellectualization.
    b. repression.
    c. rationalization.
    d. sublimation.

20

EGO PSYCHOLOGY

In the development of psychoanalysis, Freud focused on psychosexual or id drives. Others who came after him emphasized ego factors in psychoanalysis. His youngest daughter, Anna, was known for her work with children and her development of defense mechanisms. Perhaps the best known ego psychologist is Erik Erikson, who extended Freud's psychosexual stages to the entire age range and showed how the psychosexual stages could be modified to focus on developmental personal issues and crises that individuals encounter in their lives.

EGO PSYCHOLOGY CONCEPTS

identification with aggressor This is a defense mechanism in which the individual identifies with an opponent that he or she cannot master, taking on characteristics of that person.

altruism In this defense mechanism, individuals learn to become helpful to avoid feeling helpless. They learn that they can satisfy their own egos as well as the demands of society.

QUESTIONS ABOUT JUNE FROM AN EGO PSYCHOLOGY PERSPECTIVE

11. Which of these psychoanalysts is most likely to use the concept of developmental lines in understanding June's problem?

    a. Anna Freud
    b. Sigmund Freud
    c. Erik Erikson
    d. Heinz Kohut

12. June's early issues of trust with her father would be a concern most clearly articulated by

    a. Anna Freud.
    b. Sigmund Freud.
    c. Erik Erikson.
    d. Heinz Kohut

13. Which of these psychoanalysts might pay the most attention to June's early id development?

    a. Anna Freud
    b. Sigmund Freud
    c. Erik Erikson
    d. Heinz Kohut

14. Which of Erikson's 8 stages best describes June's current problem?

    a. autonomy versus shame and doubt
    b. initiative versus guilt
    c. intimacy versus isolation
    d. integrity versus despair

15. Which of Erikson's 8 stages represents development of Freud's anal stage?

    a. autonomy versus shame and doubt
    b. initiative versus guilt
    c. intimacy versus isolation
    d. integrity versus despair

21

OBJECT RELATIONS PSYCHOLOGY

Unlike drive theory, which focuses on the effects of instincts and drives on child development and ego psychology which is concerned with the adaptive aspects of the ego, object relations deals with the development of relationships between the child and love objects. As children grow older, they internalize their relationships with their parents and use these relationships as a model for interactions with those in their adolescent and adult lives. Although concerned with early childhood development, object relations psychology focuses on relationships with others rather than dealing with biological forces as Freud did. There are at least 15 psychoanalysts who have made important contributions to object relations psychology. In the text, only Donald Winnecott and Otto Kernberg are discussed. Through his work as a pediatrician, Donald Winnecott made significant contributions to object relations psychology by observing healthy and unhealthy mother-child relationships. More recently, Otto Kernberg has taken concepts from object relations and drive theory and applied them to understanding difficult personality disorders such as borderline disorder.

OBJECT RELATIONS CONCEPTS

First, concepts that explain common terms in object relations theory are described. Then concepts associated with specific object relations theorists are defined with their primary theorists or theorist indicated in parentheses.

intrapsychic processes Introduced in the object relations section, this term is used throughout psychoanalysis to refer to impulses, ideas, conflicts, or other psychological phenomenon that occur within the mind.

object A term used in psychoanalytic theory to refer, usually, to an important person in the child's life.

object relations A study of significant others or love objects in the child's life, focusing on how the child views the relationship (usually unconsciously).

separation The process that occurs when children gradually distinguish themselves from their mothers and others in their world.

individuation The process of becoming an individual, becoming aware of one's self in relationship to others.

transitional object (Winnicott) An object such as a teddy bear that serves as a transition for infants to shift from experiencing themselves as the center of the world to a sense of themselves as a person among others.

good-enough mother (Winnicott) A mother who adapts to her infant's gestures and needs during early infancy and gradually helps the infant develop independence.

true self (Winnicott) A sense of being real, whole, and spontaneous that comes from the caring of a good-enough mother; used in contrast to the false self.

false self (Winnicott) When good-enough mothering is not available in infancy, children may act as they believe they are expected to. Basically, they adopt their mother's self rather than develop their own. It is used in contrast with the true self.

splitting A process of keeping incompatible feelings separate from each other. It is an unconscious way of dealing with unwanted parts of the self or threatening parts of others. Because of problems of early development adults may have difficulty integrating feelings of love and anger and "split" their feelings by seeing others as all bad or all good.

22

16. From the information available in the case, would June's mother appear to meet Winnicott's definition of the good-enough mother?

    (a.) Yes
    b. No

17. If June's mother had been controlling, harsh, and not spontaneous, June may have developed

    (a.) a false self.
    b. an inferiority complex.
    c. a superiority complex.
    d. a true self.

18. If June were to get very angry at her boss for making her stay at work late and all of a sudden see her as hateful and vindictive when there had been no previous problem, June's action would be called

    a. identification.
    b. internalization.
    c. individuation.
    (d.) splitting.

SELF PSYCHOLOGY

The contribution of Heinz Kohut concentrates on the development of narcissism and how perceived attention, or lack of it, from parents can affect adults in later life. Freud had touched on the subject of narcissism in childhood, but Kohut develops this theme fully. For the infant, the world serves to meet his or her needs. Gradually, the child learns to attend to the influence of parents, often idealizing them. In his own therapeutic work, Kohut often worked with clients with narcissistic personality disorders. These were individuals who had difficulty being empathic to others and believed that they were very important and that others were important to the extent that they met the needs of the narcissistic individual.

CONCEPTS RELATED TO SELF PSYCHOLOGY

selfobject Unconscious thoughts, images, or representations of another person in an individual create patterns or themes called the selfobject. This representation of the person may impact the individual's self-esteem.

bipolar self This refers to the tension between the grandiose self ("I deserve to get what I want") and an idealized view of parents forming the two poles of the bipolar self.

mirroring When the parent shows the child that he or she is happy with the child, the child's grandiose self is supported. The mother or father reflects or mirrors the child's view of him or herself.

empathy Kohut used this term in a very specific sense. He believed that the therapist should be empathic with the patient's narcissistic or grandiose self. Therapist interpretations would show that the therapist understood an aspect of the development of narcissism.

23

19. In working with June, Kohut would attend most to understanding the development of her

    a. ego.
    b. id.
    (c) self.
    d. superego.

20. In helping June, Kohut would have been most interested in June's relationship with her

    a. daughter.
    b. co-workers.
    c. husband.
    (d) parents.

21. As June discusses her childhood and talks about times when she thought her mother could solve all of June's problems, Kohut would be hearing about

    a. the object.
    b. the ego.
    c. holding.
    d. the idealized parent.

22. When June talks about her view of her father taking her to a carnival when she was 5 years old, her unconscious view of him is called the _____ by self psychologists.

    a. self
    b. object
    c. selfobject
    (d) idealized parent

23. If June says, "I need my husband to pay more attention to me. My parents never did. And you certainly don't," you as a self psychology therapist will see this as an illustration of the

    (a) grandiose self.
    b. self.
    c. mirroring process.
    d. idealized parent.

RELATIONAL PSYCHOANALYSIS

Relational psychoanalysis builds on the object relations approach and self psychology. The focus is on the therapeutic relationship. The psychoanalyst is no longer seen as the authority but as a partner in the analysis. Rather than a focus on therapeutic neutrality, the therapist is seen as subjective rather than objective. Both therapist and patient have an influence on each other.

intersubjectivity The view that both analyst and patient influence each other in therapy.

one person psychology In psychoanalysis, the view that the patient is influenced by the analyst, but the analyst is not influenced by the patient

two person psychology (similar to intersubjectivity) The idea that both patient and analyst influence each other during therapy

24

24. If June sees you, her analyst, as an objective authority, June would see analysis from this point of view:

   a. one person
   b. two person
   c. three person
   d. four person

25. In relational psychoanalysis, rather than in other approaches to psychoanalysis, June's analyst would

   a. interpret id impulse
   b. focus on June's grandiosity.
   c. be aware of his/her impact on June, and June's impact on the therapist.
   d. focus on June's development of her bipolar self.

PSYCHOANALYTICAL APPROACHES TO TREATMENT

The different views of personality development and personality structure held by drive, ego, object relations, self psychology, and relational theorists can help the therapist understand or assess the patient's problems. Some therapists use one of these perspectives; others use any combination, including all of them. In making assessments of the problems, therapists pay particular attention to material that patients are unaware of (the unconscious). The general goals of treatment and the therapeutic approach or techniques that psychoanalytic therapists use are shared by drive, ego, object relations, self psychology, and relational analysts. They all make use of free association and interpretation of dreams, resistance, and transference as well as countertransference.

GOALS OF PSYCHOANALYSIS

The major purpose of psychoanalysis and psychodynamic therapy is to help individuals change their personality. By resolving unconscious conflicts within themselves, patients should be able to find more satisfactory ways of dealing with their problems. They should feel more real and more authentic within themselves as well as develop better relationships with others. The goals of therapy are reached by reconstructing, interpreting, and analyzing one's childhood experiences. Although psychoanalysts and psychodynamic therapists of all types focus on unconscious motivations and early childhood development, the five schools of psychoanalysis put different emphases on the importance of understanding different developmental issues. Drive theorists particularly emphasize individuals' awareness of their sexual and aggressive drives. Ego psychoanalysts focus on positive ways of adapting to others and external pressures. They may also focus on understanding one's own defense mechanisms. Object relations therapists listen for problems that may have developed at an early age in the relationship between the patient as a child and his or her parents. Self psychologists also listen for problems that develop in parent-child relationships but do so from the perspective of narcissism. Relational psychoanalysts attend to the effect of therapist and patient on each other.

TYPES OF TREATMENT

There are three broad approaches to treatment which differ in terms of number of meetings per week and length of time. Psychoanalysis, psychoanalytic therapy, and psychoanalytic or psychodynamic counseling are defined here.

psychoanalysis Based on the work of Freud and others, psychoanalysis includes free association, dream analysis, and working through transference issues. The patient usually lies on a couch, and sessions are conducted three to five times per week.

25

psychoanalytic therapy Free association and exploration of unconscious processes may not be emphasized as strongly as in psychoanalysis. Meetings are usually one to three times per week, and the patient sits in a chair.

psychoanalytic or ***psychodynamic counseling*** Meetings are usually once a week for a year or two, and the patient sits in a chair. Therapists may use more active techniques than those described in Chapter 2 in the text.

PSYCHOANALYTIC TECHNIQUES

Most psychoanalytic techniques are designed either to elicit information from the patient that may contain unconscious material (free association) or to help the patient develop insights about this material. Most psychoanalytic techniques focus on this latter purpose.

free association The patient relates feelings, fantasies, thoughts, memories, and recent events to the analyst spontaneously and without censoring them. These associations give the analyst clues to the unconscious processes of the patient.

interpretation The process by which the psychoanalyst points out the unconscious meanings of a situation to a patient. Analysts assess their patients' ability to accept interpretations and bring them to conscious awareness.

interpreting resistance Patients may resist uncovering repressed material in therapy. Often, through unconscious processes, patients may show aspects of themselves to the therapist which the therapist then shares with the patient.

interpreting projective identification Patients may take negative aspects of themselves, project them onto someone else, and then identify with or try unconsciously to control that person. In doing so, a part of oneself is "split off" and attributed to another in order to control that other person. When this occurs in therapy, the therapist points this out (interprets it) to the patient.

interpreting transference Transference refers to the patient's feelings and fantasies, both positive and negative, about the therapist. More specifically, it refers to responses by the patient to the therapist as though the therapist were a significant person in the patient's past, usually the mother or father. Where appropriate, the therapist informs (interprets) the patient that this is happening.

interpreting transference psychosis In transference psychosis, patients may act out early childhood destructive relationships with the therapist that they had with their parents. Interpretations are done carefully, considering the patient's ability to deal with this information.

interpreting dreams Dream interpretation may be done rather frequently as dreams represent an excellent source of unconscious material. How the therapist interprets the dream depends on whether the therapist is using a listening perspective from drive, ego, object relations, or self psychology.

countertransference An important concept in psychoanalysis, this term can be defined in three different ways: 1. The neurotic or irrational reactions of a therapist toward the patient, 2. The therapist's conscious and unconscious feelings toward the patient, 3. A way of understanding how people in the patient's past may have felt.

relational responses Comments on issues that arise in the therapeutic hour which reflect the therapist-patient relationship, rather than just making transference and countertransference interpretations.

In this section, you will be given information about June's work in therapy and asked questions about helping her from a psychoanalytic perspective.

You have been seeing June for therapy three times a week for a year. This is your 145th session with her. June sits across from you in a chair, as your approach can be described as psychoanalytic therapy. At the beginning of the session, June relates this vivid dream that she had. In the questions that follow, you will be asked to determine whether the interpretation given is from a drive, ego, object relations, or self psychology perspective.

"I was in a large church with my mother. We were kneeling next to each other right in front of the pews. There was a large plain wood cross between us with the cross piece over our heads. No one else was there, and we were both praying silently. Sun was coming through the large stained glass windows. They were beautiful. I was aware that there were several themes from the Bible and that Peter, Paul, and the Virgin Mary were there, each in a different theme. All of sudden, out of the corner of my eye right behind my mother, I could see the Virgin Mary. It was like she was a stained glass figure in dark blue, but also three dimensional at the same time. At first I was scared, but it was like at the same time, she and my mother reached out to me. My mother put her arm around me, the cross seemed to disappear, and I felt so much better. It was like the picture of the Virgin Mary seemed to dissolve into us. The feeling was very helpful and lovely. I remember a smile on my face when I woke up. I don't ever remember that happening before in a dream."

Imagine that you have given the following interpretations to the dream; indicate which school of psychoanalysis your interpretation represents.

26. "June, you seem to be returning to a time in your life when you wanted to be close to your mother in a very significant way." This interpretation reflects which of the following viewpoints?

    a. drive theory
    b. ego psychology
    (c.) object relations
    d. self psychology

27. "You seem to have a sense of your mother of being ideal, perhaps perfect. It may have felt like she was so powerful and you were insignificant. It was like everything in the world revolved around her, not you." This interpretation reflects which of the following viewpoints?

    a. drive theory
    b. ego psychology
    c. object relations
    (d.) self psychology

28. "June, having that cross, that symbol of masculinity, removed from you and your mother seemed to help you to develop trust." This interpretation reflects which of the following viewpoints?

    a. drive theory
    (b.) ego psychology
    c. object relations
    d. self psychology

27

29. "It seems that first you were afraid of the masculine phallic symbol, the cross. When it disappeared, you were less afraid to express yourself." This interpretation reflects which of the following viewpoints?

    a. drive theory
    b. ego psychology
    c. object relations
    d. self psychology

30. How would you characterize the therapist's comments in Questions 26 through 29?

    a. empathic
    b. therapeutic neutrality
    c. interpretation
    d. countertransference statements

31. After making your interpretive statement, you say to June: "As you think about this dream, I would like you to tell me anything that comes into your mind, a fragment, a thought, an image." Which technique are you using?

    a. free association
    b. eliciting a transference response
    c. providing therapeutic neutrality
    d. interpreting a dream

32. June replies to you saying, "I really don't want to do that. I feel that you are pushing this dream too far. You are trying to make too big a deal of it." You then say, "I wonder if you have some concerns about the progress that we are making in therapy." This would be an example of interpreting the

    a. dream.
    b. resistance.
    c. transference.
    d. countertransference.

33. June says, "You know, we've talked about me being depressed and uncertain, but now I find that my husband is like that. I think he's unsure of himself, and I try to help him gain control over himself. He doesn't seem to appreciate that. He says he's fine and hasn't changed, that it's me. But I really notice that he is depressed and negative like I used to be." Being the therapist, you say, "Perhaps you're seeing a part of yourself in your husband, something that you never have seen in him before." Your comment would be an example of

    a. free association.
    b. interpreting the resistance.
    c. interpreting the transference.
    d. interpreting projective identification.

34. June now says to you, "I hate it when you say I am unjustly accusing my husband of being depressed. That's what my mother always did. She never believed me and you don't believe me." You reply, "You seem to be getting angry at me just the way you were angry at your mother when you were little. You felt that she was blaming you for not doing enough at home or for not being good enough. Now you seem to be feeling that from me." As a psychoanalytic therapist, you are

    a. interpreting the resistance.
    b. free associating.
    c. interpreting the transference.
    d. providing therapeutic neutrality.

35. Hearing June's comments about you, you start to feel annoyed at her. This kind of attack reminds you of how your own father would criticize you. Your reaction could best be described as

    a. unprofessional.
    b. resistance.
    c. empathic responding.
    d. countertransference.

BRIEF THERAPY

Because traditional psychoanalysis may require meetings three or four times a week for five to eight years, many therapists have been concerned about the cost to patients and the relatively slow progress compared to other theories. More than any other theory, psychoanalysis has been the source of new creative approaches to short term work.

Typically, short term therapy lasts 12 to 40 sessions. To be successful, short term psychodynamic therapy requires that individuals be motivated, focused on one or two problems, and be experiencing anxiety or depression rather than borderline or narcissistic personality disorders. Techniques tend to be direct rather than indirect. Therapists often ask questions, restate client comments, confront clients, and deal quickly with transference issues. They tend not to use free association and lengthy dream work. In the chart shown here, psychoanalysis is contrasted with the Luborsky's Core Conflictual Theme method.

PSYCHODYNAMIC PSYCHOTHERAPY	LUBORSKY'S CORE CONFLICTUAL THEME METHOD
Free association	Listen to Relationship Episodes
Neutrality or empathy	Determine the Wish The Response From the Other
Interpreting resistance	Response From Self
Interpreting dreams	Communicate the Core Conflictual Relationship Theme
Interpreting transference	
Interpreting projective identification and other concerns	Use 5-7 Relationship Episodes Work through Response from Others and Self
	Termination
Countertransference	

OE1. Characterize the difference between long term psychodynamic psychotherapy and Luborsky's method. (63)

_____

_____

_____

_____

29

SPECIAL TOPICS

OE2. Another current trend in psychoanalysis is that toward shorter therapy. Why is this an important movement within psychoanalysis? (65)

_____

_____

_____

_____

OE3. In analytically informed therapy or counseling (psychodynamic counseling), therapists might use techniques borrowed from other theories. How could that change the practice of psychoanalysis? (66)

_____

_____

_____

_____

OE4. Why has psychoanalytic theory, specifically Freudian drive theory and object relations, been the subject of criticism for its description of the role of the development of women? (70)

_____

_____

_____

_____

OE5. In what ways have psychodynamic writers neglected multicultural issues, and in what ways have they responded to them? (72)

_____

_____

_____

_____

30

STRENGTHS AND LIMITATIONS

What do you see as the strengths and limitations of psychoanalytic therapy?

STRENGTHS	LIMITATIONS
_____	_____
_____	_____
_____	_____
_____	_____
_____	_____
_____	_____
_____	_____

PSYCHOANALYTIC THERAPY: A QUIZ

True/False items: Decide if the following statements are more "true" or more "false" as they apply to psychodynamic or psychoanalytic therapy.

T **(F)** Q1. Freud was not influenced by contemporary psychologists, psychiatrists, philosophers, or writers in the development of psychoanalysis.

(T) F Q2. It is unconscious material, rather than conscious material, that is the focus of psychoanalysis.

(T) F Q3. In drive theory, the genital stage occurs in adolescence.

T **(F)** Q4. Anna Freud is considered to be a drive theorist like her father, Sigmund.

(T) F Q5. Erik Erikson converted and further developed Freud's psychosexual stages into psychosocial stages.

(T) F Q6. Donald Winnicott emphasized the early maternal relationship as being important in healthy adult adjustment.

T **(F)** Q7. Heinz Kohut developed the term "good enough" mothering which refers to the mother being able to adapt to the infant's needs yet help the infant move toward independence.

(T) F Q8. The goals of psychoanalytic therapy are designed to bring about changes in a person's personality and character structure.

(T) F Q9. Psychoanalysts who use a couch do so to allow the patient to free-associate as much as possible. In this way, the therapist is out of view, and there is less interference in the free association process than there would be if the therapist sat across from the patient.

31

T (F)   Q10.   Psychoanalysts and psychodynamic therapists view countertransference as a hindrance
                to progress in therapy.

Multiple choice items: Select the best answer from the alternatives using a psychoanalytic or
psychodynamic perspective.

_____   Q11.   One of the techniques that Freud used in his early work but later abandoned was

           a.   free association.
           (b.) hypnosis.
           c.   behavior modification.
           d.   shock therapy.

_____   Q12.   Which of these terms fits most closely with Freud's drive theory?

           a.   individuation
           b.   relational
           (c.) oral
           d.   self

_____   Q13.   Biological forces are most closely associated with which one of these concepts?

           (a.) id
           b.   ego
           c.   superego
           d.   object

_____   Q14.   If Morris says that it is not a big deal that he is unhappy at school because all his
                  friends are unhappy at school as well, he is most likely using the defense mechanism of

           a.   repression.
           b.   reaction formation.
           (c.) projection.
           d.   sublimation.

_____   Q15.   When 6-year-old Rachel is scolded by her mother, she curls up into a fetal position and
                  sucks her thumb. She is using the defense mechanism of

           a.   repression.
           b.   reaction formation.
           (c.) regression.
           d.   sublimation.

_____   Q16.   Ralph has just broken up with his girlfriend. Rather than admit that this hurts him,
                  Ralph looks at this event philosophically as just another life event. Ralph is using the
                  defense mechanism of

           a.   regression.
           b.   reaction formation.
           c.   identification.
           (d.) intellectualization.

32

Q17. Which of Erik Erikson's psychosocial stages corresponds to Freud's oral stage?

a. trust versus mistrust
b. autonomy versus shame and doubt
c. initiative versus guilt
d. industry versus inferiority

Q18. Which of these theorists developed the idea of the "false self," defined as acting as one is expected to do by parents, rather than acting as one believes or feels?

a. Sigmund Freud
b. Otto Kernberg
c. Stephen Mitchell
d. Donald Winnicott

Q19. Self psychology is most concerned with the development of

a. ego strength.
b. separation and individuation.
c. the id.
d. normal narcissism.

Q20. Seeing the analyst as a subjective rather than objective presence in analysis is associated with

a. drive theory.
b. ego psychology.
c. object relations.
d. relational psychoanalysis.

Q21. Which school of psychoanalysis is associated with the true self?

a. drive theory
b. ego theory
c. object relations
d. self psychology

Q22. In psychoanalysis, interpretations help to bring _____ material into consciousness.

a. id
b. selfobject
c. individuated
d. unconscious

Q23. When the therapist is aware of her reactions to the client, this is typically viewed as

a. countertransference.
b. confrontation.
c. bipolar self.
d. projective identification.

33

_____ Q24.   Which of these techniques is most likely to be used in psychoanalysis and less likely to be used in psychodynamic therapy?

    a.   questions
    b.   confrontation
    ©.   free association
    d.   supportive statements

_____ Q25.   Intersubjectivity is most closely related to which one of these types of psychoanalysis?

    a.   drive theory
    b.   ego psychology
    c.   object-relations
    d.   self psychology
    ⓔ   relational psychoanalysis

ANSWER KEY

1.	b	11.	a	21.	d	31.	a
2.	a	12.	c	22.	c	32.	b
3.	c	13.	b	23.	a	33.	d
4.	c	14.	c	24.	a	34.	c
5.	a	15.	a	25.	c	35.	d
6.	a	16.	a	26.	c		
7.	a	17.	a	27.	d		
8.	b	18.	d.	28.	b		
9.	c	19.	c	29.	a		
10.	b	20.	d	30.	c		

QUIZ

Q1.	F	Q11.	b	Q21.	c
Q2.	T	Q12.	c	Q22.	d
Q3.	T	Q13.	a	Q23.	a
Q4.	F	Q14.	c	Q24.	c
Q5.	T	Q15.	c	Q25.	e
Q6.	T	Q16.	d		
Q7.	F	Q17.	a		
Q8.	T	Q18.	d		
Q9.	T	Q19.	d		
Q10.	F	Q20.	d		

34

CHAPTER 3

JUNGIAN ANALYSIS AND THERAPY

JUNGIAN THERAPY SELF-INVENTORY

Directions: By comparing your beliefs about personality to Jung's, you should have a clearer idea of how much you will need to suspend your beliefs or change attitudes to understand Jung's theory of personality. You may find it helpful to complete this section before and after you read the chapter. In this way, you can see if your views have changed. There are no correct answers, only an opportunity to express your views.

Put an "X" on the line so that it indicates how much you agree or disagree with the statement: A=Agree, D=Disagree.

D   A

_____X__ 1. Becoming more aware of thoughts and feelings that we were previously unaware of (unconscious of) will lead to personal growth.

_____X__ 2. There are themes and events that are universal for all human beings.

_____X__ 3. There are important life themes that are played out in different ways in a variety of cultures.

____X_____ 4. Understanding the religious myths and legends of different cultures gives insights into important life themes.

_____X__ 5. The concepts of introversion and extraversion are helpful in understanding people's personalities.

_____X__ 6. Knowing how people perceive events and make judgments about these events can help you understand individuals better.

_____X___ 7. Knowing that some people prefer learning by thinking and others by feeling can help you understand them better.

_X_____ 8. An important aspect of adolescence is that it is a time where young people discover their own personalities.

____X_____ 9. Middle age is as important a time of life as childhood (perhaps more so) for understanding personality development.

____X_____ 10. Old age is as important a time of life as childhood (perhaps more so) for understanding personality development.

35

D   A

_____ X____ 11. An important life goal is to become aware of one's strengths and limitations.

_____ X____ 12. An important therapeutic goal is to make previously unconscious material conscious.

X_____ 13. Dreams are among the most important material that therapists can use to help patients learn about themselves.

_____ X____ 14. Insight is an important goal of therapy.

_____ X_____ 15. Creative methods such as dance, poetry, and artwork provide insight into an individual's personality.

____ X___ X___ 16. Therapy takes time to work, often a year or more.

_____ X____ 17. Understanding a patient's culture - religion, myths, and legends - can help the therapist provide useful insight into the patient's personality.

_____ X____ 18. When patients understand their dark sides, their angry and hostile feelings, they can better understand themselves.

X_____ 19. Individual therapy is more important than group therapy for understanding oneself as an individual.

_____ X_____ 20. The therapist's unconscious awareness of a patient can be a useful therapeutic tool.

HISTORY OF JUNGIAN ANALYSIS AND THERAPY

An excellent student, Jung's background was considerably broad. He was very much influenced by his family's history of involvement in theology. His interest in spirituality, ritual, and ceremony can be seen in his childhood and adolescence. His personal experience as well as his broad knowledge of many subjects led him to develop a theoretical perspective that is quite different from any other discussed in the text.

Which influences do you think were most important in the development of Jung's theory?

PERSONAL LIFE	PROFESSIONAL LIFE
Born in 1875 Kesswil, Switzerland Childhood dreams and daydreams Rituals and ceremonies with miniature scrolls Excellent student - knowledge of Greek and Latin at early age Later studied philosophy, theology, anthropology, mythology, and science 1895 - started medical training at University of Basel	Kant's view of a priori universal forms of perception Carl Gustav Carus's view of 3 levels of unconscious including a universal level Eduard von Hartmann's ideas of a universal unconscious Gottfried Leibniz (1700's) irrationality of the unconscious Arthur Schopenhauer's irrational forces based on sexuality Johann Bachofen - anthropologist symbolism across Cultures

36

PERSONAL LIFE (Cont'd)	PROFESSIONAL LIFE (Cont'd)
1903 - married Emma Rauschenbach 1924 - visited the Pueblo of New Mexico 1925 - visited Tanganyika Studied alchemy, astrology, divination, telepathy, clairvoyance, fortune telling Built a tower at the end of Lake Zurich Died June 6, 1961	1913 - 1919 spiritual suffering, due in part to severing relationship with Sigmund Freud Adolf Bastian - anthropologist, understanding people by their rites, symbols, and mythology George Creuzer - anthropology, importance of symbolism in stories 1902 - dissertation - On Psychology and Pathology of So-called Occult Phenomenon Eugen Bleuler and Pierre Janet - psychiatrists Developed word association test with Franz Riklin 1909 - Lectured at Clark University, along with Freud 1911 - Symbols of Transformation Produced over 20 volumes of writings Honorary degrees from Harvard, Oxford, and other universities

JUNG'S THEORY OF PERSONALITY

For some students, Jung's theory of personality is the most difficult to grasp of all the theories covered in the text. This is due in part to his emphasis on the importance of the unconscious and understanding symbols of unconscious material. Additionally, his focus on the collective unconscious and its symbolism leads to the labeling of a vast array of archetypes and their symbols. The text focuses only on the most common symbols. Easier to grasp are the attitudes and functions of personality which include the concepts of introversion and extraversion. To make the material as clear as possible, I will present these definitions of concepts that help in understanding basic Jungian personality theory. Then, I will return to the dream of June, described in Chapter 2, and ask you some questions about it from a Jungian perspective. Next, I will define concepts important to learning about Jungian personality attitudes and functions. Questions about June's attitudes and functions should help to clarify these terms.

BASIC JUNGIAN PERSONALITY THEORY AND CONCEPTS

Referring to the terms below can help you understand the concepts that are most central to the ideas of Carl Jung. To separate Jung's work from that of Freud, it is important to remember that the collective unconscious is a concept used by Jung, but not by Freud. Jung emphasized the universality of the human species, symbolism, and individual development. In contrast, Freud developed a very different personality structure based on his view of the importance of psychosexual drives in early childhood.

psyche Jung's term for personality structure which includes conscious and unconscious thoughts, feelings, and behaviors.

ego An expression of personality which includes thoughts, feelings and behaviors of which we are conscious. Note that this definition is very different from Freud's, which describes the ego as a means of mediating between one's instincts or drives and the external world.

37

individuation The process of integrating opposing elements of personality to become whole. This involves, in part, bringing unconscious contents into relationship with consciousness.

personal unconscious Thoughts, feelings, and perceptions that are not accepted by the ego are stored here. Included are distant memories as well as personal or unresolved moral conflicts that may be emotionally charged.

complex A group of associated feelings, thoughts, and memories that have intense emotional content. Complexes may have elements from a personal and collective unconscious.

collective unconscious This is the part of the unconscious that contains memories and images that are universal to the human species, in contrast to the personal unconscious which is based upon individual experience. Humans have an inherited tendency to form representations of mythological motives which may vary greatly but maintain basic patterns. Thus, individuals may view the universe in similar ways by thinking, feeling, and reacting to common elements such as the moon or water.

transcendent function This function refers to a confrontation of opposites, a conscious thought and an unconscious influence. The transcendent function bridges two opposing attitudes or conditions and in the process becomes a third force, usually expressed through an emerging symbol.

archetypes Universal images that are pathways from the collective unconscious to the conscious, such as a mother (Earth Mother) or animal instincts (shadow). They take a person's reactions and put them in a pattern.

symbol The content and outward expression of archetypes. Symbols represent the wisdom of humanity and can be applied to future issues and are represented differently in a variety of cultures.

persona An archetype representing the roles that people play in response to social demands of others. It is the mask or disguise that individuals assume when superficially interacting with their environment. It may often be at variance with their true identities.

anima The archetype representing the feminine component of the male personality.

animus The archetype that represents the masculine component of the female personality.

shadow The archetype that represents unacceptable sexual, animalistic, or aggressive impulses, usually the opposite of the way we see ourselves.

Self An archetype that is the center of personality and provides organization and integration of the personality through a process of individuation.

mandala A symbolic representation of the unified wholeness of the Self. Usually, it has four sections representing an effort to achieve wholeness in the four sections (such as the four directions of the winds).

CASE EXAMPLE:
BASIC JUNGIAN PERSONALITY THEORY CONCEPTS APPLIED TO JUNE

In Chapter 2 of this manual, we discussed the case of June. In that chapter, one of her dreams was analyzed from four different psychoanalytic points of view. Let us return to that dream and examine it from a Jungian perspective. In the dream, June was in a church, kneeling next to her mother. There was a large cross between them. No one else was in the church. However, above them were large stained glass pictures of Biblical scenes. The Virgin Mary came out of one of these scenes and appeared behind June and her mother, who were facing the altar.

The following questions about this dream deal both with terms referring to important aspects of Jungian personality theory as well as to specific Jungian archetypes.

1. If June has her own thoughts, feelings, and perceptions that are unconscious but are revealed in the dream, these would be referred to as products of the

   a. conscious process.
   b. preconscious.
   c. personal unconscious.
   d. collective unconscious.

2. June's dream is one small part of her entire personality structure, called the _____ , which includes both conscious and unconscious thoughts, feelings, and behaviors.

   a. ego
   b. complex
   c. persona
   d. psyche

3. As a result of analyzing the dream, June now sees that the Virgin Mary connects common threads between her and her mother. This common bond gives her a sense of closeness with her mother that feels new. The dream may be said to have served

   a. a transcendent function.
   b. a universal function.
   c. an auxiliary function.
   d. a superior function.

4. As June brings unconscious elements into consciousness, she becomes further integrated as a person. This therapeutic goal is known as

   a. ego mediation.
   b. symbolic clarification.
   c. individuation.
   d. separation.

5. In this dream, the Virgin Mary can be viewed as a(n)

   a. archetype.
   b. anima.
   c. symbol.
   d. transcendent function.

6. If the Virgin Mary is seen as representing the Great Mother, then the Great Mother would be called a(n)

   a. archetype.
   b. religious icon.
   c. symbol.
   d. transcendent function.

7. If in the dream, a warm, caring, older man comes up behind June and gently puts his hands on her shoulders, giving her a sense of strength, one might suspect that this represents the

   a. anima.
   b. animus.
   c. persona.
   d. shadow.

39

8. When June is interacting with her fellow employees, the archetype that most likely describes her relationship with them and the roles she plays with them would be the

   a. animus.
   ⓑ persona.
   c. Self.
   d. shadow.

9. If in the dream, the Virgin Mary should turn into an aggressive, harmful monster, the archetype that is most represented by this symbol is likely to be the

   a. animus.
   b. persona.
   c. Self.
   ⓓ shadow.

10. As June and her therapist analyze the dream, June develops new insights about her personality. This process is likely to take place in the

   a. conscious part of her psyche.
   b. the preconscious.
   c. the collective conscious.
   ⓓ the collective unconscious.

PERSONALITY ATTITUDES AND FUNCTIONS

The aspect of Jung's theory of personality that is best known is the two attitudes: introversion and extraversion. Less well known are the functions: thinking, feeling, sensing, and intuiting. Inventories such as the Myers-Briggs Type Indicator have been developed to measure these concepts. This aspect of Jungian personality theory has been widely popularized and has been used by non-Jungian therapists. Jungian analysts and therapists see these attitudes and functions as related to the psyche and as expressions of the conscious and the unconscious aspects of the Self.

attitudes Introversion and extraversion are two ways of interacting with the world, or two attitudes toward the world.

introversion One of the two major attitudes or orientations of personality, introversion represents an orientation toward subjective experience and focusing on one's own perception of the external world.

extraversion One of the two major attitudes or orientations of personality. Extraversion is associated with valuing objective experience and receiving and responding to the external world rather than thinking about one's own perceptions or internal world.

functions The four ways of receiving and responding to the world (thinking, feeling, sensing, and intuiting) are called functions.

thinking A function of personality in which individuals attempt to understand the world and to solve problems. It is in contrast to feeling.

feeling A function of personality in which individuals attend to subjective experiences of pleasure, pain, anger, or other feelings. Its polar opposite is thinking.

sensing A personality function that emphasizes one's perception of one's self and one's world. Its polar opposite is intuiting.

intuiting A personality function that stresses having a hunch or guess about something, which may arise from the unconscious. Its polar opposite is sensing.

superior function The one of the four functions of personality (thinking, feeling, sensing, or intuiting) which is the most highly developed.

auxiliary function The function that takes over when the superior function is not operating. It includes thinking, feeling, sensing, and intuiting.

inferior function This is the function which is least well developed in an individual and may be repressed and unconscious, showing itself in dreams or fantasies.

QUESTIONS ABOUT PERSONALITY ATTITUDES AND FUNCTIONS AS APPLIED TO JUNE

11. June tells her Jungian analyst that she has a gut feeling that something is about to happen between her and her mother. Which of the following attitudes or functions best describes this reaction?

    a. extraversion
    b. introversion
    c. feeling
    d. intuition

12. While riding the subway to her appointment with her analyst, June was lost in thought about her dream. She couldn't figure out its meaning. Which attitude or function best represents June's way of being at that time?

    a. extraversion
    b. introversion
    c. thinking
    d. feeling

13. June very much enjoys her job because she enjoys interaction with her colleagues. Her analyst has also noticed how expressive June is of her feelings with regard to her family. Which of these is most likely to represent June's attitude towards the world?

    a. feeling
    b. thinking
    c. extraversion
    d. introversion

14. If June's feeling function is well developed, which of these functions is likely to be less well developed?

    a. intuition
    b. sensing
    c. thinking
    d. transcendent

15. Which two functions can be considered irrational functions because they relate to responding to stimuli rather than making judgments about them?

    a. feeling and intuition
    b. thinking and feeling
    c. sensation and intuition
    d. sensation and thinking

41

JUNGIAN ANALYSIS AND THERAPY

GOALS OF JUNGIAN THERAPY

The goal of Jungian analysis and therapy is, broadly speaking, to help individuals bring unconscious material into consciousness. By doing so, patients learn about their strengths and weaknesses, continually learning about new aspects of themselves of which they were previously unaware. This process is called individuation (defined previously).

ASSESSMENT IN JUNGIAN THERAPY

Assessment takes place through the analysis of dreams and other unconscious material. Assessment of personality attitudes and functions can be done through the application of objective personality inventories. The most well known is the Myers-Briggs Type Indicator. Others are the Gray-Wheelwright Jungian Type Survey, and the Singer-Loomis Inventory of Personality. Occasionally projective inventories have been used such as the Rorschach Test and the Thematic Apperception Test. Another assessment technique was developed by Jung and Franz Riklin which is known as word association. Delayed reactions to the patient's response to a word or phrase might indicate an emotional response which may be rooted in the unconscious.

TECHNIQUES OF JUNGIAN THERAPY

Like Freud and other psychoanalysts, Jungian analysts and therapists use interpretation. They may also make use of transference and countertransference. However, they tend to focus less on transference and countertransference than psychoanalysts. Jung's views of these concepts changed throughout his 50 years of writing. For Jungians, transference and countertransference, like dreams and active imagination, have archetypal components. Other creative techniques such as dance and movement therapy, poetry, artwork, and use of the sand tray help unconscious processes enter into consciousness, revealing archetypal material.

JUNGIAN THERAPEUTIC CONCEPTS

amplification A process of using knowledge of the history and meaning of symbols to understand unconscious material, like those that arise from patients' dreams.

dreams Arising from unconscious creativity, "big" dreams represent symbolic material from the collective unconscious; "little" dreams reflect day-to-day activity and may come from the personal unconscious.

active imagination A technique of analysis in which individuals actively focus on experiences or images (in dreams or fantasy), reporting changes in these images or experiences as they concentrate on them.

sand tray This is a sand box with small figures and forms that individuals can assign meaning to. Jungian therapists may attach archetypal significance to the play or stories that individuals develop as they use the figures and forms.

puer aeternus A man who may have difficulty growing out of adolescence and becoming more responsible.

puella aeterna A woman who may have difficulty accepting the responsibilities of adulthood and is likely to be still attached to her father.

synchronicity Coincidences that have no causal connection. Dreaming of seeing two snakes and then seeing snakes the next day is an example of synchronicity.

42

A JUNGIAN DREAM INTERPRETATION EXAMPLE

In this example, June will describe a dream that she had. You will play the role of a Jungian analyst and examine and interpret the dream from a Jungian perspective. Because Jungian therapy or analysis is probably the most difficult approach to learn and requires arguably more specific training than any other therapy, the questions that I will present will be followed immediately by answers and an explanation. You may wish to cover the answers as you try to answer the questions.

June comes to the therapy session with notes about a dream that she had two nights ago. As soon as she woke up in the morning, she wrote down as many details as she could remember about different aspects of the dream. However, the part that was most vivid to her was the one in which she had strong emotional reactions. She says: "I don't remember quite how I got there but I was in a hallway behind the stage of a large open air auditorium, I was puzzled by that, but a moment later I was on the stage and I was a musician. I was playing the guitar with the rock band Kiss. They were dressed in their black makeup that they usually wear and their bizarre costumes. The music was very loud, unpleasantly so, and they were screaming into the microphone. The audience of tens of thousands of people were cheering and screaming. I was playing too, more softly, but going along with them, doing what rock musicians are supposed to do. Occasionally, I was yelling too, but then I would find myself surprised at the rage in my voice. That didn't last long; most of the time I just struggled to keep going. There was a feeling of chaos in the dream, and it was confusing. I think the feeling that I had when I woke up was that I was troubled and confused by the dream."

"The dream really surprised me. I had grown up with church music. Like my mother, I had been in the choir, and we had sung hymns. Although as a teenager, I listened to other music, my mother really wanted me to only play and listen to church-related music."

I'm not sure about how this is related to my depression. I know I have felt somewhat overwhelmed lately by work and by taking care of my daughter. I worry that I'm not being a good enough mother to her or being there for her when she needs me."

QUESTIONS ABOUT JUNE'S DREAM AND RELATED ISSUES

16. An interpretation of this dream from a Jungian point of view is likely to be

    a. objective.
    (b.) subjective.

(b. the dream is likely to be a subjective interpretation because members of the audience and the band are not known or important to June.)

17. In the dream, the band, Kiss, may represent a(n)

    a. archetype.
    (b.) symbol.
    c. neither, because the band is modern and symbols and archetypes refer to myths and fairy tales.

(b. the band is a symbol of an archetype. Symbols may be modern or current characters or events. They do not necessarily have to be mythological or legendary.)

43

18. The archetype that the band Kiss represents for June is most likely to be

    a. her animus.
    b. the Wise Man.
    c. her persona.
    (d.) her shadow.

(d. June appears to be a rather restrained, now depressed, person. The aggressive behavior of the band and its loud noise and bizarre appearance represent aggressive impulses in June that are far from her conscious awareness of herself.)

19. As a Jungian therapist, which of the following statements are you most likely to make as you and June interpret her dream?

    a. "Why do you think you might be attracted to the music of Kiss?"
    b. "Perhaps the members of the rock band Kiss represent the fear that you sometimes had of your father after your mother and father divorced."
    (c.) " Perhaps your discomfort with the band and its loud and raucous music may represent an uncomfortableness with that part of yourself that is sometimes angry or aggressive (the shadow)."
    d. "Have you ever had guitar lessons?"

(c. For June, the band, Kiss, may be a symbol of the archetype of the shadow which may include unacceptable aggressive or sexual feelings. Such a response would help June to explore parts of herself that she was previously unaware of.)

20. June might respond in this way to the therapist's statement in 19.c. "I know that my mother never liked it when I got angry and I try not to. I really want to be a good wife, but sometimes my husband just does things that really irritate me."

If you were a Jungian analyst or therapist, which of these responses might you choose?

    (a.) Can you tell me more about that?
    b. Are you aware that your husband also may represent an archetypal symbol for you?

(a. Jungian therapists and analysts are likely to follow up on a new insight that patients have about their feelings, situations, or relationships. Not all comments need be directly related to archetypal imagery. The therapist and June are likely to further explore her relationship with her husband. Her awareness of her strong feelings is prompted by the dream interpretation.)

21. As a Jungian therapist, which of these techniques are you least likely to use in working with June?

    (a.) acting as if
    b. active imagination
    c. interpretation of transference
    d. the sand tray

(a. Although Jungian therapists and analysts may occasionally use Adlerian techniques, such as "acting as if", they are more likely to use the other three techniques which help to bring unconscious material into awareness.)

44

22. In interpreting a dream, a Jungian analyst is most likely to ask what the dream does for the

    a. archetype
    b. dreamer
    c. therapist
    d. patient's parents

(b. Dreams cannot be interpreted without the dreamer. The purpose of understanding the dream is to see what purpose it serves for the dreamer.)

23. Because of the archetypal imagery and new insights that June has developed about an aspect about herself, her dream is most likely to be viewed as a _____ dream?

    a. big
    b. little

(a. The dream might be called a big dream because it comes from June's collective unconscious. A little dream would reflect more day-to-day material. This dream might help June and her analyst explore more aspects of herself than a dream about a movie that she had seen which contained little archetypal material.)

SPECIAL TOPICS

OE1. Why would Jungian therapists find brief therapy inconsistent with Jungian theory? (110)

_____

_____

_____

_____

OE2. One current trend in Jungian therapy is the popularization of Jung's ideas to the general public. Why do you think Jung's ideas have achieved such popularity? (110)

_____

_____

_____

_____

OE3. In terms of using Jung's concepts with other theories, which of his concepts do you believe would be most popular among other theorists or mental health professionals? (111)

_____

_____

_____

45

OE4. In what way do the concepts of anima and animus help Jungian therapists address gender issues? (113)

_____

_____

_____

OE5. What do Jungian therapists learn in their training that helps them deal with multicultural issues in therapy? (115)

_____

_____

_____

_____

STRENGTHS AND LIMITATIONS

What do you see as the strengths and limitations of Jungian therapy?

STRENGTHS	LIMITATIONS
_____	_____
_____	_____
_____	_____
_____	_____
_____	_____
_____	_____

JUNGIAN THERAPY: A QUIZ

True or false items: Decide if the following statements are more "true" or more "false" as they apply to Jungian therapy and analysis.

Ⓣ F   Q1.   Much of Jung's life was devoted to exploring the unconscious.

T Ⓕ   Q2.   Freud and Jung had a friendly collaborative relationship that lasted until Freud died.

Ⓣ F   Q3.   Jung saw the ego as a way of organizing conscious forces.

Ⓣ F   Q4.   The collective unconscious refers to an inherited tendency of the human mind to form representations of mythological motifs, representations that vary a great deal without losing their basic pattern.

46

(T) F   Q5.   Archetypes are images with form but not content.

(T) F   Q6.   Symbols are expressions of archetypes and have content.

T (F)   Q7.   A mandala is an example of an archetype.

T (F)   Q8.   Like Freud, Jung believed that the most important focus of therapy should be early childhood development.

(T) F   Q9.   Becoming more aware of previously unconscious forces is an important goal of Jungian therapy and analysis.

T (F)   Q10. Jungian therapy pays less attention to different cultures than psychoanalysis.

Multiple choice items: Select the best answer from the alternatives using a Jungian perspective.

_____   Q11.   From the five choices below, choose the concept that Jungian therapists would consider to be most important.

     a.   anima
     b.   style of life
     c.   superego
     d.   transference
     (e.)   unconscious

_____   Q12.   The tendency of humans to form representations of mythological motifs refers to the

     a.   conscious.
     b.   preconscious.
     (c)   collective unconscious.
     d.   personal unconscious.

_____   Q13.   Which of these is not an archetype?

     a.   death
     b.   power
     c.   the persona
     (d)   Zeus

_____   Q14.   Which of these is not a symbol?

     (a)   anima
     b.   Hitler
     c.   Michael Jordan
     d.   Queen Elizabeth

_____   Q15.   Typical everyday interactions with neighbors would be representative of this archetype.

     a.   anima-animus
     (b.)   persona
     c.   Self
     d.   shadow

_____ Q16. Jung's concept of introversion refers to

 a. being shy and quiet.
 b. being concerned with one's inner world - one's thoughts and ideas.
 c. believing that others are inferior to oneself in any of these three areas: occupation, family, and society.
 d. difficulty in maintaining relationships with others.

_____ Q17. When Harvey decides that he will not take a job offer, he is using which function?

 a. introversion
 b. intuition
 c. sensing
 d. thinking

_____ Q18. To effectively use the process of Jungian analysis, a patient should have at least some of this attitude.

 a. extraversion
 b. introversion
 c. thinking
 d. feeling

_____ Q19. Which of these functions is most likely to exist in an individual's conscious level?

 a. auxiliary
 b. inferior
 c. tertiary
 d. superior

_____ Q20. Which of these is most likely to be a goal of Jungian therapy?

 a. list the archetypes most important to close family members
 b. become more extraverted while still being intuitive
 c. come to terms with unconscious factors, bringing more material into consciousness
 d. become more aware of behaviors, thoughts, and feelings of others.

_____ Q21. Which of these stages of Jungian therapy most closely fits with the contributions made by Carl Jung?

 a. catharsis
 b. elucidation or interpretation
 c. social education
 d. individuation

_____ Q22. Dreaming of a bad experience that one had at a family gathering is most likely classified as a(n) _____ .

 a. objective dream.
 b. subjective dream.
 c. inappropriate dream.
 d. nightmare.

48

_____ Q23. Which of these does NOT directly relate to gender issues in Jungian therapy or analysis?

    a. active imagination
    b. anima
    c. animus
    d. the symbol of Pandora

_____ Q24. Which of these approaches to understanding problems is most closely associated with Jungian theory?

    a. developing better communication skills
    b. establishing a holding environment
    c. using themes developed from cultural knowledge
    d. analysis of the first 5 years of life

_____ Q25. In understanding a patient's psychotic process, a Jungian therapist, more than other therapists, might

    a. take a history of physical problems.
    b. analyze speech fluency.
    c. determine effective communication patterns.
    d. examine symbolism in verbal expression.

ANSWER KEY

1. c	11. d	21. a
2. d	12. b	22. b
3. a	13. c	23. a
4. c	14. c	
5. c	15. c	
6. a	16. b	
7. b	17. b	
8. b	18. d	
9. d	19. c	
10. a	20. a	

QUIZ

Q1. T	Q11. e	Q21. d
Q2. F	Q12. c	Q22. a
Q3. T	Q13. d	Q23. a
Q4. T	Q14. a	Q24. c
Q5. T	Q15. b	Q25. d
Q6. T	Q16. b	
Q7. F	Q17. d	
Q8. F	Q18. b	
Q9. T	Q19. d	
Q10. F	Q20. c	

49

CHAPTER 4

ADLERIAN THERAPY

ADLERIAN THERAPY SELF-INVENTORY

Directions: By comparing your beliefs about personality and therapy to Adler's, you should have a clearer idea of how much you will need to suspend your beliefs or change attitudes to understand Adler's theory of personality and approach to therapy. You may find it helpful to complete this section before and after you read the chapter. In this way, you can see if your views have changed. There are no correct answers, only an opportunity to express your views.

Put an "X" on the line so that it indicates how much you agree or disagree with the statement: A=Agree, D=Disagree.

D   A

1. Developing an interest in the social welfare of others should be one of several goals of therapy.

2. Social relationships are more powerful in determining one's personality than one's drives.

3. People can be understood by examining what they want to be.

4. Individuals have a need to overcome feelings of inferiority and to strive for success.

5. Therapists should be able to understand patterns in the way clients lead their lives.

6. Therapy should focus on thinking patterns that lead to behaviors and feelings. The therapist should not focus on feelings alone.

7. It is important to understand clients' views of the world.

8. Although people are influenced by their early childhood experiences, they still may be able to improve and shape their own lives.

9. To understand clients' problems, it is helpful to ask them about their earliest memories.

10. Understanding a person's lifestyle is important in understanding his or her problems.

11. Therapeutic techniques to change beliefs and behaviors are more important than those which bring about insight.

50

_____ X X _____ 12. Clients can be seen as discouraged and in need of re-education rather than being unaware of unconscious processes.

_____ X X _____ 13. Knowing about clients' positions in their families helps to understand their problems.

_____ X _____ 14. Clients may seek help because they make mistaken assumptions about life.

_____ X X _____ 15. To bring about therapeutic change, therapy should be directed at the client's thoughts, goals, and beliefs.

_____ X _____ 16. Gathering information about the relationships among family members and then summarizing and interpreting this material will help meet therapeutic goals.

X _____ 17. Only those past events that are consistent with one's own view of oneself are going to be remembered.

_____ X _____ 18. Working with people's conscious memories is more important than trying to bring unconscious memories into current awareness.

_____ X _____ 19. Insight by itself is not enough. Clients need help in changing their beliefs.

_____ X _____ 20. Therapists and clients cooperate together to help clients change their mistaken beliefs.

HISTORY OF ADLERIAN THEORY

Which influences do you think were most important in the development of Adler's theory?

PERSONAL LIFE	PROFESSIONAL INFLUENCES
Born February 7, 1870 Hungarian Jewish parents Near Vienna Severe illnesses Traumatic events Encouragement by father helped his school work 1897 - married Wife was dedicated to socialism 1902 - joined Freud's Vienna Psychoanalytic Society 1911 - left the Society Was ophthalmologist and later a practicing physician in military hospital	Kant's approach to helping individuals learn about themselves and others Nietzsche's will to power influenced Adler's concept of superiority Vaihinger's "as if" - treating values as if they were true "Fictional finalism" ideas that are not real but help to deal with reality Freud's views of the importance of early childhood, unconscious factors, and dreams

ADLERIAN THEORY OF PERSONALITY

Adler stressed a positive view of human nature. He believed that individuals can control their fate. They can do this in part by trying to help others (social interest). How they do this can be understood through analyzing their lifestyles. Early interactions with family members, peers, and teachers help to determine the role of inferiority and superiority in their lives.

style of life or *lifestyle* A way of seeking to fulfill particular goals that individuals set in their lives. Individuals use their own patterns of beliefs, cognitive styles, and behaviors as a way of expressing their style of life. Often style of life or lifestyle is a means for overcoming feelings of inferiority.

social interest The caring and concern for the welfare of others that can serve to guide people's behavior throughout their lives. It is a sense of being a part of society and taking responsibility to improve it.

superiority The drive to become superior allows individuals to become skilled, competent, and creative.

superiority complex A means of masking feelings of inferiority by displaying boastful, self-centered, or arrogant behavior - inflating one's importance at the expense of others.

inferiority Feelings of inadequacy and incompetence that develop during infancy and serve as the basis to strive for superiority in order to overcome feelings of inferiority.

inferiority complex A strong and pervasive belief that one is not as good as other people. It is usually an exaggerated sense of feelings of inadequacy and insecurity that may result in being defensive or anxious.

birth order The idea that place in the family constellation (such as being the youngest child) can have an impact on one's later personality and functioning.

family constellation The number and birth order, as well as the personality characteristics of members of a family. Important in determining lifestyle.

CASE EXAMPLE OF AMY

At age 20, Amy is the youngest of four children. Her sister Anne is 22, and her other sister Linda is 24. Bart is 26. Although Bart has been friendly with Amy, they have not been close as Bart spent most of his time as a child with other neighborhood boys and male cousins. Linda and Anne did not get along with each other. Often they would fight for their mother's affection by telling lies about each other or show how they could help their mother. Sometimes, they would try to enlist Amy to be on their side by being nice to her and flattering her. However, when she would borrow their clothes without asking, Anne would yell at and occasionally hit her. Linda would tolerate this behavior. Amy would then cry to her mother about Anne; then her mother would discipline Anne.

Her mother stayed at home with the children until Amy was 13. Then she returned to work as a secretary at a local business. While at home, her mother tried hard to spend time with each of her children. When Anne and Linda were teenagers, she worried about their competitiveness. They were both good students and athletes. Sometimes she would take Amy to their sporting events. She noticed that Amy tried to do as well at sports as her sisters and often she struggled with math at school. Also, Amy lost interest in sports around the time she entered ninth grade. Sometimes Amy's mother would worry about Amy's moping and sullenness.

52

Amy's father owned a hardware store. Because it was busiest on Saturday, Amy rarely saw him then. During the week when the store closed at 9 p.m., her father didn't get home until 9:30. Often her father would joke with her and treat her differently than the others. He was pleased that she didn't seem to be in trouble. When she was a child, he would tell her stories and play games with her and give her stuffed animals. She was happiest when her father, and also her mother, would give her their time or gifts, even if they were small. When she entered high school, her father would talk to her about school work and tell her amusing incidents that happened at work. Although Amy enjoyed his attention and interest, it never seemed enough. She worried about whether her school work would please him. Sometimes she would work at the hardware store because she knew he appreciated that even though she didn't particularly enjoy it. She kept busy both in and out of school, in part to earn money, but also to prove that she could be successful.

QUESTIONS ABOUT AMY FROM AN ADLERIAN PERSONALITY THEORY PERSPECTIVE

1. The most overriding and important concept in understanding Amy, according to Adlerian theory, is:

   a. birth order.
   b. inferiority.
   c. life style.
   d. social interest.

2. According to Adler, Amy's worry about her school work might be an example of

   a. feeling inferior.
   b. an inferiority complex.
   c. feeling superior.
   d. a superiority complex.

3. Adler might question Amy's lack of social interest. This is most likely due to

   a. authoritative parents.
   b. poor relationship between parents.
   c. pampering by parents and siblings.
   d. socially isolating Amy.

4. According to Adler, Amy seems to be developing many feelings of

   a. inferiority.
   b. industriousness.
   c. introvertedness.
   d. separation anxiety.

5. Adlerian therapists' interest in Amy's relationships with Bart would refer to which of these concepts?

   a. birth order
   b. inferiority
   c. social interest
   d. separation anxiety

6. According to Adler, the relationship between Amy and her family can be described by the term

   a. cathartic.
   b. family constellation.
   c. holding environment.
   d. social interest.

53

7. Examining Amy's relationship with her father, one could conclude that Amy has not sufficiently developed her

   a. inferiority complex.
   b. super ego.
   c. social interest.
   d. superiority complex.

8. According to Adlerians, which of these is not likely to be considered in understanding Amy's life style?

   a. her relationship with her father
   b. her repression of memories of not being as successful as her sisters
   c. her lack of social interest in others
   d. her family constellation

ADLERIAN THERAPY AND COUNSELING

GOALS OF ADLERIAN THERAPY

Amy is depressed and does not feel that her life is going well. She sees other women as being more attractive, more interesting, and brighter. She does not have a boyfriend and is upset that her friends spend too much time with their boyfriends. She feels that her professors do not make her courses interesting enough and that they make the courses too difficult.

9. The major focus of counseling or therapy for an Adlerian would be Amy's

   a. feelings of inferiority.
   b. feelings of superiority.
   c. lifestyle.
   d. social interest.

10. Amy seems to expect others to do things for her, but she does not do much for others. Thus, one goal of therapy may be to

    a. explore her feelings of superiority.
    b. explore her feelings of inferiority.
    c. examine her family constellation.
    d. work on her lack of social interest.

11. Which of these is LEAST likely to be a goal of Adlerian therapy or counseling for Amy?

    a. bring unconscious material into conscious awareness
    b. help her resolve problems with her sisters
    c. consider ways to be involved in community service
    d. deal with day-to-day problems

12. In Adlerian therapy and counseling, most practitioners consider themselves to do

    a. only counseling.
    b. only psychotherapy.
    c. both counseling and psychotherapy.
    d. Adlerian psychoanalysis.

54

ASSESSMENT IN ADLERIAN THERAPY

Adlerians usually use a lifestyle analysis to assess their clients. Projective techniques, questionnaires, and interviews are a part of this process. Material includes information about the family, early recollection, and dreams. Adlerians determine individuals' strengths and basic mistakes from this material. The following are key concepts to know about assessment:

early recollections Memories of actual incidents that patients recall from their childhood. Adlerians use this information to make inferences about current behavior of children or adults.

basic mistakes Self-defeating aspects of individuals' lifestyle that may affect their later behavior are called basic mistakes. Such mistakes often include avoidance of others, seeking power, a desperate need for security, or faulty values.

assets Assessing the strengths of individuals' lifestyles is an important part of lifestyle assessment, as is assessment of early recollections and basic mistakes.

EXAMPLE OF A LIFESTYLE ANALYSIS

Several lifestyle questionnaires have been developed by Adlerians. A modified version of a lifestyle analysis is presented here. Much of it is adapted from Mosak and Shulman's Life Style Inventory (1988). Such a questionnaire could be completed by the client, for the client by the therapist, or both working together.

ADLERIAN LIFESTYLE ANALYSIS OF AMY
(Amy's responses are noted in italics.)

FAMILY CONSTELLATION: BIRTH ORDER AND SIBLING DESCRIPTION

List your brothers and sisters from oldest to youngest and describe them briefly.

Bart +6	Linda +4	Ann +2	Amy
handsome	aggressive	attractive	slow
very social	athletic	sneaky	insecure
rugged	attractive	small	loner
likes outdoors	independent	good in science	overprotected
mature	well-liked	protective sometimes	sensitive
protective	respected	picked on me	exaggerates
likeable	looked down on me	sometimes	self-critical
		in trouble with Mom	

1. Which of your siblings is the most different from you and how? *They all are. Bart maybe, because he's the oldest and a guy. They all seemed to accomplish so much more than me. Linda did the best in school and sports. Bart was ok at school. I'm struggling.*

2. Which of your siblings is most like you? *None really. Maybe Anne as she would get in trouble with Mom for lying. I don't do that, but Anne seemed less perfect than Bart and Linda.*

3. Which played together? *Anne and Linda sometimes. I would get included for some activities.*

4. Which fought each other? *Anne and Linda definitely.*

5. Who took care of whom? *Mainly, Linda took care of me. Once in a while Bart did.*

6. Any unusual achievements? *Bart was an Eagle Scout. Linda was captain of field hockey and softball in high school.*

7. Any accidents or sickness? *Bart had spinal meningitis when he was 12 and almost died. I was in an automobile accident when I was 9 and sprained my neck. Lots of bruises too.*

8. What kind of child were you? *I was lonely sometimes, but I would get my sisters to do things for me. I always seemed to be tagging behind my sisters.*

9. What was school like for you? *It was hard; I didn't feel like I did as well as my sisters. I often went to them for help.*

10. What scared you when you were a child? *I didn't like being alone. I was scared of monsters in my closet. Sometimes I was worried about something bad happening to my mother.*

11. What were your childhood ambitions? *I wanted to be an actress or a singer and be very famous.*

12. What was your role in your peer group? *I had a few friends that I confided in, but we were never a part of the "in" group.*

13. Any significant events in your physical and sexual development? *I wanted to be beautiful like Linda. I was afraid I'd never develop breasts and that I would be flat chested. When I did mature, boys teased me and I didn't like it.*

14. How would you summarize your social development? *I felt slow, shy often. Others seemed to know the right thing to say and I didn't.*

15. What were the most important values in your family? *To be successful, academically and athletically, to make hard work pay off.*

16. What stands out the most for you about family life? *I never seemed to be able to do as well as my brother and sisters even though they would help me out.*

FAMILY CONSTELLATION: PARENTAL FIGURES AND RELATIONSHIPS

	Father	*Mother*
1.Current age	*55*	*51*
2. Occupation	*Hardware store owner*	*Secretary*
3. Kind of person	*Hardworking, kind, busy*	*Harried, loving*
4. Ambitions for the children	*Go to college, get a prestigious job*	*Stay out of trouble, do well in school*
5. Your childhood view	*I idolized him before I was 9, very fond of him*	*Felt she worried most about my sisters fighting*
6. Relationship to children	*Closest to Bart, then maybe me next*	*Appreciated Linda's accomplishments, seemed to favor her.*
7. Sibling most like	*Bart was very much like my father: looks, behavior*	*Anne was like my mother, often frustrating*

8. Describe your parents' relationship to each other? *Got along well. Not too affectionate. Dad wasn't in the house a lot.*

9. How did your brother and sisters view your parents? *Anne fought, especially with Mom. Bart got along well with both. Sometimes Linda barely noticed them.*

10. What was your parents' relationship to the children? *Dad didn't get too involved in discipline. Very warm. We could drive Mom nuts.*

11. Besides your parents, who was another parental figure in your life? *My grandmother. She often came to visit in the afternoons, and Mom would go out shopping. She was great. She was very loving and had a lot of patience with me.*

EARLY RECOLLECTIONS AND DREAMS

1. What is your earliest single specific memory? *I remember when I was about 4 playing in the snow and then coming into a warm kitchen to lick the pan when my Mom made brownies. My Mom laughed and cleaned me up when I had chocolate all over my face.*

2. What are some other early recollections?
   a. *I was about 5 and I was riding my tricycle. An older boy, maybe 7 or 8, started teasing me and grabbed the handlebars. Bart saw this and made him go home.*
   b. *I had a room next to Anne's. When I was about 6 she took cookies into her room at night. I told on her, and she punched me in the chest.*

57

3. What feelings are associated with these early memories? *I feel protected by Mom and Bart, but I don't feel confident. I felt hurt by Anne; it seemed she didn't like me.*

4. Any recurring dreams? *I am nominated for an award at the Academy Awards - best supporting actress. My name is mentioned as a nominee, and then the entire audience starts to hoot and jeer. It feels awful.*

LIFESTYLE SUMMARY

1. Summary of Amy's family constellation: Amy is the youngest of four children. She is somewhat like Adler's description of the youngest child. She was taken care of by Linda and Bart but picked on somewhat by Anne. She felt inferior in terms of accomplishments to Bart, Anne, and especially Linda. Amy's family values success, academic and athletic, and now job success. Amy does not feel that she is meeting these values. Amy has tried to show her parents that she can achieve but has not felt that she has done so. She feels somewhat isolated from her family in terms of achievement but has felt loving attention from her father. Amy feels love from her mother but resents that it is shared with her siblings. To get attention, Amy might get hurt or wounded.

2. Summary of Amy's early recollections: Amy enjoys the warmth and protectiveness of family members. She says: "I like the feeling of being cared for, but sometimes I don't think people will care for me or love me because I'm not good at much."

3. Summary of Amy's basic mistakes: Amy has some beliefs about herself that cause problems for her in her daily life.

   a. When I set out to do things, I never really do them well enough.

   b. You have to be very bright and talented (like Linda) to be a successful person.

   c. People will see through to my failings and never really care about me.

   d. If I were a stronger person, nothing would bother me.

   Summary of Amy's assets: Some of her assets are not obvious from the lifestyle analysis as Amy tends to be self-deprecating.

   1. Amy is a better than average student. A's and B's in high school.

   2. Amy is willing to challenge her beliefs about being inferior to others.

   3. She is sensitive to the needs of other people and caring in her relations. Exceptions to this occur when Amy is feeling very inferior to others or afraid she will say the wrong thing.

   4. Amy works hard both at school and in her part-time jobs.

   5. She takes responsibility when involved in activities like the sociology club or organizing activities for the Student Activities Association.

58

QUESTIONS ABOUT AMY'S LIFESTYLE ANALYSIS

13. Which of Amy's beliefs would you want to help her change? (Select more than one. Answers follow).

    a. Belief that she is inferior to others.
    b. Belief that she won't be successful.
    c. Belief that she will not find someone who cares about her.
    d. Belief that she is better than others.
    e. Belief that if you try hard enough you can do anything you want.

(Answer: a, b, and c because they are consistent with Amy's lifestyle analysis and her feelings of inferiority or lack of self worth. "d" suggests a feeling of superiority that is not evident in the analysis. "e" suggests more confidence than Amy has.)

14. Which of the following are not important in Amy's lifestyle analysis? (Answer follows)

    a. family constellation
    b. early recollections
    c. basic mistakes
    d. assets
    e. all are important

(e. All are essential to an Adlerian lifestyle analysis. However, information about family constellation and early recollections form the raw data from which inferences about basic mistakes and assets are made.)

TECHNIQUES FOR CHANGE

A lifestyle analysis helps the Adlerian therapist to gain insights into client problems by determining the clients' basic mistakes and assets. These insights are based on assessing family constellation, dreams, and social interest. To help the client change, Adlerians may use a number of active techniques that focus to a great extent on changing beliefs and reorienting the client's view of situations and relationships. These techniques are defined here.

interpretation Adlerians express insights to their patients that relate to patients' goals. Interpretations often focus on the family constellation and social interest.

immediacy Communicating the experience of the therapist to the patient about what is happening in the moment.

encouragement An important therapeutic technique that is used to build a relationship and to foster client change. Supporting clients in changing beliefs and behaviors is a part of encouragement.

acting as if In this technique, patients are asked to "act as if" a behavior will be effective. Patients are encouraged to try a new role, the way they might try on new clothing.

catching oneself In this technique, patients learn to notice that they are performing behaviors which they wish to change. When they catch themselves, they may have an "Aha" response.

spitting in the client's soup Making comments to the client to make behaviors less attractive or desirable.

creating images The techniques to form a mental picture of doing something, which can have more impact than reminding oneself mentally.

avoiding the tar baby Although the term "tar baby" has come to have racial and other meanings, Adler used tar baby to refer to the therapist being careful when discussing a sticky (tar) issue that is both significant for the patient and causes problems for the patient. This way the therapist does not fall into a trap that the patient sets by using faulty assumptions.

59

paradoxical intention A therapeutic strategy in which clients are instructed to engage and exaggerate behaviors that they seek to change. By prescribing the symptom, therapists make patients more aware of their situation and help them achieve distance from the symptoms. For example, a patient who is afraid of mice may be asked to exaggerate his fear of mice, or a patient who hoards paper may be asked to exaggerate that behavior so that living becomes difficult. In this way individuals can become more aware of and more distant from their symptoms.

homework Specific behaviors or activities that clients are asked to do after a therapy session.

life tasks There are five basic obligations and opportunities: occupation, society, love, self development, and spirituality development. These are used to help determine therapeutic goals.

push-button technique Designed to show patients how they can create whatever feelings they want by thinking about them, the push-button technique asks patients to remember a pleasant incident that they have experienced, become aware of feelings connected to it, and then switch to an unpleasant image and those feelings. Thus patients learn that they have the power to change their own feelings.

QUESTIONS ABOUT HELPING AMY

In the following examples, you are an Adlerian therapist and are using different techniques to help Amy change her beliefs and (sometimes) her behaviors. Identify the techniques.

15. Amy has often gotten her father and also friends to feel sorry for her. Now she is telling you how terrible her week was. Instead of talking to her about the week being really awful, you identify strengths in her behavior. You are

    a.   avoiding the tar baby.
    b.   spitting in the client's soup.
    c.   using paradoxical intentions.
    d.   using the push button technique.

16. Amy has met a man that she likes but she is afraid to talk to him because she is afraid he won't be interested in her. You tell her to pretend that she knows he likes her. You are using

    a.   the push-button technique.
    b.   the acting as if technique.
    c.   paradoxical intention.
    d.   life tasks

17. Amy says that she has been fighting with her sister Anne a lot. Now when she sees Anne she starts to feel angry even before she talks to her. You tell her to imagine a pleasant time that she has spent with Anne and feel the accompanying feelings. Then she is to imagine an unpleasant scene with Anne and the feelings that go with it. You show Amy how she can create different feelings by changing what she is thinking about. You are using this technique:

    a.   catching oneself
    b.   avoiding the tar baby
    c.   acting as if technique
    d.   the push-button technique

60

18. Amy has developed mental pictures of herself talking easily and articulately with a popular friend. Which technique is Amy using?

    a. catching oneself
    b. creating imagery
    c. paradoxical intention
    d. avoiding the tar baby

19. Amy has had difficulty in talking to Alicia, a friend she admires. You remind her of the abilities she has in talking to other friends. You suggest she use these abilities when talking to Alicia. You are using

    a. avoiding the tar baby.
    b. encouragement.
    c. catching oneself.
    d immediacy.

20. Amy comes to a therapy session excited that she has noticed several times that she has felt sorry for herself when she started to complain about all of the homework she had. She was able to see what she was doing and go right to her homework. Which technique did Amy use?

    a. acting as if
    b. avoiding the tar baby
    c. catching oneself
    d. creating imagery

21. Being an Adlerian, you are interested in how Amy deals with five important life tasks. Which is NOT an important life task?

    a. love
    b. dreams
    c. work
    d. spiritual development

SPECIAL TOPICS

*OE1. How do Adlerians make therapy briefer? (148-149)

_____

_____

_____

_____

*OE2. What are current trends in Adlerian therapy? (149-150)

_____

_____

_____

_____

61

*OE3. How are gender issues in Adlerian therapy related to Adler's concept of masculine protest? (152-153)

_____

_____

_____

_____

OE4. How can multicultural issues affect individuals' family constellation, social interest, and early recollections? (153-154)

_____

_____

_____

_____

OE5.   What is the Adlerian approach to group therapy? (154)

_____

_____

_____

_____

STRENGTHS AND LIMITATIONS

What do you see as the strengths and limitations of Adlerian therapy?

STRENGTHS	LIMITATIONS
_____	_____
_____	_____
_____	_____
_____	_____
_____	_____
_____	_____

ADLERIAN THERAPY: A QUIZ

True/false items: Decide if the following statements are more "true" or more "false" as they apply to Adlerian therapy.

T **F** Q1. The Adlerian approach is primarily behavioral.

T **F** Q2. Adler was a devoted student of Freud's as reflected by the similarity of his theory to Freud's drive theory.

T F Q3. Striving for superiority is appropriate for all people.

T F Q4. Early recollections are helpful to Adlerians in determining life style.

T F Q5. Confronting and changing faulty beliefs are important aspects of Adler's therapy.

T **F** Q6. Adlerians should have neutral relationships with their clients and not encourage them to change their beliefs.

T **F** Q7. Lifestyle is formed in adulthood.

T F Q8. The "as if" technique can help a client try out a behavior that she may be afraid of.

T **F** Q9. Id forces determine an individual's lifestyle.

T **F** Q10. Assessment is not important in Adlerian therapy.

Multiple choice items. Select the best answer from the alternatives using an Adlerian perspective.

_____ Q11. The most comprehensive concept in Adlerian therapy is

   a. birth order.
   b. inferiority.
   c. superiority.
   d. style of life.

_____ Q12. If a person has strong and pervasive feelings of inadequacy which effect his life, he may

   a. have feelings of inferiority.
   b. have an inferiority complex.
   c. have a superiority complex.
   d. lack social interest.

_____ Q13. Which is most important for Adlerians?

   a. changing beliefs
   b. changing behaviors
   c. making unconscious processes concerns
   d. interpreting early childhood family interactions

63

_____ Q14. Which of these individuals had the least influence on Adler?

a. Freud
b. Jung
c. Kant
d. Nietzsche

_____ Q15. Which of the following is not a part of lifestyle assessment?

a. acting as if
b. dreams
c. early recollections
d. mistaken beliefs

_____ Q16. Charles has few friends, and he does little but play computer games. An Adlerian goal for Charles would be to increase his

a. feelings of superiority.
b. early recollections.
c. dream activity.
d. social interest.

_____ Q17. "All men are created equal" is an example of

a. lifestyle.
b. fictionalism.
c. striving for superiority.
d. an expression of social interest.

_____ Q18. Which of these is NOT an Adlerian life task?

a. love
b. lifestyle
c. occupation
d. spiritual development

_____ Q19. Which of the following ideas did Adler share with Freud?

a. Oedipus complex
b. emphasis on early childhood
c. educational emphasis in treatment
d. importance of psychosexual stages

_____ Q20. Allison is scared to talk to her boss but pretends that she can do it. This is called

a. encouragement.
b. acting as if.
c. catching oneself.
d. immediacy.

64

_____ Q21. Which Adlerian concept has generated the most research?

     (a)   birth order
     b.   creating imagery
     c.   social interest
     d.   masculine protest

_____ Q22. Which of these is least likely to occur in Adlerian group therapy?

     a.   education of clients
     (b)   interpretation of transference
     c.   improving communication style
     d.   discussion of family relationships

_____ Q23. Which of these is most likely to be a goal of Adlerian therapy?

     a.   modifying behavior
     b.   removing symptoms
     (c)   changing beliefs
     d.   developing a holding environment

_____ Q24. Which of these is a basic source of data for Adlerian therapists?

     a.   encouragement
     b.   lifestyle
     (c)   early recollections
     d.   social interest

_____ Q25. A lifestyle analysis uses information about

     a.   early childhood
     b.   relationships with peers
     c.   dreams
     (d)   all of the above

ANSWER KEY

1.	c	11.	a
2.	a	12.	c
3.	c	13.	a, b, c
4.	a	14.	e
5.	a	15.	a
6.	b	16.	b
7.	c	17.	d
8.	b	18.	b
9.	c	19.	b
10.	d	20.	c
		21.	b

QUIZ

Q1.	F	Q11.	d	Q21.	a
Q2.	F	Q12.	b	Q22.	b
Q3.	T	Q13.	a	Q23.	c
Q4.	T	Q14.	b	Q24.	c
Q5.	T	Q15.	a	Q25.	d
Q6.	F	Q16.	d		
Q7.	F	Q17.	b		
Q8.	T	Q18.	b		
Q9.	F	Q19.	b		
Q10.	F	Q20.	b		

ANSWERS TO OPEN ENDED QUESTIONS

OE1*   They may limit time for the lifestyle analysis. They may focus work on one life task.

OE2*   Trends include focusing on social change and issues such as AIDS and family violence; developing an educational thrust.

OE3*   Adler believed that some men would focus on masculinity to prove they were superior to women. He was concerned about the social roles that limited women's striving for equality.

CHAPTER 5

EXISTENTIAL THERAPY

EXISTENTIAL THERAPY SELF-INVENTORY

Directions: By comparing your beliefs about personality and therapy to those of existential therapists, you should have a clearer idea of how much you will need to suspend your beliefs or change your attitudes to understand existential therapy. You may find it helpful to complete this section before and after you read the chapter. In this way you can see if your views have changed. There are no correct answers, only an opportunity to express your views.

Put an "X" on the line so that it indicates how much you disagree with the statement: A = Agree, D = Disagree.

D   A

_____ 1. Understanding the qualities of human existence is important in therapy.

_____ 2. Expanding self-awareness and increasing one's potential for making choices in life is an important goal of therapy.

_____ 3. Psychotherapy should concentrate on human relationships rather than on techniques.

_____ 4. It is not techniques themselves that are important in therapeutic change but the resolution of important life issues.

_____ 5. To understand individuals, one must understand how they make important life choices.

_____ 6. The special humanness of the therapeutic relationship is one of the most important determinants in assessing the helpfulness of therapy.

_____ 7. Therapists must truly know themselves, their strengths, and weaknesses to be effective.

_____ 8. Self awareness is one of the most important aspects of humanness. It is this which makes effective therapy possible.

_____ 9. Being responsible for one's choices and actions is an important goal of therapy. To seek freedom and to act responsibly within it is also an important goal of therapy.

_____ 10. A special aspect of being human is the freedom to choose and to be responsible for one's life.

67

D   A

_____ 11. Freedom and responsibility are important issues in therapy. Individuals are thrown into an environment which can be hostile. It is their responsibility to make the best of it.

_____ 12. Relationships with others are one of the most essential qualities of being human.

_____ 13. Individuals seek meaning and purpose in their life.

_____ 14. To have poor or ineffective relationships in one's life is to experience alienation and isolation.

_____ 15. Anxiety can be normal as well as a type of psychological disorder.

_____ 16. Being aware of the reality of death helps individuals attribute significance to their own lives and those of others.

_____ 17. An important therapy goal is to strive to be authentic, to be self aware.

_____ 18. An important therapy goal is to try to be all that one is capable of becoming.

HISTORY OF EXISTENTIAL THERAPY

Nineteenth century philosophy forms the basis for existential therapy. A number of philosophers contributed many ideas to the development of existential philosophy. Writers and theologians have also made significant contributions. To help you better understand the basic contributions of these individuals, they are listed along with their most significant contributions.

PHILOSOPHERS	THEOLOGIANS	WRITERS
Søren Kierkegaard conflicts and problems of human existence Freidrich Nietzsche search for a "will to power" Edmund Husserl phenomenology, the study of objects as experienced in the consciousness of individuals Martin Heidegger emphasized the awareness of existence and time Karl Jaspers humans must transcend suffering, struggle, and guilt through decisions	Martin Buber Jewish; I-thou relationships Gabriel Marceau Catholic; relationships that focus on love, hope, and faithfulness Paul Tillich Protestant; emphasized courage and people's capabilities to make life meaningful	Jean-Paul Sartre French philosopher, novelist, and playwright; humanity is freedom, people should find a reason to exist Fyodor Dostoevsky Russian novelist; awareness of one's actions Albert Camus French novelist and philosopher; the absurdity of understanding a meaningless world Franz Kafka German novelist and essayist; despairing and frustrating situations that question the mean- ingfulness of existence

68

QUESTIONS ABOUT EXISTENTIAL ROOTS

1. Which group had the most hopeful view of humanity?

    a. philosophers
    b. theologians
    c. writers
    d. all were similar

2. Which group had the least hopeful view of humanity?

    a. philosophers
    b. theologians
    c. writers
    d. all were similar

ORIGINATORS AND MORE RECENT CONTRIBUTORS TO EXISTENTIAL THERAPY

Unlike many other theories of psychotherapy, there is no single individual who developed existential therapy. The original contributors were the Swiss psychiatrists Ludwig Binswanger and Medard Boss. Other important contributors include Viktor Frankl, Rollo May, Irvin Yalom, James Bugental, R. D. Laing, and Emmy van Deurzen.

ORIGINATORS	MORE RECENT CONTRIBUTORS

Ludwig Binswanger
  Swiss psychiatrist;
  helped patients understand the meaning of their behavior; become authentic
	Rollo May
	  American psychiatrist;
	  author of many books on existential therapy; integrated psychoanalysis and existential therapy

Medard Boss
  Swiss psychiatrist;
  concerned with existential themes and being-in-the- world
	Irvin Yalom
	  American psychiatrist;
	  influential textbook and casebook on existential therapy; developed existential themes

Viktor Frankl
  Psychiatrist born in Vienna;
  developed logotherapy; concerned with finding meaning in life
	James Bugental
	  American psychiatrist;
	  humanistic focus on awareness and self-actualization

	R. D. Laing
	  English psychiatrist;
	  established a therapeutic community for severely disturbed patients' understanding a meaningless world

	Emmy van Deurzen
	  English psychologist;
	  actively involved in writing on existential therapy; developed British School of Existential Psychotherapy

3.   Match the existential therapist with an important contribution.

A.   James Bugental   s.   developed therapeutic community in England
B.   Viktor Frankl   t.   Swiss; helped patients understand meaning of theirs lives
C.   Medard Boss   u.   Swiss; focused patients on being-in-the-world
D.   Rollo May   v.   wrote influential textbook on existential therapy
E.   Ludwig Binswanger   w.   started British School of Existential therapy
F.   Emmy van Deurzen   x.   American; wrote many books on existential themes
G.   R. D. Laing   y.   developed logotherapy
H.   Irvin Yalom   z.   humanistic focus on awareness

Answers: A, z, B, y, C, u, D, x, E, t, F, w, G, s, H, v.

EXISTENTIAL PERSONALITY THEORY

Existence and themes related to existence form the core of existential personality theory. Perhaps the most central concept is Dasein or being-in-the-world. Existential therapists have identified four ways of being in the world: Ümwelt, Mitwelt, Uberwelt, and Eigenwelt. Existing in the world can bring about both normal and neurotic anxiety. Anxiety occurs as individuals deal with important life themes such as living and dying; freedom, responsibility, and choice; isolation and loving; and meaning and meaninglessness. In dealing with these themes, individuals strive for authenticity and self-transcendence.

existentialism A philosophical view that emphasizes the importance of existence, including one's responsibility for one's own psychological existence. Related themes include living and dying, freedom, responsibility to self and others, meaningfulness in life, and authenticity.

being-in-the-world Derived from the German word Dasein that refers to examining oneself, others, and one's relationship with the world, thus attaining higher levels of consciousness.

Umwelt Relating to the environment, the objects and living beings within it; attending to the biological and physical aspects of the world.

Mitwelt A way in which individuals relate to the world by interacting socially with others. The focus is on human relationships rather than relationships that are biological or physical Umwelt.

Überwelt Religious or spiritual beliefs about the ideal world, the way an individual wants the world to be.

Eigenwelt A way of relating to one's "own world." It refers to being aware of oneself and how we relate to ourselves.

kairos A Greek word that refers to the critical point at which a disease is expected to get better or worse. In psychotherapy, it refers to the appropriate timing of a therapeutic intervention.

thrown condition Unforeseen forces or events in the world that one does not cause.

existential anxiety Anxiety arising from the nature of being human and dealing with unforeseen forces (the thrown condition). Existential anxiety is a significant subset of normal anxiety.

neurotic anxiety Anxiety that is out of proportion to a particular event. It is often an indication that an individual is not living authentically and may fail to make choices and assume responsibility.

boundary situation An urgent experience that compels an individual to deal with an existential situation.

70

I-sharing The concept of "I-sharing," a positive term, is one which produces a sense of intimacy. In "I-sharing" a sense of connection or fondness develops when people experience a moment in the same way that another does. This creates a sense of existential connectedness that is in contrast to existential isolation.

self-transcendence Going beyond one's immediate situation to understand one's being and to take responsibility for that being. Going beyond one's own needs to take responsibility for others or to see the world in different ways.

authenticity Being genuine and real, as well as aware of one's being. Authentic individuals deal with moral choices, the meaning of life, and being human.

CASE EXAMPLE OF DAVID

David is a 28-year old truck driver who makes local deliveries in Las Vegas, the city where he has been living for the last five years. After he graduated high school in Seattle, Washington, he joined the Marines. He received a general discharge from the Marines rather than an honorable discharge due to fights that he had been in with some of his fellow Marines. David finds his truck driving responsibilities routine and boring.

When work is done, David looks forward to spending evenings in the casinos. Gambling and the entertainment that is offered in the casinos takes up his evening and much of his weekend leisure time. In the last year, David has been drinking more heavily. He has been less satisfied with his life and things in general. This is a vague sense which he is aware of only a few times during the week when he is sober and not working, gambling, or being entertained.

Growing up in Seattle, David had an undistinguished high school career. He graduated with C's, while his older brother, an excellent student, became a mechanical engineer. Twice during high school, David was arrested for vandalism and brought before juvenile court. His father, a long-distance truck driver became very angry and distant from David, giving up on him. His mother, who worked in a plastics manufacturing factory, seemed to David to be more concerned about her sisters and their families than about her own family.

About eight months ago, David heard that his father was diagnosed with prostate cancer. He had been complaining of physical problems for months but never went to a doctor. After diagnosis of the problem, David's father learned that the cancer was inoperable. Furthermore, David's father had not responded well to either chemical or radiation therapies.

David had talked to his father a few times, but their conversations had been rather brief. David's view is "stuff happens." He has not returned to Seattle to visit his father.

David had gone out with Melinda for about two years. They broke up about a year ago, as it became evident to Melinda that their relationship would not lead to marriage. Although he has tried to contact her since, she has not been interested in resuming the relationship and has become engaged to someone else.

QUESTIONS ABOUT DAVID FROM AN EXISTENTIAL PERSONALITY THEORY VIEWPOINT

4. Regarding being-in-the-world, David would be seen by existential therapists as

   a. barely aware of his existence.
   b. consumed by questions about his existence.
   c. too individuated from his parents.
   d. lacking in social interest.

71

5. David seems to be most preoccupied with the

    a.   Umwelt.
    b.   Mitwelt.
    c.   Überwelt.
    d.   Eigenwelt.
    e.   equally present in all four.

6. Existential therapists are particularly concerned with how their patients deal with the

    a.   Umwelt.
    b.   Mitwelt.
    c.   Überwelt.
    d.   Eigenwelt.

7. David's relationship with his parents and Melinda occur in the

    a.   Umwelt.
    b.   Mitwelt.
    c.   Überwelt.
    d.   Eigenwelt.

8. The fact that David's father unexpectedly developed cancer could be called

    a.   Mitwelt.
    b.   Überwelt.
    c.   kairos.
    d.   a thrown condition.

9. David is barely aware of discomforts in his life. As he becomes more aware, then _____ is likely to increase.

    a.   kairos
    b.   existential anxiety
    c.   neurotic anxiety
    d.   all of the above

10. For David to take responsibility for his life, to become more involved in family and other relationships, would be to start on the path to

    a.   the Ümwelt.
    b.   the thrown condition.
    c.   self-transcendence.
    d.   neurotic anxiety.

11. Which of these existential themes present challenges for David?

    a.   living and dying
    b.   freedom, responsibility, and choice
    c.   isolation and loving
    d.   meaning and meaninglessness
    e.   all of the above

12. If David were to deal with responsibilities in his life and were to become more genuine, he would become more

    a.   authentic.
    b.   neurotic.
    c.   involved in the Ümwelt.
    d.   immersed in his thrown condition.

13. Which of these would help David become more authentic?

    a.   Win $25,000 at poker-slots.
    b.   Get a 20% pay raise.
    c.   Become more self-aware and open to changing his feelings about his father.
    d.   Visit his father.

GOALS OF EXISTENTIAL THERAPY

Existential therapists believe the goals of therapy are to help clients find a purpose to their life, to make it more meaningful. By doing so they become more authentic, more aware of their own being. They become better able to deal with moral choices and decisions.

David is becoming unhappier. His involvement in gambling is not making him richer, nor is it helping him become more satisfied with his life. David is more aware of being lonely. His friendships at work and in the casinos seem superficial and unfulfilling. His phone calls to his mother leave him dissatisfied, whereas in the past he just hung up and went about his business.

QUESTIONS ABOUT DAVID'S GOALS

14. The goals of David's therapy are likely to focus most on the

    a.   Umwelt.
    b.   Mitwelt.
    c.   Überwelt.
    d.   Eigenwelt.

15. A goal of existential therapy for David is to help him

    a.   become more aware of his need to gamble.
    b.   stop his gambling immediately.
    c.   gradually cut back on his gambling.
    d.   do more for his parents.

16. An existential therapist is most likely to be concerned with how detached David is from

    a.   himself.
    b.   God.
    c.   his parents.
    d.   his work responsibilities.

ASSESSMENT IN EXISTENTIAL THERAPY

Typically assessment in existential therapy takes place throughout the course of therapy. Therapists assess progress on current existential themes or follow the emergence of new themes. For existential therapy to be effective, clients must be willing to work in developing authenticity and dealing with existential themes. Material that is discussed can include dreams and responses or scores on projective or objective tests.

17. If David wants help only on stopping his gambling behavior, an existential therapist is most likely to

    a.   refer him to another type of therapist.
    b.   point out that he is being narrow-minded in his outlook.
    c.   convince him that his issues can only be approached by becoming more authentic.
    d.   none of the above.

18. In using dream material in assessment of patient problems, the important aspect is

    a.   the therapist's interpretation of the dream.
    b.   the client's experience of the dream.
    c.   the thrown conditions in operation at the time.
    d.   the therapist's sense of timing.

EXISTENTIAL APPROACH TO THERAPEUTIC CHANGE

The therapist is fully present in the relationship. Her mind does not wander, at least not for long. She brings her attention immediately back to the patient. The relationship is that of therapeutic love - a loving friendship. The therapist genuinely cares for the client and is accepting even though the client may be angry, hostile, or untruthful. The therapist is understanding of client fears that may be expressed as resistance to therapeutic change.

In the following sections, you will be David's existential therapist. Select the response that best fits that of an existential therapist. We will use examples from each of the four existential themes.

LIVING AND DYING

19. David: I'm hearing from my mother that my father's health is getting worse. It bothers me just a little. I wonder why it doesn't bother me more.

    Therapist: a.   What bothers you about his illness?
                 b.   Are you concerned your mother isn't taking better care of him?
                 c.   You may be looking at him from a new point of view. Can you tell me about it?
                 d.   You have focused only on yourself, not on him.

20. David: Knowing that he may be dying has helped me to start to look at my life differently.

    Therapist: a.   How are you looking at it differently?
                 b.   You might be looking not only at how you may be living differently, but also at the possibility of death.
                 c.   Your father's dying might make you realize that now is the time to take responsibility for him and your mother.
                 d.   How do you know he is dying? Maybe there is a chance for him to live.

21. David: Although we didn't get along, I always assumed my father would be here.

    Therapist: a.   You always felt that he would be here and take care of your mother.
                 b.   Looking at the possibility of your father's death seems to give you the opportunity to look at your own life differently.
                 c.   Do you see this as an opportunity for the two of you to get along better?
                 d.   This is an opportunity now for you to change your relationship and try to get along better with him.

22. David: I could change my job. Just because I don't like it, I don't have to change. Lots of people do things they don't like. I can keep it and be bored.

    Therapist: a.   Your job is really boring you. You don't know what to do.
                 b.   You may never get another good chance. You're still young, and there are a number of opportunities for you.
                 c.   Now is the time for you to take responsibility for yourself. Get out of the rut. Go back to school or contact an employment agency. Those actions will pay off for you.
                 d.   You have the freedom to change your job, but acting on that freedom can be overwhelming.

23. David: My job really isn't that bad.

    Therapist: a.   You've given the job a lot of thought, and it seems right to stay with it.
                 b.   How do you know what else is out there? Other options might be better.
                 c.   At times it is really difficult to examine how you react to something, like this job.
                 d.   When you consider the pay, there are other jobs that are a lot worse.

24. David: What should I do?

    Therapist: a.   Stay at your old job. It's secure. You don't know what's out there.
                 b.   Look for a new job. There is a bright future ahead of you.
                 c.   You really don't know what to do, do you?
                 d.   Making a choice is really difficult. It's hard when two difficult choices present themselves to you.

ISOLATION AND LOVING

25. David: I think I really cared for Melinda. When I was with her, I am not sure I wanted her. Now that we've broken up, I miss her.

    Therapist: a.   Being alone is difficult, and now you're experiencing the loneliness in a way you have not done before.
                 b.   It is time for you to be decisive. Decide what is best and act on it.
                 c.   Do you think Melinda wants you back?
                 d.   When you are indecisive, there is a price to pay. That price is being lonely and being isolated.

26. David: It's hard for me to believe anyone cares for me.

    Therapist: a.   It's hard for me to believe that too. Why would anyone care for you?
                 b.   You are really wondering why anyone would care?
                 c.   I know it's hard for you to believe that I care for you, that I really want to help you.
                 d.   I'm sure your mother and father cared for you. Even though your relationship with your father isn't good, I am sure he cared.

27. David: Maybe you could call Melinda. Maybe she'll listen to you if you tell her I've changed.

    Therapist: a.   Sure. What's her phone number.
                 b.   You haven't changed much yet. You've got a lot of work to do in therapy.
                 c.   It's hard being alone, and you really want me to fix things for you.
                 d.   What makes you think she will listen to me making the request for you?

75

28. David: Every once in a while when I'm at a casino, I'll stop. I'll look around. Everyone is so busy. And why? Everything starts to look silly.

    Therapist: a. That's a special moment. You are aware of yourself, and you can look at yourself as well as the others.
                b. Don't lose your concentration on the cards you're playing.
                c. You've been gambling again. I thought you were going to stop.
                d. You are starting to feel as if gambling is not right for you

29. David: I like the sense I have that I can choose not to gamble and I can leave at that moment.

    Therapist: a. Life has meaning at that point. You have the choice to leave or to stay.
                b. There are many questions that present themselves to you.
                c. You can act as if you are not going to gamble.
                d. Why don't you just say "no" to gambling and leave?

30. David: When I decided to leave the casino, I was thinking about my father all the way home in the car.

    Therapist: a. You could get into an accident if you aren't careful.
                b. Being aware of yourself at that moment helped you think of your father's life and possible death. It had meaning.
                c. You were really thinking a lot about your father.
                d.   Did you decide to call your father?

LOGOTHERAPY: FRANKL

Viktor Frankl was particularly concerned about the need for individuals to find meaning in their lives. Unlike most existential therapists, he developed a form of therapy that includes specific techniques that the therapist might use with clients.

LOGOTHERAPY CONCEPTS

logotherapy A type of existential therapy that focuses on challenging clients to search for meaning in their lives. It is associated with the techniques of attitude modulation, dereflection, and paradoxical intention.

Socratic dialogue A series of questions designed to help the client arrive at logical answers to and conclusions about a certain hypothesis; also called guided discovery.

dereflection A technique in which clients focus away from their problems instead of on them to reduce anxiety.

paradoxical intention A therapeutic strategy in which clients are instructed to engage in and exaggerate behaviors they seek to change. By prescribing the symptom, therapists make patients more aware of their situation and help them achieve distance from symptoms.

OE1. Most existential therapies do not use specific techniques. What are the advantages and disadvantages of this?

_____

_____

_____

_____

OE2. What is your reaction to the specific techniques used in logotherapy? (185)

_____

_____

_____

_____

SPECIAL TOPICS

OE3. Are Bugental's six phases of existential therapy a useful model? Explain. (191-192)

_____

_____

_____

_____

OE4. One current trend in existential therapy is Viktor Frankl's logotherapy. Why do you think it has been popular? (193)

_____

_____

_____

_____

OE5. A second current trend in existential therapy is its similarity to postmodern thought. In what way are the two similar and dissimilar? (193)

_____

_____

_____

OE6. In what ways do you think existential therapy could be integrated with other theories of therapy? (194)

_____

_____

_____

_____

OE7. Do men and women experience death, freedom, responsibility, and choice, loving, and meaningfulness differently? Explain. (196)

_____

_____

_____

_____

OE8. Are the existential themes multicultural? Are the themes universal and relevant for all cultures? Explain. (196)

_____

_____

_____

_____

STRENGTHS AND LIMITATIONS

As you review existential therapy and the concepts that it is based on, what do you view its strengths and limitations to be?

STRENGTHS	LIMITATIONS
_____	_____
_____	_____
_____	_____
_____	_____
_____	_____
_____	_____

EXISTENTIAL THERAPY: A QUIZ

True/false items: Decide if the following statements are more "true" or more "false" as they apply to existential therapy.

T   F   Q1.   Much of existential therapy has its roots in 19th century Western European philosophy.

T   F   Q2.   As a group, existential therapists focus on techniques to bring about change.

T   F   Q3.   The goal to become more expert at manipulating others is consistent with existential therapy.

T   F   Q4.   Existential therapy is based on a thorough grounding on the research into psychotherapy effectiveness.

T   F   Q5.   Logotherapy is one form of existential therapy.

T   F   Q6.   The therapist should feel "therapeutic love" for her client.

T   F   Q7.   The client should feel "therapeutic love" for his therapist.

T   F   Q8.   Existentialists believe that part of peoples' problems comes from dealing with a world that is not of their making.

T   F   Q9.   Part of being human is to make choices and take responsibility for them.

T   F   Q10. Existential therapy is both behavioral and cognitive in its focus.

Multiple choice items: Select the best answer from the alternatives given. Answer each question from the point of view of existential therapy.

_____   Q11.   Which of these philosophers could be considered the grandfather of existential therapy?

    a.   Søren Kierkegaard
    b.   Franz Kafka
    c.   Edmund Husserl
    d.   Gabriel Marcel

_____   Q12.   The "I-thou" relationship was a contribution to existential therapy made by

    a.   Karl Jasper.
    b.   Martin Buber.
    c.   Freidrich Nietzsche.
    d.   Jean-Paul Sartre.

_____   Q13.   Ludwig Binswanger and _____ could be considered the first existential therapists.

    a.   Medard Boss
    b.   Rollo May
    c.   Paul Tillich
    d.   R. D. Laing

79

_____ Q14. Logotherapy was developed by

    a.   Medard Boss.
    b.   Ludwig Binswanger.
    c.   Rollo May.
    d.   Viktor Frankl.

_____ Q15. Which of these is not an important existential theme?

    a.   love
    b.   death
    c.   animosity
    d.   meaning

_____ Q16. Existential anxiety can be viewed as a (an)

    a.   expression of repressed sexuality.
    b.   neurotic symptom.
    c.   part of being human.
    d.   result of early traumatic childhood experience.

_____ Q17. The basic goal(s) of existential therapy is (are)

    a.   to make free choices.
    b.   to become more authentic.
    c.   to make responsible choices.
    d.   to find meaning in life.
    e.   all of the above.

_____ Q18. An important issue in existential therapy is

    a.   finding meaning in life.
    b.   resistance.
    c.   countertransference.
    d.   separation from parents.

_____ Q19. Which of these most clearly exemplifies existential therapy?

    a.   Umwelt
    b.   Mitwelt
    c.   Überwelt
    d.   Eigenwelt

_____ Q20. The existential condition that most concerned Viktor Frankl was

    a.   anxiety.
    b.   fusion.
    c.   judgmentalness.
    d.   meaningfulness.

_____ Q21. "Being authentic" is best defined by

    a.   a central genuineness and awareness of being.
    b.   general agreement about what constitutes the subjective self.
    c.   general agreement about what constitutes the objective self.
    d.   being able to go beyond the immediate situation.

Q22. In dealing with a patient's problem in making choices, an existential therapist would

a. point out possible solutions.
b. show why one solution was better than others.
c. help the client understand it is important that the client make the decision.
d. describe decision-making techniques.

Q23. To focus away from one's own problems is

a. an example of kairos
b. to use dereflection, a logotherapy technique.
c. to be in the Überwelt.
d. to be authentic.

Q24. In existential therapy, a therapist might

a. discuss difficult issues.
b. conduct a lifestyle analysis
c. make archetypal interpretations.
d. use statements highlighting the superego.

Q25. Existential therapy deals with a(an)

a. objective approach to reality.
b. subjective approach to reality.
c. behavioral approach to reality.
d. cognitive approach to reality.

ANSWER KEY

1.	b	11.	e	21.	b
2.	c	12.	a	22.	d
3.	-	13.	c	23.	c
4.	a	14.	d	24.	d
5.	a	15.	a	25.	d
6.	d	16.	a	26.	c
7.	b	17.	a	27.	d
8.	d	18.	b	28.	a
9.	b	19.	c	29.	a
10.	c	20.	b	30.	b

QUIZ

Q1.	T	Q11.	a	Q21.	a
Q2.	F	Q12.	b	Q22.	c
Q3.	F	Q13.	a	Q23.	b
Q4.	F	Q14.	d	Q24.	a
Q5.	T	Q15.	c	Q25.	b
Q6.	T	Q16.	c		
Q7.	F	Q17.	e		
Q8.	T	Q18.	a		
Q9.	T	Q19.	d		
Q10.	F	Q20.	d		

81

CHAPTER 6

PERSON-CENTERED THERAPY

PERSON-CENTERED THERAPY SELF-INVENTORY

Directions: By comparing your beliefs about personality and therapy to the person-centered approach, you should have a clearer idea of how much you will need to suspend your beliefs or change attitudes to understand the person-centered theory of personality and approach to therapy. You may find it helpful to complete this section before and after you read the chapter. In this way, you can see if your views have changed. There are no correct answers, only an opportunity to express your views.

Put an "X" on the line so that it indicates how much you agree or disagree with the statement: A=Agree, D=Disagree.

D   A

_____ 1. Creating a safe atmosphere for clients to express themselves is a major goal of therapy.

_____ 2. The answer to problems lies within the client rather than with the therapist.

_____ 3. People strive to function fully in their world.

_____ 4. It is the therapist rather than the therapist's techniques that are important.

_____ 5. Clients develop problems in their childhood because of inconsistent or inappropriate relationships with others.

_____ 6. As the relationship between the therapist and the client develops, so does progress in therapy.

_____ 7. The essential qualities of effective therapy are genuineness, caring, and unconditional positive regard.

_____ 8. Empathy is a healing condition.

_____ 9. Tests and inventories do not help progress in therapy.

_____ 10. The therapist accepts rather than judges the client's experiences.

82

_____ 11. Therapeutic change depends on the client's perceptions of the experience with the therapist and the therapist's basic attitudes.

_____ 12. Being genuine is essential for therapeutic change.

_____ 13. Giving advice is not consistent with the role of the therapist.

_____ 14. Although the therapist must accept the client, it is not necessary to agree with the client on all or even most issues.

_____ 15. As a result of therapy, individuals learn how to be more open and responsible.

_____ 16. Clients become more creative as a result of the relationship with the therapist.

_____ 17. The client determines the direction of therapy, not the therapist.

_____ 18. Acceptance by the therapist helps to reduce client defenses.

_____ 19. Relating to the therapist in an open manner helps the client relate better to others.

_____ 20. Diagnosis is not an important part of the therapeutic relationship.

HISTORY OF PERSON-CENTERED THERAPY

Person-centered therapy is very much embodied in the work of Carl Rogers. He is mainly responsible for the development of person-centered therapy. His focus on the importance of the client-counselor relationship has had an influence on both theorists and practitioners. The following chart describes the personal and professional development of Carl Rogers. As he changed and developed, so did person-centered therapy.

PERSONAL DEVELOPMENT AND POSITIONS	PROFESSIONAL INFLUENCES
Developmental Stage	

Born in 1902 in a suburb of Chicago
Fourth of six children
Religious fundamental upbringing
Adolescent interest in agriculture
Early career goal: the ministry
Graduated from the University of Wisconsin
Married Helen Elliott
Attended Union Theological Seminary
Received Ph.D. from Columbia University Teacher's
College in 1931 in clinical psychology
12 years at the Society for Prevention of Cruelty to Children in Rochester, NY
1940 - academic career at Ohio State University
	Early work influenced by psychoanalysis
	   Rogers was influenced by Rank through his work with Jessie Taft and Elizabeth Davis.
	   Rank focused on the uniqueness of the individual, as did Alfred Adler
	Goldstein and Maslow wrote about self-actualization - a humanist idea
	Rogers read writings of existentialists
	The Clinical Treatment of the Problem Child, 1939

Non-directive Stage	
1945 - worked at the University of Chicago	At Ohio State, started writing about the importance of the therapeutic relationship

Client-centered Stage 1945	
1957 - University of Wisconsin psychology department, later psychiatry department	*Counseling and Psychotherapy*, 1942 *Client-Centered Therapy: Its Current Practice, Implications and Theory*, 1951 Focus on empathy, genuineness, unconditional positive regard APA Distinguished Contribution awarded 1956 Research with hospitalized patients with schizophrenia
Person-Centered Stage	
1968 - formed the Center for Studies of the Person at La Jolla, California Traveled to South Africa, Northern Ireland, and other countries to help others bring about political change Died in 1987	*On Becoming a Person*, 1961 Writings were more philosophical, more concerned about social issues than before Concerned about education and global peace; led encounter group *Carl Rogers on Personal Power*, 1977 *A Way of Being*, 1980

QUESTIONS ABOUT THE HISTORY OF PERSON-CENTERED THERAPY

1. Rogers's early exposure to theological training led him to

   a. espouse Christian values in his therapy.
   b. train pastoral counselors to be therapists.
   c. a psychology program where he did not have to profess certain beliefs.
   d. become an ordained minister.

2. Rogers was most influenced by the writings of

   a. Freud.
   b. Jung.
   c. Nietschze.
   d. Rank.

3. The development of the philosophical underpinnings of Rogers' work and its subsequent publication occurred during the _____ phase of his work.

   a. developmental
   b. nondirective
   c. person-centered
   d. client-centered

4. Rogers was influenced by writings on self-actualization by Kurt Goldstein and

   a. Alfred Adler.
   b. Sigmund Freud.
   c. Abraham Maslow.
   d. Otto Rank.

PERSON-CENTERED THEORY OF PERSONALITY

Carl Rogers was concerned about the way people treated each other and how they cared for or didn't care for each other. This is reflected in his writings on childhood development (which are quite limited). He

84

believed that children would develop a good sense of their own self-worth or self-regard if others (parents, teachers, or friends) treated them as valuable and worthy.

When individuals treated others in a way that was sometimes harsh, manipulative, or self-serving, then the person was treated conditionally. Conditions of worth (conditionality) develop from conditional positive regard from others. Such conditions can make it difficult for a person to become a fully functioning person.

conditionality or conditions of worth The process of evaluating one's own experience based on values or beliefs that others hold.

conditional positive regard Receiving praise, attention, or approval from others as a result of behaving in accordance with the expectations of others.

fully functioning person A person who meets his or her own need for positive regard rather than relying on the expectations of others. Such individuals are open to new experiences and not defensive.

Questions about you from a person-centered perspective.

OE 1. Describe an experience that you have had, in which after a conversation with a person, you felt bad about yourself. How does that experience fit with the concept of "conditions of worth?"

_____

_____

_____

OE 2. Think of a situation in which you only received approval from someone if you did what he or she wanted you to do. How does that experience fit with Rogers' description of conditional positive regard?

_____

_____

_____

_____

PERSON-CENTERED THEORY OF PSYCHOTHERAPY

Rogers' theory of psychotherapy grew out of his experiences with clients. Regardless of their problems, Rogers cared for and accepted his clients. In the process of understanding clients, Rogers helped them to better understand and appreciate themselves. The focus of his work was on the process of therapy not assessment.

GOALS OF PERSON-CENTERED THERAPY

As the terms "client-centered" and "person-centered" imply, the goals of therapy come from the client. The therapist often helps the client to articulate the goals. Goals typically are consistent with helping an individual become a fully functioning person.

85

ASSESSMENT IN PERSON-CENTERED THERAPY

Inventories and tests are not a part of person-centered counseling. In some cases, tests or inventories may be used in career counseling. Assessment is a part of the therapeutic relationship with the client.

NECESSARY AND SUFFICIENT CONDITIONS FOR CHANGE

Rogers believed that therapeutic change could result if six conditions were met. These conditions form the essence of his approach to therapy.

1. *Psychological contact* A relationship must exist so that two people may have impact on each other.

2. *Incongruence* For change to take place, a client must be in a state of psychological vulnerability. There is a discrepancy between individuals' views of themselves and their actual experience. Included would be depression, anxiety, or a wide variety of problems. Although individuals may not be aware at first of their incongruence or vulnerability, they will become aware if therapy continues.

3. *Congruence and genuineness* Therapists are aware of themselves. They are aware of their feelings, their experiences as they relate to the client, and their general reaction to the client. Therapists are open to understanding their own experiences as well as those of the client.

4. *Unconditional positive regard or acceptance* The therapist does not judge the client but accepts the client for who he or she is. Accepting the client does not mean that the counselor agrees with the client. With acceptance often comes caring and warmth.

5. *Empathy* The therapist enters the world of the client, leaving behind, as much as possible, his or her own values. Since it is not possible to be "value free," the therapist monitors his or her own values and feelings. The therapist tries to understand the experience of the client, what it is to be the client. Caring and warmth are expressed often in statements of empathy.

6. *Perception of empathy and acceptance* Not only must the therapist unconditionally accept and understand the client, the client must perceive that he or she is being understood and accepted. Therapists' voice tone and physical expression contribute to the communication of empathy and acceptance. Thus, they are part of the client's perception of empathy.

PERSON-CENTERED THERAPY: KEY CONCEPTS

The following concepts define the words that Rogers uses in his six necessary and sufficient conditions for client change.

incongruence The disharmony that takes place when there is a disagreement between individuals and their view of themselves and their actual experience.

congruence The harmony that takes place when there is no disagreement between individuals' experience and their views of themselves. For therapists, congruence refers to matching one's inner experiencing with external expressions.

genuineness Similar to congruence, genuineness in the therapist refers to being one's actual self with the client, not phony or affected.

86

unconditional positive regard Accepting and appreciating clients as they are, regardless of whether the therapist agrees with the person. Positive regard is not contingent on acting or thinking in a specific way. It is essentially appreciating clients for being themselves.

empathy To enter the world of another individual without being influenced by one's own views and values is to be empathic with the individual. The therapist, when being empathic, is attuned to the experience, feelings, and sensitivities of the client.

acceptance Appreciating clients for who they are without valuing or judging them.

A PERSON-CENTERED APPROACH TO RESPONDING TO CLIENTS

Rogers believed that responses to clients should be empathic and genuine. However, non-person-centered therapists who train counselors find it helpful to use exercises to help students learn empathic responding. Because they are exercises, the responses sometimes seem artificial. The exercises here will help you learn some ways of responding empathically.

The responses are sometimes called "reflections". Rogers found that this term sometimes misled counselors into thinking that repeating the essence of a client's statement was adequate. Rogers emphasized the importance of showing the client that he understood the client's experience or feelings.

Read the two examples to get an idea of the exercise. Next, write down the important words or phrases that describe the client's feelings. In the next line, write what situation or event the feeling refers to. Last, put the feeling and event together to make a reflection or empathic response.

Example: A 30-year-old man says: Since my wife left me, I feel all alone. I just go through the motions at work.

a. What is he feeling? *Lonely. Sad. Uninvolved. Unloved*

b. What is the situation or event? *His wife has left him*

c. Give an empathic response. *You seem to be feeling lonely since your wife left. It's hard to put your heart into your work.*

Example: A 43-year-old woman says: My boss really lost his temper and started screaming at me for being a half-hour late for work. Who does he think he is!

a. What is she feeling? *Angry. Upset. Resentful*

b. What is the situation or event? *Her boss yelled at her for being late.*

c. Give an empathic response. *You are really angry that your boss would yell at you for coming to work late.*

In the following examples, answer the questions as best you can. Note from the example above that there is often more than one feeling that may be present. In an empathic response you pick the one or two that seem most significant to you. Also notice that the response reflects the client's meaning back to the client. The response does not repeat what the client said. Suggested correct responses are on the last page of this chapter.

*OE3. A girl, 13, says: My father came home from work really drunk. As soon as he came into the house yelling and screaming, he threw a book at my mother. I ran to my room and locked the door.

    a. What is she feeling?_____

_____

    b. What is the situation or event? _____

_____

    c. Give an empathetic response. _____

_____

*OE4. An 18-year-old male college freshman says: I am so excited. I just got an A on my biology exam. I really had studied hard for it.

    a. What is he feeling? _____

_____

    b. What is the situation or event? _____

_____

    c. Give an empathic response. _____

_____

*OE5. A 19-year-old female college sophomore says: Here it is 6 weeks into the semester and I haven't gone to classes for 2 weeks. I just haven't felt like leaving my room or doing much of anything.

    a. What is she feeling? _____

_____

    b. What is the situation or event? _____

_____

    c. Give an empathic response. _____

_____

88

*OE6. A man, 45, says: My wife thinks she is so smart! Like she has all the answers. Whatever I do is wrong.

a. What is he feeling? _____

_____

b. What is the situation or event? _____

_____

c. Give an empathic response. _____

_____

OE7. An 11-year-old girl says: My mother stinks and she's mean. She won't let me wear makeup to
school. Other kids' moms let them do it.

a. What is she feeling? _____

_____

b. What is the situation or event? _____

_____

c. Give an empathic response. _____

_____

CASE EXAMPLE OF SHEILA

Sheila is a 23-year-old secretary working for a trucking firm near Cleveland, Ohio. She is single and
lives at home with her mother. When in high school, Sheila was a C student and did not care much for
school. She did the minimal amount of homework and spent most of the afternoons and evenings either
working at a women's clothing store or with her friends. She has been working for this firm for a year. The
work is somewhat boring, but she enjoys the other clerical staff and tolerates her bosses.

When she was seven, Sheila's mother and father were divorced. Her father, a carpenter, moved to
California to be closer to his family. When she was younger and in school, she talked to him weekly and
visited him for one week each summer. Now, she talks to him about every three months and has not seen
him for two years. He has remarried and has two young boys.

Sheila has two older brothers, four years older and six years older. Bob, the oldest, is a roofing supply
salesman, and Paul is a plumber. Both are married and live in the Cleveland area.

Sheila's mother has worked in many retail jobs throughout her life. Since the divorce, she has had many
boyfriends but has not remarried. Her cocaine abuse is part of the problem that is affecting Sheila. Many of
Sheila's mother's boyfriends have also been cocaine abusers and have been the source of cocaine for her
mother. Having seen the effects of cocaine on those close to her, Sheila has avoided all drug and alcohol use.

Her current problem is what to do about her mother. Sheila lives at home because the rent is cheap.
Sheila's mother does not ask for a specific amount but takes whatever Sheila gives her. However, Sheila has
been taking care of her mother since she was in high school. She has prepared the meals and cleaned the
house. Sheila is growing resentful of this and is not sure what to do.

89

QUESTIONS ABOUT DOING THERAPY WITH SHEILA

Problem: The next set of questions is a dialogue between Sheila and her counselor. You are to be her person-centered counselor and pick the response that most closely fits a person-centered response.

5.   Sheila: I don't know what to do. My mother is driving me nuts. She doesn't do anything around the house. I never know which boyfriend is gonna to show up. I can't stand it.

   a.   You want to know what to do?
   b.   You feel angry at your mother's lack of responsibility in the house.
   c.   Your mother has no right to ask more of you than she is willing to give of herself.

6.   Sheila: She never has lived up to her end of the bargain. Sometimes it seemed like I was the mother and she was the child. She didn't take care of me or herself.

   a.   You're angry at your mother for not being there when you needed her when you were a child.
   b.   You know that your mother really loves you and really cares for you.
   c.   Sometimes you wonder where your father was in all this.

7.   I never knew whether I was doing the right thing at home. Particularly when I was about 14, I had to cook all the meals and have dinner ready when she would get home. If I didn't, nothing would get done.

   a.   You felt you were unsure of yourself when you were young. It was so hard to know what to do at home.
   b.   Why couldn't your mother take responsibility for the problems that she was making for you at home?
   c.   Sometimes you really felt dumb.

8.   When she would come home, sometimes she was just really silly. Until I was about 13 or 14, I didn't know what this was about. Later, I got to recognize when she was high and when she wasn't. And when she was high I knew I could get nowhere with her. I couldn't reason with her.

   a.   You wondered whether she might get caught for using cocaine.
   b.   Being around her was so incredibly depressing.
   c.   Sometimes it was so frustrating not being able to talk to her when you really wanted to.

9.   When her boyfriend of the week was at the house, it was really bad. Mainly my mother and her boyfriend ignored me, but it was real tense.

   a.   You were really scared of your mother's boyfriend.
   b.   You wondered where did she get this one now.
   c.   You felt tense not knowing this person and yet having him right there in your house.

10.   Sheila: The same thing is happening now, and it is really frustrating. I don't know how I can stand it. I want to move out, but I can't afford to.

   a.   It's such a difficult struggle for you being caught between dealing with your mother's behavior and the financial responsibility of being on your own.
   b.   Living expenses are not so high in the Cleveland area. Have you thought about sharing expenses with a roommate?
   c.   Living at home with your mother need not be so bad after all.

   The purpose of the above example has been to give you a chance to think like a person-centered therapist. Besides the appropriate person-centered responses listed above, there are many others that could be given. If you want to, see if you can generate some that you think are better than the ones given here.

THE CLIENT'S EXPERIENCE IN THERAPY

Students often wonder about using reflections continually in therapy. They may wonder if the client gets bored or if reflections sound repetitious to the client. Many clients are likely to experience therapy differently than this. They may feel understood, value the chance to grow and explore issues, appreciate the safety to explore difficult problems, and feel the opportunity to make positive changes in their lives.

In answering the following questions, try to speculate how a continuing dialogue with Sheila might help her.

OE8. How could person-centered therapy help Sheila take responsibility for herself?

_____

_____

_____

_____

OE9. How might the process of exploring issues dealing with her mother be helpful to Sheila?

_____

_____

_____

_____

SPECIAL TOPICS

*OE10. Why is it difficult for person-centered therapy to be time-limited? (226)

_____

_____

_____

_____

OE11. One current trend of person-centered therapy is its appeal to people of many different cultures. Why do you think this is? (232)

_____

_____

_____

_____

91

OE12. Would you find Rogers's six necessary and sufficient conditions too restrictive? Explain. (214-218)

_____

_____

_____

_____

OE13. Why do you think so many therapists find Rogers's emphasis on empathic listening so appealing
that they want to incorporate his reflecting approach into their theory? (216-217)

_____

_____

_____

_____

STRENGTHS AND LIMITATIONS

What do you believe are the strengths and limitations of person-centered therapy?

STRENGTHS	LIMITATIONS
_____	_____
_____	_____
_____	_____
_____	_____
_____	_____
_____	_____
_____	_____

92

PERSON-CENTERED THERAPY: A QUIZ

True/false items: Decide if the following statements are more "true" or more "false" as they apply to person-centered therapy.

T   F   Q1.   The influence of Maslow's self-actualization theory can be found in person-centered theory.

T   F   Q2.   Ego formation in childhood determines later functioning.

T   F   Q3.   Conditions of worth bring about ego growth.

T   F   Q4.   Being listened to and understood can give individuals a sense of positive regard.

T   F   Q5.   Therapists choose appropriate goals from the ones that clients present.

T   F   Q6.   Rogers valued assessment instruments for research but not therapy.

T   F   Q7.   An initial assessment is a major part of person-centered therapy.

T   F   Q8.   Advice-giving adds to empathic responding in person-centered therapy.

T   F   Q9.   A feature of person-centered therapy is its brief therapy approach.

T   F   Q10.   Accurate empathy is one of the most significant concepts in person-centered therapy.

Multiple-choice items: Select the best answer from the alternatives given. Answer each question from the point of view of person-centered therapy.

_____   Q11.   Person-centered therapy is a form of

      a.   psychoanalysis.
      b.   humanistic therapy.
      c.   behavioral therapy.
      d.   reality therapy.
      e.   cognitive therapy.

_____   Q12.   The founder of person-centered therapy is

      a.   Kurt Goldstein.
      b.   Abraham Maslow.
      c.   Fritz Perls.
      d.   Carl Rogers.
      e.   Emmy van Deurzen.

_____   Q13.   Rogers interest in world peace is reflected in which of these phases?

      a.   developmental
      b.   nondirective
      c.   client-centered
      d.   person-centered

Q14. An important developmental issue in childhood in person-centered therapy is the

a. development of authenticity.
b. development of the ego.
c. need for positive regard.
d. need for incongruence.

Q15. Which one of these concepts is NOT congruent with being a fully functioning person?

a. being non-defensive
b. being self-absorbed
c. being creative
d. being adaptable

Q16. In person-centered therapy, the goals are chosen by

a. the client.
b. the therapist.
c. neither a nor b.
d. both a and b.

Q17. Which of these receives the LEAST attention in person-centered therapy?

a. client-therapist relationship
b. client goals
c. diagnosis
d. all are important

Q18. When a therapist is congruent, she is

a. genuine.
b. empathic.
c. reliable.
d. respectful.
e. accepting.

Q19. A child molester who is in therapy with a person-centered therapist would find that the therapist would _____ the child molester.

a. accept
b. not accept
c. agree with
d. condemn

Q20. If a client says, "You know, you really are stupid. You haven't done anything right," the person-centered therapist might respond in this way:

a. Well, you're not so bright yourself.
b. You seem angry and disappointed that I haven't been more helpful.
c. The anger you feel toward your father seems to be directed toward me.
d. There are several things that I have done right. I have been genuine and empathic.

94

_____ Q21. Unconditional positive regard refers to

    a. accepting the client as a worthy person.
    b. approving of the client's decisions.
    c. agreeing with the client's values.
    d. approving of the client's behavior.

_____ Q22. A criticism of person-centered therapy is that

    a. the client is not accepted.
    b. the therapist does not listen to the client.
    c. the client is not shown how to solve her problems.
    d. client feelings are not attended to.

_____ Q23. As a result of person-centered therapy, the client should NOT expect to

    a. experience change.
    b. experience the empathy of the therapist.
    c. experience the process of exploration.
    d. experience awareness of contact boundaries.

_____ Q24. Which of these concepts is NOT associated with Carl Rogers?

    a. acceptance
    b. empathy
    c. interpretation
    d. unconditional positive regard

_____ Q25. Rogers contributed to

    a. pioneering research in the process and outcome of therapy.
    b. fostering world peace.
    c. understanding the client-therapist relationship.
    d. the development of encounter groups.
    e. all of the above.

ANSWER KEY

1. c
2. d
3. c
4. c
5. b
6. a
7. a
8. c
9. c
10. a

QUIZ

Q1.	T	Q11.	b	Q21.	a
Q2.	F	Q12.	d	Q22.	c
Q3.	F	Q13.	d	Q23.	d
Q4.	T	Q14.	c	Q24.	c
Q5.	F	Q15.	b	Q25.	e
Q6.	T	Q16.	a		
Q7.	F	Q17.	c		
Q8.	F	Q18.	a		
Q9.	F	Q19.	a		
Q10.	T	Q20.	b		

ANSWERS TO OPEN ENDED QUESTIONS

The following answers to the Open Ended Questions 3 through 6 may not be exactly like yours. That doesn't mean your responses are wrong. People have different perceptions and will see events differently.

OE3.   a.   What is she feeling? *Scared. Frightened. Worried about her mother.*

b.   What is the situation or event? *Her father is drunk, angry, and throwing things at her mother. She ran to her room.*

c.   Give an empathic response. *You were so frightened that your father might come after you that you ran to your room. OR You were worried that your father might hurt your mother and you are scared of him.*

OE4.   a.   What is he feeling? *Excited. Happy. Ecstatic. Happily surprised.*

b.   What is the situation or event? *Getting an A on the biology test. Studying hard for the test.*

c.   Give an empathic response. *An A! That's so exciting to have all your hard work pay off that way!*

OE5.   a.   What is she feeling? *Very depressed. Despair. Worried.*

b.   What is the situation or event? *Not going to class for two weeks.*

c.   Give an empathic response. *You are feeling so down that you haven't gone to class for two weeks.*

OE6.   a.   What is he feeling? *Angry. Hurt. Insulted. Lacking in confidence.*

b.   What is the situation? *Wife's criticism of him.*

c.   Give an empathic response. *When your wife criticizes you, it really hurts. Then you may feel bad about yourself.*

OE10.   In person-centered therapy, the client chooses the problem and is likely to define the length of therapy. The therapist does not want to artificially restrict the length of the therapeutic exploration process.

CHAPTER 7

GESTALT THERAPY

> Gestalt therapy is the most well-known of several experiential therapies. Experiential therapists help clients experience the problem, not just tell about it. Besides gestalt therapy, there are three other established experiential therapies. Mahrer's experiential therapy focuses on intense emotional moments in the client's life. Gendlin's focusing therapy guides clients to become more aware of their inner selves. Greenberg and his colleagues have developed process experiential therapy and emotion focused therapy that combine person-centered and gestalt therapies. Because gestalt therapy is so widely used this chapter explains the gestalt approach.

GESTALT THERAPY SELF-INVENTORY

Directions: By comparing your beliefs about personality and therapy to those of gestalt therapy, you should have a clearer idea of how much you will need to suspend your beliefs or change attitudes to understand gestalt therapy. You may find it helpful to complete this section before and after you read the chapter. In this way you can see if your views have changed. There are no correct answers, only an opportunity to express your views.

Put an "X" on the line so that it indicates how much you agree or disagree with the statement: A=Agree, D=Disagree.

D   A

_____ 1. The whole is greater than the sum of its parts.

_____ 2. Relationships between events are important, not just the events themselves.

_____ 3. Focusing on the present in therapy is more important than focusing on the past or the future.

_____ 4. Knowing what is happening and how it happened is more important than knowing why it happened.

_____ 5. Rather than talking about experiences, clients should attempt to relive experiences as though they were happening now.

_____ 6. The past should be viewed in terms of how it affects present functioning.

_____ 7. Dwelling in the past can prevent people from taking responsibility for their own growth.

_____ 8. Self-awareness should be a primary goal of therapy.

_____ 9. Therapy should help clients become less phony.

D   A

_____   10. Unfinished business from the past can result in problems in the present.

_____   11. Therapeutic support is helpful in encouraging self-support.

_____   12. For a client, acting out and experiencing his or her problem can be more therapeutic than just talking about it.

_____   13. Therapy should help clients become more truly alive and aware of their true selves.

_____   14. Awareness of client feelings and feelings within one's body will help clients grow and develop.

_____   15. The therapist should be empathic as well as help the client gain self awareness.

_____   16. Diagnosis should focus on present rather than past events or behavior.

_____   17. Body language and other nonverbal cues are important information for the therapist.

_____   18. Increased responsibility for client thoughts, feeling, and behaviors are associated with progress in therapy.

_____   19. Group therapy can be as helpful as individual therapy and can be a useful adjunct to it.

_____   20. Therapy should help clients become more aware of aspects of themselves that have interfered with their functioning and which they were not aware of previously.

HISTORY OF GESTALT THERAPY

Which influences do you think were most important in Fritz Perls's development of gestalt therapy?

PERSONAL LIFE	PROFESSIONAL LIFE
Born in 1893 in Berlin, Germany	Assistant to Kurt Goldstein at Institute for
German Jewish parents	Brain Damaged Soldiers
A sister killed in a concentration camp	Influenced by Wilhelm Reich, his analyst, who
Failed seventh grade twice	was interested in facial and body position
Worked for a merchant, returned to school at 14	Trained as a psychoanalyst at the Vienna and
Studied medicine	Berlin Institute of Psychoanalysis
At 23, volunteered as a medic in World War I	Sigmund Friedlander's work in polarities
Left Germany for South Africa in 1934	Alfred Korzybiski's work on semantics
Established South African Institute for	Kurt Lewin's field theory
Psychoanalysis in 1935	Influenced by several existential therapists
Moved to New York in 1947	Gestalt psychology background
Established gestalt training centers in several	Influenced by Jan Smut's writings on holism
cities	*Ego, Hunger, and Aggression*, 1942/1947
Associate psychiatrist in residence at the Esalin	Laura Perls, Fritz's wife, influenced gestalt
Institute, 1964-1969	therapy directly through her emphasis on
Died in 1970	relationships
	Gestalt Therapy Excitement and Growth in the Human Personality, 1951, coauthored with Hefferline and Goodman
	Gestalt Therapy Verbatim, 1969
	The Gestalt Approach, 1973, was published after his death

GESTALT PERSONALITY THEORY CONCEPTS

Several concepts that are important in the gestalt theory of personality are related to concepts developed by gestalt psychologists who then distanced themselves from gestalt therapy. Other concepts deal with connection or contrast with others. Contact brings with it a sense of self and a differentiation from others. When there are disturbances in the contact boundaries, several difficulties result. Awareness of these disturbances is one focus of gestalt therapy.

CONCEPTS FROM GESTALT PSYCHOLOGY

gestalt psychology A psychological approach that studies the organization of experience into patterns or configurations. Gestalt psychologists believe that the whole is greater than the sum of its parts and study, among other issues, the relationship of a figure to its background.

ground The background that contrasts with the figure in the perceptions of a field.

figure That part of a field that stands out in good contour clearly from the ground.

CONCERNS RELATED TO CONTACT

contact The relationship between "me" and others. Contact involves feeling a connection with others or the world outside oneself while maintaining separation from it.

contact boundaries The boundaries that distinguish between one person (or one aspect of a person) and an object, another person, or another aspect of oneself. Examples include body-boundaries, value-boundaries, familiarity- boundaries, and expressive-boundaries.

CONTACT BOUNDARY DISTURBANCES

introjection This occurs when individuals accept information or values from others without evaluating them or without assimilating them into one's personality.

projection When we ascribe aspects of ourselves to others, such as when we attribute some of our own unacceptable thoughts, feelings, or behaviors to friends, projection takes place.

retroflection When we do to ourselves what we want to do to someone else or do things for ourselves that we want others to do for us, then we experience retroflection.

deflection When individuals avoid meaningful contact by being indirect or vague rather than being direct, deflection occurs.

confluence When the separation between one's self and others becomes muted or unclear, we experience confluence. Thus, it can be difficult to distinguish one's own perceptions or values from those of another person.

OTHER IMPORTANT PERSONALITY THEORY CONCEPTS

awareness Attending to and observing what is happening in the present. Types of awareness include sensations and actions, feelings, wants, and values or assessments.

unfinished business Unexpressed feelings from the past that occur in the present and interfere with psychological functioning. They may include feelings, memories, or fantasies from earlier life (often childhood) that can be dealt with in the present.

QUESTIONS ABOUT GESTALT PERSONALITY THEORY

1. As you read this question and look at it, this question is the

    a. field.
    b. figure.
    c. ground.
    d. gestalt.

2. The rest of this page is then called the

    a. field.
    b. figure.
    c. ground.
    d. gestalt.

3. Which of these terms is the most inclusive?

    a. field
    b. figure
    c. ground

4. Which of these is the weakest gestalt?

    a.
    b.
    c.
    d.

5. Greeting a friend on the way to class is an example of this level of contact.

    a. phony
    b. phobic
    c. impasse
    d. implosive
    e. explosive

6. Which of these statements about gestalt psychology is correct?

    a. Gestalt psychology and gestalt psychotherapy are one and the same.
    b. Gestalt psychology is based on principles of behavior therapy.
    c. Gestalt psychologists have been critical about the way in which Perls applied gestalt psychology to gestalt therapy.
    d. Existential therapists developed gestalt psychology through focus on authenticity.

7. At this level of contact, individuals are the most authentic.

    a. phony
    b. phobic
    c. impasse
    d. implosive
    e. explosive

100

8. Wanting to change an aspect of oneself but not being able to do so is likely to be experienced at this level.

   a. phony
   b. phobic
   c. impasse
   d. implosive
   e. explosive

9. Which of these is not a contact boundary?

   a. body
   b. expressive
   c. familiarity
   d. property
   e. value

10. Contact boundary disturbances represent problems that are always significant ones for individuals.

    a. true
    b. false

GESTALT THEORY OF PSYCHOTHERAPY

Gestalt psychotherapy combines a good working relationship with a client and respect for the client with methods that help clients become self aware. Gestalt therapists have developed a number of approaches to helping their clients become more aware of their feelings, attitudes, and verbal and nonverbal behavior. They work in the present, paying attention to changes in the client as therapy progresses.

GOALS OF GESTALT THERAPY

Developing fuller awareness of oneself is the basic goal of gestalt therapy. Patients should become more aware of their bodies, feelings, experiences, needs and skills, sensations, and their environment. As they do this, they develop the ability to further support themselves and to become more responsible for their actions.

ASSESSMENT IN GESTALT THERAPY

Assessment takes place in the present moment, as gestalt therapists attend to bodily movements, feelings, sensations, or other aspects of their clients. Therapists' prior experience attending to other clients gives them creative ways of assessing the problems of their clients. Gestalt therapists and those who use a gestalt approach as a part of their work may include assessment approaches derived from other theories. Some use diagnostic categories and projective or objective tests in their approach to therapy.

GESTALT THERAPY: KEY CONCEPTS

For change to take place in gestalt therapy, there must be a fully functioning I-Thou relationship. The empathic relationship with the client allows the therapist to use a variety of exercises and experiments that will help the client develop self awareness. Therapeutic approaches include statements and questions that bring about awareness as well as emphasis on behavior or language. Clients not only become more aware of their own feelings and behaviors but become more aware of their relationships with others. Self dialogue through use of the empty chair and enactment are among the more powerful approaches to self-awareness. Awareness is directed not only to what one may be doing but also to what one may be avoiding.

101

exercises Specific techniques that have been developed to be used in group or individual gestalt therapy.

experiments Creative approaches or techniques used by the therapist to deal with an impasse in therapy brought about by the client's difficulty in achieving awareness.

empty chair A technique developed by gestalt therapists and adapted by other theorists in which the patient is asked to play different roles in two different chairs. Dialogues between different aspects of the client or between client and others who are not present can then take place.

enactment In enactment, the patient may act out a previous experience or a characteristic. If the patient says he feels like a rat for cheating on his wife, the therapist may ask him to act like a rat.

CASE EXAMPLE OF JUAN WITH QUESTIONS

The purpose of the following case example is to help you become more familiar with gestalt approaches to enhancing awareness. Helping clients become more aware of themselves is done in a context of a caring relationship. Thus gestalt therapists may choose less confrontational comments or awareness exercises over more creative ones because of the impact on the relationship. In actual gestalt therapy, the number and type of awareness experiments that are done vary greatly. To keep this example brief, client statements will be given to you, and then you, playing the role of the gestalt therapist, will give a response that enhances the client's awareness. Because some of the questions are difficult, answers and explanations will be given after most of the questions.

Juan is a 42-year-old man who has been married for 12 years and has no children. For the past 15 years, he has driven a parcel delivery truck in his city. He daydreams constantly and has had several near misses and one minor accident. He would like to return to school to study to be a nurse but has not felt that he would be successful. His wife is an executive secretary who works for a large packaging company. She often compares Juan's lack of success and ambition to that of her bosses' financial and managerial success.

Whenever possible, Juan spends time watching baseball, basketball, ice hockey, and football on television. He avoids talking to his wife about their relationship. He prefers to talk about sports with her. However, this has only moderate interest for her, and she tolerates it.

Juan's parents and his three sisters live in different parts of the country. His parents, living 40 miles away, are the closest to him. Juan and his wife, Marita, visit his parents about ten times a year. His mother often speaks to Juan about how successful his sisters have been in both their careers and marriages. Juan feels criticized by this and is upset that he has been the one child in the family who has not been successful.

Juan has sought therapy because of his low self-esteem. He is very critical of himself and feels that he has been a failure. He would make changes in his life but feels that nothing will come of them. He does not feel that he will ever be successful. In the last three years, he has become more and more depressed. Marita has become annoyed by his sullenness and irritability. She has started to bring up the subject of a possible divorce, a subject that Juan tries to avoid. The idea of a divorce has frightened Juan very much, and he has sought therapy.

11. Which of the following contact boundary disturbances would best seem to describe Juan's level of awareness about his wife's desire to discuss divorce?

    a. introjection
    b. projection
    c. retroflection
    d. deflection
    e. confluence

    (Deflection "d" is a term that can be used to describe his avoidance of dealing with important issues within himself or with his wife.)

102

12. Which of the following concepts would gestalt therapists attend to in understanding Juan?

   a. his awareness
   b. his hatching
   c. his inferiority complex
   d. the thrown world

13. In reading the information about Juan, which of these people or events would seem to represent the "figure" for Juan?

   a. his job
   b. his religion
   c. his entire environment
   d. Marita

In the first session, Juan complains of his frustration with his job and his relationship with Marita. He is very upset, to the point of tears, about his failure to be successful. His head is buried in his hands, his elbows are resting on his knees, and he is looking at the floor. He says to you: "Sometimes I can't stand myself. I feel like I am just going through the motions. I want to make progress but I feel so stuck."

14. Which of the following gestalt therapeutic comments do you feel would be most appropriate to say in responding to Juan?

   a. Could you please push your face even further into your hands and tell me what you are feeling?
   b. You're so upset with yourself for not having done more with your life that it is hurting you very much.
   c. Could you "go through the motions", make motions now that might express how you feel?
   d. How has your wife been responding to you?

(This is a hard question. At this point in gestalt therapy, a gestalt therapist is likely to respond with a relationship-based response such as "b" rather than responses "a" and "c" that call the client's attention to his awareness. At a later time in therapy, such responses may be appropriate. Now is the time to be empathic to Juan's pain.)

Now you are working with Juan about his problems at work. It is the third session, and Juan is trying to make progress in understanding his problems at work and doing something about them.

15. He says to you: "You know, they never give you a break. My bosses, they're always questioning what you do and why you do it." Which of the following responses might be most appropriate in helping Juan develop his awareness in the moment?

   a. Do you think they would talk that way to Marita?
   b. Could you say that again, but use the word "I" instead of "you"?
   c. Can you tell me how you feel your bosses are treating "you"?
   d. Both b and c.

(Both answers "b" and "c" help Juan to take more responsibility for his situation with his bosses. "b" is somewhat more confrontational and direct than "c". Response "c" is more subtle than "b" and redirects Juan's attention to himself.)

In his distress about his boredom with work and his lack of progress, Juan says that it is about time for him to return to school and leave his job.

103

16. Juan says to you, "I need to do something more meaningful with my life and return to school." Which of these phrases would best replace the word "need"?

   a. have to
   b. must
   c. choose to
   d. am required to

As Juan continues to discuss his frustration with his job, he says to you in a loud voice, while beating his right fist against the arm of his chair: "I've got to stop letting life overwhelm me. Now is the time to do something about it".

17. In response to Juan's emotional frustration to his job situation, which response would seem to be most appropriate?

   a. Could you stop beating on my furniture please?
   b. Could you hit the arm of the chair again with your fist, like you just did? Can you describe what you are aware of?
   c. When you hit your fist against the chair, I believe you are acting out some of the rage that you felt as a child when your parents would not buy you a toy.
   d. Why are you hitting your fist against the arm of the chair?

Now Juan talks about how Marita feels about his job. "When Marita points out that my job is a dead end, I feel like I am all washed out, like I can't do anything. There is just that feeling of helplessness that I really dislike."

18. Respond now to Juan, using a statement that most closely fits a gestalt awareness approach.

   a. Be that washed out self and talk in a wishy-washy voice.
   b. You could tell her that it does not help you to have her complain about your work.
   c. You could say to her, "I am responsible for myself and you are responsible for yourself."
   d. You are projecting your anger at your father onto Marita.

19. As Juan is describing his concern about his job and Marita's interference in his career plans, he says to you, "I'd like to tell Marita to back off and leave me alone." Pick the statement that most closely fits a gestalt awareness response.

   a. Why don't you tell her to leave you alone, then?
   b. So Marita doesn't seem to think that you're very capable.
   c. Imagine, if you would, that Marita is sitting in this chair across from you; tell her what you would like to say to her.
   d. There are times when husbands and wives don't listen carefully to each other. Perhaps, you can listen more carefully to the underlying meaning of what she has to say.

Juan now describes the conflict that he feels between wanting to take a risk and return to school or being safe and staying with his current job. He describes how often he prefers to be safe, and yet more and more that he is able to take a risk and do something new or different.

20. The conflict that is described in the previous paragraph is seen by gestalt therapists as representing a(n)

    a. boundary contact disturbance.
    b. exercise.
    c. experiment.
    d. polarity.

    (d. Gestalt therapists often become aware of a variety of polarities in their clients' description of their problems.)

In dealing with a polarity such as the one described previously, gestalt therapists use self-dialogues so that individuals can play out the roles of the polarity.

21. Which of the following roles best describes the polarities that Juan is experiencing now?

    a. bossy self - submissive self
    b. masculine self - feminine self
    c. good boy - bad boy
    d. cautious self - risky self

22. In using the empty chair technique to play out the polarity, which choice would be the appropriate gestalt therapeutic approach?

    a. Free associate to the chair on the other side of the room.
    b. Would you be the cautious self in that chair and express how you feel, then you can respond in the other chair as the risky self?
    c. Tell me more about how you feel when you want to take risks. I think you need to take more risks.
    d. The conflict between the risky and the cautious self is incongruent. In the future, you must compromise between these two. I would like you to play the role of the compromise and express those feelings to the other chair.

Some gestalt therapists find dreams to be particularly meaningful in understanding issues in one's life. Rather than interpret the dream to the patient, they may ask the patient to enact the dream. Juan reports that he has dreamt about speeding down a highway in the middle of the night. He is going about 80 miles an hour and the scenery is whizzing by him quickly. Behind him he hears a loud siren and in his rear view mirror sees the lights of a police car chasing him. The chase continues through desert scenery. And the sound of the siren grows louder. Finally, the police car crashes into the back of Juan's car with terrible sounds and force.

23. As a gestalt therapist, you might ask Juan to be (and act the role of)

    a. his car.
    b. the police car.
    c. the road.
    d. the desert scenery.
    e. any or all of the above

The preceding case of Juan should help you to become more familiar with therapeutic approaches or concepts in gestalt therapy. Because these are presented in a brief amount of space, they can make gestalt therapy appear gimmicky. When gestalt therapists make interventions, it is in the interest of helping their patients. Interventions are not made for dramatic effect. They are made to help individuals become more self-aware in a constructive way that helps them become more responsible for themselves, more creative, and less anxious. Respect for the client and the relationship with the client are paramount in gestalt therapy.

SPECIAL TOPICS

OE1. Do you think it would be easy or difficult to do gestalt therapy in a time limited manner? Explain. (268)

_____

_____

_____

_____

OE2. An ongoing and current trend in gestalt therapy is the focus on the client-counselor relationship. Why do you think gestalt therapists have addressed this topic with so much interest? (268)

_____

_____

_____

_____

OE3. The two theories that have most recently been integrated with gestalt therapy are person-centered and psychoanalytical theories. What do you believe they have to offer gestalt therapy? (269)

_____

_____

_____

_____

OE4. How do you think gestalt therapy can empower women? (271-272)

_____

_____

_____

_____

OE5. How do gestalt therapists integrate cultural influences in helping clients to become more aware of themselves? (272-273)

_____

_____

_____

_____

STRENGTHS AND LIMITATIONS

What do you see as the strengths and limitations of gestalt therapy?

STRENGTHS   LIMITATIONS

_____   _____

_____   _____

_____   _____

_____   _____

_____   _____

_____   _____

_____   _____

GESTALT THERAPY: A QUIZ

True/false items: Decide if the following statements are more "true" or more "false" as they apply to gestalt therapy.

T   F   Q1.   Enhancing awareness is a major goal of gestalt therapy.

T   F   Q2.   The ground encompasses the field.

T   F   Q3.   Disturbances in contact boundaries mean that individuals have dysfunctional personality problems.

T   F   Q4.   The present, rather than the past, is the focus of gestalt therapy.

T   F   Q5.   Knowledge of archetypes is important in assessment in gestalt therapy.

T   F   Q6.   Awareness, not the therapeutic relationship, is important in gestalt therapy.

T   F   Q7.   Body language and other non-verbal behaviors are important therapeutic data in gestalt therapy.

T   F   Q8.   Interpretation is a major therapeutic technique in gestalt therapy.

T   F   Q9.   Group therapy is highly valued by gestalt therapists.

T   F   Q10.   Enactment is an approach to awareness used by gestalt therapists.

107

Multiple choice items. Select the one best answer from the alternatives using a gestalt therapy perspective.

_____ Q11. Gestalt therapy focuses on

    a. early childhood development.
    b. developing rational thinking.
    c. the here and now.
    d. the holding environment.

_____ Q12. Which of the following is NOT important in gestalt therapy?

    a. awareness
    b. acceptance of responsibility
    c. dealing with impasse
    d. exploring the collective unconscious
    e. unfinished business

_____ Q13. Which of these sentences is least consistent with developing awareness?

    a. I have to do my homework.
    b. I won't do my homework.
    c. I want to do my homework.
    d. I choose to do my homework.

_____ Q14. Which of these statements is most consistent with the goal of gestalt therapy?

    a. I need to be nicer to my sister.
    b. I can't be nice to my sister.
    c. I want to be nice to my sister.
    d. I have to be nicer to my sister.

_____ Q15. Gestalt therapists work with dreams through

    a. free association.
    b. enactment.
    c. interpretation of contact boundary disturbances.
    d. interpretation of I-thou relationships.

_____ Q16. Gestalt therapists view avoidance as a(n)

    a. active process.
    b. passive process.
    c. resistance to therapeutic love.
    d. transference resistance.

_____ Q17. Which of these is not a topic of interest for gestalt therapists?

    a. forgiveness
    b. mindfulness
    c. shame
    d. birth order

108

_____ Q18. Which of these statements is least consistent with gestalt therapy?

    a. Could you hold your fist there for a moment?
    b. Could you say that using the word "I" instead of "you".
    c. You should not express your anger to your wife.
    d. You seem to be feeling upset that your wife is angry with you.

_____ Q19. Gestalt therapy can be best characterized as

    a. experiential therapy.
    b. cognitive therapy.
    c. behavior therapy.
    d. therapy focused on the unconscious.

_____ Q20. The process of turning back to ourselves what we would like to do to someone else is called

    a. introjection.
    b. projection.
    c. retroflection.
    d. confluence.
    e. deflection.

_____ Q21. When Joe starts to talk about problems with his wife, he goes from one detail to another without drawing a conclusion. What type of contact boundary disturbance is this?

    a. introjection
    b. projection
    c. retroflection
    d. deflection
    e. confluence

_____ Q22. Mary has had a great level of trouble finding a job. She believes this is due to employers being angry and disdainful. Mary is angry that she has to look for work. What type of contact boundary disturbance is this?

    a. introjection
    b. projection
    c. retroflection
    d. deflection
    e. confluence

_____ Q23. The focus of gestalt therapy is on the

    a. past.
    b. present.
    c. future.

_____ Q24.   Unfinished business concerns

    a.   feelings from the past that will impact the future.
    b.   feelings from the past that are buried and are out of awareness.
    c.   unexpected feelings from the past that are dealt with in the present.
    d.   feelings in the present that will be dealt with in the future.

_____ Q25.   Gestalt therapy is most concerned with _____ boundaries.

    a.   borderline
    b.   depressed
    c.   I
    d.   thou

ANSWER KEY

1. b	11. d	21. d
2. c	12. a	22. b
3. a	13. d	23. e
4. d	14. b	
5. a	15. d	
6. c	16. c	
7. e	17. b	
8. c	18. a	
9. d	19. c	
10. b	20. d	

QUIZ

Q1. T	Q11. c	Q21. d
Q2. F	Q12. d	Q22. b
Q3. F	Q13. a	Q23. b
Q4. T	Q14. c	Q24. c
Q5. F	Q15. b	Q25. c
Q6. F	Q16. a	
Q7. T	Q17. d	
Q8. F	Q18. c	
Q9. T	Q19. a	
Q10. T	Q20. c	

CHAPTER 8

BEHAVIOR THERAPY

BEHAVIOR THERAPY SELF-INVENTORY

Directions: By comparing your beliefs about personality and therapy with those of behavior therapy, you should have a clearer idea of how much you will need to suspend your beliefs and change attitudes to understand behavior therapy's theory of personality and approach to therapy. You may find it helpful to complete this section before and after you read the chapter. In this way, you can see if your views have changed. There are no correct answers, only an opportunity to express your views.

Put an "X" on the line so that it indicates how much you agree or disagree with the statement: A = Agree, D = Disagree.

D   A

_____ 1. Changing and improving symptoms is sufficient to bring about therapeutic change.

_____ 2. Psychotherapy should be based on scientific principles which are supported by research results.

_____ 3. Clients should be informed about the therapy process and be involved in setting treatment goals.

_____ 4. Research on psychotherapy should help to refine concepts and the practice of therapy so that new approaches can be confirmed and developed.

_____ 5. Clients should be informed about the therapy process and be involved in setting treatment goals.

_____ 6. Clients control what behaviors are to be changed. Therapists and clients control how behavior is to change.

_____ 7. Past history is important only to the degree that it directly contributes to a client's current difficulties.

_____ 8. A detailed and comprehensive assessment is necessary for behavior change to occur.

_____ 9. Psychotherapy should focus on overt and specific behaviors rather than clients' feelings about a situation.

111

_____ 10. The outcomes of therapy should be assessed to determine the degree of success or failure of treatment.

_____ 11. The focus of psychotherapy should be changing behavior, not developing insight into problems.

_____ 12. Positive reinforcement enhances client learning.

_____ 13. The roles of the therapist should include being a teacher, consultant, facilitator, coach, model, director and/or problem solver.

_____ 14. Client change can take place using imagination or going out into the actual environment.

_____ 15. Both therapist and client can control the pace at which therapeutic change takes place.

_____ 16. Clients should be actively involved in the analysis, planning, process, and evaluation of a treatment program.

_____ 17. Therapy should be made available to all people including those who are severely limited due to psychological or physical functioning.

_____ 18. Therapeutic procedures should be aimed at behavior change.

_____ 19. The client and the therapist should have a good working relationship in order to ensure behavior change.

_____ 20. Cognitive and behavior therapy can compliment each other to bring about therapeutic change.

HISTORY OF BEHAVIOR THERAPY

Which influences do you think were most important in the development of behavior therapy?

PSYCHOLOGISTS AND THEIR CONTRIBUTIONS		
CLASSICAL CONDITIONING	*OPERANT CONDITIONING*	*SOCIAL COGNITIVE THEORY*
Ivan Pavlov - classical conditioning late 19th century John Watson - applied classical conditioning to the treatment of human behavior, 1910-1926 Mowrer and Mowrer - applied classical conditioning to the treatment of bed wetting using a urine alarm system, 1938	E. L. Thorndike - studied the learning of new behaviors – Law of Effect - emphasized adaptive nature of learning, 1890s-1920s B. F. Skinner - selectively reinforced different behaviors – applied behavioral principles to animals and humans, 1930s-1980s	Mary Cover Jones - used models and observation to treat Peter's fear of rabbits, 1924 Albert Bandura - developed social cognitive theory, included beliefs, preferences, self-perceptions, sense of self-efficacy as regulators of behavior, described observations and modeling, 1960

BEHAVIOR THEORY OF PERSONALITY

No single person is responsible for the development of a behavioral theory of personality. Rather, the foundation for a theory of personality is based on principles of behavior that have been developed by the research of many different behavioral psychologists. The principles can be divided into two very broad categories. One category is principles derived mainly from operant conditioning but also classical conditioning. The other is derived from observational learning, the work of Albert Bandura. Behavior therapists build on these principles in developing techniques of behavior change.

OPERANT AND CLASSICAL CONDITIONING CONCEPTS

classical conditioning A type of learning in which a neutral stimulus is presented repeatedly with one that reflexively elicits a particular response so the neutral stimulus will eventually elicit the response itself (also called respondent conditioning).

operant conditioning A type of learning in which behavior is increased or decreased by systematically changing its consequences.

overt behavior Actions that can be directly observed by others.

positive reinforcement The process by which the introduction of a stimulus has a consequence of a behavior that increases the likelihood that the behavior will be performed again.

negative reinforcement An unpleasant or undesirable consequence of a behavior is removed. This increases the likelihood that the behavior will be repeated.

extinction The process of no longer presenting a reinforcement. It is used to decrease or eliminate certain behaviors.

generalization Transferring the response from one type of stimuli to similar stimuli.

discrimination Responding differentially to stimuli that are similarly based on different cues or antecedent events.

shaping Gradually reinforcing certain parts of a behavior to more closely approximate the desired behavior.

OBSERVATIONAL LEARNING CONCEPTS

observational learning A type of learning in which people are influenced by observing the behaviors of others.

covert behavior Behavior that others cannot directly perceive, such as thinking or feeling.

attentional processes The act of perceiving or watching something and learning from it.

retention processes This basically refers to remembering that which has been observed.

motor reproduction processes This refers to translating what one has seen into action using motor skills.

motivational processes For observations to be put into action and then continued for some time, reinforcement must be present. Reinforcement brings about motivation.

self-efficacy The individuals' perceptions of their ability to deal with different types of events.

113

QUESTIONS ABOUT BEHAVIORAL PERSONALITY CONCEPTS

1. If Jill is no longer praised for doing her homework, then this process may take place.

    a. positive reinforcement
    (b.) extinction
    c. generalization
    d. discrimination

2. Now that Bradley has been bitten by a dog, he is afraid of all dogs. This process has taken place.

    a. positive reinforcement
    b. extinction
    (c.) generalization
    d. discrimination

3. The type of learning in which the researcher or experimenter has the most control is

    (a.) classical conditioning.
    b. operant conditioning.
    c. social cognitive theory.
    d. negative reinforcement.

4. Covert behavior would most closely be associated with which of these concepts?

    a. negative reinforcement
    b. discrimination
    c. shaping
    (d.) attentional processes

5. When Millie uses self-talk to describe to herself how she is going to visit a friend at her new apartment and not get lost, she is using

    a. attentional processes.
    (b.) retention processes.
    c. motor reproduction processes.
    d. motivational processes.

BEHAVIORAL APPROACHES TO THERAPY

Methods used for change in behavior therapy have been developed by a variety of practitioners using approaches that are consistent with basic principles of behavior. All aspects of behavior therapy including goals, assessments, and techniques are well defined and specified.

GOALS OF BEHAVIOR THERAPY

There may be several goals in behavior therapy. The client and the therapist work together to develop goals, often referred to as target behaviors.

functional analysis Specifying goals and treatment by assessing antecedents and consequences of a behavior. Analyze what is maintaining the behavior and propose hypotheses about contributors to the behavior. Use this information to guide treatment of the behavior and to further specify goals.

target behavior A part of the client's problem that can be clearly defined and easily assessed. It is the focus of treatment in behavior therapy.

114

ASSESSMENT IN BEHAVIOR THERAPY.

The focus of behavioral assessment is current behavior. Past behavior is useful to the extent that it helps in specifying current behavior. Common methods for assessment are interviews, reports and writings, observations, and physiological measurements.

INTERVIEWS	REPORTS AND RATINGS	OBSERVATIONS	PHYSIOLOGICAL MEASUREMENTS
ask about antecedents and consequences	brief ratings, yes or no or on a scale	naturalistic simulated	blood pressure heart rate respiration

interrater reliability The degree of agreement among raters about their observations of an individual or individuals.

reactivity This occurs when clients change their behaviors because they know that they are being observed.

The fact that behavioral therapists are concerned about interrater reliability and reactivity shows the importance that they place on accuracy, specificity, and scientific principles.

GENERAL BEHAVIORAL TREATMENT APPROACHES

Many behavioral approaches have been developed to reduce fear and anxiety, but they also can be applied to other concerns. Systematic desensitization and implosive therapy are particularly designed to reduce anxiety. Modeling techniques help individuals learn new behaviors. Donald Meichenbaum has developed two approaches that combine cognitive and behavioral methods: self-instructional training and stress inoculation.

ANXIETY TREATMENT APPROACHES

Several strategies have been developed, such as systematic desensitization, virtual reality, and implosive therapy, to reduce fear and anxiety. One useful dimension to examine these approaches determines if the client is to make changes using imagination, a virtual reality situation, or in the real situation (in vivo). A second dimension concerns the speed of type of delivery of the approach. Is it to be done gradually or all at once to evoke high levels of anxiety? The following chart describes these dimensions and places systematic desensitization and implosive therapy within the chart.

ANXIETY TREATMENT APPROACHES

	Imagination	Virtual Reality	In Vivo
Gradual	Systematic Desensitization		
Flooding	Implosive Therapy		

systematic desensitization A specific procedure for replacing anxiety with relaxation while gradually increasing the imagined exposure to an anxiety-producing situation.

flooding Prolonged in vivo or imagined exposure to stimuli that evoke high levels of anxiety, with no ability to avoid or escape the stimuli. Implosive therapy uses flooding.

115

in vivo The Latin term for "in life", which refers to therapeutic procedures that take place in the client's natural environment.

implosive therapy A type of prolonged intense exposure therapy in which the client imagines exaggerated scenes that include hypothesized stimuli.

virtual reality therapy This therapy takes place in a computer-generated environment. Typically, the client can interact with this environment by using a joystick, a headband, a glove with physiological sensors, or a similar device. Although used most frequently for anxiety, especially phobias, virtual reality therapy can also be used with other disorders.

MODELING TECHNIQUES

Based on Bandura's social cognitive theory, modeling techniques provide an opportunity for clients to observe the behavior of another person (a model) and then use the results of their observations. There are several types of modeling that behavior therapists use:

live Watch a model (can be the therapist).

symbolic Includes films, videotapes, photographs, or pictures.

role playing Acting the part of someone, something else, or oneself under different conditions. Clients may practice different situations. Therapists and clients can play different roles.

participant modeling Therapists model a behavior and guide the client in the use of the behavior.

covert modeling The client imagines a model. The therapist describes the activities of the model which the client follows in her imagination.

COGNITIVE-BEHAVIORAL APPROACHES

Donald Meichenbaum has developed two approaches that combine cognitive and behavioral methods. These are self-instructional training and stress inoculation.

self-instructional training A cognitive-behavioral therapy that teaches patients to instruct themselves verbally so that they may cope with difficult situations.

stress inoculation training Clients use coping skills for dealing with stressful situations and then practice the skills, while being exposed to the situation. In the conceptual phase, the therapist gathers information and educates the client about the problem. In the skills acquisition phase, new cognitive and behavioral skills are taught such as relaxation training, cognitive restructuring, problem-solving skills, and self-reinforcement. In the application phase, clients apply these skills to their problems. Specific homework assignments are given.

FOUR OTHER SPECIFIC BEHAVIORAL APPROACHES

exposure and ritual prevention (EX/RP) A treatment method used primarily with obsessive-compulsive disorders in which patients are exposed to the feared stimulus for an hour or more at a time. They are then asked to refrain from participating in rituals such as continually checking the door to see if they have closed it.

eye movement desensitization and reprocessing (EMDR) Designed first for post traumatic stress, EMDR requires that the patient visualize a most upsetting memory and accompanying physical sensations. The clients repeat negative self-statements that they associate with the scene. The patient follows the therapist's finger as it moves rapidly back and forth. After completing the eye movements, the client stops thinking about the scene. This procedure is repeated again and again until the client's anxiety is reduced.

116

acceptance and commitment therapy Behavioral techniques are combined with a focus on clients' use of language to reduce distress. The focus is on accepting a feeling, event, or situation rather than avoiding it. Therapists help clients commit to behaviors that fits with their values.

dialectical behavior therapy A research supported therapy designed for the treatment of suicidal patients and those with borderline disorder. Mindfulness values and meditation techniques have been incorporated into this treatment.

CASE EXAMPLE OF JUDY'S ANXIETY

Judy is a 22-year-old college student majoring in business administration. She is in her senior year at a midwestern university. Except for her freshman year when she received C's and D's, she has been a B+ student. Very conscientious, she worries that her work will not be good enough. There are many things that Judy worries about. Not only is she fearful that she will do poorly on exams, but she worries about how she will be perceived in social situations. About one year ago, she and her boyfriend broke up. Since then, she has dated several times but usually worries about how her date will view her.

Although Judy's concerns about how others see her and her academic performance are important to her, she is most worried about driving. About two years ago, Judy was in a bad accident in which her leg was broken. She was driving near her home when another driver smashed into the driver's side of her car. She was in the hospital overnight and on crutches for about a month. Since that time, she has been very afraid of driving. Living near suburban Chicago, about four hours from her university, Judy often worries about the trips home. She worries even more about driving in the Chicago traffic when she goes to visit friends who live in apartments there.

Judy's father is an orthodontist working in Chicago. Her mother is a computer programmer. When Judy went to college, she was glad to get away. She finds that her mother is overprotective, often asking her if she will be all right when she goes out at night. She worries too about Judy when Judy is driving home. For the last 20 years, Judy's mother has been treated on and off for symptoms of anxiety. For the last four years, she has been taking anti-anxiety medication.

QUESTIONS ABOUT TREATING JUDY'S FEARS

6. Which of Judy's presenting problems would you, as a behavior therapist, most easily be able to define as target behaviors, along with Judy's help?

    a. her academic anxiety
    b. her fear in social situations
    c. anxiety when driving

7. Which of the following questions is most consistent with determining goals in behavior therapy?

    a. What dreams have you had about driving?
    b. What thoughts do you have when you start to drive?
    c. In what type of driving situation are you the most anxious?
    d. How does your mother feel about your driving alone?

8. Which questions seem most appropriate in determining goals for behavior therapy with regard to Judy's driving behavior?

    a. How anxious are you when you are the passenger and a friend is driving?
    b. Are there any driving situations in which you feel little anxiety?
    c. Does the type of car that you are driving affect your problem with driving?
    d. All of the above.

117

9. Which of the following methods of behavioral assessments will most likely give you the most information in assessing appropriate target behaviors for Judy's concerns about driving?

    a. behavioral interviews
    b. behavioral reports and ratings
    c. behavioral observations
    d. physiological measurements

10. Behavioral observations of Judy's driving could come from

    a. Judy.
    b. her mother.
    c. a friend.
    d. all of the above.

As you and Judy discuss her problems, the two of you decide to devote attention at first to her fears about driving. Judy tells you that she is most fearful when driving alone, slightly less fearful when there is a passenger in the car, and not fearful when she is a passenger. Furthermore, she tells you that it doesn't matter what type of car she is driving, as long as it is not a truck, something she has only driven once. She is most comfortable driving along streets near her college and through small towns. Highway driving isn't as hard for her as driving in downtown Chicago traffic. The more traffic there is, either in the city or on a highway, the more anxious she is.

11. Which of the following treatment approaches that you could discuss with Judy are likely to be the most gentle, yet take the most time?

    a. implosive therapy
    b. in vivo flooding
    c. explosive therapy
    d. systematic desensitization

12. If you and Judy decided to use systematic desensitization, what would be one of the first aspects of treatment?

    a. have her drive her car in downtown Chicago
    b. initiate relaxation training
    c. have Judy imagine a scene that is slightly anxiety producing
    d. have Judy imagine a scene that is very anxiety producing

13. Which of the following instructions fits most closely with a relaxation instruction that you might give to Judy?

    a. Just relax more and more.
    b. Keep relaxing, and tell me when you're done.
    c. Clench both fists together tightly. Feel the tension in both fists. Now tense up your forearms and feel the tension in your forearms.
    d. Think of a lovely day, and just let yourself relax as much as possible.
    e. Tense your biceps. Make your biceps quite hard. Feel the tension in your forearms, upper arms, and into your shoulders. Now let yourself relax. Let your arms become loose and heavy, and feel the relaxation all over your arms.

14. Which of the following items is likely to have the highest rating on Judy's subjective units of discomfort scale (SUDs)?

    a.   driving around her college town
    b.   driving around home
    c.   driving on a highway
    d.   driving in downtown Chicago in rush hour

15. Once Judy has learned how to relax, you will ask her to write a number of items on a hierarchy, and then ask her to imagine them. Which item are you likely to have her imagine first?

    a.   driving in an unfamiliar city
    b.   driving around home
    c.   driving on a highway
    d.   driving in downtown Chicago in rush hour

16. What type of behavioral treatment would you be using with Judy if you said to her: "Imagine you are in downtown Chicago, driving alone. Your car is stalled at a light and drivers are honking all around you, trying to get you to move. No matter how much you try, the car is still stalled. Someone knocks at you window and asks you to get your car moving."

    a.   virtual reality
    b.   gradual in vivo
    c.   flooding-imagination
    d.   flooding-in vivo

17. If you decide to have Judy sit in a car seat in a laboratory with a steering wheel and view simulated traffic situations projected onto a screen by a computer, you would be using this behavioral treatment approach.

    a.   gradual in vivo
    b.   virtual reality
    c.   flooding-imagination
    d.   flooding-in vivo

Rather than use any of these approaches, you may prefer to use modeling techniques. This would allow Judy to observe someone else driving and make use of her knowledge of others' driving. Judy may reply to that idea, "Well, I drive with others all the time, and that doesn't seem to help." For modeling to work in a situation such as this, Judy would need to watch the other person carefully and learn how she controls her anxiety. Even so, it may not provide sufficient anxiety reduction.

18. If Judy were watching her father drive in Chicago through heavy traffic, while being relatively calm, she would be participating in

    a.   live modeling.
    b.   symbolic modeling.
    c.   role playing.
    d.   participant modeling.
    e.   covert modeling.

19. If you were to say to Judy: "I want you to imagine your father driving through Chicago. Picture the street he is on and the stores on either side. Notice how relaxed and calm he is as he drives the car. He is breathing slowly and easily. His muscles are relaxed, yet there are cars in front of him at the stop light." Which of the following types of modeling is he likely to be using?

    a. live modeling
    b. symbolic modeling
    c. role playing
    d. participant modeling
    e. covert modeling

Donald Meichenbaum has developed two methods that combine behavioral approaches with a cognitive technique. In using the techniques, clients are often told to give instructions to themselves or to reinforce their own behaviors by saying positive statements to themselves. His two methods are self-instructional training and stress inoculation.

20. If Judy were to practice new skills in the office with you, then plan to apply them in actual traffic situations by repeating instructions to herself, she would be using

    a. self-instructional training.
    b. stress inoculation.
    c. cognitive restructuring.
    d. none of the above.

21. If you teach Judy how to replace a statement such as "I'm afraid I'm going to get into an accident" with "When I am afraid, I will take a breath and be able to handle the traffic," you are using

    a. self-instructional training.
    b. stress inoculation.
    c. cognitive restructuring.
    d. none of the above.

22. If Judy said to herself, "I am almost there. I am driving well in Chicago traffic," this statement would be called

    a. classical conditioning.
    b. implosive therapy.
    c. role playing.
    d. self-reinforcement.

SPECIAL TOPICS

OE1. What factors influence the duration of behavior therapy? (309)

_____

_____

_____

_____

OE2. What do you see as the advantages and disadvantages of using treatment manuals in behavior therapy?

_____

_____

_____

_____

OE3. What type of ethical issues face behavior therapists that do not face most other therapists? (316)

_____

_____

_____

_____

OE4. What difficulties would a therapist have in using behavior therapy with psychoanalysis? (316-317)

_____

_____

_____

_____

OE5. What approaches do behavior therapists use to avoid gender bias in their treatment of clients? (320)

_____

_____

_____

_____

OE6. How can the identification of antecedents and consequences of behavior help therapists avoid cultural bias? (321)

_____

_____

_____

_____

121

STRENGTHS AND LIMITATIONS

What do you believe are the strengths and limitations of behavior therapy?

STRENGTHS	LIMITATIONS
_____	_____
_____	_____
_____	_____
_____	_____
_____	_____
_____	_____
_____	_____

BEHAVIOR THERAPY: A QUIZ

True/false items: Decide if the following statements are "more true" or "more false" as they apply to behavior therapy.

T (F) Q1. Behavior therapy is derived from principles of psychoanalysis.

T (F) Q2. B. F. Skinner developed the process of learning called classical conditioning.

T (F) Q3. Behavior therapy is concerned with changing only visible behaviors.

(T) F Q4. Behavior therapy is based on scientific principles derived from human and animal learning.

(T) F Q5. Newer developments in behavior therapy have focused on cognitive as well as behavioral factors.

(T) F Q6. Client and therapist work together to choose goals of behavior therapy.

(T) F Q7. Questions are an important technique of behavior therapists.

(T) F Q8. Behavioral assessment could include the measurement of the client's blood pressure.

T (F) Q9. The client-therapist relationship is not important in behavior therapy.

(T) F Q10. Clients' sense of self-efficacy is important in social cognitive theory.

122

Multiple choice items: Select the one best answer from those alternatives given. Consider each question within the framework of behavior therapy.

_____ Q11. Behavior therapy is based on

    a. principles of learning.
    b. action oriented techniques.
    c. principles of self-actualization.
    d. classical conditioning.

_____ Q12. Observational learning is a part of

    a. classical conditioning.
    b. operant conditioning.
    c. social cognitive theory.
    d. desensitization.

_____ Q13. The Law of Effect was derived by

    a. Pavlov.
    b. Skinner.
    c. Thorndike.
    d. Bandura.

_____ Q14. When you get an A on an exam, the A serves as

    a. a focus in acceptance and commitment therapy
    b. an unconditioned stimulus.
    c. a positive reinforcer.
    d. an attentional process.

_____ Q15. Which of these terms is most closely associated with social cognitive theory?

    a. positive reinforcement
    b. generalization
    c. shaping
    d. motivational processes

_____ Q16. Which of these is most likely to be a goal of behavior therapy?

    a. increase amount of talking to opposite sex peers
    b. decrease social anxiety
    c. increase awareness of facial movements when anxious
    d. develop a stronger sense of confidence when with peers of the opposite sex

_____ Q17. Which of these is NOT a behavioral assessment technique?

    a. interviews
    b. ratings
    c. observations
    d. virtual reality
    e. physiological measures

123

_____ Q18. In which of these methods of behavioral assessment is reactivity most likely to be a potential concern?

    a.   interviews
    b.   reports
    c.   measures of physical functioning
    (d.) observations

_____ Q19. Relaxation training is an important part of

    (a.) desensitization.
    b.   modeling.
    c.   virtual reality therapy.
    d.   in vivo flooding therapy.

_____ Q20. Examining painful thoughts and feelings are characteristic of this type of behavior therapy.

    (a.) acceptance and commitment therapy
    b.   eye-movement desensitization reprocessing
    c.   dialectical behavior therapy
    d.   virtual reality therapy

_____ Q21. Which disorder is dialectical behavior therapy designed to treat?

    a.   bi-polar disorder
    b.   narcissistic disorder
    c.   phobias
    (d.) borderline disorder

_____ Q22. Using films of spiders that get increasingly closer and larger in size could be characteristic of this type of therapy.

    a.   acceptance and commitment therapy
    b.   eye-movement desensitization therapy
    c.   stress inoculation
    (d.) virtual reality therapy.

_____ Q23. Which of these disorders can usually be treated more briefly by behavior therapy than can the other disorders?

    a.   depression
    b.   obsessive-compulsive disorder
    c.   general anxiety
    (d.) phobias
    e.   posttraumatic stress disorder

124

Q24. Exposure and ritual prevention is a behavioral treatment most commonly applied to

a. depression.
b. obsessive-compulsive disorder.
c. general anxiety.
d. borderline disorder.
e. posttraumatic stress disorder.

Q25. Which of these techniques is most likely to be used in behavioral group therapy?

a. assertiveness training
b. empathic listening skills
c. eye movement desensitization
d. motivational processing
e. classical conditioning

ANSWER KEY

1.	b	11.	d	21.	c
2.	c	12.	b	22.	d
3.	a	13.	e		
4.	d	14.	d		
5.	b	15.	b		
6.	c	16.	c		
7.	c	17.	b		
8.	d	18.	a		
9.	a	19.	e		
10.	d	20.	a		

QUIZ

Q1.	F	Q11.	a	Q21.	d
Q2.	F	Q12.	c	Q22.	d
Q3.	F	Q13.	c	Q23.	d
Q4.	T	Q14.	c	Q24.	b
Q5.	T	Q15.	d	Q25.	a
Q6.	T	Q16.	a		
Q7.	T	Q17.	d		
Q8.	T	Q18.	d		
Q9.	F	Q19.	a		
Q10.	T	Q20.	a		

125

CHAPTER 9

RATIONAL EMOTIVE BEHAVIOR THERAPY

RATIONAL EMOTIVE BEHAVIOR THERAPY SELF-INVENTORY

Directions: By comparing your beliefs about personality and therapy to those of Albert Ellis, you should have a clearer idea of how much you will need to suspend your beliefs or change attitudes to understand REBT's theory of personality and approach to therapy. You may find it helpful to complete this section before and after you read the chapter. In this way, you can see if your views have changed. There are no correct answers, only an opportunity to express your views.

Put an "X" on the line so that it indicates how much you agree or disagree with the statement: A=Agree, D=Disagree.

D   A

_____ 1. Individuals have the potential for both rational thinking and irrational thinking.

_____ 2. Biological factors as well as social factors are important in determining personality.

_____ 3. It is desirable to be loved and accepted but not necessary.

_____ 4. We have irrational ideas without realizing it.

_____ 5. Seeking pleasure and avoiding pain is an appropriate philosophy of life.

_____ 6. Because of their irrational beliefs, individuals largely create their own emotional disturbances.

_____ 7. Therapy preferably should reduce clients' self-defeating outlook, helping them to acquire a rational philosophy of life.

_____ 8. Human interests are more important than theological ones.

_____ 9. Therapy preferably should challenge clients' illogical ideas and teach clients how to think rationally.

_____ 10. Being directive and attacking faulty thinking is an appropriate therapeutic approach.

_____ 11. Being efficient, logical, and flexible can help people get more from life.

126

D   A

_____ 12. Dysfunctional beliefs can interfere with an individual's enjoyment of life.

_____ 13. Irrational thoughts play a large role in many psychological disorders.

_____ 14. Teaching clients new ways to think can be a valuable tool in therapy.

_____ 15. Problem solving is an appropriate therapeutic technique.

_____ 16. Forceful self-statements that represent rational beliefs are helpful for clients to learn so that they may change self-defeating behaviors.

_____ 17. Understanding the origins of our disturbances can yield insight that will be helpful in solving future problems.

_____ 18. Therapy should attend to clients' thinking, feeling, and behavior.

_____ 19. Disputing clients' irrational thoughts can be a helpful approach to client change.

_____ 20. Although desirable, an empathic relationship between a client and therapist is neither necessary nor sufficient for change in therapy.

HISTORY OF RATIONAL EMOTIVE BEHAVIOR THERAPY

Which influences do you think were most important in the development of Ellis's Rational Emotive Behavior Therapy?

PERSONAL LIFE	PROFESSIONAL LIFE
Born in Pittsburgh in 1913 Moved to New York City in 1917 Oldest of three children Hospitalized nine times as a child for kidney disease Became self-sufficient at an early age Used rational approaches to deal with rejection as a young man Undergraduate degree from City College of New York in 1934 Continues to work at the Albert Ellis Institute Very active in professional practice Many awards and honors	Interested in philosophy of the Stoics Influenced by European philosophers who wrote about happiness and rationality – Spinoza, Nietszche, Kant Studied modern philosophers' emphasis on cognition - Dewey, Russell, and Popper. Influenced by Adler's focus on beliefs. Started the *Journal of Rational-Emotive Behavior and Cognitive-Behavior Therapy* Wrote over 800 articles and 75 books, including *Reason and Emotion in Psychotherapy*, 1962, *Humanistic Psychotherapy: The Rational Emotive Approach*, 1973

127

RATIONAL EMOTIVE BEHAVIOR THEORY OF PERSONALITY

Philosophical viewpoints as well as attention to biological and social factors have influenced the development of rational emotive behavior's theory of personality. Ellis's A-B-C model is the basis of his personality theory. Ellis believes that it is not the activating event (A) that causes positive or emotional and behavioral consequences (C), but rather it is the individual's belief system (B) that helps cause the consequences (C). When activating events are unpleasant, irrational beliefs may develop. The concepts basic to REBT's theory of personality are defined here.

REBT'S PHILOSOPHICAL VIEWPOINTS

Throughout his life, Ellis has had an interest in the study of philosophy. This interest influenced his focus on irrational beliefs as being a major problem for individuals. He encourages patients to consider and adopt a sensible philosophy so that it will help them enjoy their lives. Responsible hedonism, humanism, and rationality are philosophical ideas that can be seen in REBT's approach to psychotherapy.

hedonism A philosophical term referring to the concept of seeking pleasure and avoiding pain. In REBT, responsible hedonism refers to maintaining pleasure over the long-term by avoiding short-term pleasures that may lead to pain, such as alcohol or cocaine.

humanism A philosophy or value system in which human interests and dignity are valued and that takes an individualist, critical, and secular perspective as opposed to a religious or spiritual perspective.

Unconditional Self Acceptance (**USA**) Individuals have worth. They should accept that they make mistakes and that some of their assets and qualities are stronger than others. Individuals' acts or performances should be criticized, not their personal worth.

rationality Thinking, feeling, and acting in ways that will help individuals attain their goals. This is in contrast to irrationality in which thinking, feeling, and acting are self-defeating and interfere with goal attainment.

FACTORS BASIC TO REBT THEORY OF PERSONALITY

Ellis recognized that individuals' personality developments and their emotional disturbances were not independent of biological social aspects. Ellis believes that individuals have a biological tendency to severely disturb themselves and to prolong their emotional dysfunction. One reason that Ellis uses such powerful and direct therapeutic techniques is his view of the strength in which individuals hold irrational beliefs. Some of this is due to biological factors. Social factors refer to the effect of interpersonal relationships on beliefs about self. Criticism from others contributes to negative self-beliefs. Likewise, caring too much about what others think of you can negatively affect your own beliefs about yourself.

Being vulnerable to emotional disturbance for both social and biological reasons is a core view of Albert Ellis. Although individuals desire to be successful and happy, many irrational beliefs interfere with these goals. Examples of some of these are irrational beliefs about competence and success, about love and approval, about being treated unfairly, and about safety and comfort.

irrational belief Unreasonable views or convictions that produce emotional and behavioral problems.

THE RATIONAL EMOTIVE BEHAVIOR A-B-C THEORY OF PERSONALITY

Ellis's philosophical viewpoints and his focus on biological and social factors are concepts that support his basic personality theory, the A-B-C model.
> A- ACTIVATING EVENT
> B- BELIEF SYSTEM
> C- CONSEQUENCES

Briefly stated, the A-B-C model refers to what happens when an activating event (A) leads to emotional and behavioral consequences (C). The emotional and behavioral consequences are not caused by (A) the activating event but by the individual's belief system (B). Irrational beliefs occur when the activating event (A) is an unpleasant one. Irrational beliefs (B) can then partly cause difficult emotional and behavioral consequences (C).

According to Ellis, it is bad enough that individuals have irrational beliefs, but they turn these beliefs into new activating events which cause new irrational beliefs. Ellis refers to this as disturbances about disturbances. Thus, if an individual does not get a job promotion that he wants, he may say to himself, "I feel terrible and hopeless," and feels depressed. This consequence can then turn into a new activating event, and the individual can say, "This is really awful that I'm so depressed and hopeless." Now a new consequence is even greater than the original consequence. For Ellis, words such as "have to" and "must" are consequences that lead to more irrational beliefs.

musterbation Albert Ellis' phrase to characterize the behavior of clients who are inflexible and absolutistic in their thinking, maintaining that they must not fail or that they must have their way.

low frustration tolerance Inability or difficulty in dealing with events or situations that do not go as planned, for example, getting very angry because someone does not do as you ask.

discomfort anxiety When individuals' comfort level is threatened and they feel they must get what they want (low frustration tolerance). There is a belief that if individuals don't get or do what they want, the results will be awful or catastrophic.

ego anxiety Individuals' sense of self worth is threatened and they feel that they must perform well. There is a belief that if individuals don't get or do what they want, the results will be awful or catastrophic.

RATIONAL EMOTIVE BEHAVIOR THEORY OF PSYCHOTHERAPY

The A-B-C theory of personality affects the way REBT therapists determine goals for their clients, assess their clients, and select therapeutic techniques. Disputing irrational beliefs is a most important therapeutic intervention. Being aware of how vulnerable individuals are to disturbance, Ellis has used a variety of cognitive, affective, and behavioral methods to help clients change.

GOALS OF REBT

A general goal of REBT is to help clients minimize emotional disturbances, decrease self-defeating behaviors, and become happier. If individuals can think rationally and have fewer irrational beliefs, Ellis believes they will live happier lives. REBT teaches individuals how to deal with negative feelings such as sorrow, regret, frustration, depression, and anxiety. Virtually all client problems are viewed from the perspective of the contribution of their irrational beliefs.

ASSESSMENT IN REBT

REBT therapists try to assess which thoughts and behaviors create problems for their clients. They may listen for themes that repeat themselves. They can conceptualize these themes more specifically by using the A-B-C theory of personality. Identifying activating events (A), rational and irrational beliefs (B), and emotional and behavioral consequences (C) is the most basic form of assessment in REBT. This assessment continues in each session and is not limited to the first few sessions. The REBT Self-Help Form that is shown on pages 341 and 342 provides a specific method for following the A-B-C theory in assessing a client. Other objective personality inventories may be used, but they yield information that only indirectly applies to the A-B-C theory of personality.

THE A-B-C-D-E THERAPEUTIC APPROACH

Described in detail in the text, the A-B-C-D-E therapeutic approach is briefly summarized here. The therapeutic interventions referred to by D are three parts of disputation. When irrational beliefs are disputed, the client will experience E, a new effect. In essence, the client will have a logical philosophy that allows her to challenge her own irrational beliefs.

A (Activating Event) Therapists often divide activating events into two parts: what happened and what the patient perceived happened. Typically, therapists focus only on a few activating events at a time. Sometimes previous consequences (C) become activating events.

C (Consequences) Sometimes it is difficult for therapists to distinguish between consequences and beliefs. Consequences tend to be feelings such as "I feel so stressed out." Feelings cannot be disputed, but beliefs that bring about feelings can. Changing beliefs (B) can alter consequences (C).

B (Beliefs) Irrational or self-defeating rather than rational or self helping beliefs are the focus of therapy. Changing irrational beliefs can change consequences.

D (Disputing) Disputing irrational beliefs is the major therapeutic technique in REBT. Disputing is often done in three parts.

1. Detecting - the client and therapist detect the irrational beliefs that underlie activating events.
2. Discriminating - the therapist and client discriminate irrational from rational beliefs.
3. Debating - the therapist uses several different strategies to debate the client's irrational beliefs. These include the lecture, the Socratic debate, humor, and self-disclosure.

E (Effect) Developing an effective philosophy in which irrational beliefs have been replaced by rational beliefs is the product of successful REBT.

OTHER THERAPEUTIC APPROACHES

REBT does not limit itself to using disputing methods. Other cognitive approaches, as well as affective and behavioral methods are used. Some of the more common approaches are listed here.

OTHER COGNITIVE APPROACHES	EMOTIVE TECHNIQUES	BEHAVIORAL METHODS
coping self-statements cost-benefit analysis psychoeducational methods teaching others problem solving	imagery role playing shame-attacking exercises forceful self-statements forceful self-dialogue	activity homework reinforcement and penalties skill training

INSIGHT

Three types of insight develop from REBT that can lead to behavioral change.

1. Acknowledging that disturbances largely come from irrational beliefs not from the past.
2. Learning how one has reindoctrinated oneself with irrational beliefs from the past.
3. Accepting 1 and 2, knowing that insight does not automatically change people, and working hard to effect change.

Ellis believes that when clients have achieved all three types of insight, "elegant" change takes place. Clients have thus made changes and know why they have made the changes.

CASE EXAMPLE OF CHARLES

Charles is an 11-year-old fifth grade student. His parents have referred him to counseling because Charles seems to be very worried. He reports difficulty sleeping and tries to eat throughout the day. He seems to have very few friends that he plays with either in the neighborhood or at school. When he gets off the bus, he typically goes right to the television set and turns it on, watching soap operas and cartoons.

Charles is a heavy set young man who has been teased because he is overweight. Few things seem to make him happy. When he is watching cartoons, he will laugh as they seem to help him take his mind off his problems.

His younger brother is in third grade and is very active. In fact, his parents think that Jack might have attention deficit disorder. Charles's father is a supervisor in an automobile parts plant, and Charles's mother is an electronics technician in another factory. Neither of Charles's parents has gone to college, but both would like to see their two sons become professionals as they find their own jobs physically and emotionally draining. Charles's mother worries that she has had to leave Jack and Charles in the care of neighbors or occasionally with her mother. Now that both boys seem to be having problems at school, she worries about being an inadequate mother and feels that she may have made a mistake to keep working. However, the family has a high mortgage on their house and are overdue on some of their bills.

Charles has been sent to see you because he is having trouble at school. You will try to help him using the A-B-C-D-E theory of REBT.

When you see Charles, he tells you that he hates school and hates the kids at school. His academic work is at the B level, but he would like it to be higher. He does spend some time helping some of his teachers with tasks like cleaning the blackboard. He tries to stay close to them and worries about being physically beaten by bullies when he goes out onto the playground. His self-esteem is quite low, and he doesn't feel that he is doing well in school at all. In terms of social relationships at school, Charles thinks that the other children consider him to be a nerd and boring. He feels isolated and does not think that other children will want to be with him. He hates when he is teased about his weight, called "fatty" and "big butt."

QUESTIONS ABOUT ASSESSING AND TREATING CHARLES'S PROBLEMS

1. Using rational emotive behavior theory, which of the following statements best describes appropriate goals for Charles to further understand why he is so defensive?

   a. to learn to stand up for himself
   b. to think more rationally about this situation and to act more effectively in achieving goals of living happily
   c. to understand his angry feelings
   d. to speak more assertively to his peers

2. If Charles says to you, "I get so upset when I get a C on a math test at school, I feel like such a moron," a sub-goal that you might have for Charles might be to

   a. change his irrational beliefs about his academic performance.
   b. involve his parents in a parent-teacher conference.
   c. do family therapy with Charles and his parents.
   d. help Charles express his feelings about mistreatment at school.

3. As you try to assess Charles's problems at school and with peers, what types of information are you likely to listen for?

   a. the activating events that cause problems for Charles
   b. the hurtful, angry, and frustrating feelings that are a consequence of the activating events
   c. Charles's belief about the activating events
   d. all of the above

131

4. When you work with Charles to help him with his problems, which of the following are you most likely to concentrate on helping him change and improve?

   a. the activating events that cause problems for Charles
   b. the hurtful, angry, and frustrating feelings that are a consequence of the activating events
   c. Charles's beliefs about the activating events.
   d. all of the above.

5. In trying to develop a good relationship with Charles, one of the most important things to do is

   a. intervene with his teachers, telling them how to behave with Charles.
   b. let Charles know that you really care for him and want to help him with his problems.
   c. help Charles solve some of his immediate problems as quickly as possible.
   d. help Charles improve his relationship with Jack and his parents.

6. When Charles says, "All of the other boys in my class ignore me except Ralph," his statement refers to a(n)

   a. activating event.
   b. belief.
   c. consequence.
   d. disputing.
   e. effect.

7. His statement, "I feel terrible that nobody but Ralph will play with me" refers to a(n)

   a. activating event.
   b. belief.
   c. consequence.
   d. disputing.
   e. effect.

8. Charles's statement, "I have to have these kids like me" is best described by which of the following terms?

   a. activating event
   b. belief
   c. consequence
   d. disputing
   e. effect

To dispute Charles's negative beliefs, it is helpful first to detect when there is a belief, next to discriminate rational from irrational beliefs and third, to debate the irrational belief.

9. Which of the following would be an appropriate REBT debating statement in reply to Charles saying, "I must do well at school or I'll never be able to do well next year"?

   a. Don't worry, this year has been difficult, but next year will be better.
   b. You really are very conscientious and want to do so well at school, it's admirable.
   c. You are upset that school isn't going well and fearful that next year will be just as bad.
   d. You say you must do well. It would be nice to do well, but you can manage all right, and accept yourself as a person even if you don't live up to your expectations.

The following three statements express irrational beliefs. Write down an appropriate REBT response that debates Charles's belief, and then check it with the answer at the end of the chapter to see how similar your response is.

132

*OE1. "I have to do well on this book report for English. If I don't, I'll just about die."

_____

_____

_____

_____

*OE2. "If I have to sit by myself at lunch again, I will stand out as the stupidest kid in the cafeteria."

_____

_____

_____

_____

*OE3. "I have to do better at school than Ralph. He really isn't that bright. When he gets a better grade on a paper, I just can't stand it."

_____

_____

_____

_____

The answers that I have given at the end of the chapter are just examples of ways to respond to Charles's irrational beliefs. Your answer does not have to be the same as mine, but it should show that you're disputing Charles's irrational beliefs.

REBT therapists use many other approaches besides disputing. In the following questions, identify the type of approach that an REBT therapist is using with Charles.

QUESTIONS ABOUT REBT TECHNIQUES WITH CHARLES

10. "Charles, I would like you to learn more about the REBT method so you can apply it yourself when situations come up with other children or at school." This is an example of

    a. imagery.
    b. problem solving.
    c. psycho-educational methods.
    d. cost-benefit analysis
    e. coping self-statements.

11. "Charles, when you are in a situation when you can identify an irrational belief about getting a poor grade at school, say to yourself several times, 'I won't be killed if I get a bad grade. I have done well at school and can do well again.'" This technique is an example of

    a. imagery.
    b. problem solving.
    c. psycho-educational methods.
    d. cost-benefit analysis
    e. coping self-statements.

12. "Charles, when you get upset before a test, say to yourself, 'I want to get an A, but I don't have to!' Make that last part of the sentence powerful as you say it to yourself." This is an example of

    a. role playing.
    b. a shame attacking exercise.
    c. a forceful self-statement.
    d. a forceful self-dialogue.

13. "When you don't criticize yourself for doing poorly on an exam, I would like you to reward yourself. What do you think would be a good reward for you?" This method is an example of

    a. imagery.
    b. forceful self-statements.
    c. skill training.
    d. a reinforcement.

14. When Charles realizes that his problems are not from being teased and having difficulty at school but from having irrational beliefs about these events, he is

    a. having insight into his problems from an REBT point of view.
    b. successfully making use of a shame-attacking exercise.
    c. effectively disputing major irrational beliefs that he has encountered.
    d. able to teach others how they too may dispute irrational beliefs.

SPECIAL TOPICS

OE4. What aspects of REBT would tend to make it a brief form of therapy? (355)

_____

_____

_____

_____

OE5. In what ways can REBT be seen as a constructivist approach to therapy? (356)

_____

_____

_____

_____

134

OE6. In which other theories do you think the REBT disputational technique could be applied? Explain. (356)

_____

_____

_____

_____

_____

OE7. Would REBT be as applicable for women as for men? Explain. (359)

_____

_____

_____

_____

_____

OE8. Would you agree with Ellis that REBT would be applicable to people from all cultures? Explain. (361)

_____

_____

_____

_____

STRENGTHS AND LIMITATIONS

What do you believe are the strengths and limitations of REBT therapy?

<table>
<tr><th>STRENGTHS</th><th>LIMITATIONS</th></tr>
<tr><td>_____</td><td>_____</td></tr>
<tr><td>_____</td><td>_____</td></tr>
<tr><td>_____</td><td>_____</td></tr>
<tr><td>_____</td><td>_____</td></tr>
<tr><td>_____</td><td>_____</td></tr>
<tr><td>_____</td><td>_____</td></tr>
</table>

REBT THERAPY: A QUIZ

True/false items. Decide if the following statements are more "true" or more "false" as they apply to REBT.

(T) F   Q1.   REBT is primarily a cognitive therapy but also attends to feelings and behavior.

T (F)   Q2.   To help individuals improve their psychological functioning, therapists should help clients change the activating events rather than their beliefs about the events.

T (F)   Q3.   REBT is a mechanistic rather than a humanistic approach.

(T) F   Q4.   Vulnerability to disturbance is a factor in determining the extent to which individuals may have psychological problems.

T (F)   Q5.   According to REBT, beliefs that individuals hold are all, to some degree, irrational.

(T) F   Q6.   Helping individuals minimize emotional disturbance is a major goal of REBT.

(T) F   Q7.   REBT has philosophical underpinnings that include responsible hedonism.

(T) F   Q8.   Disputation is the most important technique in REBT.

T (F)   Q9.   Disputation is the only technique in REBT.

(T) F   Q10. Most REBT techniques have been developed to deal with individuals' irrational beliefs.

136

Multiple choice items. Select the best answer from the alternatives using an REBT perspective.

_____ Q11. Which of the following is not a part of REBT philosophy?

    a. responsible hedonism
    b. humanism
    (c.) existentialism
    d. rationality

_____ Q12. Activating events can be

    a. pleasant.
    b. unpleasant.
    c. rational.
    d. irrational.
    (e.) all of the above.

_____ Q13. An individual's vulnerability to disturbance depends on

    a. social factors.
    b. biological factors.
    c. neither a or b.
    (d.) both a and b.

_____ Q14. "I feel terrible now that my husband left me," is likely to be a(n)

    a. activating event.
    b. belief.
    (c.) consequence.
    d. all of the above.

_____ Q15. "My husband left me" refers to a(n)

    (a.) activating event.
    b. belief.
    c. consequence.
    d. all of the above.

_____ Q16. "My husband wouldn't have left me if I weren't so terrible a wife" refers to a(n)

    a. activating event.
    (b.) belief.
    c. consequence.
    d. all of the above.

_____ Q17. Having disturbances about disturbances refers to turning a(n)

    (a.) consequence into a new activating event.
    b. activating event into a new consequence.
    c. activating event into a new activating event.
    d. consequence into a new consequence.

_____ Q18. Which of the following words or phrases would turn this statement into an irrational belief? "I _____ go to graduate school."

a. would like to
b. would not like to
c. can afford to
d. must

_____ Q19. "I have to find the right solution to my marital problems" is an example of a(n)

a. rational belief.
b. irrational belief.
c. low frustration tolerance statement.
d. disputation.

_____ Q20. In assessing client problems, therapists listen mainly to

a. clients describing biological factors to determine which are most important.
b. clients describing social factors to determine which are most important.
c. clients describing their feelings and behaviors that they feel are caused by specific experiences and the beliefs that clients have about the specific experience.
d. none of the above.

_____ Q21. In REBT, the goal of therapy may be reached if the client has achieved

a. A.
b. B.
c. C.
d. D.
e. E.

_____ Q22. The most important treatment technique in REBT is the use of

a. coping self-statements.
b. disputing.
c. role playing.
d. forceful self-statements.

_____ Q23. In REBT, skills training is a(n) _____ technique.

a. behavioral
b. cognitive
c. emotive
d. all of the above

_____ Q24. Which of the following shows that the client has a philosophical understanding of REBT?

a. imagery
b. insight
c. disputing
d. teaching others

138

_____ Q25. From a multicultural perspective, REBT can be criticized as placing an overemphasis on

    a.   assessment.
    b.   beliefs.
    c.   existentialism.
    d.   self-sufficiency.

ANSWER KEY

1.	b	11.	e
2.	a	12.	c
3.	d	13.	d
4.	c	14.	a
5.	c		
6.	a		
7.	c		
8.	b		
9.	d		
10.	c		

QUIZ

Q1.	T	Q11.	c	Q21.	e
Q2.	F	Q12.	e	Q22.	b
Q3.	F	Q13.	d	Q23.	a
Q4.	T	Q14.	c	Q24.	b
Q5.	F	Q15.	a	Q25.	d
Q6.	T	Q16.	b		
Q7.	T	Q17.	a		
Q8.	T	Q18.	d		
Q9.	F	Q19.	b		
Q10.	T	Q20.	c		

ANSWERS TO OPEN ENDED QUESTIONS

*OE1.   It would be nice to get an A, but you don't have to. You won't die. How bad would a B or B+ be?

*OE2.   You say that if you eat alone, others will think you are stupid. Do you believe that's accurate?

*OE3.   How terrible could it be if Ralph does better on a paper than you?

CHAPTER 10

COGNITIVE THERAPY

COGNITIVE THERAPY SELF-INVENTORY

Directions: By comparing your beliefs about personality and therapy to those of cognitive therapy, you should have a clearer idea of how much you will need to suspend your beliefs or change attitudes to understand the cognitive theory of personality and approach to therapy. You may find it helpful to complete this section before and after you read the chapter. In this way, you can see if your views have changed. There are no correct answers, only an opportunity to express your views.

Put an "X" on the line so that it indicates how much you agree or disagree with the statement: A=Agree, D=Disagree.

D　　　　　A

_____ 1. People have thoughts that they are not aware of which influence their behavior.

_____ 2. The way individuals think about themselves and their world very much influences how they feel about themselves.

_____ 3. An individual develops a set of beliefs in early childhood that influences later development.

_____ 4. When an individual starts to have strong negative thoughts or dysfunctional thoughts, this thinking can sometimes be seen in the person's facial or bodily movements.

_____ 5. Basic sets of beliefs that individuals have can lead to several types of psychological disorders later on.

_____ 6. Dysfunctional thinking can lead to depression.

_____ 7. Exaggerating an event so that it becomes a catastrophe can contribute to psychological problems.

_____ 8. A basic goal of therapy is to remove biases or distortions in thinking.

_____ 9. In therapy, it is important to have specific goals and prioritize those.

_____ 10. Goals are developed in collaboration with the client.

_____ 11. Keeping track of thoughts outside of therapy can be a useful adjunct to therapy.

140

_____ 12. Scales and questionnaires are very helpful in assessing psychological problems.

_____ 13. Guiding individuals to understand how they distort their thoughts can be helpful in therapy.

_____ 14. Studying the effectiveness of therapy is essential in the development of a theory of psychotherapy.

_____ 15. The best way to change dysfunctional feelings and behaviors is to modify inaccurate and faulty thinking.

_____ 16. Challenging absolutes such as "always" and "never" is a helpful therapeutic technique.

_____ 17. When starting therapy, it is helpful to plan for the end of therapy.

_____ 18. Different cognitive techniques should be used for different psychological disorders.

_____ 19. Putting labels on types of dysfunctional thinking can be useful in therapy.

_____ 20. The therapist's role is to help clients find evidence that either supports or refutes their hypotheses and views.

HISTORY OF COGNITIVE THERAPY

Which influences do you think were most important in the development of Beck's cognitive therapy?

PERSONAL AND PROFESSIONAL LIFE	THEORETICAL INFLUENCES
Born in 1921 1946 - M.D. from Yale 1948 - Internship and Residency at Rhode Island Hospital Resident in neurology and psychiatry at Cushing VA Hospital in Framingham, Massachusetts Fellow in psychiatry at Austen Riggs Center in Stockbridge, Massachusetts 1953 - Certified by American Board of Psychiatry and Neurology Joined Department of Psychiatry of the Medical School of the University of Pennsylvania 1958 - Graduated from Philadelphia Psychoanalytic Institute Research on depression Founded Beck Institute for Cognitive Therapy and Research	Trained as a psychoanalyst Freud's emphasis on unconscious processes Adler's focus on beliefs and ways to change them Ellis's active and challenging approaches to irrational beliefs Kelly's theory of personal constructs Piaget's developmental approach to the study of cognition Cognitive science models of intellectual functioning

141

COGNITIVE THEORY OF PERSONALITY

Beck believes that psychological disorders are caused by a combination of biological, environmental, and social factors. Rarely is one of these a cause for a disorder. In understanding psychological disturbance, Beck uses a cognitive model of development that includes the impact of early childhood experiences on the development of cognitive schemas and automatic thoughts. Beliefs and schemas are subject to cognitive distortions, a key concept in cognitive therapy.

THE COGNITIVE MODEL OF THE DEVELOPMENT OF SCHEMAS

As individuals develop, they think about their world and themselves in different ways. Their beliefs and assumptions about people, events, and themselves are cognitive schemas. Individuals have automatic thoughts that are derived from these beliefs that they may not be aware of. How individuals shift from adaptive beliefs to dysfunctional beliefs is referred to as cognitive shifts in Beck's system. These concepts are defined below.

automatic thoughts Notions or ideas that occur without effort or choice, which can be dysfunctional, and lead to emotional responses. Automatic thoughts provide data about core beliefs.

schemas or cognitive schemas Ways of thinking that comprise a set of core beliefs and assumptions about how the world operates.

early maladaptive schemas Long-standing schemas that individuals assume to be true about themselves and their world. These schemas are resistant to change and cause difficulties in individuals' lives.

active schemas Cognitive schemas occurring in everyday events.

inactive schemas These are cognitive schemas that are triggered by special or unusual events.

cognitive shift Basically a biased interpretation of life experiences, occurring when individuals shift their focus from unbiased to more biased information about themselves or their world.

negative cognitive shift A state in which individuals ignore positive information relative to themselves and focus on negative information about themselves.

affective shift A shift in facial or bodily expressions of emotion or stress indicating that a cognitive shift has just taken place, often a negative cognitive shift. Often an indication of a hot cognition.

hot cognitions A strong or highly charged thought or idea that produces powerful emotional reactions.

COGNITIVE DYSFUNCTIONS

Automatic thoughts are subject to cognitive distortion. Cognitive therapists have identified a variety of cognitive distortions that can be found in different psychological disorders. Eleven of these are described in the text and are defined here along with "cognitive distortions".

cognitive distortions Systematic errors in reasoning, often stemming from early childhood errors in reasoning; an indication of inaccurate or ineffective information processing.

all-or-nothing thinking Engaging in black-or-white thinking. Thinking in extremes, such as all good or all bad, with nothing in the middle.

selective abstraction Selecting one idea or fact from an event while ignoring other facts in order to support negative thinking.

142

mind reading Believing that we know the thoughts in another person's mind.

negative prediction Believing that something bad is going to happen even though there is no evidence to support this prediction.

catastrophizing Exaggerating the potential or real consequences of an event and becoming fearful of the consequences.

overgeneralization An example of dysfunctional thinking that occurs when individuals make a rule based on a few negative or isolated events and then apply it broadly.

labeling Creating a negative view of oneself based on errors or mistakes that one has made. It is a type of overgeneralizing which affects one's view of oneself.

magnification A cognitive distortion in which an imperfection is exaggerated into something greater than it is.

minimization Making a positive event much less important than it really is.

personalization A cognitive distortion in which an individual takes an event and relates it to himself or herself when there is no relationship. An example would be, "Whenever I want to go skiing, there is no snow." Wanting to go skiing does not cause a lack of snow.

Discriminating one type of cognitive distortion from another is sometimes difficult. Individuals may present distortions that may fall into more than one category or have elements of more than one distortion.

CASE EXAMPLE OF BETH

Beth is a 20-year-old college sophomore majoring in marketing. She is very concerned about her grades and her performance in class this semester. Particularly, she is worried about her accounting course which is necessary for her to complete in order to continue with her program in marketing. She dislikes it so much that she finds it difficult to stay in class without being upset.

Throughout her schoolwork, in elementary, middle, and high school, she has been worried about doing well. An only child, she worries about displeasing her parents who would like to see her finish college and have a successful career. Her father is an accountant, and her mother is a chemical engineer. Although neither parent has pressed her to enter a particular career, the pressure seems to come from Beth herself.

Sometimes she gets very upset with herself for not doing well and feels like a failure. Although she maintained a B- average in her first year of college, this was not satisfactory to her.

Beth has had trouble making friends at college. Living at school three hours away from home has been difficult for her. She misses her parents and her boyfriend who is at a local community college. Although she was friendly with women on her floor last year, she has not kept up these friendships and has few friendships in her new dormitory. When people ask her to go out with them, she often declines and stays inside. She is feeling lonely and worthless.

QUESTIONS ABOUT BETH'S COGNITIVE DISTORTIONS

1. Beth says to you: "I have to get an A on the economics exam, otherwise, everything is lost." This is an example of

   a. all-or-nothing thinking.
   b. negative prediction.
   c. labeling.
   d. personalization.

2. In talking about her problems, Beth says: "I know my accounting professor doesn't like me. He has never spoken to me, but I can just tell." This is an example of

    a. all-or-nothing thinking.
    b. mind reading.
    c. negative thinking.
    d. catastrophizing.

3. In discussing her schoolwork, Beth says, "I got a D on my first accounting exam. I know I can't do accounting at all." This is an example of

    a. irrational thinking.
    b. selective abstraction.
    c. overgeneralization.
    d. mislabeling.

4. Beth says, "I know when I go home this weekend and see my boyfriend, things will go badly. He's going to tell me I don't spend enough time with him, and I will just get mad at him. I know that I'm going to get furious and things will go terribly." This is an example of

    a. catastrophizing.
    b. all-or-nothing thinking.
    c. minimization.
    d. personalization.

5. Throughout school, Beth has come to believe that she will not do well academically. She believes that other students are smarter that she is. Furthermore, she believes that no matter how hard she works, she won't do well. This set of beliefs can be called a(n)

    a. critical incident.
    b. automatic thought.
    c. cognitive schema.
    d. cognitive shift.

THEORY OF COGNITIVE THERAPY

In cognitive therapy, client and therapist combine to examine thinking patterns and behaviors and change them so that the client can function more effectively. The focus of therapy is often on dysfunctional thinking, such as that shown in the five previous questions. Assessment is quite detailed, more so than in REBT. Techniques challenge the client's dysfunctional thoughts and replace them with more effective thinking.

GOALS OF COGNITIVE THERAPY

Cognitive therapy focuses on dysfunctional or biased thinking. Removing such thinking is the goal of cognitive therapy. Since clients often have many negative thoughts, therapists and clients prioritize goals and examine thoughts specifically.

6. Which of these is most likely to be a goal for Beth?

    a. to become a more fully functioning individual.
    b. to identify her catastrophic thinking and overgeneralizations, replacing them with more accurate thinking.
    c. to become more aware of her unconscious motivation to fail.
    d. to be able to relax when studying.

144

ASSESSMENT IN COGNITIVE THERAPY

Attention to detail is a hallmark of cognitive therapy. In interviews, therapists ask many questions about the presenting problem, past problems, past traumatic experiences, and medical history. Questions elicit details to help therapists make assessments about dysfunctional thinking. Scales and questionnaires, several developed by Aaron Beck, assess for depression, suicide, and other concerns. These may be administered to clients prior to each session. Another method is self monitoring that uses forms such as the Dysfunctional Thoughts Record. Still other methods are used for sampling thoughts.

self-monitoring A method of assessing thoughts, emotions, or behaviors outside of therapy in which clients are asked to keep records of events, feelings, and/or thoughts. An example is the Dysfunctional Thought Record.

thought sampling A means of obtaining samples of thoughts outside of therapy by asking the client to record thoughts on tape or in a notebook at different intervals.

A cognitive therapist might explain the concept of automatic thoughts to Beth and ask her to write them down on a Dysfunctional Thought Record.

7. Which of these items would not be found on a Dysfunctional Thought Record?

   a. automatic thoughts
   b. actual events
   c. emotions
   d. rational response to the automatic thought
   e. all would be found on the Dysfunctional Thought Record

8. If Beth records her thoughts randomly on a tape recorder and brings them in to discuss with the therapist, she is using the technique of

   a. self-monitoring.
   b. thought sampling.
   c. scaling.
   d. specifying automatic thoughts.

THERAPEUTIC TECHNIQUES

Cognitive therapy techniques are often challenging and specific. Socratic dialogue helps to challenge maladaptive beliefs and assumptions. Basically, it is a series of questions that are designed to help the client arrive at logical answers to and conclusions about a certain hypothesis. The three-question technique is a form of guided discovery. Clients are often asked to specify automatic thoughts by recording them on the Dysfunctional Thought Record or through thought sampling. The client can then bring material to therapy so that the client and therapist can challenge maladaptive assumptions or ineffective beliefs. Several different techniques are used for challenging different dysfunctional beliefs. The ones that are listed in the text are defined here.

challenging absolutes Statements that include words such as "everyone", "never", "no one", and "always" are usually exaggerations which therapists point out to the client.

reattribution Helping clients distribute responsibility for an event (such as an argument) so as to equally place responsibility for the event.

decatastrophizing A "what if" technique, in which clients are asked, "What if X happened, what would you do?" It is designed to explore actual rather than feared events.

145

scaling   A technique of turning a dichotomy into a continuum so that individuals do not see things as "all or nothing." It is used in challenging dichotomous thinking.

cognitive rehearsal   A means of using imagination to think about having a positive interaction or experience. For example, to imagine a positive interaction with one's future in-laws.

Some cognitive therapy concepts are associated primarily with certain disorders. For example, the cognitive triad is associated with depression but also may be used to describe negative views or beliefs as they apply to other disorders.

cognitive triad   The negative views that individuals have about themselves, their world, and their future.

QUESTIONS ABOUT DOING COGNITIVE THERAPY WITH BETH

Respond as if you are Beth's cognitive therapist:

9. Beth says to you, "All the other students can learn accounting better than I can."

    a.   Why do you think the course is so difficult for you?
    b.   Have you considered getting tutoring so that you can do better?
    c.   You seem to assume that all the students in the class do better than you. How do you know?
    d.   Accounting is so frustrating for you.

10. Beth says to you, "I never understand anything that's going on in class." The cognitive technique that you are most likely to use is

    a.   challenging absolutes.
    b.   challenging all-or-nothing thinking.
    c.   labeling of distortions.
    d.   reattribution.

11. Beth says to you, "Whenever I go to accounting class, everything is so blah." You reply to her, "What do you mean by blah? Can you tell me more about how you feel?" You are using the technique of

    a.   challenging absolutes.
    b.   labeling of distortions.
    c.   reattribution.
    d.   understanding idiosyncratic meaning.

12. Beth says, "If I fail my accounting exam, I don't know what I will do. There's no reason to stay in school or to keep on living." Which of the following techniques are you most likely to use?

    a.   understanding idiosyncratic meaning.
    b.   decatastrophizing.
    c.   reattribution.
    d.   cognitive rehearsal.

13. Which of the following would help Beth decatastrophize her statement in question 12?

    a.   Have you ever considered killing yourself before?
    b.   You seem to be thinking that things will be all good or all bad.
    c.   Getting an F is a big assumption. Let's really take a look at what would happen if you got an F in accounting and what you would do.
    d.   What do you mean by "failing?"

14. Beth is planning to talk to her professor about her difficulty in the accounting course. She is very much afraid of his potential criticism of her for doing badly. Which technique are you most likely to use in helping her prepare for her talk with her professor?

    a. challenging absolutes
    b. reattribution
    c. decatastrophizing
    d. cognitive rehearsal

In working with Beth, you are likely to have an opportunity to challenge her dysfunctional thinking on many occasions. It is not necessary for you to challenge her each time. You would also help her develop new alternative responses to her automatic thoughts. You are also likely to use behavioral techniques such as reinforcing her successes and teaching her new skills. There are also times when you may respond to her empathically using person-centered techniques.

SPECIAL TOPICS

OE1. What aspects of patients and their problems are likely to make cognitive therapy brief? (399)

_____

_____

_____

_____

OE2. Why do you think treatment manuals can be effective in cognitive therapy? (401)

_____

_____

_____

_____

OE3. How are REBT and cognitive therapy different from each other? (401-402)

Both approaches try to make changes in the clients' belief system. Ellis focuses on irrational beliefs and uses the A-B-C-D-E theory to challenge irrational beliefs of all types. Beck identifies different types of cognitive distortions (a concept similar to irrational beliefs) and has developed different methods for challenging these distortions. Ellis applies his approach to all disorders. Beck has different suggestions and techniques for different disorders. In many ways, their approaches seem to be quite similar, but the language that they use is rather different. Both tend to challenge the clients' belief system. Beck uses different challenging methods for different disorders, whereas Ellis uses disputing, primarily, for most disorders.

OE4. How can cognitive therapy help women and sexual minorities dispute their dysfunctional beliefs while at the same time recognizing the value of their own views? (406)

_____

_____

_____

_____

OE5. How can therapists separate their own cultural beliefs from their view of what constitutes dysfunctional beliefs? (407)

_____

_____

_____

_____

STRENGTHS AND LIMITATIONS

What do you believe are the strengths and limitations of cognitive therapy?

STRENGTHS	LIMITATIONS
_____	_____
_____	_____
_____	_____
_____	_____
_____	_____
_____	_____
_____	_____

COGNITIVE THERAPY: A QUIZ

True/false items: Decide if the following statements are more "true" or more "false" as they apply to cognitive therapy.

T   F   Q1.   Freud's psychoanalysis had an indirect influence on the development of cognitive therapy.

T   F   Q2.   Beck's cognitive therapy uses techniques similar to psychoanalysis.

T   F   Q3.   Cognitive schemas develop from childhood beliefs about oneself and one's world.

148

T   F   Q4.   Automatic thoughts can be exaggerated or inaccurate.

T   F   Q5.   Socratic dialogue is an example of dysfunctional thinking.

T   F   Q6.   Removing biases and distortions so that individuals can think more effectively is a major goal of cognitive therapy.

T   F   Q7.   The Beck Depression Inventory is used for thought sampling.

T   F   Q8.   Different therapeutic techniques are used for different psychological disorders.

T   F   Q9.   The cognitive triad is a helpful concept in understanding depression.

T   F   Q10. Cognitive therapists assess patients' thoughts, not their feelings or behaviors.

Multiple choice items. Select the best answer from the alternatives using a cognitive therapy perspective.

_____   Q11.   A developmental approach to understanding how children think was pioneered by

    a.   Ellis.
    b.   Kelly.
    c.   Liese.
    d.   Piaget.

_____   Q12.   Beck's cognitive schemas bear a resemblance to the personal construct theory of

    a.   Ellis.
    b.   Kelly.
    c.   Liese.
    d.   Piaget.

_____   Q13.   Individuals may have a number of different cognitions such as "I run slowly," "I'm uncoordinated," "I can't play baseball," "I am always chosen last for a team." These cognitions may exist without a person being aware of them. These thoughts are called

    a.   automatic thoughts.
    b.   cognitive schemas.
    c.   hot cognitions.
    d.   negative prediction.

_____   Q14.   When the statements from Question 13 are viewed as a whole and represent a belief such as "I'm no good at sports," this belief may represent

    a.   automatic thoughts.
    b.   cognitive schemas.
    c.   hot cognitions.
    d.   negative prediction.

_____   Q15.   Which of the following is NOT a cognitive distortion?

    a.   catastrophizing
    b.   cognitive schema
    c.   magnification
    d.   personalization

_____ Q16. "I know that I will have a bad day today" is an example of which type of cognitive distortion?

a. all-or-nothing thinking
b. selective abstraction
c. negative prediction
d. mislabeling

_____ Q17. The Dysfunctional Thought Record is an example of

a. an interviewing technique.
b. a scale.
c. self-monitoring.
d. thought sampling.

_____ Q18. Which of the following questions is not used in the three-question techniques?

a. What is the evidence for the belief?
b. How do you feel about your belief?
c. How else can you interpret the situation?
d. If it is true, what are the implications?

_____ Q19. Jim: If it hadn't been for me, Bob wouldn't have hit me.
Therapist: You said Bob was very drunk. That would seem to play a large role in Bob hitting you.

What cognitive therapy technique is the therapist using?

a. understanding idiosyncratic meaning
b. challenging absolutes
c. reattribution
d. decatastrophizing

_____ Q20. Carla: I can't do anything right.
Therapist: Let's talk about some of the things that you do that work well for you.

Which cognitive technique is the therapist using?

a. understanding idiosyncratic meaning
b. challenging absolutes
c. reattribution
d. scaling

_____ Q21. Mary: My boss criticizes me constantly on all of my projects.
Therapist: I believe you may be overgeneralizing from that one time your boss reprimanded you.

Which cognitive technique is the therapist using?

a. scaling
b. reattribution
c. labeling of distortions
d. cognitive rehearsal

150

_____ Q22. The cognitive schema of hypervigilance is associated with

    a. depression.
    b. general anxiety disorder.
    c. obsessive-compulsive disorder.
    d. drug abuse.

_____ Q23. Schema focused cognitive therapy differs from Aaron Beck's cognitive therapy because of its emphasis on

    a. believes that developed in early childhood.
    b. working with depressed clients.
    c. use of the Dysfunctional Thought Record.
    d. transference and countertransference.

_____ Q24. The view that thoughts are just thoughts not reality is a significant aspect of

    a. Aaron Beck's cognitive therapy.
    b. schema focused cognitive therapy.
    c. mindfulness-based cognitive therapy.
    d. REBT.

_____ Q25. Which of these techniques is most likely to be used in cognitive group therapy?

    a. Examining belief systems of group members.
    b. Reflect the silence of group members.
    c. Analyze the feelings of the therapist towards group members.
    d. Educate members about contact boundary disturbances.

ANSWER KEY

QUIZ

#	Ans	#	Ans	Q	Ans	Q	Ans	Q	Ans
1.	a	11.	d	Q1.	T	Q11.	d	Q21.	c
2.	b	12.	b	Q2.	F	Q12.	b	Q22.	b
3.	c	13.	c	Q3.	T	Q13.	a	Q23.	a
4.	a	14.	d	Q4.	T	Q14.	b	Q24.	c
5.	c			Q5.	F	Q15.	b	Q25.	a
6.	b			Q6.	T	Q16.	c		
7.	e			Q7.	F	Q17.	c		
8.	b			Q8.	T	Q18.	b		
9.	c			Q9.	T	Q19.	c		
10.	a			Q10.	F	Q20.	b		

CHAPTER 11

REALITY THERAPY

REALITY THERAPY SELF-INVENTORY

Directions: By comparing your beliefs about personality and therapy to those of reality therapy, you should have a clearer idea of how much you will need to suspend your beliefs or change attitudes to understand the reality theory of personality and approach to therapy. You may find it helpful to complete this section before and after you read the chapter. In this way, you can see if your views have changed. There are no correct answers, only an opportunity to express your views.

Put an "X" on the line so that it indicates how much you agree or disagree with the statement: A=Agree, D=Disagree.

D   A

_____ 1. Understanding how people make choices helps in understanding their personalities.

_____ 2. A major goal of therapy is for clients to become responsible for their actions.

_____ 3. To be responsible means to meet one's own needs so that the needs of others are not interfered with.

_____ 4. Individuals are responsible for the choices that they make.

_____ 5. Focusing on unconscious motivation gives clients excuses for avoiding responsibility.

_____ 6. Clients should evaluate their own behavior and decide what changes to make.

_____ 7. Therapy should focus on present behavior rather than past behavior.

_____ 8. Our perceptions of the world are more important than reality itself.

_____ 9. We choose behaviors that keep us anxious and depressed.

_____ 10. The therapist does not judge the client's behavior. This should be left to judges, school administrators, and others.

_____ 11. The therapist's role includes teaching and educating.

_____ 12. The therapist should take a friendly and involved approach to helping clients.

152

D   A

_____   13. The major focus in therapy should be changing behavior rather than thoughts and feelings.

_____   14. Discussion of transference distracts from the therapeutic focus on clients' choices and plans.

_____   15. In therapy, clients should evaluate the quality of their behavior.

_____   16. Planning for actions and following through with plans is an important part of therapy.

_____   17. Making excuses, blaming, or explaining why a particular plan failed should be minimized or not discussed in therapy.

_____   18. Focusing on the client's positive aspects is more helpful than focusing on negative aspects.

_____   19. Punishment is not an effective therapeutic technique.

_____   20. Positive addictions, like running, can be helpful for some clients.

HISTORY OF REALITY THERAPY

Which influences do you think were most important in the development of William Glasser's reality therapy?

PERSONAL AND PROFESSIONAL LIFE	BOOKS	PROFESSIONAL ORGANIZATIONS
Glasser born in Cleveland, Ohio in 1925. 1944 - undergraduate degree in chemical engineering 1953 -MD from Case Western Reserve; Psychiatric residency at VA Center in Los Angeles and the University of California at Los Angeles. 1956 - consulting psychiatrist at a state institution for delinquent adolescent girls Consulted in the California school system. 1962 - Influenced by Harrington's active approach with chronic and regressed psychotic patients.	1965 - *Reality Therapy* 1969 - *Schools Without Failure* 1981 - *Stations of the Mind* A book influenced by William Power's *Behavior: The Control of Perception* (1973) 1986 - *Control Theory in the Classroom* 1990 - *The Quality School* 1998 - *Choice Theory: A New Psychology of Personal Freedom* 2000 - *Counseling with Choice Theory* 2000 - *Every Student Can Succeed* 2000 - *Getting Together and Staying Together* 2003 – *Warning: Psychiatry can be Hazardous to Your Health* 2007- *Eight Lessons for a Happier Marriage*	1967 - Institute for Reality Therapy, founded 1968 - Educator's Training Center (a branch of the Institute for Reality Therapy), founded 1973 -Training and certification for reality therapists initiated 1981 - International organization for Reality Therapists started – annual meetings Current - The William Glasser Institute is now the new name for the Institute for Reality Therapy.

PERSONALITY THEORY: CHOICE THEORY

Glasser believed that individuals have control over their lives and make choices about their lives for which they are responsible. His first theory of personality was called control theory, focusing on the control that individuals have in handling their emotional problems. To differentiate this theory from Powers' control theory and to make clear that he is not talking about controlling other people, Glasser changed the name for his personality theory to Choice Theory with his 1998 book, *Choice Theory: A New Psychology of Personal Freedom*. Glasser believes that individuals have perceptions of reality which determine their behavior - actions, thoughts, and feelings. Perceptions or pictures of our world are used to satisfy needs (belonging, power, freedom, and fun). Individuals make choices to meet their needs. Acting on these choices accounts for an individual's total behavior - doing, thinking, feeling, and physiology. If we have choices about how we behave, why would we choose to behave in ways that make ourselves unhappy? Glasser describes a number of reasons why depression, anxiety, and other disorders serve to meet individual's needs in limiting ways.

PICTURES OF REALITY

The perceptions and images that individuals have of the world around them influences how individuals' needs are met. We cannot know reality itself but only our perceptions which we then can compare to others' perceptions of reality.

NEEDS

To satisfy needs that we have, we develop pictures of our reality. These are perceptions of people, objects, or events. Glasser believes that our perceptions that are used to satisfy our needs are primarily visual. The four basic psychological needs according to Glasser are belonging, power, freedom, and fun.

belonging The need to love, to share, and to cooperate with others.

power The need to control others and be better than others.

freedom How we wish to live our lives, express ourselves, and worship. Included also are choices about who we associate with, what we wish to read or write, and how we wish to create or behave.

fun Included are hobbies and things we do for amusement such as sports, reading, collecting, laughing, and joking.

Needs often conflict with each other. In romantic relationships, the need for belongingness and the need for power are often negotiated so that couples can work out harmonious relationships. In political situations, a person's need for power may conflict with someone else's need for freedom. We meet these needs through our perceptions of the world around us.

CHOICE

Often choices are made without awareness that we are choosing. According to Glasser, we choose to be depressed. He prefers to say a person is not depressed but chooses to depress or is in the act of depressing. These choices are made without awareness. However, Glasser believes individuals can control their choices to depress, to anger, or to be anxious.

BEHAVIOR

For Glasser, behavior is how we act to deal with ourselves and the world around us. Individuals respond in very creative ways, sometimes very positive such as through music or art, and sometimes in negative ways such as through suicide or murder.

total behavior Refers to four components in reality therapy: doing, thinking, feeling, and physiology.

doing These are active behaviors such as walking, talking, writing, or eating.

thinking Voluntary and involuntary thoughts, including daydreams and night dreams, make up this aspect of total behavior.

feelings Included are emotions such as happiness, satisfaction, pleasure, anger, and irritation.

physiology Voluntary and involuntary mechanisms such as sweating and urinating make up this aspect of total behavior.

For Glasser, the key to changing behavior is in changing our doing, in particular, and also our thinking. These will bring about emotional and physiological changes.

CHOOSING BEHAVIOR

Why would someone choose to depress, to be anxious, or otherwise to be miserable?

1. By choosing to depress or anxietize, individuals can keep angering under control.

2. People may choose to depress or anxietize to get others to help them.

3. Choosing pain and misery can excuse an individual's unwillingness to do something more effective.

4. Choosing to depress or anxietize can help individuals gain power or control over others.

Glasser sees hallucinations, delusions, and/or active behaviors as creative ones. These are behaviors that individuals choose (without awareness) to deal with various aspects of their lives.

Should people who are "crazy" be responsible for their actions? Glasser's view is that criminals should not be tried until they have enough control over their lives to stand trial. When they have this control, they should be responsible for their actions.

CASE EXAMPLE OF JAKE

Jake is a 16-year-old high school sophomore living in a suburb of Philadelphia. He has been arrested for stealing cars. Although this is his first arrest, it is the fifth time that he has stolen a car with friends. He and three friends have done this for fun. Because none of them are licensed drivers, this has been a way for them to practice their driving. Last week, one of Jake's friends was speeding in a stolen car, and Jake was in the back seat. All four of the young men in the car were arrested.

Jake's parents were very upset. His mother was surprised because Jake had not been in trouble before except for poor grades in school. Although teachers had commented about Jake's not doing homework and not paying attention in class, Jake had never been suspended from school. Jake's father saw Jake as a lazy kid who probably would not amount to much. He thought that all that Jake was interested in was sports. Jake's father is a roofer, and his mother is a chef.

Although Jake does not see a problem with his behavior, his mother does. Jake thinks that he was just unlucky and got caught. His mother is afraid that Jake is headed for more trouble, possibly jail, if something is not done. She made an appointment for him to see a counselor.

Jake tells the counselor: "I don't see what the big deal is. We'd just been driving around. It's been a lot of fun except for getting caught. I have a hearing next week. My mother really worries. She thinks it's the first time I've been in a stolen car. It's not. We just like to have fun. Visit girls. Stuff like that."

155

"Anyway, it's not my idea. My friend is really good at hot wiring cars, so I go along with him, so do the other guys. Maybe if I didn't hang around with them I wouldn't get into trouble. Joe is the one with the good ideas. Or maybe I should say the bad ideas. My mother always says, 'Jake, what do you think will happen to you when you grow up? At this rate, you might not even graduate high school.' I don't know. Maybe, she's right. My father never graduated from high school and he's done okay."

QUESTIONS ABOUT CHOICE THEORY AS IT RELATES TO JAKE

1. Which of the following four needs are being met by Jake's activities?

    a. belonging
    b. power
    c. freedom
    d. fun
    e. all of the above

    (e. Currently all four are being met by Jake's activities. He has a feeling of belonging by being with his friends. There is probably a sense of power in being able to get away with stealing a car and doing things that other people don't do. Also, there is a sense of freedom in being able to do things that other people say is wrong. Finally, he is having fun as he seems to enjoy this activity.)

2. Which of the two following needs is Jake not likely to meet in the near future?

    a. belonging
    b. power
    c. freedom
    d. fun

    (b and c. Jake is likely to be arrested, and his freedom and power to do what he wants are likely to be limited in terms of rules and guidelines by a juvenile court. Incarceration is likely to be threatened if he continues to do this activity.)

*OE1. List two choices that Jake has made, probably without being aware of them.

_____

_____

*OE2. Jake says, "It's not my fault; it's the guys that I hang around with." Change Jake's statement so that it shows that he is in control and is aware of his choice.

_____

_____

3. Which of the following does not meet Glasser's criteria for "total behavior"? All are Jake's comments.

    a. I ride in the car.
    b. Joe drives the car.
    c. I'm thinking how fast can we go?
    d. I'm feeling pleasantly excited by this.
    e. I can feel butterflies in my stomach.

    (b. "b" represents Joe's behavior, not Jake's. "a" refers to doing, "c" to thinking, "d" to feeling, and "e" to physiology.)

156

THEORY OF REALITY THERAPY

Reality therapy puts the responsibility of choosing goals and following through with them on clients. A good relationship with clients ensures that clients see that therapists are there to help them make changes which will make positive improvements in their lives. Techniques are directed toward changing behaviors and focusing on strengths and accomplishments.

GOALS OF REALITY THERAPY

The basic goal of reality therapy is to help individuals meet their psychological needs for belonging, power, freedom, and fun. These goals are met in such a way that they do not infringe on the needs of others. The focus is on responsible choices.

4. Which of the following is most likely to be a reality therapy goal for Jake?

   a. To steal cars without getting caught
   b. To improve relationships with his friends
   c. To get better grades at school
   d. To become more aware of his unconscious anger at his parents

ASSESSMENT IN REALITY THERAPY

Reality therapists ask their clients what they want, what they "really want." A glib answer is likely to be challenged by reality therapists. They would want clients to consider their future.

For example, if the counselor asks Jake what he wants and Jake replied, "I want to be able to go on a joy ride in other people's cars anytime I want," the counselor is apt to challenge that and ask Jake if it is possible, and look at why that is not possible. Such a discussion can lead to examining "total behavior" so that Jake can look at what he wants to do, how he wants to think, and how he wants to feel emotionally and physiologically. The counselor can talk to Jake about this and examine how his behaviors can change without impinging on the needs of others.

5. If Jake says, "Riding in stolen cars is fun; I want to keep doing it," you as a reality therapist may reply

   a. What else do you like to do that's fun?
   b. You mentioned sports. What sports do you like?
   c. How does your choice affect the lives of others?
   d. All of the above.

(d. Choices "a" and "b" can help to assess other activities that may meet the need for fun. Choice "c" can help Jake see that his need for fun may interfere with other people's need to keep their cars. Then the therapist can continue to assess what activities may meet Jake's need for fun.)

6. Which of the following comments by Jake would help the therapist assess that Jake does not see choices in his life?

   a. I can steal cars if I want to.
   b. I can hang out with Joe.
   c. I can make noise in the classroom if I want.
   d. I can just sit in the car, and all of a sudden I get arrested for no good reason.

Assessment of how needs (belonging, power, freedom, and fun) are being met and of total behavior (doing, thinking, feeling, and physiology) are done throughout therapy. This is an on-going assessment that takes place from the first session through the last.

THE PROCESS OF REALITY THERAPY

When changing behavior and making plans to change that behavior, the therapist establishes him or herself as someone wanting to help with that process. A friendly approach that shows that the counselor is concerned and wants to be helpful continues throughout therapy. That provides an opportunity to explore client wants, needs, and perceptions. This then further provides an opportunity to examine total behavior, especially doing. With that as a basis, plans can be made to improve behavior. Then commitment to plans can be obtained.

FRIENDLY INVOLVEMENT

The therapist is open to talking about anything that the client and the counselor can consider changing. There should be an atmosphere of openness, optimism, and honesty. There would be more emphasis on what the client is doing rather than what the client is feeling. However, counselors do attend to the client's feelings and will not ignore them. Friendly involvement builds the relationship and establishes a commitment to counseling and planning.

7. Which of the following statements would you as a reality therapist be least likely to say to Jake when he says, "I'm only here because my mom said I needed to be."

    a. Well, since you're here, let's see what we can do.
    b. I know you don't want to be here, but let's see what I can do to help.
    c. Let's see what your Mom may have had in mind when she said come see me.
    d. You haven't been acting very responsibly, and that's why your mom sent you here.

(d. Although "d" is probably true, it is not going to help set up a relationship between you and Jake in which Jake is willing to listen to you and make changes.)

QUESTIONS ABOUT EXPLORING TOTAL BEHAVIOR

8. In exploring Jake's total behavior, which of the following questions are you most likely to ask?

    a. What did you do when your teacher asked you to get back into your seat?
    b. How did you feel when your teacher asked you to get back into your seat?
    c. What did you think when your teacher asked you to get back into your seat?
    d. How did you feel physically when your teacher asked you to get back into your seat?

(a. Although a reality therapist might ask any of those questions, when asking about total behavior, the reality therapist is more likely to ask about doing rather than thinking, feeling, or a physiological state.)

9. If Jake says that he got in trouble in school yesterday, which of these questions are you least likely to ask?

    a. Where at school did it happen?
    b. Who did it happen with?
    c. Why did it happen?
    d. When did it happen?

(c. Although the question may be answered, questions such as what, who, and when provide more information about what took place or what the client did.)

Reality therapists will explore thinking, feeling, and physiology but focus on doing. They believe that changes in doing will bring about changes in thinking, emotional feeling, and physical feeling.

EVALUATING BEHAVIOR

Self evaluations are a part of therapy. Clients make value judgments about their own behavior as do therapists. However, it is the therapist's goal to help clients see values that are embedded in their behavior. It is not the role of the therapist to criticize the values of the client. One way in which the therapist's values impact counseling in reality therapy is through the questions that the therapist asks. The reality therapist will ask about how the needs of the client and the needs of others are being met. Also the therapist will ask about how the client's behaviors are helping or hurting the client or others.

The text lists questions that Wubbolding (1988) asks clients to help them evaluate their behaviors. Because they communicate the role of evaluation in reality therapy so well, they are listed here.

Does your behavior help you or hurt you?
By doing what you're doing, are you getting what you want?
Are you breaking the rules?
Are your wants realistic and attainable?
How does it help to look at it like that?

10. If Jake says to you, "I guess stealing a car is against the rules, but it's a stupid rule," you as a reality therapist might reply:

   a. Yes, but rules are meant to be kept.
   b. What do you think the rule does for people you know?
   c. What would your mother say if she knew you broke this rule?
   d. Look what happened to Joe when he got arrested.

MAKING PLANS TO DO BETTER

Making plans provides a way for clients to change what they are doing. The emphasis is on doing rather than thinking, feeling, or physiology. In making plans, clients' needs should be met.

11. Which of these plans would probably work best for Jake?

   a. to behave better in school
   b. to play basketball after school with new friends
   c. to clean his parents' house
   d. to tell the police about the other times he stole a car

(b. Playing basketball should help Jake meet his need for fun. "a" is too vague, as "being better" is not defined. "c" and "d", while being laudable goals, may be plans that fulfill other people's needs, not Jake's. If Jake really wants to do something for his mother or really wants to tell the police what he did before, then these choices will meet a need.)

12. When you and Jake make a plan to help him meet his need for fun by playing basketball, which of these statements would be least effective from a reality therapy point of view?

   a. Meet Dan and Pedro in the front hall of school when the final bell rings.
   b. Sign up for intramural basketball at lunch time today.
   c. Plan to meet on Saturday at 1:00 in the afternoon. Pedro will bring the basketball.
   d. Plan to play basketball after school each day next week.

(d. The plans for "d" are vague, too far in advance. The plans describe what Jake will do but do not describe clearly who he will do them with or exactly when.)

COMMITMENT TO PLANS

For a client to commit to a plan, it should be feasible. In question 12, choices "a", "b", and "c" are more feasible than choice "d". In some instances, it can be helpful to use a verbal or written contract to ensure commitment. Depending on your relationship with Jake, you might ask for a written commitment. An advantage of the written commitment with Jake would be that it is clear, and you can refer to it again in a later session. A disadvantage is that it is formal and such formality may affect the relationship that you have with him.

THERAPIST ATTITUDES

Throughout reality therapy, therapists are consistent about their attitudes toward their work with clients. Because the focus of therapy is on planning and carrying out plans, the therapist takes attitudes that will help him or her deal with clients when they do not follow through on plans.

Don't accept excuses.
No punishment or criticism.
Don't give up.

With Jake, it is likely to expect that he will not follow through on all the plans that you and he come up with.

13. If Jake says, "I talked to Dan but not Pedro about playing basketball, and then I just forgot about it," how might you reply?

   a. Why didn't you talk to Pedro?
   b. Why didn't you get Dan to talk to Pedro?
   c. How did you feel about not following through with your plans?
   d. Let's talk about playing basketball with Dan and Pedro soon. When would be a good time?

(d. You don't accept excuses from Jake, nor do you punish or criticize him. You would make another plan with him, not giving up on him.)

REALITY THERAPY STRATEGIES

Reality therapists do not emphasize specific techniques. However, they are more likely to use some techniques than others. Because of the focus on exploring and evaluating behavior, reality therapists are likely to ask many questions. They may also listen to client metaphors and make use of them when talking to clients. Because much of reality therapy focuses on making plans and commitment to them, using humor and being positive can be helpful in encouraging clients. Confrontation helps therapists deal with clients when they do not follow up on plans. Paradoxical techniques are ways to help clients when they may be resistant to carrying out plans.

QUESTIONING

Questions can be used to help clients explore their wants, needs, and perceptions. They are also good approaches to understanding how the client thinks, to gathering information, to giving information and making sure it's understood, and in helping clients take more effective control.

BEING POSITIVE

Reality therapists take many opportunities to reinforce the constructive planning of their clients and their success in following through on the plans. Reality therapists may turn negative occurrences into positive ones by taking advantage of opportunities to communicate hope to clients.

METAPHORS

When clients talk, they sometimes use metaphors such as "When I got caught, the whole world fell apart." Therapists listen to those metaphors and may respond to the metaphor such as, "What happened when the world fell apart?"

HUMOR

Because humor is spontaneous and idiosyncratic, it can only occur at the moment so that it can fit in naturally. Humor is a part of friendly involvement as therapists can sometimes laugh at themselves which encourages clients to do the same.

CONFRONTATION

When clients don't follow through on plans, confrontation is unavoidable. Not accepting excuses, being positive, and using humor can be ways of confronting clients.

PARADOXICAL TECHNIQUES

When clients are reluctant to carry out plans or resist making plans, sometimes paradoxical techniques can be used. They are among the most difficult techniques for therapists to use because they are counter-intuitive. Reframing the way clients think about a topic can help them believe a previously undesirable behavior is desirable. Another paradoxical technique is to prescribe a symptom such as telling an anxious person to schedule times when they are anxious.

To prescribe a paradoxical technique with Jake would be difficult. Encouraging an illegal behavior by saying, "Why don't you steal more cars?" could have disastrous effects if Jake does in fact follow up on your request.

Reframing might work better with Jake. For example, if he says, "My teacher got upset with me for looking out the window during class. I just sat there and listened to him. Then he went on with the math problems." You can reframe this by saying, "You chose to control your behavior and not talk back to your teacher. You showed good restraint."

QUESTIONS ABOUT USING THERAPEUTIC TECHNIQUES WITH JAKE

14. If Jake comes in during the following session and says to you, "I played basketball twice with Dan and Pedro. The third time I couldn't do it because Dan was sick, so Pedro and I went to the mall." Which of the following strategies are you most likely to take?

    a. questioning
    b. being positive
    c. using metaphors
    d. humor
    e. confrontation

15. In developing new plans with Jake to go over Spanish vocabulary words with Alice, which techniques are you likely to use most frequently?

    a. questioning
    b. being positive
    c. using metaphors
    d. humor
    e. confrontation

SPECIAL TOPICS

OE3. Why do you think a certification program is a good or bad idea for reality therapy? (442)

_____

_____

OE4. Why do you think reality therapy may be difficult to integrate with other theories? (443)

_____

_____

_____

OE5. Does reality therapy ignore gender issues by focusing on personal choice and responsibility? Explain. (444-445)

_____

_____

_____

OE6. Does reality therapy ignore individuals' multicultural background by focusing on personal choice and responsibility? Explain (445-446)

_____

_____

_____

STRENGTHS AND LIMITATIONS

What do you believe are the strengths and limitations of reality therapy?

STRENGTHS	LIMITATIONS
_____	_____
_____	_____
_____	_____
_____	_____
_____	_____
_____	_____
_____	_____

REALITY THERAPY: A QUIZ

True/false items: Decide if the following statements are more "true" or more "false" as they apply to reality therapy.

T F   Q1.   Reality therapy emphasizes the way clients perceive the world rather than reality itself.

T F   Q2.   The theory of personality that reality therapy is based on is choice theory.

T F   Q3.   Reality therapy is concerned primarily with changing negative self-concepts.

T F   Q4.   Use of questioning is discouraged as a technique in therapy.

T F   Q5.   The Dysfunctional Thought Record is an important assessment tool in reality therapy.

T F   Q6.   Education on how to be a responsible person is the essence of reality therapy.

T F   Q7.   Reality therapy is a form of psychodynamic therapy.

T F   Q8.   Establishing a friendly working relationship is important in reality therapy.

T F   Q9.   Client excuses for not following through on plans should be challenged.

T F   Q10. Written contracts to follow through on plans is one approach in reality therapy.

Multiple choice items. Select the best answer from the alternatives using a reality therapy perspective.

_____   Q11. The clients that reality therapy was originally used with were

     a.   alcoholics.
     b.   delinquent adolescent women.
     c.   depressed clients.
     d.   middle-class white men.

_____   Q12. Reality therapy is grounded in

     a.   Freud's psychoanalysis.
     b.   behavior theory.
     c.   person-centered therapy.
     d.   Power's control theory.

_____   Q13. According to reality therapy, which of the following is not one of the four basic needs?

     a.   belonging
     b.   power
     c.   freedom
     d.   self-actualization
     e.   fun

_____ Q14. In describing Harry's depression, which sentence would a reality therapist use?

a. Harry is depressed.
b. Harry is experiencing many dysfunctional thoughts.
c. Harry chooses to depress.
d. Harry is nuts.
e. Harry is delusional.

_____ Q15. Which of the following is not a component of "total behavior"?

a. doing
b. dreaming
c. thinking
d. feeling
e. physiology

_____ Q16. Which of the following do reality therapists believe is most important in making therapeutic change?

a. doing
b. dreaming
c. thinking
d. feeling
e. physiology

_____ Q17. Betty chooses to anxietize. Which of the following is likely to be a reason for choosing to anxietize, according to Glasser?

a. She learned to be anxious from her neurotic mother.
b. She chooses to anxietize to get others to help her.
c. She chooses to anxietize to get disability payments.
d. She chooses to anxietize because it is more interesting than choosing to be depressed.

_____ Q18. Miranda chooses to hit her husband over the head with a frying pan and throw his clothes out the window after she finds out he has cheated on her. Unique to reality therapy would be viewing her behaviors as

a. creative.
b. criminal.
c. excessively jealous.
d. psychotic.

_____ Q19. Which of these would NOT be a necessary goal of therapy according to reality therapy?

a. I want to have more fun.
b. I want to feel loved.
c. I want to understand my problems.
d. I want to feel more powerful at work.

_____ Q20. In reality therapy, the basis of a therapeutic relationship is

a. therapeutic control.
b. friendly involvement.
c. therapeutic love.
d. unconditional positive regard.

164

_____ Q21. Which of the following is NOT one of Wubbolding's procedures or processes in his model of reality therapy?

   a.   wants
   b.   direction and doing
   c.   evaluation
   d.   catharsis
   e.   planning

_____ Q22. In evaluating behavior, which of these questions is a reality therapist most likely to ask?

   a.   Why did you smoke at school?
   b.   What did your mother say when the principal called?
   c.   Did you break school rules?
   d.   Who else was with you when you got caught smoking?

_____ Q23. Glasser supports the notion of a positive addiction because it

   a.   gives access to one's creativity.
   b.   provides additional strength to help with problems.
   c.   neither a or b.
   d.   both a and b.

_____ Q24. Which of the following is not a technique used in reality therapy?

   a.   questioning
   b.   active imagination
   c.   humor
   d.   metaphor
   e.   confrontation

_____ Q25. Reality therapy is a system which helps clients learn

   a.   how to make responsible choices for themselves.
   b.   how to make responsible choices for others.
   c.   how to control events in their lives.
   d.   all of the above.

165

ANSWER KEY

QUIZ

1.	e	11.	b	Q1.	T	Q11.	b	Q21.	d
2.	b, c	12.	d	Q2.	T	Q12.	d	Q22.	c
3.	b	13.	d	Q3.	F	Q13.	d	Q23.	d
4.	c	14.	b	Q4.	F	Q14.	c	Q24.	b
5.	d	15.	a	Q5.	F	Q15.	b	Q25.	a
6.	d			Q6.	F	Q16.	a		
7.	d			Q7.	F	Q17.	b		
8.	a			Q8.	T	Q18.	a		
9.	c			Q9.	F	Q19.	c		
10.	b			Q10.	T	Q20.	b		

ANSWERS TO OPEN ENDED QUESTIONS

*OE1.   To steal cars, to act out in school, to not do school work, to pick friends, to spend time with certain friends.

*OE2.   I choose to be with friends who steal cars. I choose to go with them when they steal cars.

166

CHAPTER 12

CONSTRUCTIVIST APPROACHES

In constructivist approaches, the therapist focuses on understanding problems, not from theory, but from the client's point of view. Solution-focused therapy concentrates on new solutions for a problem rather than understanding the origin of the problem. Narrative therapy examines patients' stories to learn how they view their lives. Therapists help clients change their stories to find more positive outcomes.

In this chapter of the Student Manual, the case of Wanda is used to help you better understand two constructivist theories, solution-focused and narrative therapy. Both are summarized and questions are asked about each.

CONSTRUCTIVIST APPROACHES SELF-INVENTORY

Directions: By comparing your beliefs about personality and therapy to those of the constructivist approaches, you should have a clearer idea of how much you will need to suspend your beliefs or change attitudes to understand constructivist approaches. You may find it helpful to complete this section before and after you read the chapter. In this way you can see if your views have changed. There are no correct answers, only an opportunity to express your views.

Put an "X" on the line so that it indicates how much you agree or disagree with the statement: A=Agree, D=Disagree.

D   A

_____ 1. Theories can get in the way of understanding a client.

_____ 2. Therapists can learn much about a client by understanding her story from her point of view.

_____ 3. Theory does not help clients move toward solving their problems.

_____ 4. Approaching a client's problems as if they are short stories or novels can be helpful.

_____ 5. Solutions to problems should be the therapist's focus, not underlying reasons for the problem.

_____ 6. Complimenting the client is a useful therapeutic technique.

_____ 7. It is helpful to know what changes have taken place in solving a specific problem prior to therapy.

_____ 8. Finding exceptions to when the problem presents itself can be helpful in therapy.

_____ 9. Organizing goals and solutions to problems by using a diagram can be helpful.

_____ 10. A few sessions of therapy may be enough for many clients.

_____ 11. I enjoy understanding themes and characters in novels.

_____ 12. For some client problems, theories of psychotherapy are not necessary.

_____ 13. Individuals have basic ways they see or construct the world.

_____ 14. A client's view of the world is more important than the therapist's theory of psychotherapy.

_____ 15. In therapy, subjective perceptions that clients have are more important than an objective diagnostic system like the DSM-III-TR.

_____ 16. Blaming the problem rather than looking at the client's difficulty with the problem is a useful technique.

_____ 17. Examining what could happen in the client's future can facilitate positive change.

_____ 18. Sharing the successful experiences of former clients in dealing with similar problems is helpful.

_____ 19. Examining those aspects of a client's life that are going well can help the client with her problem.

_____ 20. I like to help clients solve problems quickly.

HISTORY OF CONSTRUCTIVIST APPROACHES

The following influences were important in the development of both solution-focused and narrative therapies.

- Epictetus Greek philosopher. People are disturbed by their own views of reality.

- Immanual Kant 1700s. Human mind transforms and coordinates data that is then integrated into thoughts.

- Hans Vaihinger. "Fictionalisms" do not exist in reality, but help individuals deal with reality.

- Alfred Korzybiski Linguist. Examined how individuals present their perceptions as reality.

- George Kelly Psychologist. Studied how individuals use personal constructs.

- Milton Erickson Psychiatrist. Had extraordinary ways of viewing patients and then making suggestions to help them.

- Early family therapy approaches. Members of the Mental Research Institute studied communication and hidden messages and patterns within types of communication.

168

To varying degrees these philosophers and writers influenced those who developed solution-focused and narrative therapies.

SOLUTION-FOCUSED THERAPY	NARRATIVE THERAPY
Steve de Shazer - social worker, wrote Keys to Solutions in Brief Therapy (1985), Clues: Investigating Solutions in Brief Therapy (1988) as well as other books and articles (married to Insoo Kim Berg) *Insoo Kim Berg* - social worker, executive director of Brief Family Therapy Center in Milwaukee, Wisconsin, author of solution-focused writings	*Michael White* - social worker, worked at the Dulwich Centre in Adelaide, South Australia, contributed to Narrative Means to Therapeutic Ends (1990), developed narrative therapy. *David Epston* - social worker, co-director of the Family Therapy Centre in Auckland, New Zealand. Developed the concept of "leagues". Contributed to several books including Narrative Means to Therapeutic Ends (1988)

SOLUTION-FOCUSED THERAPY

Therapists want to know how individuals view possible solutions to the problem. They are not particularly interested in discussing the causes of the problem. The focus is on the expectations that family members have for change.

GOALS OF SOLUTION-FOCUSED THERAPY

Goals should be clear, specific, and small. Therapists want to know how things would be different in life if the goals were met. Progress on goals is often measured in therapy using a 0 to 10 scale. At the end of a session, the therapist may ask for feedback about meeting goals as well as give written or oral feedback to clients about their progress in meeting goals.

TECHNIQUES USED IN SOLUTION-FOCUSED THERAPY

Most techniques used in solution-focused therapy are questions. These are usually goal related, often dealing with progress in meeting goals. Some questions inquire about ways the individual may have tried to solve the problem and when they were successful, even if briefly, in making their problems better. Questions may try to focus on what worked rather than what didn't work.

mindmaps Diagrams or outlines of the session that are made during or after the session and used for the therapist to focus on organizing the goals and solutions to the problems.

complimenting The client is encouraged as the therapist makes positive statements about client actions. Berg and De Jong discuss three types of complimenting: direct, indirect, and self-compliments.

pretherapy change Change that takes place before the client arrives at the therapist's office. The therapist asks about and comments on this change.

coping questions These questions ask about successful experiences that individuals have had in dealing with the problem. They highlight the person's ability to cope with problems.

miracle questions What would be different if a miracle happened? Questions like this help to further define the goal.

scaling questions Asking individuals to rate their progress on a goal from 0 to 10 is the basic approach in using scaling questions.

169

assessing motivation Attention paid to the degree of client motivation to make changes. Scaling questions are often used to assess the motivation for change.

"The message" Giving the client a written message with instructions and/or compliments at the end of a session.

exception-seeking questions Therapists ask about exceptions to the problem. When is the problem not there and what is life like when the problem is not there?

CASE EXAMPLE OF WANDA

Wanda is a 9-year-old girl who is in the third grade. She has a 12 year-old-sister, Jill, who is in the sixth grade. Wanda's parents have been concerned because Wanda has started to scream at Jill and at Wanda's classmates if Wanda does not get her way.

Wanda's parents, Harry and Mary Balto, have become concerned because the relationship between Jill and Wanda has gotten worse. Because Mary works at a chemical plant as a technician and Harry is a self-employed electrician, they have depended on Jill to take care of Wanda after school. Wanda complains about Jill being mean to her and Jill complains about Wanda's rudeness and uncooperativeness.

Harry and Mary have sought help in dealing with Wanda because they have seen her becoming more defiant and less cooperative recently.

QUESTIONS ABOUT USING SOLUTION-FOCUSED THERAPEUTIC TECHNIQUES WITH WANDA

1. When listening to Wanda and her parents describe the problems, what method of diagramming their problem are you most likely to use?

   a. mindmap
   b. road map
   c. genogram
   d. telegram

2. If you ask Mary, how Wanda's behavior has changed since she made the appointment to see you, you would be asking about

   a. miracles.
   b. compliments.
   c. pre-therapy change.
   d. leagues.

3. As a solution-focused therapist, which of the following questions are you most likely to ask in counseling the Balto family?

   a. How did Wanda's angry behavior start?
   b. When have you noticed that Wanda plays well and is cooperative?
   c. What has happened at home that has caused Wanda to act out angrily?
   d. When did Jill start to have difficulty with Wanda?

170

4. The answer to question 3 is "b", because all other questions deal with causes rather than solutions. What type of solution-focused question is "b"?

   a. change
   b. miracle
   c. exception finding
   d. coping

5. When you ask, "When have you noticed that Wanda plays well and is cooperative?", Wanda replies "I helped Jane and Bill when they were working on math at school and my teacher said nice things to me." As a solution-focused therapist, you might reply

   a. Mary, did you know about this?
   b. Mary, why do you think Wanda made this change?
   c. Wanda that is great that not only were you helpful to Jane and Bill, but your teacher appreciated your helpfulness, too.
   d. Wanda, since you can be cooperative at school, do you think that you can do it at home?

6. The answer to question 5 is "c. What type of solution-focused question is "c"?

   a. a coping question
   b. complimenting
   c. a miracle question
   d. scaling

7. As a solution-focused therapist, which of the following questions are you most likely to ask in counseling the Balto family?

   a. Jill, how do you feel when Wanda is angry at you?
   b. Mary, were you at all like Wanda when you were growing up?
   c. Mary, if something wonderful could happen with your family and there were no longer any problems, how would your family be different?
   d. Wanda, the solution to the problem can be easy if you want it to be. Do you need to control your temper when you are angry?

8. The answer to question 3 is "c", because all other questions deal with feelings, past behavior, or simplistic solutions. What type of solution-focused question is "c"?

   a. change
   b. miracle
   c. exception finding
   d. coping

9. If you say to Jill, "How were you able to talk calmly to Wanda and get her to enjoy playing with her Barbies rather than have a tantrum?", you would be asking a(n) _____ question.

   a. change
   b. miracle
   c. exception finding
   d. coping

10. If you ask Wanda to rate her improvement in being cooperative using 1 as no change and 10 as a large amount of change, you would be using this solution-focused technique.

    a. assigning blame
    b. coping
    c. mindmapping
    d. scaling

NARRATIVE THERAPY

Changing or retelling stories so that more positive resolutions can occur is the basis of narrative therapy. The narratives can deal with issues in people's lives that are political, cultural, economic, or social. Negative or problem-oriented stories can affect the attitudes or lives of families.

CONCEPTS OF NARRATIVE THERAPY

Clients' perceptions of events and the world around them are of great interest to narrative therapists. They listen for problem-oriented or problem-saturated stories, thinking about how these can be reconstructed so that the solutions can be changed to be more productive. Attending to themes and meanings of stories is a major focus of narrative therapists. Many narrative therapists use terms that are used in literature classes to analyze stories or novels:

setting When and where the story takes place. This promotes a background for understanding the client's description of the problem.

characterization The people in the story are the characters. The client is often the protagonist as well as the narrator. People who have conflicts with the client are often the antagonists.

plot The plot refers to actions that take place in the story. Plots may have several episodes and/or actions. The story may be told more than once. Different plots or views of the plot may develop.

themes The themes are the meanings that the story has for the client. What does the client find important or meaningful in the story? Clients may understand the story in one or more of these ways: cognitively, emotionally, or spiritually.

GOALS OF NARRATIVE THERAPY

A significant goal of narrative therapy is to help clients see their lives or stories from a more positive rather than a problem saturated point of view. Clients try to derive meaning from examining the characters and plots in their lives. Achieving a resolution to a problem can come from examining a story in new ways to bring about new alternatives to events in the story.

TECHNIQUES OF NARRATIVE THERAPY

Narrative therapy techniques are all related to the telling of stories. Narrative therapists have developed new ways to look at stories and retell them.

externalizing the problem Making the problem, not the child or family, the opponent. Thus, removing Guilt becomes the focus of therapy rather than the person's guilty feelings.

unique outcomes Sometimes called sparkling moments, unique outcomes are thoughts, feelings, or actions that occur when the problem starts to dissolve.

alternative narratives The process of exploring strengths, special abilities, and aspirations of the family to tell a positive story with good outcomes rather than a problem-saturated story.

positive narratives Clients' stories about what is going well. Such positive stories can give clients a sense of empowerment.

questions about the future As change takes place, therapists can assist the client in looking into the future and at potentially positive new stories. For example: "If the problem were to continue next week, what meaning would it have for you?"

172

leagues Lists of former clients with similar problems who can give encouragement to battle the problem that the client and others have in common through sharing their stories by letters, email, or a similar means of communicating. Typically therapists organize and manage leagues.

testimony therapy An African-centered therapy that focuses on stories of the African experience in the United States.

narradrama The combination of drama therapy and narrative therapy in which individuals can act out their stories.

QUESTIONS ABOUT USING NARRATIVE THERAPEUTIC TECHNIQUES WITH WANDA

11. Mary tells of a time recently when the four of them went to a large shopping mall. Wanda went with Jill into a toy store and patiently listened to Jill give her opinion of some toys. Narrative therapists would call this a(n)

    a. reflective moment.
    b. alternative narrative.
    c. scaling.
    d. unique outcome.

12. When Wanda says " I liked showing the toys to Jill and when she seemed bored, I didn't get angry, but let her find one she liked." A narrative therapist would view Wanda's statement as a definite change that is helpful to Wanda and the family. In narrative therapy this would be referred to as a

    a. league.
    b. miracle.
    c. positive narrative.
    d. setting based statement.

13. When Wanda describes how she just got so angry at a classmate and yelled at her, you, as a narrative therapist, might say:

    a. Weren't there any other alternatives?
    b. What were you feeling at the moment?
    c. What would you like to do when Anger appears?
    d. Wanda, what would you like to say to that girl now?

14. "C" is the correct answer. In narrative therapy saying " What would you like to do when Anger appears?" is referred to as

    a. developing a positive narrative
    b. externalizing the problem.
    c. internalizing the problem.
    d. developing the problem.

15. As a narrative therapist, you would try to find a(n) _____ for the Balto family that would lead to Wanda dominating Anger.

    a. reflective moment
    b. alternative narrative
    c. mindmap
    d. unique outcome

173

16. If you say to Wanda, "I have notes from other girls your age about how they conquered Anger. I think you might like to see the notes. What do you think?" As a narrative therapist you are making reference to

    a. a division.
    b. a league.
    c. modeling.
    d. a theme.

17. As a narrative therapist, which theoretical background would seem the most similar to using narrative therapy with a family?

    a. psychoanalytic theory
    b. person-centered theory
    c. structural therapy
    d. strategic therapy
    e. no theory

(e. This may seem like a trick question, but a narrative therapist would not want theoretical or other preconceptions to interfere with her understanding the family's story.)

18. At the conclusion of narrative therapy, a narrative therapist would like Wanda to replace her problem saturated stories with

    a. exceptions.
    b. a miracle.
    c. new leagues.
    d. positive narratives.

SPECIAL TOPICS

OE1. How do you think clients would respond to solution-focused therapy?

_____

_____

OE2. How do you think clients would respond to narrative therapy?

_____

_____

OE3. How does the construct of gender fit into the techniques of solution-focused therapies? (476)

_____

_____

174

OE4. How does the construct of gender fit into the techniques of narrative therapies? (477)

_____

_____

OE5. What multicultural issues can hinder the application of solution-focused therapy when using languages other than English? (477)

_____

_____

OE6. What multicultural issues can hinder the application of narrative therapy when using languages other than English? (477)

_____

_____

STRENGTHS AND LIMITATIONS

What do you believe are the strengths and limitations of solution-focused therapy?

STRENGTHS	LIMITATIONS
_____	_____
_____	_____
_____	_____
_____	_____
_____	_____
_____	_____
_____	_____

What do you believe are the strengths and limitations of narrative therapy?

STRENGTHS   LIMITATIONS

_____   _____

_____   _____

_____   _____

_____   _____

_____   _____

_____   _____

_____   _____

CONSTRUCTIVIST AND INTEGRATIVE APPROACHES: A QUIZ

True/False Items. Decide if the following statements are "more true" or "more false" as they apply to constructivist and integrative therapies.

T   F   Q1.   George Kelly believed most people, not just scientists, construct hypotheses and test them against their view of reality.

T   F   Q2.   Solution-focused therapists can work with vague and unclear goals as well as those that are specific.

T   F   Q3.   Reflections of feelings rather than questions are a basic tool of solution-focused therapy.

T   F   Q4.   Mindmapping is a way of organizing goals and solutions to the problem in solution-focused therapy.

T   F   Q5.   In solution-focused therapy, assessing client motivation by having clients use rating scales is a means of assessment.

T   F   Q6.   In narrative therapy, clients' problems can be analyzed the way one would analyze a novel.

T   F   Q7.   Externalizing the problem by asking "What do you do to fight Procrastination?" is a solution-focused technique.

T   F   Q8.   Narrative therapists ask only about what is happening in the present, not what might happen in the future.

T   F   Q9.   In narrative therapy, offering a certificate for client progress and achievement in therapy can be seen as support for this progress.

T   F   Q10.   Narrative therapists and solution-focused therapists look for times in their patients' lives when the problem did not occur or when the problem started to dissolve.

Multiple choice items: Select the best answer from the alternatives given. Many of the questions ask you to choose the constructivist or integrative therapy that most closely fits the question.

_____ Q11. In narrative therapy, therapists try to determine the meaning of the story the client tells. The therapist is listening for the

    a. miracle.
    b. theme.
    c. solution.
    d. unconscious.

_____ Q12. Externalizing the problem is a technique used in

    a. solution-focused therapy.
    b. narrative therapy.

_____ Q13. Which of the following therapies is most likely to ask about positive changes in solving a problem that took place prior to therapy?

    a. solution-focused therapy.
    b. narrative therapy.
    c. psychoanalysis.
    d. REBT.

_____ Q14. Rating the client's progress on a goal from one to ten is a technique called

    a. coping.
    b. laddering.
    c. modeling.
    d. scaling.

_____ Q15. What would be different if a miracle happened? is a question most likely to be used in

    a. narrative therapy.
    b. solution-focused therapy.
    c. both a and b.
    d. neither a and b.

_____ Q16 In solution-focused therapy, if the therapist says "Submitting your homework every day for the past week is an important accomplishment. What can you say to yourself that recognizes this accomplishment?" This would be referred to as

    a. a miracle question.
    b. complimenting.
    c. pre-therapy change.
    d. "the message".

_____ Q17. In solution-focused therapy, the therapist may give written instructions for the client to follow before the next session. This is referred to as

  a. a miracle question.
  b. complimenting.
  c. pre-therapy change.
  d. "the message".

_____ Q18. Solution-focused therapists are concerned with client _____ strategies.

  a. coping
  b. modeling
  c. dereflecting
  d. reinforcement.

_____ Q19. What presenting problem would seem most appropriate for solution-focused therapy? One where the client is

  a. seeking to understand who he really is.
  b. trying to understand his place in the world..
  c. trying to change self-defeating behaviors.
  d. trying to solve a specific problem.

_____ Q20. Solution-focused and narrative therapies have in common this factor. They both

  a. examine the client's problem as if it is a story.
  b. focus on changing thoughts rather than feelings.
  c. focus on the client's perception of her problem.
  d. are concerned with the role of unconscious factors on the presenting problem.

_____ Q21. The development of personal constructs is associated with the work of

  a. Immanuel Kant.
  b. Erik Erikson.
  c. Milton Erikson.
  d. George Kelly.

_____ Q22. Which of the following are constructivist approaches to therapy?

  a. narrative
  b. solution-focused.
  c. both and b
  d. neither a or b.

_____ Q23. If a narrative therapist asks a client, "If the problem was to continue next week, what would that mean for you?" The therapist is asking a question about

  a. the future.
  b. a miracle.
  c. coping.
  d. a positive narrative.

_____ Q24. Testimony therapy is therapy which focuses on the experience of

    a.   Africans.
    b.   Caucasians.
    c.   Asians.
    d.   Native Americans.

_____ Q25. David Epston has developed the narrative therapy called "leagues". Which of the following refers to the type of league that he would be interested in developing?

    a.   bulimia
    b.   baseball
    c.   authentic
    d.   reality-focused

ANSWER KEY   QUIZ

1.	a	11.	d	Q1.	T	Q11.	b	Q21.	d
2.	c	12.	c	Q2.	F	Q12.	b	Q22.	c
3.	b	13.	c	Q3.	F	Q13.	a	Q23.	a
4.	c	14.	b	Q4.	T	Q14.	d	Q24.	a
5.	c	15.	d	Q5.	T	Q15.	b	Q25.	a
6.	b	16.	b	Q6.	T	Q16.	b		
7.	c	17.	e	Q7.	F	Q17.	d		
8.	b	18.	d	Q8.	F	Q18.	a		
9.	d			Q9.	T	Q19.	d		
10.	d			Q10.	T	Q20.	c		

CHAPTER 13

FEMINIST THERAPY: A MULTICULTURAL APPROACH

FEMINIST THERAPY SELF-INVENTORY

Directions: By comparing your beliefs about personality and therapy to feminist therapy, you should have a clearer idea of how much you will need to suspend your beliefs or change attitudes to understand the feminist theory of personality and approach to therapy. You may find it helpful to complete this section before and after you read the chapter. In this way, you can see if your views have changed. There are no correct answers, only an opportunity to express your views.

Put an "X" on the line so that it indicates how much you agree or disagree with the statement: A=Agree, D=Disagree.

D   A

_____ 1. Therapeutic issues are different for men than for women.

_____ 2. Therapeutic issues differ depending on one's cultural background.

_____ 3. The sexism of psychotherapists is a concern in the practice of psychotherapy.

_____ 4. Consciousness-raising groups can bring about productive social change.

_____ 5. Violence to women is much more common than violence to men.

_____ 6. Strong identification with one's gender can limit the way individuals view themselves and others.

_____ 7. Cultural role interventions can be important therapeutic methods.

_____ 8. In general, women tend to focus more on relationships and men more on achievement.

_____ 9. Women and culturally diverse populations are placed in a position in which they are subordinate to men in Western society.

_____ 10. Building self-esteem should be a goal of therapy.

180

D   A

_____ 11. Accepting one's body can be an important goal in therapy.

_____ 12. Social action should be a goal in therapy.

_____ 13. "The person is political."

_____ 14. Psychological classification systems like the DSM-IV encourage social adjustment to norms, reinforcing stereotypes rather than questioning social injustice.

_____ 15. Cultural interventions can be important therapeutic techniques.

_____ 16. Power role and gender role interventions can be important therapeutic techniques.

_____ 17. Therapists and clients should have a relationship in which both are equals, rather than the therapist being in a more powerful position.

_____ 18. Assertiveness is often an appropriate goal for female clients.

_____ 19. Openness to gay, lesbian, bisexual and transgendered people (GLBT) is an important characteristic of a therapist.

_____ 20. Therapists should be politically active.

HISTORY OF FEMINIST PERSONALITY THEORY

Which influences do you think were most important in the development of feminist personality theory?

HISTORICAL AND PROFESSIONAL INFLUENCES
Chesler's (1972) criticism of the relationship between the female patient and the male therapist; critical of male therapists' gender bias Criticisms of gender bias in psychoanalysis Concerns about the social and political rights of women, as expressed by groups such as the National Organization for Women Consciousness-raising groups Encouragement of therapist involvement in social action groups Many contributors to feminist therapy; no single leader Concerns about the social and political rights of culturally diverse populations

CONCEPTS BASIC TO FEMINIST THERAPY

multiple identities There are many forces that affect the way that gender is seen; these include ethnicity, social class, gender orientation, disabilities, and other characteristics.

consciousness-raising groups (CR) A creation of the women's movement, in which women met regularly to discuss their lives and issues in them.

alpha bias The bias that occurs by separating women and men into two specific categories, running the risk of treating women as unequal to men.

beta bias Bias that occurs when treating men and women as identical, thus ignoring important differences between the lives of women and men.

181

FEMINIST THEORIES OF PERSONALITY

There is not one theory of personality for feminist therapy. Rather researchers have studied differences between the development of women and men. Theories that deal with a subset of development or personality do exist. These include Bem's gender schema theory, Gilligan's ethic of care, and the relationship model.

GENDER DIFFERENCES AND SIMILARITIES ACROSS THE LIFE SPAN

To understand broad differences between the life experiences of men and women, describe your own development (or those of friends) as it relates to common concerns that children, adolescents, and adults face as they relate to gender issues.

CHILDHOOD - YOURS OR OTHERS	COMMON CHILDHOOD GENDER ISSUES
	Parental preference for a son (sometimes a daughter)
	Clothing and toys of young children
	Gender segregation (playing with children of one's own gender)
	Devaluing characteristics of the other gender.
	Adults encouraging independence and efficacy in boys, nurturing in girls
	Exposure to stereotypes by peers, movies, magazines

ADOLESCENCE - YOURS OR OTHERS	COMMON ADOLESCENT GENDER ISSUES
	Onset of puberty (for girls, breast development and menarche; for boys, voice change, sexual development)
	Emphasis on attractiveness and appearance
	Dating and regulating sexual activity
	Females competing with other females for boys
	Focus on academic and athletic accomplishments
	Relationships with parents

182

ADULTHOOD - YOURS OR OTHERS	COMMON ADULT GENDER ISSUES
	Child bearing and child raising
	Full time vs. part time work
	Leaving the workforce
	Sexual harassment at work
	Income
	Housework
	Violence - sexual abuse, rape, and physical attack
	Aging process - losing sexual attractiveness

SCHEMA THEORY AND MULTIPLE IDENTITIES

Schemas are a cognitive concept of referring to ways of thinking, core beliefs that individuals hold.

cultural schema Beliefs about one's own culture as it relates to other cultures.

gender schema A set of mental associations in which individuals are seen from the point of view of their gender, as opposed to other characteristics.

GILLIGAN'S ETHIC OF CARE

Carol Gilligan built upon Lawrence Kohlberg's model of moral development. In Kohlberg's model, a high level of morality of justice is determined by individuals' ability to understand rules and the need to obey them as they relate to a need for social order. Gilligan's morality of care deals with being responsible to self and others. There is an emphasis on compassion and the relationship or interdependence between self and others. Research has not shown clear evidence that males fit more closely with Kohlberg's model and females with Gilligan's model.

THE RELATIONAL CULTURAL MODEL

Developed by Miller and other writers at the Stone Center at Wellesley College, the relational model emphasizes the importance for women of finding a sense of identity through the context of relationships. Miller and her colleagues believe that women (as well as minorities and poor people) have been subordinate to dominant groups (generally white males). As a subordinate group, they have had to please the dominant group and thus improve their relationships with both men and women by tending to the emotional and physical needs of others. Rather than see the need for relatedness as a weakness, the relational model sees this as a strength that should be valued and appreciated.

relational resilience Refers to growing in a relationship and being able to move forward despite setbacks. Resilience also concerns recognizing when relationships are not mutual and moving on from them.

relational competence Refers to being able to be empathic toward self and others. It also includes the ability to participate in and build a sense of strength in a community.

FEMINIST PERSONALITY THEORY: AN EXAMPLE

The following example is a conversation between April and her three roommates. April, a 23-year-old secretary in a manufacturing firm, has been date raped and is discussing this with Bonita, Clara, and Denise. At the end of the example, there are questions about feminist personality theory. The purpose of these questions is to help you review your knowledge and understanding of feminist personality theory.

April: Last night Dave and I had been at a party drinking. You know Dave, he's the guy in the transportation department who I sometimes see at lunch. I had known him a little bit but not very well. He seemed like a nice guy. Well, we were at this party, and then he took me home. I was tired and sort of interested in him, but not too. Anyway, he asked if he could come in for a soda. I said sure. Actually, I thought maybe some of you would be there, but nobody was there. So we start to kiss, and all of a sudden, he starts to put his hand down my blouse. So I told him to stop it. He did for a while - like about thirty seconds. Then he started again. So I started to get up and push him away. As I did that, he really leaned into me, pushed my head down into the sofa and my hands under my head and told me, "Shut up, you'll enjoy it." Then he really leaned hard on me, took off my panties and raped me. I didn't know what to do. I was afraid that no one would believe me.

Bonita: You know how men are. You find a cop and they don't believe you. They will think that because you knew him and were kissing him that you were asking for it. They're all jerks.

April: I know. That's what I'm afraid of. I don't know what to do.

Clara: I'm really worried about you. What a terrible thing! You must be feeling awful!

April: I am. I'm in shock. I don't know what to do. Nothing like this has ever happened to me before.

Denise: That's not right. We've got to do something about it. We can call a support hot line and get advice about what to do. This slime ought to go to jail. And we've got to get him charged.

April: I know I need to do something. But I feel at such a loss right now. I just feel dirty.

Bonita: It's not you who are dirty. It's men who are. They do something like this and then they tell themselves "Hey, it's okay. She really wanted it." Real slime.

Clara: Oh April! (She moves next to her and hugs her). How devastating for you to have to experience that last night.

April: I know. (crying)

Denise: Don't worry. We're gonna make sure Dave doesn't get away with this. One way or another, he's going to pay.

1. Which of the four women has the strongest gender schema?

    a. April
    b. Bonita
    c. Clara
    d. Denise

2. Which of the four women is using a frame of reference that is most similar to Kohlberg's view of moral development?

   a. April
   b. Bonita
   c. Clara
   d. Denise

3. Which of the four women most closely resembles Gilligan's views of moral development?

   a. April
   b. Bonita
   c. Clara
   d. Denise

4. The behavior of which of these four women most closely fits the relational model?

   a. April
   b. Bonita
   c. Clara
   d. Denise

5. Of April's three friends, who fits least well with Kohlberg's model of moral development?

   a. Bonita
   b. Clara
   c. Denise

6. If I had written this example using the names of Bill instead of Bonita, Carl instead of Clara, and Dennis instead of Denise, I might be guilty of

   a. alpha bias.
   b. beta bias.
   c. gamma bias.
   d. delta bias.

   The answer to question 6 is "a". By separating women and men into two categories, my example would indicate alpha bias. Men do not always respond to situations using Kohlberg's morality of justice, and women do not always use Gilligan's morality of care. Likewise, women are not always relational in their comments, nor are men always non-relational and achievement-oriented. However, these models do provide a means for understanding how social factors tend to impact men and women differently.

THEORIES OF FEMINIST THERAPY

   Feminist therapy is a theory that is combined with others rather than used strictly on its own. Feminist goals of therapy are goals that reflect how society's institutions affect women. They are not the only possible goals for therapy. Assessment also reflects the therapist's awareness of social and cultural background and events as they affect their clients. Techniques of feminist therapy tend to reflect an awareness of women's lack of power in society in general and our approaches to resolving problems in effective ways.

185

GOALS OF FEMINIST THERAPY

The goals that are listed in the text are not the only goals of feminist therapy, but they are ones that put a focus on social change. Unlike other therapies, feminist therapies point out that the problem is often in the culture or society rather than in the client.

1. *Symptom removal (adjustment)* Although symptom removal may be appropriate in therapy and is a traditional goal, feminist therapists are aware that the problem can be with others, such as a spouse or boss. If a client has headaches that result from an angry and hostile superior, dealing with the boss is preferable to taking headache medication. Adjusting to social pressures is often not a good solution.

2. *Self-nurturance and self esteem* A goal is to help people take care of themselves and meet their own needs.

3. *Balancing instrumental and relational strengths* Clients should become more independent and take actions in their lives but also develop meaningful relationships with others.

4. *Body image and sensuality* Because of pressures from men that women should be attractive and the focus of many types of media on attractiveness, accepting one's body and sexuality is a frequent goal of feminist therapy.

5. *Affirming diversity* Therapists should value the client's cultural differences. This includes acknowledging multiple identities such as class, age, race, power, gender orientation, disabilities, and other characteristics.

6. *Empowerment and social action* These are goals that separate feminist therapy from other therapies. For clients and therapists to work toward making social change by being an advocate for clients is very consistent with the feminist therapy view that the "person is political."

ASSESSMENT IN FEMINIST THERAPY

Feminist therapists have been critical of the major diagnostic system (DSM-IV) because of its absence of consideration of social factors and its development by the dominant group (white men). Feminist therapists are wary of encouraging adjustment to social norms and reinforcing stereotypes.

TECHNIQUES OF FEMINIST THERAPY

Although feminist therapists use many methods and techniques in their work, gender-role analysis and intervention, and power analysis and intervention are methods that reflect the need to help people deal with and overcome social inequalities. These methods will be a focus of this section.

CASE EXAMPLE OF APRIL

To apply gender-role analysis and interventions along with power analysis and interventions, let us continue with the case of April. Let's assume that a month after her conversation with her three friends, April is still very much disturbed by being date raped by Dave. She seeks your help to deal with her feelings of confusion and depression that she has had for the last month. In her first meeting with you, she reveals more information about herself.

She was born in a small town about 50 miles from where you are living now. After graduating high school, she moved to the town or city where you live and took a job as a secretary in a medium-sized firm. Both of her parents were farmers. They both moved to the United States from Vietnam shortly after the conclusion of the Vietnam War. They worked on the farm for an elderly widow, who willed the farm to them. They have owned the farm for 15 years. April grew up with her younger brother and sister on the farm. Neither of her parents had gone to college, and both lived on farms for several years in Vietnam.

186

April went to a fairly small high school where she was active as a cheerleader and in student government. Most of her friends were boys and girls whom she met in church or lived on nearby farms. She felt accepted by her friends and did not feel discriminated against because she was Vietnamese-American. She had relatively little dating experience. During the first few months of her senior year, she dated a boy whom she knew in her church. However, that relationship seemed to fall apart and did not distress her. Her sexual experience has been quite limited.

When she came to your area, she had few friends. However, she was able to make friends at work and has appreciated spending time with Bonita, Clara, and Denise after work. She has had few dates in the two years that she has been here. Most of the social functions that she has attended have either been at a church or with large groups of people.

She tells you that she feels very differently than she did before the date rape. She feels dirty and tarnished. She wonders if someone would ever want to marry her. When she was home last weekend, she felt different from her family in a way that she had never felt before.

When returning to work this past week, she found it difficult to concentrate on her assignments. It was hard to pay attention to her colleagues and superiors. After work, she would sometimes go back to her apartment, turn on the television, and cry.

In the following sections, read the cultural analysis, gender-role analysis, and power analysis for April. Use the information that is provided about April to answer the questions that follow the analyses.

CULTURAL ANALYSIS

1. Talk with April about the extent to which the dominant culture affects her difficulties in dealing with the rape.

2. Ask April how she views being sexually assaulted as it relates to her culture. For example, does she blame herself?

3. Explore with April myths about being from a Vietnamese background that might affect how others view her and her concerns.

GENDER ROLE ANALYSIS

1. Identify gender role messages that April may have received at home or at school.

2. Identify positive and negative consequences of April's gender-related messages.

3. Identify statements that April says to herself based on gender-related messages.

4. Decide which of April's messages you want to change.

5. Develop a plan to help April make changes in her behavior.

POWER ROLE ANALYSIS

1. Have April choose a definition for "power" and apply it to different kinds of power.

2. Describe ways that April can become more powerful (e.g. financial control, self-defense classes, the legal system).

187

3. Discuss with April different ways to bring about changes in power.

4. Examine gender role messages that interfere with April becoming more powerful.

5. Decide how to be powerful in certain situations. Plan behavioral changes with April.

FEMINIST THERAPY INTERVENTIONS

Many interventions and techniques in feminist therapy empower clients to deal with social and political inequities. They also seek to inform and educate clients about ways of dealing with environmental stresses and events. In doing this, they often seek to create equality between themselves and their clients. One method of doing this is to use appropriate self-disclosures. Feminist therapy interventions and methods are defined here.

cultural intervention Understanding the client's culture and helping him or her make use of interventions that may include the use of lawyers, social agencies, or families, or taking action in some way.

gender role intervention Such interventions deal with reinforcing or helping clients' interventions or helping them deal with gender role obstacles in their lives. Some interventions provide insight into social or political issues that serve as obstacles to clients.

power intervention Empowering clients can occur in the course of therapeutic discussion. Often encouragement and reinforcement are ways to help clients become more powerful.

assertiveness training A technique to teach clients to effectively express positive and negative feelings to others so that they may achieve desired purposes.

bibliotherapy A therapeutic technique in which the therapist suggests readings for the client for purposes such as gaining insight into problems, learning new information, and increasing self esteem.

reframing Looking at an individual's behavior from a different point of reference. This helps individuals understand how social pressures can affect their problems.

relabeling Attaching a new name to a problem so that therapeutic progress can be made. For example, saying that a client is overwhelmed by an issue rather than "depressed" may allow the client to develop methods to deal with the problem.

therapy-demystifying strategies Providing information about the process of therapy and sharing information about theoretical orientation and client rights.

self disclosure The process in which therapists or counselors discuss aspects of their own lives in order to enhance therapeutic progress with clients.

QUESTIONS ABOUT THERAPY WITH APRIL

7. April says, "Girls are supposed to be quiet and not contradict boys. Sometimes it's hard just to sit there and take it." Which of the following would be an appropriate gender role intervention?

   a. How do you know that girls are just supposed to be quiet?
   b. How did you learn that girls are supposed to be quiet?
   c. What would happen if you were not quiet?
   d. All of the above.

(d. All of the answers help April explore her assumptions about gender role. They do so without making her resist further exploration)

8. As you talk with April, she shares her view of how sexual assaults on women are viewed in her (Vietnamese) culture. This discussion can be seen as a part of a

    a. cultural analysis.
    b. power analysis.
    c. psychoanalysis.

9. April says, "Sometimes, I want my mother to listen to me, to see that I am not a little girl any more. I certainly don't feel like one now." Which of the following would be an appropriate power intervention?

    a. Why don't you just tell her what's on your mind?
    b. I would like to hear what you would say to her. Then we might talk about how you could say some of this to her.
    c. You can let her know how difficult it has been to have learned gender roles from her that are not helpful to you.
    d. Don't you think you should respect your mother's views?
    e. All of the above.

(b. For April, this statement may be best as it is a way of being more powerful without alienating her from her mother. Statements "a" and "c" may backfire on April. They don't encourage her to both listen to her mother and to express herself. Statement "d" does not acknowledge April's power.)

10. Which of these techniques is most likely to directly help April with her passivity?

    a. assertiveness training
    b. bibliotherapy
    c. reframing
    d. therapy-demystifying

11. Which of the following methods of feminist therapy is most likely to help April learn new approaches to relationships, sexual violence, and the importance of women's achievement?

    a. assertiveness training
    b. bibliotherapy
    c. reframing
    d. therapy-demystifying

12. April says to you, "My roommates drink and they pressure me to drink. I really don't like it. I'm afraid of getting out of control, and I'm afraid of being with guys who might get out of control with me when they're drinking." Which would be an appropriate feminist therapy response?

    a. You can ignore them and do whatever you want.
    b. Let's examine the pressures on women to drink and how drinking could affect you.
    c. If a guy is too drunk and starts to get obnoxious, mace him.
    d. You seem to be worried about losing control of yourself and being vulnerable to being hurt.

(b. The therapist takes an opportunity to educate April about options having to do with alcohol use and abuse. She also supports April's decision.)

189

13. Response "b" in question 11 is called

    a. assertiveness training.
    b. bibliotherapy.
    c. reframing.
    d. therapy-demystifying.

("c" is a way of framing the reference for looking at April's behavior. It shifts the focus from April to look at society and alcohol as a social issue.)

14. When April introduces herself to you, she says, "I am April Smith." In introducing yourself, you would use your

    a. first name.
    b. first and last name.
    c. Mr. or Ms. followed by your first and last name.
    d. Dr. followed by your first or last name.

(b. An equal relationship between client and therapist is important in feminist therapy. A feminist therapist would not call herself Dr. and call the client April.)

15. April says, "Sometimes I'm so angry at what Dave did to me that I want to make sure that it doesn't happen to anyone else or at least help decrease the chances that other women will experience that."

    Would it be an appropriate feminist therapy response for you to say, "I am glad to hear of your interest and commitment to trying to prevent date rape. Let me give you the number of the local chapter of the National Organization for Women. You may want to contact them as they are working on education about rape?"

    a. yes
    b. no

(a. Yes. Empowering clients and getting them involved in social action would be an appropriate feminist therapy technique.)

SPECIAL TOPICS

OE1. To what extent do cultural, gender, and power analysis perspectives overlap? (500-503)

_____

_____

_____

OE2. Describe your view of the helpfulness of applying cultural, gender, and power analysis to April's problems. (500-503)

_____

_____

_____

OE3. How do feminist therapists suggest that the following theories can be modified to be consistent with feminist therapy principles?

a. psychoanalytic theory (507) _____

_____

_____

b. behavioral and cognitive therapy (508) _____

_____

_____

c. gestalt therapy (509) _____

_____

_____

d. narrative therapy (509)

_____

_____

_____

OE4. Why is it difficult to determine the length of feminist therapy? (510-511)

_____

_____

OE5. How are the principles of social constructionism consistent with feminist therapy? (517)

_____

_____

OE6. Do you think the advocacy of social action has a place in therapy? (518)

_____

_____

OE7. How can feminist therapy be helpful for the treatment of men? (520)

_____

_____

191

OE8. How does feminist therapy address these two concepts? (522)

homophobia The dislike, fear, or hatred of GLBT people.

heterosexism The view that being heterosexual is more normal and better than being GLBT thus devaluing the lifestyle of GLBT individuals.

_____

_____

_____

OE9. In what ways is feminist therapy a good or a poor model for counseling people with a variety of multicultural backgrounds? (523)

_____

_____

STRENGTHS AND LIMITATIONS

What do you see as the strengths and limitations of feminist therapy?

STRENGTHS	LIMITATIONS
_____	_____
_____	_____
_____	_____
_____	_____
_____	_____
_____	_____
_____	_____

FEMINIST THERAPY: A QUIZ

True/false items. Decide which of the following statements are more "true" or more "false" as they apply to feminist therapy.

T F Q1. Feminist therapy should be applied to women, not men.

T F Q2. Feminist therapy is independent from multicultural therapy.

T F Q3. Feminist therapists are concerned with social injustice.

T F Q4. The stronger a person's gender schema is, the more gender aware he or she is.

192

T F   Q5.   Kohlberg's work on morality is concerned with the ethics of care.

T F   Q6.   Relational cultural theory focuses on finding a sense of identity through the context of relationships.

T F   Q7.   Assertiveness training teaches women how to be more aggressive.

T F   Q8.   Power interventions may be used in feminist therapy.

T F   Q9.   Feminist therapists are concerned with the need to regulate who can call themselves a feminist therapist.

T F   Q10. Feminist therapists work to help GLBT individuals combat societal discrimination.

Multiple choice items: Select the best answer from the alternatives given. Answer each question from the point of view of feminist therapy.

_____ Q11.   Which of these is a major issue of consideration for feminist therapists?

   a.   cultural issues
   b.   search for meaning
   c.   objectivity
   d.   unconscious factors

_____ Q12.   In her study of therapy, Chesler pointed to concerns about

   a.   male therapists working with female patients.
   b.   the destructiveness of therapists' sexual relations with patients.
   c.   gender-biased values of therapists.
   d.   all of the above.

_____ Q13.   Therapists have been particularly concerned about gender-biased values in

   a.   cognitive therapy.
   b.   gestalt therapy.
   c.   psychoanalytic therapy.
   d.   all of the above.

_____ Q14.   According to _____ feminist therapists, men cannot be feminist therapists.

   a.   biased
   b.   liberal
   c.   non-sexist
   d.   radical

_____ Q15.   In which period of life do gender role pressures tend to be the most severe?

   a.   childhood
   b.   adolescence
   c.   adulthood
   d.   old age

193

_____ Q16. Which type of intervention is not a focus of feminist therapy?

    a.   authenticity
    b.   cultural
    c.   gender
    d.   power

_____ Q17. Which of these goals are feminist therapists most cautious about?

    a.   symptom-removal
    b.   self-esteem
    c.   quality of personal relationships
    d.   body image

_____ Q18. Which of these is NOT a technique of feminist therapy?

    a.   gender-role analysis
    b.   power analysis
    c.   biological analysis
    d.   therapist demystifying strategies

_____ Q19. Which of the following responses would feminist therapists see as appropriately assertive?

Statement: "Would you mind working late for me now? I want to go home early."

    a.   Sure. I would be glad to.
    b.   I would be glad to work for you, but later I would like for us to arrange a time for you to do the same.
    c.   Don't ask me at the last minute to work for you. Show some consideration.
    d.   No.

_____ Q20. Feminist therapists seek to

    a.   enhance the feminine mystique in therapy.
    b.   demystify therapy for clients.
    c.   educate male clients about social injustice.
    d.   reframe therapy as consciousness-raising.

_____ Q21. Societal pressures are likely to cause women to be more prone to _____ than men.

    a.   anorexia
    b.   bulimia
    c.   depression
    d.   all of the above

_____ Q22. Feminist therapy with men is likely to include observations about

    a.   men abusing their power with their wives.
    b.   the Oedipus complex.
    c.   societal effects on men's behavior.
    d.   men's body boundaries.

_____ Q23. Feminist therapists tend to be sensitive to gender issues as well as to

    a.   cultural views.
    b.   existential issues.
    c.   choice theory.
    d.   the use of problem solving methods.

_____ Q24. _____ groups were responsible for the development of other groups for women.

    a.   Alcoholics anonymous
    b.   Body image
    c.   Consciousness-raising
    d.   Male/female

_____ Q25. Which of these issues are feminist therapists most concerned with?

    a.   literary
    b.   psychodynamic
    c.   political
    d.   organizational

ANSWER KEY

1. b	11. b		
2. d	12. b		
3. c	13. c		
4. c	14. b		
5. b	15. a		
6. a			
7. d			
8. a			
9. b			
10. a			

QUIZ

Q1.	F	Q11.	a	Q21.	d
Q2.	F	Q12.	d	Q22.	c
Q3.	T	Q13.	c	Q23.	a
Q4.	F	Q14.	d	Q24.	c
Q5.	F	Q15.	b	Q25.	c
Q6.	T	Q16.	a		
Q7.	F	Q17.	a		
Q8.	T	Q18.	c		
Q9.	T	Q19.	b		
Q10.	T	Q20.	b		

195

CHAPTER 14

FAMILY THERAPY

This chapter has a different format from the others. Four different family systems therapies are presented along with brief information about several others and information about early work leading to the development of systems therapy. A brief inventory that is general in nature will be presented first. One case will be explained, and then you will have the opportunity to answer questions about it from different family points of view. The sections will focus on basic concepts, goals, and therapeutic techniques. Also, the application of individual therapies to family therapy will be discussed.

FAMILY THERAPY SELF-INVENTORY

Directions: By comparing your beliefs about personality and therapy to those of family therapy, you should have a clearer idea of how much you will need to suspend your beliefs or change attitudes to understand family therapy. You may find it helpful to complete this section before and after you read the chapter. In this way you can see if your views have changed. There are no correct answers, only an opportunity to express your views.

Put an "X" on the line so that it indicates how much you agree or disagree with the statement: A = Agree, D = Disagree.

D   A

_____ 1. Individuals should be viewed from the perspective of their family rather than from the perspective of a single individual.

_____ 2. Individuals' problems can best be understood by understanding their family problems.

_____ 3. Change in one part of a family system is likely to result in changes in other family members.

_____ 4. Changes within a person can only be made if significant others do not interfere with these changes.

_____ 5. A family therapist should be a teacher and coach as well as a therapist.

_____ 6. The major goal of family therapy is to help the family to solve the presenting problems.

_____ 7. To understand a family's problems, therapists should attend to who says what to whom and how they communicate.

_____ 8. Being active and often directive is a part of the therapist's role in family therapy.

D   A

_____ 9. Attending to both verbal and nonverbal communications within the family are important aspects of family therapy.

_____ 10. An important goal of family therapy is the growth of individuals, not just the growth of the family.

HISTORY OF FAMILY THERAPY

EARLY APPROACHES TO FAMILY COUNSELING
Before the 1930s advice was provided by clergy, friends, doctors, and lawyers The first centers for marriage counseling were in New York and Los Angeles In 1930s and 1940s different therapists saw different members of the family or couple Conjoint therapy in the 1950s became more common Children often were dealt with in guidance clinics separately from the parents Some blaming of parents for the child's problems In the 1950s a shift to helping parents and children relate better to each other

EARLY PSYCHOANALYTIC INFLUENCES
Sigmund Freud's work with five-year-old Hans and other children using a drive theory perspective Anna Freud's work with children in a clinic in England Donald Winnicott was a pediatrician and object relations therapist who made recommendations to parents as well as working with children Erikson specialized in working with children Alfred Adler developed and was involved with child guidance clinics in Vienna Harry Stack Sullivan studied how children and their families behaved in interpersonal situations Nathan Ackerman was the first to treat children and families as a single unit, making use of psychoanalytical techniques

BASIC FAMILY THERAPY CONCEPTS

The following terms distinguish types of work with families. Family therapy that is described in other chapters is distinguished from family systems therapy described in this chapter.

family therapy Any psychotherapeutic treatment of the family to improve psychological functioning among its members. Most major theories of psychotherapy have applications to family therapy.

family systems therapy A type of family therapy in which the entire family is seen as a unit or as a system. Focus is often on the interaction of family members.

conjoint therapy A type of couples therapy in which one therapist sees both members of the couple at the same time.

identified patient The person who other members of the family identify as having the problem for which treatment is sought.

CASE EXAMPLE OF THE GREEN FAMILY

The following case will be used for each of the next four sections. By using the same example, you will be able to see the different perspectives of different family therapists. You will be asked questions about the Green family from each of the perspectives.

Sara and her husband, Ron, have sought help for Charles, their 12-year-old son. Charles is in the sixth grade at a local public elementary school. The principal at the school asked Sara and Ron to meet with him because of his concern about Charles' behavior with his classmates. Basically, Charles is described as a bully. He picks fights with his classmates and argues with them. Recently, he hit Jonnie so hard that Jonnie suffered a concussion. He also has been fighting with other children at recess and on the way home from school.

This has not come as a surprise to Sara and Ron as they received a call from Jonnie's father's lawyer about paying the cost of his injuries and possible civil charges against Charles as well as a complaint to be filed regarding Charles in juvenile court.

Sara and Ron have talked to Charles about his behavior which is not limited to school. His nine-year-old sister, Vivian, is terrified of him. When Charles is angry and upset with Vivian, he swats her rather than talks to her. This behavior has been going on for two years.

Although he does not respond physically to his parents, he is surly and sullen. They have had difficulty getting Charles to clean up his room and put away toys or sports equipment that he uses. Similarly, Charles does little of his homework on time. He does write English papers when prodded. Surprisingly, he does his math homework. His A's in math contrast with C's and D's in other subjects. His behavior has not always been like this. As Sara points out, Charles used to have a gentler disposition, although he has always been rather physical and rough with toys and other children.

Charles is large for his age. He is about 5'6" tall and weighs almost 170 pounds. His large, sloppy appearance tends to put off other children. His athletic skills are average for his age. He has more difficulty in sports like baseball or tennis than in football and running.

Vivian is a third grader who is doing well at school. She enjoys playing with friends who live across the street. On weekends she can be found at her friends' houses. At home she is quiet, often going up to her room to play with her dolls. She avoids the conflict that exists between Charles and her parents.

Sara is a manager of a small jewelry store in their town. This puts strong time demands on her as the store is open until 9 PM every evening except Sunday. She works until 9:30 three evenings a week. She has arranged for an after-school program for Vivian and Charles. Because she grew up in a situation in which her mother took care of her two brothers and sisters while her father traveled frequently, she feels guilty about having made such arrangements. Her father was a wholesale auto parts salesman.

Ron is a lawyer, working mainly with wills and estates. His father died when he was seven. His mother, a seamstress, raised Ron and his older brother by herself. She was a religious woman who believed that one of her main goals in life was to see that her children were educated. Both Ron and his brother, a surgeon, worked their way through college and professional school.

INFLUENCES ON FAMILY SYSTEMS THERAPY

There have been two major influences on family systems theory that are more specific in nature than the influence of psychoanalysis. The first is observations of communication styles in schizophrenic families. The second influence is general systems theory.

COMMUNICATION PATTERNS IN SCHIZOPHRENIC FAMILIES

Although most family therapists believe that physiological factors play a much greater role in schizophrenia than was believed to be the case in the 1950s, work on family communication patterns has had a lasting contribution. Some of the most important concepts are defined here.

double bind A view that when an individual receives an important message with two different meanings and is unable to respond to it, the individual is in an impossible situation. If such messages are repeated over time, individuals may begin to show signs of schizophrenia.

marital schism A situation in which one parent tries to undermine the worth of another by competing for sympathy or support from the children.

marital skew A situation in which the psychological disturbance of one parent dominates the family's interactions. An unreal situation for family members is created so that the family can deal with one member's disturbance.

pseudomutuality Presenting an appearance of open relationships in a family so as to conceal distant or troubled relationships within the family. Members develop roles that they play rather than relating honestly.

GENERAL SYSTEMS THEORY

Systems theory is based on the work of Wiener, a mathematician, and Bertalanffy, a biologist. Systems theory provides several concepts that deal with changes in the system. In the case of family systems therapy, this refers to how changes in one family member can bring about changes in another. Thus, general systems theory has helped therapists look at the entire family as a unit. All of these concepts deal with changes in the system.

systems theory A study of the relationship of parts in their context, emphasizing their unity and their relationship to each other. It is applied to biology, medicine, and other fields and is a basis for family systems therapy.

feedback A communication pattern in which information about the consequences of an event is reintroduced into the system.

negative feedback Information that flows back to a system to reduce behavior that causes disequilibrium.

positive feedback Information that leads to deviation from the system's norm, bringing about change and a loss of stability.

equifinality The ability of a system to arrive at the same destination from different paths or conditions.

homeostasis Balance or equilibrium in a system. Such a balance can bring about a stable environment in the system.

QUESTIONS APPLYING GENERAL SYSTEMS THEORY TO THE GREEN FAMILY

1. If Sara says to Charles in a very exasperated voice, "Now, Charles you are such a nice boy," there is evidence that Charles may be experiencing

    a. a double bind.
    b. marital schism.
    c. marital skew.
    d. pseudomutuality.

2. If Ron were to become very depressed, then we might expect _____ to occur in the family.

    a.   a double bind
    b.   a marital schism
    c.   a marital skew
    d.   pseudomutuality

3. The family member who is most likely to behave in a way that demonstrates pseudomutuality is

    a.   Ron.
    b.   Sara.
    c.   Charles.
    d.   Vivian.

4. The identified patient in this case example is

    a.   Ron.
    b.   Sara.
    c.   Charles.
    d.   Vivian.

5. When Ron gets mad at Charles for getting in trouble at school and this argument escalates into a shouting match, then _____ is occurring in the system.

    a   homeostasis
    b.   positive feedback
    c.   negative feedback
    d.   equifinality

6. Which of these concepts refers to the many ways that Ron could interact with Charles to discuss the problems that he is having at school?

    a.   homeostasis
    b.   positive feedback
    c.   negative feedback
    d.   equifinality

BOWEN'S INTERGENERATIONAL APPROACH

Murray Bowen developed a system that is based on an individual's ability to differentiate his or her own intellectual functioning from his or her feelings. He examined relationships among family members. One concept not shared by other family systems theories is his view of passing psychological characteristics from one generation to another.

THEORY OF FAMILY SYSTEMS

Bowen's view of how families interact is shown in his development of significant concepts. Perhaps the key concept is differentiation of self. A major problem in families can occur when there is fusion, indicating a lack of differentiation.

fusion   A merging or meshing of thoughts and feelings in a family member; the opposite of differentiation.

200

differentiation The process of differentiating one's thinking from one's feeling; the opposite of fusion.

pseudoself An expression of values or opinions that other family members may find acceptable rather than one's own values or opinions.

triangulation A process in which two people who are in conflict involve a third person in order to reduce the tension in the relationship between the original two people.

family projection process A means of projecting or transmitting a parental conflict to one or more children.

emotional cut-off Given too much stress in a family due to over-involvement of parents, children may withdraw or cut themselves off emotionally from the family.

GOALS OF BOWENIAN THERAPY

Bowen tried to help family members become more differentiated and thus reduce their general stress level. He felt that it was helpful to try to get family members to detriangulate.

TECHNIQUES OF BOWENIAN FAMILY THERAPY

In Bowenian therapy, taking a history of the family and using a genogram is a part of the evaluation interview. Later, interpreting information from the genogram and from observations about dynamics in the family takes place. Detriangulation and the use of genograms are among the most important of Bowenian therapeutic approaches.

detriangulation The process of withdrawing from a family member or therapist, so as not to be drawn into alliances of one person against another.

genogram A method of charting a family's relationship system. It is essentially a family tree in which ages, sex, marriage dates, and similar information may be diagrammed.

QUESTIONS APPLYING BOWEN'S THEORY TO THE GREEN FAMILY

7. As a Bowenian therapist, you would ask for information about Ron and Sara's

    a. parents.
    b. grandparents.
    c. aunts and uncles.
    d. all of the above.

8. The individual in the family who is probably least differentiated is

    a. Ron.
    b. Sara.
    c. Charles.
    d. Vivian.

9. When Vivian is challenged by Charles, she tries to involve her mother as soon as possible. This is called

    a. differentiation of self.
    b. triangulation.
    c. family projection process.
    d. emotional cutoff.

10. The family member most likely to experience an emotional cut off is

    a. Ron.
    b. Sara.
    c. Charles.
    d. Vivian.

11. As a Bowenian therapist, a goal that you might have for this family is to

    a. help the parents deal with their own emotional stress that they feel from dealing with Charles.
    b. help Vivian become more emotional when dealing with Charles.
    c. help the principal become more effective in dealing with Charles.
    d. become more aware of alignments and coalitions within the family.

12. Which of these comments are you most likely to make to Charles when he says: "If the kids at school don't behave the way I like, I push them around"?

    a.   It is the teacher's role to discipline the other children, not yours.
    b.   When you act as angry as you like, where does it get you?
    c.   What do you feel when other children don't do as you ask?
    d.   Try something different next time. Pick a child that you might like just a little bit, and say something nice to him or her.

STRUCTURAL FAMILY THERAPY

One of the most influential therapies, Minuchin's structural family therapy, deals with alignments and coalitions within the family. Observing and changing relationships in the family is a focus of this system of family therapy.

CONCEPTS OF STRUCTURAL THERAPY

Minuchin was an astute observer of family interactions. He would observe their verbal and nonverbal behavior. He would also inquire about subsystems, smaller units within the family such as the husband and wife. He would learn about the circumstances under which members of the family would join with one another. He would also try to learn the rules within the family. His focus was on current functioning rather than past relationships.

family structure The rules that have been developed in the course of family life to determine which members interact with which other members and in what way.

boundary permeability The degree to which boundaries are flexible among family members, and the nature of the contact that family members have with each other.

enmeshed A reference to families in which members are overly concerned and overly involved in each other's lives. Boundaries are highly permeable.

disengaged A reference to families, where members are isolated or feel unconnected to each other. Boundaries are rigid and non-permeable.

alignment The way in which family members join or oppose each other in dealing with events.

coalitions Alliances or affiliations between family members against another family member.

202

GOALS OF STRUCTURAL THERAPY

Structural therapists try to bring about changes in the family that will alter coalitions and change alliances to help a family function more effectively.

TECHNIQUES OF FAMILY THERAPY

Structural therapists often join with the family to focus on present issues. They may accommodate themselves to family customs to better understand the family and to be accepted by them. Enacting a problem helps the therapist observe coalitions and alliances which they then may map using diagrams to describe the ways that the family relates. Techniques are often active, sometimes subtle, and sometimes directive. The intensity of an intervention may be varied in order to bring about a certain reaction.

mimesis A process by which a therapist appears similar to family members by imitating body language, styles, or other features. A way of joining a family system and getting cooperation from a family.

tracking Staying attuned to a family's style of relating and understanding symbols of a family's life.

enactment A therapeutic procedure in which families are asked to act out a conflict so that the therapist can work with the actual conflict rather than a report of it.

boundary marking A technique to change boundaries or interactions among individual family members. An example would be to change the seating of family members in therapy.

reframing Giving a new or different explanation for an event so that constructive change can occur in the family.

QUESTIONS APPLYING STRUCTURAL THERAPY TO THE GREEN FAMILY

13. The relationship between Charles and Vivian can be viewed as a

    a. family structure.
    b. family subsystem.
    c. family boundary.
    d. family coalition.

14. When all four members of the family are together, Ron tends to give orders, and the others are expected to follow. Sara is often expected to see that the orders are carried out. This is an example of a(n) _____ family.

    a. fused
    b. coalesced
    c. enmeshed
    d. disengaged

15. As you talk to and observe the family, you notice that they all sit up very straight in their chairs. You also decide to do this. This is an example of

    a. family sculpting.
    b. enactment.
    c. mimesis.
    d. tracking.

203

16. As you are watching Sara and Ron talk about Charles, you notice that Charles is looking out the window. You are likely

    a. to ask him to pay attention to what his parents are saying.
    b. to have him move his chair close to or between his parents.
    c. ignore him and listen to his parents.
    d. ask him what he is feeling now.

17. When Sara and Ron talk about how they had a difficult time with Charles at home about not doing his history assignment, you may

    a. suggest that they be more encouraging.
    b. act out the situation right now with Charles, having his parents talk to him now about history.
    c. suggest that he start first with math (something he likes) and later do history.
    d. get Charles' attention and explain why it is important for him to listen to his parents.

18. After the session is over and you make a map of the family, the map would include

    a. a diagram of Sara and Ron's relationship to their parents.
    b. lines to indicate the type of boundaries that exist within the family.
    c. changes in the seating that took place within the session.
    d. directions to the family's house.

STRATEGIC THERAPY

Strategic therapy focuses on the clients' symptoms or problems that they describe to the therapist. Like structural therapists, strategic therapists attend to relationships within families and triangles that exist. However, strategic therapists concentrate on symptoms, often seeing them as metaphors for problems within the family.

GOALS OF STRATEGIC THERAPY

The basic goals are to remove the symptoms that families bring to therapy. The goals must be specific so that the therapist can find out which family member is experiencing which symptoms, in what ways, and in which situations. There must be enough information so that the therapist can decide how to reach the goals.

TECHNIQUES OF STRATEGIC THERAPY

Strategic therapy is one of the most difficult of the therapies covered in this text for therapists to learn and implement. The therapist devises and assigns tasks to the family. Such tasks would be ones that the family has not implemented. The two types of tasks that are used to bring about change are straightforward and paradoxical. The tasks are often metaphors for solving family problems. For example, asking a father and daughter to go shopping together would be a metaphor for improving the relationship between the father and daughter. Paradoxical tasks are particularly difficult to devise.

straightforward task A task that the family is intended to accept and perform as stated.

paradoxical task A task in which a therapist gives a client or family a directive that is likely to be resisted. Change takes place whether or not the task is completed.

204

QUESTIONS APPLYING STRATEGIC THERAPY TO THE GREEN FAMILY

Because strategic therapy is complex, you are likely to find questions OE2 and OE3 very difficult to answer. Take a guess and don't worry if you can't think of possible solutions. Some solutions are offered at the end of the chapter.

*OE1. State the goal of strategic therapy for the Green family.

_____

_____

*OE2. Describe a straightforward task that you would give to the family.

_____

_____

*OE3. Describe a paradoxical task that you would give to the family.

_____

_____

EXPERIENTIAL AND HUMANISTIC THERAPY

Both Carl Whitaker and Virginia Satir used approaches that encouraged open communications within the family. Whitaker used an intuitive approach, trusting his reactions to the family. Whitaker used confrontation, exaggeration, and absurdity as techniques. His approach was creative and energetic.

Noted for her communication skills, Virginia Satir was often empathic with the family. She identified five styles of relating within the family. To explore relationships within the family, she used techniques such as family sculpting and taking a family life chronology.

family sculpting A technique in which family members are physically molded or directed to take characteristic poses to represent a view of family relationships.

family life chronology A way of recording significant events in a family's development.

QUESTIONS APPLYING EXPERIENTIAL AND HUMANISTIC THEORY TO THE GREEN FAMILY

19. If Charles says "Nobody pays attention to me unless I'm in trouble," a humanistic therapist might respond in this way:

    a.   Why don't you sit closer to Vivian.
    b.   Sometimes you really hurt inside if you feel your parents are too busy to be with you.
    c.   When you are at school and the teacher asks a question, raise your hand and try to answer it.
    d.   Sara, did you feel ignored by your mother when you were Charles' age? What did you do to feel closer to her?

205

20. When Vivian starts to cry because of Charles's outbursts in therapy, a humanistic or experiential family systems therapist might

    a. tell Charles to be careful not to shout so as not to upset Vivian.
    b. ask Ron to caution Charles not to shout.
    c. ask whether what has just happened in therapy happens at home.
    d. empathize with Vivian, discussing her fear of Charles' shouting.

INTEGRATIVE APPROACHES

Several of the different family systems theories may seem quite distinct from each other. However, many family therapists make use of some of these approaches or even all of them. The training of family therapists and the perception that family therapists have of the best approach to treating the family is likely to influence the therapists' approaches. Also, their own personalities are likely to influence which theories they choose to use.

THEORIES OF INDIVIDUAL THERAPY AS APPLIED TO FAMILY THERAPY

Each of the theories in the text, with the exception of Jungian therapy, applies its theoretical approach to helping families. The method for doing this is summarized in the following chart that lists the chapter, the theory, and the basic approach to family therapy.

Chapter 2	Psychoanalysis	The object relations approach is influential in focusing on nurturing and caring provided by family members to each other. Interpretation of past behavior and therapeutic resistance is common.
Chapter 4	Adlerian Therapy	Using an educational approach, Adlerians teach parents how to deal with children by pinpointing the problem and reaching agreement.
Chapter 5	Existential Therapy	Therapists are aware not only of relationships between family members but also each member's sense of being in the world. Keeping diaries is an example of an existential method.
Chapter 6	Person-Centered Therapy	Family therapists may empathize with family members who are present at the session, as well as those who are not.
Chapter 7	Gestalt Therapy	Gestalt therapists help members to be aware of their own issues. They may also have family members enact problems.
Chapter 8	Behavior Therapy	Behavioral family therapists often teach parents how to use behavioral methods with their children.
Chapter 9	REBT	Family therapists identify irrational beliefs among family members. They then dispute *shoulds* and *musts* and other irrational beliefs. They also use cognitive and behavioral change techniques.

206

Chapter 10	Cognitive Therapy	Education is a part of family therapy as is challenging and changing distorted beliefs. Suggestions for changing beliefs are given to family members.
Chapter 11	Reality Therapy	Reality therapists observe the choice systems of family members. They help family members meet their own needs while promoting harmony in the family. They focus on activities family members can do together.
Chapter 12	Constructivist Therapies	Solution-focused therapy, frequently used with families, may use miracle, exception-finding, scaling, and other questions. Narrative therapists often externalize the problem, engaging the whole family in a struggle with the externalized problem.
Chapter 13	Feminist Therapy	Feminist family therapists may focus on how political and social factors influence the family. They attend to the effect of gender and cultural issues that affect the family.

BRIEF FAMILY SYSTEMS THERAPIES

Although most family therapeutic approaches tend to be brief, some were designed to produce change quite quickly or to require relatively few sessions. Even though the approaches are symptom-focused (first-order change), they are designed to bring about lasting change (second-order). Brief family therapy may be for fewer than 5 or 10 sessions.

first-order change A temporary change in the family system to solve a specific problem. Such changes do not alter the basic system of the family.

second-order change A change that produces a lasting change in the family as well as fundamental changes in the family's structure and organization.

THE MENTAL RESEARCH INSTITUTE BRIEF FAMILY THERAPY (MRI) MODEL

One of the earliest approaches, the MRI model, focused on communication patterns. Its goal was to resolve problems in the family and relieve symptoms. Often MRI therapists try to make small changes and build on them. As Haley does in structural therapy, they make use of straightforward and paradoxical tasks. Some of their communication concepts include the following:

complimentary communication A relationship in which there is inequality in two or more members. One is usually submissive to the other.

symmetrical communication A type of communication characterized by equality among individuals. Such communication can result in one angry remark following another, leading to an argument.

punctuation The concept that each person in a transaction believes what he or she says is caused by what the other person says. Basically, the individual holds the other responsible for his or her reactions.

Focus is more on communication patterns rather than on coalitions and alliances as used by Minuchin in structural therapy or on parental hierarchies as in Haley's strategic therapy.

Although there are several different approaches within the Milan group in Italy, their focus has been somewhat similar to the MRI model. They have used dramatic interventions. They also have had consulting therapists watch sessions of the family therapy and then make suggestions to the therapists. Two techniques that they are particularly known for are circular questioning and the invariant prescription.

circular questioning An interviewing technique designed to elicit differences in perceptions about events or relationships from different family members.

invariant prescription A single directive given to parents, designed to create clear boundaries between parents and children.

SPECIAL TOPICS

OE4. Why do you think psychoeducational approaches have become more popular recently in working with families with members with schizophrenia than have traditional therapeutic approaches? (567)

_____

_____

OE5. Why is it helpful for family therapists to have knowledge of legal issues? (568)

_____

_____

OE6. What impact can feminist therapy's view of gender roles have on the practice of family therapy? (572)

_____

_____

OE7. If you were a family therapist, in what ways would knowledge of your clients' family background and culture be helpful to you? (573-575)

_____

_____

OE8. How can ideas from family systems therapy be applied to individual therapy? (575)

_____

_____

STRENGTHS AND LIMITATIONS

What do you believe are the strengths and limitations of family systems therapy?

STRENGTHS   LIMITATIONS

_____   _____

_____   _____

_____   _____

_____   _____

_____   _____

_____   _____

_____   _____

FAMILY THERAPY: A QUIZ

True/False Items. Decide if the following statements are "more true" or "more false" as they apply to family systems therapy.

T F Q1. Family systems therapy focuses on each individual equally.

T F Q2. The genogram would be a useful assessment device in Haley's strategic therapy.

T F Q3. Only family systems therapies try to help families with problems.

T F Q4. Only family system theories of therapy work with families.

T F Q5. Bowenian therapies are interested in family relationships that may include grandparents.

T F Q6. In the 1930s, it was almost unheard of for a family therapist to meet with the whole family.

T F Q7. Experiential therapy has a set of specific techniques that are applied to the experiences of different family members.

T F Q8. A structural therapist might ask a family member to move closer to another member in order to realign boundaries.

T F Q9. Psychoeducational approaches have been developed to help families with members with schizophrenia develop methods for coping with and helping the member with schizophrenia.

T F Q10. In family systems therapy, positive feedback refers to giving positive reinforcement to a family member.

Multiple choice items: Select the best answer from the alternatives given. Most of the questions ask you to choose the theory of family therapy that most closely fits the question.

_____ Q11. How do other theories of family therapy differ most clearly from family systems therapy?

    a. do not apply as many directive techniques
    b. do not adhere to the same strict code of ethics
    c. do not view the family as a single system
    d. are less likely to use paradoxical interventions

_____ Q12. A family that has a severely depressed parent is most likely to experience

    a. a double bind.
    b. marital schism.
    c. marital skew.
    d. pseudomutuality.

_____ Q13. Family systems therapists view the communication within the family as

    a. linear.
    b. contrived.
    c. dysfunctional.
    d. circular.

_____ Q14. In assessing family problems, which type of family therapy is most likely to use family mapping?

    a. Bowen's intergenerational therapy
    b. existential therapy
    c. structural therapy
    d. strategic therapy

_____ Q15. In assessing family problems, which type of family therapy is most likely to examine dysfunctional thoughts of family members?

    a. Bowen's intergenerational therapy
    b. cognitive therapy
    c. structural therapy
    d. strategic therapy

_____ Q16. The use of straightforward tasks to create change in the family is most often used in

    a. Bowen's intergenerational therapy.
    b. cognitive therapy.
    c. structural therapy.
    d. strategic therapy.

_____ Q17. Discussion of family interaction style of grandparents is most likely to occur in

    a. Bowen's intergenerational therapy.
    b. rational emotive behavioral therapy.
    c. structural therapy.
    d. strategic therapy.

210

_____ Q18. Having a family act out a conflict is a technique that is most commonly associated with structural family therapy and

   a.   Bowen's intergenerational therapy.
   b.   existential therapy.
   c.   gestalt therapy.
   d.   psychoanalytic therapy.

_____ Q19. Which of these theorists was most concerned about education as a way of helping families with problems?

   a.   Adler
   b.   Bowen
   c.   Freud
   d.   Jung

_____ Q20. Determining the degree to which family members are differentiated is most likely to be done in

   a.   Adlerian therapy
   b.   Bowen's intergenerational therapy.
   c.   structural therapy.
   d.   strategic therapy.

_____ Q21. Focusing on helping families develop authenticity and meaningfulness in their lives is most associated with

   a.   Adlerian therapy.
   b.   existential therapy.
   c.   psychoanalytic therapy.
   d.   strategic therapy.

_____ Q22. Empathy and warmth in relating to the family are most often associated with the work of

   a.   Murray Bowen.
   b.   Jay Haley.
   c.   Virginia Satir.
   d.   Carl Whitaker.

_____ Q23. The use of the invariant prescription is an approach associated with

   a.   Murray Bowen.
   b.   Jay Haley.
   c.   Virginia Satir.
   d.   Carl Whitaker.

_____ Q24. Which of these approaches to family therapy is the most difficult for therapists to use well?

   a.   Adlerian therapy
   b.   Bowenian therapy
   c.   person-centered therapy
   d.   strategic therapy

211

_____ Q25. Which of the following is NOT a current issue in family systems therapy?

    a.   the impact of medication on family therapy
    b.   psychoeducational methods with families with members who have severe psychological disturbances
    c.   concern about vulnerability to malpractice suits
    d.   the impact of intersubjectivity theory on the therapeutic relationship with the family

ANSWER KEY

1.	a	11.	a
2.	c	12.	d
3.	d	13.	b
4.	c	14.	d
5.	b	15.	c
6.	d	16.	b
7.	d	17.	b
8.	c	18.	b
9.	b	19.	b
10.	d	20.	d

QUIZ

Q1.	F	Q11.	c	Q21.	b
Q2.	F	Q12.	c	Q22.	c
Q3.	F	Q13.	d	Q23.	e
Q4.	F	Q14.	c	Q24.	d
Q5.	T	Q15.	b	Q25.	d
Q6.	T	Q16.	d		
Q7.	F	Q17.	a		
Q8.	T	Q18.	c		
Q9.	T	Q19.	a		
Q10.	F	Q20.	b		

ANSWERS TO OPEN ENDED QUESTIONS

*OE1.   The goal of strategic therapy would be to have Charles act friendly and verbally with his peers and sister. Another goal would be for him to complete his homework on time.

*OE2.   Straightforward tasks might be to
      have him play football and have his father involved in coaching the team.
      have his father play sports with him.
      have Charles help Vivian with her math homework.
      have Charles teach Vivian an athletic activity.
      have Sara take Charles to school, go to a sports event, or do an activity with him.

(Most of these activities would be designed to channel Charles' aggressiveness into socially acceptable activities or to have Charles have a closer coalition with members of his family.)

212

*OE3. Paradoxical tasks might include

telling Charles to continue to act out aggressively so he can make others do what he wants.
telling Charles not to do his homework so he can be even more independent.
telling the family to encourage Charles to not be friendly with children at school so he can be even more independent.

(Because the Green family is cooperative, paradoxical tasks may not be necessary. The paradoxical tasks above could have negative consequences that the therapist does not intend.)

CHAPTER 15

OTHER PSYCHOTHERAPIES

Because this chapter contains relatively brief explanations of five different therapies, the format of this chapter in this manual is different from the other chapters. For each of the five theories, five questions are given to compare your views of therapeutic issues with those of the theory. Then the theory is summarized and important concepts are described. A quiz follows which includes five true and false questions and five multiple choice questions.

ASIAN THERAPIES

SELF-INVENTORY

To compare your views of therapy with those who use Asian therapeutic approaches, put an "X" on the line that indicates how much you agree or disagree with the statement.

D   A

_____ 1. Spiritual healing and therapy are closely related.

_____ 2. Clients can learn responsibility by learning how to act ethically.

_____ 3. To understand oneself, one has to understand other aspects of the universe.

_____ 4. Attending to one's own being and thoughts can be therapeutic.

_____ 5. Helping clients become less self-centered is an important goal of therapy.

BACKGROUND OF ASIAN THERAPIES

Dating back more than 3,000 years, Asian philosophy and psychology have been influenced by Hindu and Buddhist teachings. In Indian psychology, four concepts have been key to understanding philosophical beliefs that relate to Asian psychology.

dharma Rules that describe goodness and appropriate behavior.

karma Movement from past incarnations that affect the present.

214

maya A concept referring to the distorted perception of reality and experience. Only by directing attention to one's awareness, through concentration or meditation, can reality and experience be perceived more accurately.

atman A concept of universality in which the self is not seen as an individual but as part of the entire universe.

These concepts are learned, in part, through yoga and Hatha-yoga.

yoga Hindu teachings dealing with ethics, life-style, body postures, breath control, intellectual study and meditation.

Hatha-yoga Deals with the physiological discipline required in separating the self from thought processes.

Other concepts that are derived from Buddhist teachings are the four noble truths and the eightfold path. These values have had a major influence on Asian psychology and philosophy.

ASIAN THEORIES OF PERSONALITY

Thousands of years of the history of Asian philosophy and religion are condensed into less than eight pages on Asian therapy. There are major differences between several Asian philosophies and religions. The commonalities between these philosophies, rather than the differences, are described in the text. These include:

The self is closely related to the universe.

Deemphasis on the individual, emphasis on the whole of humanity.

Interdependence as seen by involvement with the family and the extended family is important.

There are different states of consciousness.

Psychological health can be seen as freedom from fears, compulsions, and anxieties.

Being able to observe one's fears, compulsions, and anxieties is helpful in being psychologically healthy.

ASIAN THEORIES OF PSYCHOTHERAPY

Three Asian therapies are described in the text. They can be called "quiet" therapies because of their focus on spending time in isolation to deal with thoughts and varied states of awareness. Meditation is the most ancient and is closely associated with Buddhism and Hinduism. Naikan and Morita therapies were both developed in Japan.

MEDITATION AND MINFULNESS MEDITATION

Used widely in Asia to seek higher psychological or religious levels of self-development, meditation is used much less commonly in the West. In the West, it is often used for stress management and relaxation. Mindfulness meditation is used in therapies such as acceptance and commitment therapy and dialectical behavior therapy. By focusing on consciousness itself, individuals can become aware of distortions in perceptions (maya).

meditation Methods for controlling one's mental processes. In concentration meditation, the focus is on a stimulus such as the act of breathing. In awareness meditation, the purpose is to examine consciousness and the mind.

215

mindfulness A way of experiencing oneself in the present. In doing so, one is relaxed, open, and alert.

mindfulness meditation Focusing awareness on breathing. By focusing on breathing, following the inhale and exhale, feelings and images are likely to arise.

dialectical behavior therapy An evidence-based therapy designed for the treatment of suicidal patients and those with borderline disorder. Mindfulness values and meditation techniques have been incorporated into this treatment.

NAIKAN THERAPY

A Japanese therapy in which patients focus on their mistakes in past relationships, Naikan therapy helps patients improve relationships with others so that they may contribute to society. In Japan, it is a strict inpatient therapy. In the West, it has been modified so that isolation and activity restriction is not so strict. Three important questions guide patients in their self-observations of past relationships:

1. What did I receive from this person?
2. What did I return to the person?
3. What troubles and worries did I cause this person? (Reynolds, 1993, p.124)

MORITA THERAPY

Originated around 1915, Morita therapy is designed to help patients redirect tension away from themselves. It is an inpatient therapy lasting 4 to 5 weeks. There are four phases starting with isolation and moving towards doing mundane tasks.

Following this regimen, patients learn to be practical and specific so that actions can be taken to reduce symptoms. Originally designed to treat obsessive-compulsive, panic, and phobic disorders, it has been used for other psychological disturbances as well. When used in the United States, the severe isolation aspects are modified. Writing down one's thoughts and the therapist's comments are an aspect of Morita therapy.

ASIAN THERAPIES: A QUIZ

True/false items. Decide if the following statements are more "true" or more "false".

T F Q1. Asian therapies are derived from Western existential philosophy.

T F Q2. Meditation is viewed in Asia as a form of psychotherapy.

T F Q3. Mindfulness meditation interferes with the ability to observe one's own fears.

T F Q4. Assertiveness training is very different in focus than Naikan therapy.

T F Q5. The purpose of isolation in Morita therapy is to help patients experience their symptoms and appreciate the need for changing their lifestyles.

Multiple choice items. Select the best answer from the alternatives given.

_____ Q6. Which of the following concepts refers to distortions of perceptions of experience?

   a. dharma
   b. karma
   c. maya
   d. atman

216

_____ Q7. Which of the following concepts refers to seeing oneself not as an individual but as a part of the universe?

  a. dharma
  b. karma
  c. maya
  d. atman

_____ Q8. Which of these therapies sees overcoming self-centeredness as an important therapeutic goal?

  a. mindfulness meditation
  b. Naikan therapy
  c. Morita therapy
  d. existential therapy

_____ Q9. Learning to be more practical and less idealistic is an important therapeutic goal for

  a. meditation.
  b. Naikan therapy.
  c. Morita therapy.
  d. existential therapy.

_____ Q10. In Naikan therapy, the therapist's role is similar to that of a

  a. coach.
  b. confessor.
  c. evaluator.
  d. facilitator.

BODY PSYCHOTHERAPIES

SELF-INVENTORY

To compare your views of therapy with those who use body therapy approaches, put an "X" on the line that indicates how much you agree or disagree with the statement.

D   A

_____ 1. Bodily and psychological processes are one and the same.

_____ 2. Attending to patients' breathing, posture, and physique is useful in assessing patients' problems.

_____ 3. Touching the patient is appropriate in therapy as long as it is done in accordance with ethical guidelines.

_____ 4. The personalities of individuals can be assessed by attending to how patients move and stand.

_____ 5. Early traumatic experiences can affect how people breathe, stand, walk, or run.

217

BACKGROUND OF BODY THERAPY

Developed by Wilhelm Reich, body therapies seek to integrate the body and mind. Reich developed vegetotherapy in which he sought to release life forces so that they could flow through the body. He did this by observing and manipulating the body. For Reich, orgone was a central concept.

Alexander Lowen, a patient and student of Reich's, developed bioenergetic analysis. It differed from Reich's method in that it used a more varied approach to treatment, was more closely aligned with psychoanalysis, and attended to grounding. Lowen's work has been popularized to some degree through his writings. The most significant concepts from Reich's and Lowen's work are described here.

body armor or *muscular armor* A protective mechanism in the individual to deal with the punishment that comes from acting on instinctual demands such as defecating in public.

orgone A physical force that powers all physiological and psychological functions. Developed by Wilhelm Reich.

bioenergetic analysis Developed principally by Alexander Lowen, this is a method of understanding personality in terms of the body and its energy flow. Attention is given to physiology, breathing, and bodily movement.

grounding A concept developed by Alexander Lowen which emphasizes being in contact with the ground literally, through feet and legs, as well as figuratively being grounded in the real world.

PERSONALITY THEORY AND THE BODY

Attending to the ways that individuals conduct themselves physically is an essential aspect of understanding personality. Body therapists especially attend to the ways in which individuals breathe. Changing breathing patterns can bring about momentary changes in affect. Likewise, changing other bodily positions and movements can bring about other changes. Psychological disorders are affected by physiology. Physiology may be affected by past events.

Lowen described five types of character structures. They are explained in the text along with their psychological attributes. The physiological characteristics associated with them are pointed out here.

schizoid character The individuals' upper and lower body parts may not seem to go together. The head may be held to one side, and there may be a lack of energy in face, hands, and feet.

oral character The legs and feet are likely to be underdeveloped and thin. Tension in the shoulders and legs may symbolize that the person has been left alone or abandoned.

narcissistic character A sense of superiority may appear in the overdevelopment of the upper half of the body. Tension appears in the legs and back of the person when standing.

masochistic character Because such individuals tend to hold in feelings, tension can be seen in the arms and legs. Often the eyes have a look of suffering, and the individual has a whining voice.

rigid character The posture is erect, with rigidity in the back muscles and stiffness in the neck.

It is important not to take these descriptions out of context. They are provided to show how Lowen makes a link between the physical and the psychological. As he points out, he treats people not character types. Individuals combine different character types.

218

TECHNIQUES AND ASSESSMENT IN BODY PSYCHOTHERAPY

Body therapists integrate assessment with therapy. As individuals change their body positions and breathing, body therapists reassess these changes, and therapists use this information to make therapeutic interventions. Body reading and body awareness methods are used for assessment. Soft and hard techniques are used for helping individuals with their psychological problems.

body reading Systematic observations used to understand energy blockages and tensions within the body.

body awareness Patients may move or change positions and develop more awareness of their body.

soft techniques A way of asking the patient to assume a gentle posture or softly touching a patient so that psychological awareness or change may occur.

hard techniques A method of asking the patient to assume an uncomfortable or painful position or touching a patient in a somewhat painful way which may bring about intense emotional responses.

ETHICS AND BODY PSYCHOTHERAPY

Because of the use of touch, ethics are of primary importance in body psychotherapies. Focus is on patient growth. Therapists should not use therapy to satisfy their own needs. Erotic intentions are prohibited. Ethics also apply to group workshops. Therapists must be aware when members are in therapy that contact with all workshop participants may be limited to the single event.

BODY PSYCHOTHERAPIES: A QUIZ

True/false items. Decide if the following statements are more "true" or more "false".

T F Q11. Body psychotherapists use similar techniques to those of physical therapists.

T F Q12. The concept of muscular armor is a protective mechanism to deal with punishment for acting on instinctual demands.

T F Q13. In the assessment process, body psychotherapists may touch the patient's body to assess blockages in energy flow.

T F Q14. The use of the orgone box to help a variety of patients' problems led to Reich's eventual imprisonment.

T F Q15. Because of their use of touch, body therapists are particularly concerned with following ethical guidelines closely.

Multiple choice items. Select the best answer from the alternatives given.

_____ Q16. To have firm contact with the real world refers to the concept of

a. orgone.
b. grounding.
c. soft therapeutic techniques.
d. hard therapeutic techniques.

219

_____ Q17. Vegetotherapy is a technique associated with the work of

    a.   Lowen.
    b.   Reich.
    c.   Sheldon.
    d.   Smith.

_____ Q18. Which of the following is not a part of Lowen's group of character structures?

    a.   schizoid
    b.   grounding
    c.   oral
    d.   masochistic

_____ Q19. Calling attention to when a patient stops breathing for a moment is an example of a body therapy

    a.   soft technique.
    b.   hard technique.
    c.   grounding technique.
    d.   use of a technique from a different theory.

_____ Q20. In body therapy, touching a female patient's breast would be an example of

    a.   a soft technique.
    b.   a hard technique.
    c.   grounding.
    d.   unethical behavior.

INTERPERSONAL PSYCHOTHERAPY

SELF-INVENTORY

To compare your views of therapy with those who use interpersonal therapy, put an "X" on the line that indicates how much you agree or disagree with the statement.

D   A

_____ 1. Therapy should be designed to treat specific disorders.

_____ 2. In developing a theory of therapy, attention should be paid to research that supports the use of certain methods rather than relying solely on clinical hunches.

_____ 3. Treatment of depression should focus on interpersonal relationships.

_____ 4. Encouragement and support are essential elements of therapeutic treatment.

_____ 5. Treatment manuals are a valuable asset in the application of psychotherapy.

BACKGROUND OF INTERPERSONAL PSYCHOTHERAPY

Developed by Gerald Klerman and his colleagues, interpersonal therapy differs from other therapies in several respects. It was designed using a medical model, being exposed rather quickly to tests of its effectiveness. Not only was it designed to be subject to research, but its rationale and techniques were built on prior research. Its original application was to depression. Other applications have generally been to

220

disorders that are somewhat similar to depression such as dysthymia. Because it was designed to be subject to research, treatment manuals that clearly spell out procedures for therapists to follow were implemented and refined. The manuals plan for therapy to be completed in approximately 12 to 16 sessions.

A psychiatrist, Klerman was influenced by medical research and, more specifically, research into the treatment of depression. Three theorists were particularly important in the early development of interpersonal therapy.

Adolf Meyer emphasized the importance of both physiological and psychological forces on treatment of psychiatric disorders.

Harry Stack Sullivan showed how peer relationships in childhood and adolescence affect later interpersonal relationships.

John Bowlby's work on attachment explained the importance of early bonding with the mother.

One of the most important influences on Klerman's development of interpersonal psychotherapy was his review of specific factors that contributed to depression.

INTERPERSONAL THERAPY PERSONALITY THEORY

Designed for assisting depressed patients, Klerman's theory focused on those factors that contributed specifically to depression. He asked what problem areas contribute to depression, and after reviewing literature on depression, identified four: grief, interpersonal disputes, role transitions, and interpersonal deficits.

grief   Although a normal process, grief can contribute to depression. When the loss is severe and lengthy or there is more than one loss, depression can last a long time.

interpersonal disputes   Ongoing struggles, disagreements, or arguments with others can contribute to depression. The disputes may occur in the family, at school, at work, or in other situations.

role transitions   Life changes such as illness, divorce, marriage, or having children leave home can create stress and contribute to depression.

interpersonal deficits   Social isolation or the lack of social skills may cause loneliness and related problems.

Note that all four of these categories deal in some way with interpersonal relationships.

GOALS OF INTERPERSONAL THERAPY

The goals of interpersonal therapy are developed from the four types of problems that relate to depression. Typically, interpersonal therapists will only work on one or two of these goals due to the short duration of interpersonal therapy.

grief   To reestablish interest in relationships and become more involved with others and to help with the mourning process.

interpersonal disputes   To understand how disputes and arguments relate to depression and to resolve these disputes to bring about change.

role transitions   To move from one role to another. To mourn the loss of one role and develop mastery of a new role, resulting in increased self-esteem.

interpersonal deficits   To reduce isolation from others, develop new relationships and improve old ones.

TECHNIQUES OF INTERPERSONAL THERAPY

Interpersonal therapy is done in three phases: the initial, the intermediate, and the termination phase. The first and third phases last for two or three sessions each. All phases focus, in different ways, on one or two of the four problem areas.

Initial phase Diagnosis of depression is made. Referral may be made if interpersonal therapy is not appropriate. Assessment is focused on placing the problem into one or more of the four problem areas. Diagnosis is shared with the patient. Encouragement and hope for the problem are given to the patient.

Intermediate phase In this phase, attention is addressed to the four problem areas. A good therapeutic relationship not only encourages participation in therapy but provides a model for outside relationships. Techniques for change are not very different than those used by other therapies, but the techniques are designed to address those problem areas as appropriate.

starting the session Klerman suggested that therapists ask: "How have things been since we last met?" Because the question focuses on recent events, it helps to focus the patient on specific problem areas.

encouragement of affect Expression of painful emotions is encouraged so that the therapist can show understanding and explore ways to remedy the situation.

clarification Interpersonal relationships are clarified so that patients can better understand an interpersonal situation.

role playing This is one of several techniques used to help the patient try out or explore new methods for improving interpersonal relationships.

Termination phase Explicitly discussing the approaching end of therapy, a focus is put on the patient becoming more independent. Emphasis on gains and discussion of relapse prevention also takes place.

Interpersonal therapy flows from one phase to another. The attention to the appropriate problem areas (grief, interpersonal disputes, role transitions, or interpersonal deficits) occurs in all three phases.

Although interpersonal therapy was designed for the treatment of depression, it has been applied to other problem areas. Before it is applied to a new area, a new treatment manual is developed. The new areas of treatment are often quite close to the original area: distressed but not clinically depressed individuals, people depressed by marital disputes, individuals with panic symptoms, depressed adolescents with medical concerns, and depressed elderly individuals. In general, results have been more positive when interpersonal therapy was applied to these groups than when it was applied to substance addictions.

INTERPERSONAL PSYCHOTHERAPY: A QUIZ

True/false items. Decide if the following statements are more "true" or more "false".

T   F   Q21. Klerman's interpersonal therapy focuses on unconscious communication.

T   F   Q22. Interpersonal therapy was developed to treat anxiety disorders.

© 2012 Cengage Learning. All Rights Reserved. May not be scanned, copied or duplicated, or posted to a publicly accessible website, in whole or in part.

T F   Q23. The duration of interpersonal therapy is approximately three months.

T F   Q24. Past interpersonal relationships are the major emphasis of interpersonal therapy.

T F   Q25. Treatment manuals were written in such a way to encourage the use of support rather than to explore unconscious motivations.

Multiple choice items. Select the best answer from the alternatives given.

_____   Q26. A significant aspect of interpersonal therapy is its

    a.   tie to existentialism.
    b.   grounding in constructivism.
    c.   focus on enactment.
    d.   use of treatment manuals.

_____   Q27. Which of the following is not a problem area that interpersonal therapy addresses?

    a.   anti-social behavior
    b.   grief
    c.   interpersonal disputes
    d.   interpersonal deficits

_____   Q28. In interpersonal therapy, which of the following areas is considered the most difficult to address?

    a.   anti-social behavior
    b.   role transitions
    c.   interpersonal disputes
    d.   interpersonal deficits

_____   Q29. Which of the following problems is interpersonal therapy LEAST likely to address?

    a.   loss of a spouse
    b.   borderline disorder
    c.   disputes at work
    d.   lack of friends

_____   Q30. Which of the following techniques is most likely to be used by an interpersonal therapist?

    a.   behavioral analysis
    b.   boundary analysis
    c.   communication analysis
    d.   psychoanalysis

223

PSYCHODRAMA

SELF-INVENTORY

To compare your views of therapy with those who use psychodrama, put an "X" on the line that indicates how much you agree or disagree with the statement.

D   A

_____ 1. Individuals learn about themselves by examining the different roles that they play in life.

_____ 2. Spontaneity and creativity are characteristics of living a full and healthy life.

_____ 3. Enacting one's problems can provide new and creative solutions to individuals.

_____ 4. Expressing feelings that have been held in is a significant goal of therapy.

_____ 5. Other people can provide valuable insights into your problems by playing roles of important people in your life.

BACKGROUND OF PSYCHODRAMA

The theatrical nature of psychodrama reflects the flair for the dramatic and the interest in drama of its founder, Jacob Moreno. As a student of philosophy, he enjoyed watching the play of children. While a medical student in Vienna, he was interested in social injustice and in helping socially disenfranchised groups. His development of psychodrama in the 1930s laid the groundwork for group therapies that were to follow. The technique of role playing, adopted by many theories, was developed by Moreno as he created new therapeutic techniques to be used in psychodrama.

Moreno worked in a variety of settings. He developed impromptu theater in Vienna. In 1925, he moved to the United States. In one sanitarium, he built a theater to be used for psychodrama. He brought psychodrama to schools, prisons, and hospitals. Moreno's focus on the different roles people play and the use of the group in therapy provided an impetus for other therapeutic interventions that were to follow.

THEORY OF PERSONALITY

In his view of personality, the roles that people played at various times in their lives with other people were of paramount importance. He developed sociometry as a way of studying roles and the relationships between people. He was interested in activity that was taking place in the present. The past is important as it influences the present. Noted for his spontaneity and creativity, Moreno valued these characteristics in others and saw them as a part of acting in a healthy way. His major concepts of personality relate to roles, the present, creativity, and energy.

sociometry A method of learning the nature of relationships between people in a group by getting feedback from members about their interpersonal preferences.

role distance By playing parts connected to or associated with an event, individuals become more objective (or more distant) from their roles.

encounter The dialogue that takes place between two individuals or two aspects of the same individual meeting another individual or another part of themselves.

tele The energy that is present in an interaction between two people in an interpersonal exchange. Moreno frequently used tele to refer to a sense of caring that developed in group members in the process of psychodrama.

PSYCHODRAMA THEORY OF PSYCHOTHERAPY

The basis of psychodrama is role playing. By playing different roles through the use of enactment, individuals can view their lives differently. They can experience catharsis, the expression of feelings that have been previously repressed. In psychodrama, individuals can play different roles. The therapist functions as a director.

director The person who manages the participants in a psychodrama. The director initiates and organizes a psychodrama and works with the protagonist, auxiliaries, and the audience.

protagonist The individual who presents a problem that will be the focus of a psychodrama.

auxiliaries Members of a group or audience who play significant roles in the life of the protagonist.

audience People present during the enactment who observe the psychodrama. They may be involved at some point as protagonists or auxiliaries.

In psychodrama there are three basic phases: the warmup, action, and discussion and sharing. During all of these phases, the therapist creates an atmosphere of sharing and trust.

warm-up Describes the purpose of psychodrama and encourages sharing among participants, often in small groups.

action Auxiliaries and the protagonist work through the protagonist's issues guided by the director.

sharing and discussion Auxiliaries and the audience share their observations with the protagonist. The director guides the process so that the feedback is helpful rather than critical.

A variety of psychodrama techniques are used to help individuals learn about their relationships with others through enactment. These can involve just the protagonist or the protagonist and one or more auxiliaries.

monodrama A dialogue with oneself in which an individual plays both parts in a scene by alternating between them.

role reversal A technique in which individuals play the part of someone else in their life to get a better perspective of their relationships with others.

double technique A role in which an auxiliary takes the part of the protagonist and expresses his or her perception of the protagonist's thoughts or feelings.

mirror technique A process in which the auxiliary tries to copy the postures, expressions, and words of the protagonist so that the protagonist can view the perceptions of his or her behavior as held by another person.

surplus reality Experiences that are not physical reality but rather may refer to fantasies, dreams, hallucinations, or relationships with imagined people.

future projection Playing a situation that could occur at some time in the future. For example, playing out an interaction with a future mother-in-law.

225

PSYCHODRAMA: A QUIZ

True/false items. Decide if the following statements are more "true" or more "false".

T F Q31. Understanding one's relationships with others is a primary focus of psychodrama's approach to understanding personality.

T F Q32. The role of the director is to encourage the audience and auxiliaries to express their unchecked emotional feelings regarding the protagonist's problems.

T F Q33. Bringing past experiences and relationships into the present through enactment is a primary purpose of psychodrama.

T F Q34. Sociometry is a systematic way of studying the relationships between people.

T F Q35. Assessment in psychodrama occurs throughout the entire process of the psychodrama, not just at the beginning.

Multiple choice items. Select the best answer from the alternatives given.

_____ Q36. Which of the following does NOT describe psychodrama?

    a. creative
    b. cognitive
    c. encounter
    d. spontaneous

_____ Q37. Psychodrama is based on a belief that individuals' personality is based in large part on

    a. each individual's relationships with his or her parents.
    b. responsibility for one's own actions.
    c. the different roles that individuals play in their lives.
    d. how individuals cope with choices that concern behaving authentically.

_____ Q38. In studying roles, Moreno used _____ as a method for determining how individuals related to each other.

    a. genograms
    b. sociograms
    c. diagrams
    d. anagrams

_____ Q39. When Mary plays the role of Margaret's grandmother and then gives up the role so that Margaret, the protagonist, can play her own grandmother, the director is using

    a. the double technique.
    b. surplus reality.
    c. future projection.
    d. role reversal.

_____ Q40. If Mary, an auxiliary, now plays the role of Margaret, the protagonist, the director is using

    a.   the double technique.
    b.   surplus reality.
    c.   future projection.
    d.   role reversal.

CREATIVE ARTS THERAPIES

SELF-INVENTORY

To compare your views of therapy with those who use creative arts therapies, put an "X" on the line that indicates how much you agree or disagree with the statement.

D   A

_____ 1. Non-verbal expressions by patients as acted out in art, music, dance, or drama can be a helpful adjunct to therapy.

_____ 2. Acting out one's problems can be a helpful therapeutic approach.

_____ 3. Listening to music or watching drama and discussing its relevance or value for individuals can contribute to personal growth.

_____ 4. Social skills can be learned by interaction with the therapist and group members while using a variety of creative arts therapies, such as art, music, or dance.

_____ 5. Having artwork that can be looked at from time to time and discussed in therapy provides a dimension that verbal expression does not.

OVERVIEW OF CREATIVE ARTS THERAPIES

By expressing themselves through the use of creative arts therapies, individuals can understand their feelings and beliefs in new ways, become more productive, develop self-esteem, develop new forms of self-expression, and/or improve their social interaction with others. The most common creative arts therapies are art, drama, dance movement, and music. The text describes each briefly, giving one or two case examples of each. The use of an artistic medium or form of expression is an element that all four have in common.

Creative arts therapy training programs exist for each of these areas. More recently there has been a trend for creative arts therapists to learn more than one form of the creative arts therapies.

Creative arts therapists often work as a part of a team. Although the traditional area of employment is psychiatric hospitals, this trend is changing with creative arts therapists working in a variety of employment settings. Regardless of setting, creative arts therapists combine their knowledge of an area of artistic skill with knowledge of psychotherapy to help patients. The four types of creative arts therapies are defined here.

art therapy A method of helping patients deal with emotional conflicts and awareness of their feelings by using a variety of art media such as paints, crayons, paper, or sculpting materials.

dance movement therapy A method of helping individuals integrate psychological and physiological processes so that they can better understand their own feelings, thoughts, and memories by expressing themselves through movement or dance.

227

dramatherapy A means of making psychological change by involving individuals in experiences that are related to theater. Sometimes patients may enact their own spontaneous drama, play the parts of a play that has been written, or observe a play and discuss it. Psychodrama is considered to be one form of dramatherapy.

music therapy Patients may listen or participate in musical experiences through singing or using musical instruments to improve emotional expression, reduce stress, or to deal nonverbally with a variety of issues.

CREATIVE ARTS THERAPIES: A QUIZ

True/false items. Decide if the following statements are more "true" or more "false".

T F Q41. Art therapists should use their art work as examples to stimulate client creativity.

T F Q42. An advantage of art therapy is that it can create physical works that can be discussed, whereas words are lost once they are spoken.

T F Q43. More than most therapists, creative arts therapists often work as part of a team.

T F Q44. Video recording equipment is too complex to be used in art therapy.

T F Q45. Music therapy involves making sounds or music, not listening to it.

Multiple choice items. Select the best answer from the alternatives given.

_____ Q46. Exaggeration is a technique that is most likely to be used in

    a. art therapy.
    b. dance movement therapy.
    c. dramatherapy.
    d. music therapy.

_____ Q47. Psychodrama can be viewed as a subset of

    a. art therapy.
    b. dance movement therapy.
    c. dramatherapy.
    d. music therapy.

_____ Q48. Dance movement therapy is least likely to include

    a. movement exercises.
    b. spontaneous movement by patients.
    c. dancing with other patients.
    d. structured dances.

_____ Q49. In creative arts therapies, suggestions for creative expression come from

    a. the client.
    b. the therapist.
    c. treatment manuals.
    d. both a and b.

228

_____ Q50. Issues of boundaries, transference, and ethics are most likely to be found in

   a.   art therapy.
   b.   dramatherapy.
   c.   music therapy.
   d.   all of the above

ANSWER KEY

Q1.	F	Q11.	F	Q21.	F	Q31.	T	Q41.	F
Q2.	F	Q12.	T	Q22.	F	Q32.	F	Q42.	T
Q3.	F	Q13.	T	Q23.	T	Q33.	T	Q43.	T
Q4.	T	Q14.	T	Q24.	T	Q34.	T	Q44.	F
Q5.	T	Q15.	T	Q25.	T	Q35.	T	Q45.	F
Q6.	c	Q16.	b	Q26.	d	Q36.	b	Q46.	b
Q7.	d	Q17.	b	Q27.	a	Q37.	c	Q47.	c
Q8.	b	Q18.	b	Q28.	b	Q38.	b	Q48.	d
Q9.	c	Q19.	a	Q29.	b	Q39.	d	Q49.	d
Q10.	b	Q20.	d	Q30.	c	Q40.	a	Q50.	b

CHAPTER 16

COMPARISON AND CRITIQUE

Because this final chapter seeks to summarize and integrate the theories discussed in previous chapters, the format in this study guide is different from that of other chapters. I provide a format for you to make notes about pertinent information that will help you prepare for a final exam.

To help you identify concepts from theories, I will give you a case example and follow it with a dialogue with the client. You will be asked to identify the theory that best fits the therapist's response. Finally, a quiz with 25 multiple choice questions will help you test your knowledge of theoretical concepts and therapeutic techniques.

BACKGROUND

Perhaps the best way to review the background for each theory is to go over the section in this study guide that summarizes the background for each theory. Doing this prior to completing the following section may be helpful.

PERSONALITY THEORY, GOALS, ASSESSMENT, AND THERAPEUTIC TECHNIQUES

These four sections represent the core of the textbook and of theories of psychotherapy and counseling in general. Personality theory, goals, assessment, and therapeutic techniques are summarized in Chapter 16 separately. Reviewing these sections should prove useful. Another way to further review the material is to test yourself on it by filling out the following charts which are designed to summarize the four areas for each chapter. Using this section to make notes and to list important concepts in the text may be helpful.

DIFFERENTIAL TREATMENT

You may find it helpful to review cases in the text to better understand the application of theory to actual psychotherapy. Table 16.5 on page 640 in the text provides a useful overview of the ways each theory can be applied to depression and anxiety. Cognitive therapy and psychoanalysis are two theories that have developed different techniques for different disorders. Behavior therapy and Adlerian therapy have done this also but to a lesser degree. Other theories apply similar approaches to different disorders, focusing more on attending to patient issues and problems than on diagnostic classification systems.

230

PSYCHOANALYSIS

PERSONALITY THEORY	GOALS AND ASSESSMENT	THERAPEUTIC TECHNIQUES
Drive Theory		
Ego Psychology		
Object Relations		
Self Psychology		
Relational Psychoanalysis		

231

JUNGIAN ANALYSIS

PERSONALITY THEORY	GOALS AND ASSESSMENT	THERAPEUTIC TECHNIQUES

ADLERIAN THERAPY

PERSONALITY THEORY	GOALS AND ASSESSMENT	THERAPEUTIC TECHNIQUES

EXISTENTIAL THERAPY

PERSONALITY THEORY	GOALS AND ASSESSMENT	THERAPEUTIC TECHNIQUES

PERSON-CENTERED THERAPY

PERSONALITY THEORY	GOALS AND ASSESSMENT	THERAPEUTIC TECHNIQUES

GESTALT THERAPY

PERSONALITY THEORY	GOALS AND ASSESSMENT	THERAPEUTIC TECHNIQUES

BEHAVIOR THERAPY

PERSONALITY THEORY	GOALS AND ASSESSMENT	THERAPEUTIC TECHNIQUES

RATIONAL EMOTIVE BEHAVIOR THERAPY

PERSONALITY THEORY	GOALS AND ASSESSMENT	THERAPEUTIC TECHNIQUES

COGNITIVE THERAPY

PERSONALITY THEORY	GOALS AND ASSESSMENT	THERAPEUTIC TECHNIQUES

REALITY THERAPY

PERSONALITY THEORY	GOALS AND ASSESSMENT	THERAPEUTIC TECHNIQUES

CONSTRUCTIVIST APPROACHES

PERSONALITY THEORY	GOALS AND ASSESSMENT	THERAPEUTIC TECHNIQUES
Solution-focused therapy		
Narrative therapy		

FEMINIST THERAPY

PERSONALITY THEORY	GOALS AND ASSESSMENT	THERAPEUTIC TECHNIQUES

FAMILY THERAPY

PERSONALITY THEORY	GOALS AND ASSESSMENT	THERAPEUTIC TECHNIQUES
Bowen's intergenerational		
Minuchin's structural		
Haley's strategic		
Experiential		

INTEGRATIVE THERAPIES

PERSONALITY THEORY	GOALS AND ASSESSMENT	THERAPEUTIC TECHNIQUES
Prochaska's transtheoretical approach		
Wachtel's cyclical psychodynamics		
Lazarus's multimodal therapy		

BRIEF THERAPIES

More than any other theory, psychoanalysis has been applied to short term psychotherapeutic treatment. Brief psychodynamic therapy varies in length from 12 to 50 sessions. Most brief psychoanalytical approaches are 12 to 20 sessions. One of over a dozen short-term psychoanalytical therapies is described in the text.

Brief approaches have not usually been applied to Jungian or person-centered therapies. Gestalt, Adlerian, and reality therapy tend to be briefer than psychodynamic and Jungian therapies.

Cognitive, behavioral, and REBT therapies are generally brief. However, the number of problems, their severity, and their strength influence the length of therapy for these theories.

238

Family systems therapies tend to be brief. A few, the MRI model and the long brief therapy of the Milan school, are very brief, often less than 6 to 10 sessions. Solution-focused and narrative therapy are also brief, meetings may not be weekly and may become less frequent as therapy proceeds.

CURRENT TRENDS AND INNOVATIONS

The text has focused on three specific trends in terms of the way they affect many theories: treatment manuals, common factors, and research-supported psychological treatments and constructivism. Common factors and the two major types of common factors are defined here.

common factors Factors that are common to changes that take place in psychotherapy and counseling. These include participant and relationship factors.

participant factors In a common factors approach, characteristics of the client or therapist, such as gender, ethnicity, attachment style, coping style, resistance, and expectations.

relationship factors In a common factors approach, attributes of the therapeutic interaction that include the therapist's skills that affect the client's improvement.

Reviewing answers to questions about current trends and innovations in this study guide will help to remind you of specific trends within each theory.

USING THE THEORY WITH OTHER THEORIES

Most practitioners of a theory often look outside of it to add new techniques or concepts. A notable exception is person-centered theory that continues to focus on genuineness, empathy, and unconditional positive regard as the only conditions that are necessary and sufficient for change. Reality therapy has a focus on responsibility and planning that tends to limit its use of techniques from other theories. Feminist and existential therapies tend to borrow heavily from other theories as they have relatively few of their own techniques. The three integrative approaches in Chapter 17 demonstrate different ways of incorporating concepts and methods from various theoretical approaches.

RESEARCH

Research has not been addressed in this study guide, in part because research is summarized briefly in the text and is difficult to summarize or abstract further. However, I have done this in Table 16.7 on page 647. As this table shows, much research has been done with cognitive, behavior, and REBT therapies. Some research has been conducted with psychoanalysis, person-centered, and family systems therapies. Relatively little research has been done with other theories of therapy. Two specific concepts that are useful in understanding research issues are process and outcome research.

process research The study of various aspects of how psychotherapy works. Examples include comparing two or more psychotherapeutic techniques and monitoring a change in personality as a result of the introduction of a technique. It is used in contrast to outcome research.

outcome research A systematic investigation of the effectiveness of a theory of psychotherapy or a comparison of techniques or theories of psychotherapy, in contrast to process research.

GENDER ISSUES

Feminist therapy has had the greatest influence on gender issues within the field of psychotherapy. However, within each theory this issue has been addressed to varying degrees. The earliest theory, psychoanalysis, was the one that was most often criticized by theorists and practitioners for its gender bias. Many feminist psychodynamic writers have added to the literature on psychoanalysis.

239

In the following space, it would be helpful for you to summarize your comments from the Special Topics section of this study guide that refers to gender to provide you with an overview of how gender issues affect therapy.

_____

_____

_____

_____

_____

MULTICULTURAL ISSUES

Clients who sought therapy prior to the 1950s tended to be White and have at least a moderate income. In recent years, there has been an emphasis on the need to provide therapy for individuals from a variety of cultures. Feminist therapy has probably done more than other theories to provide techniques and support for mental health services to people from a variety of backgrounds. Asian therapy, discussed in Chapter 15, has also had an influence on an awareness of cultural differences and the application of meditation and other methods. Jung and Erikson were particularly interested in studying other cultures and learning about how these cultures could help inform their own theoretical development.

Family systems therapists have been quite aware of the different traditions and customs that affect family interaction. Behavioral, cognitive, and REBT theories have been slower to study the relationship between culture and their theoretical approaches.

In the following space, it would be helpful for you to summarize your comments from the Special Topics section of this study guide that concerns multicultural issues to provide you with an overview of how culture affects therapy.

_____

_____

_____

_____

_____

GROUP THERAPY

Some theories, such as person-centered, gestalt, and feminist therapy clearly value the importance of group therapy. Others provide group approaches to a variety of problems. Jungian therapists tend to see group as an adjunct to individual therapy. Table 16.8 on pages 651 and 652 summarizes each theory's approach to group therapy.

CASE EXAMPLE OF CHRIS

The purpose of the following case study is for you to practice identifying personality theory concepts and techniques from different theories that have been described in the text. This case is not meant as a demonstration of how to do therapy, but merely as a way to learn about and test your ability to identify theoretical concepts and techniques. I will briefly describe a case, then I will provide a client statement followed by a therapeutic statement or question. I will ask you to choose the theory that fits with that therapeutic response.

240

Chris is a 42-year-old married woman with a 10-year-old son and a 12-year-old daughter. She works part-time in an insurance office, mainly when her children are in school. Before she was married, 12 years ago, she had worked at a small office. Her employers were pleased to have her back when she decided three years ago that she wanted to return to work part time.

Her husband, Desmond, is currently unemployed. He had worked for the phone company until nine months ago. After repeated warnings and a suspension, he was terminated for drunkenness on the job. His drinking has been a considerable problem for the past five years. When drunk, he gets violent, yelling at Chris and hitting her. At those times, he blames her for his problems. He is particularly critical of her cooking and complains about the lack of cleanliness in the house. He also blames her for the problems that their daughter, Amanda, is having at school which include not doing her work and talking in class.

Chris agrees that she is responsible for many of these problems. Since childhood, she has had low self-esteem. Her father, like Desmond, was an alcoholic. He was often critical of Chris, her brother, and their mother. Her father died in an automobile accident when Chris was 17. A shy child, Chris often hid in her room, sometimes in her closet, when she heard her father come home drunk. She could tell by the way he opened the back door to the house, how drunk he was. As a child, Chris was often sickly. She complained of a nervous stomach and heart palpitations. She has had these symptoms all of her life.

Chris has been very anxious since she was hospitalized for a concussion. Desmond hit her with his fist. She fell back and hit her head against the refrigerator, causing her to be hospitalized overnight for observation. Since she has come home, she has been very anxious. She complains of headaches, possibly related to the concussion. Her stomach is upset, and she has little appetite. At 5'4", she is very thin, weighing 101 pounds. She feels tense in her neck and shoulders and has heart palpitations frequently. She now seeks help from a therapist for her anxiety symptoms, her lack of self-esteem, and her fears of Desmond's violent behavior.

In the following questions, choose the theory that most closely fits the therapist's conceptualization or response.

QUESTIONS ABOUT CHRIS USING DIFFERENT THEORIES OF PSYCHOTHERAPY AND COUNSELING

1. C: I seem to live in constant fear of doing something wrong or saying something wrong. I feel miserable.

    T: Chris, tell me more about what you are afraid of. (T thinks: I want to learn specific details about Chris's fears.)

    a. behavior therapy
    b. gestalt therapy
    c. existential therapy
    d. person-centered therapy

2. C: I am afraid of the stove boiling over, of my children getting sick, of giving the wrong phone messages at work, and of Desmond hitting me.

    T: Be aware how you clench your fist now. Could you put words to that clenched fist?

    a. behavior therapy
    b. gestalt therapy
    c. existential therapy
    d. person-centered therapy

3. C: I feel so angry. I want to do something, but I don't think anything will work. I have got to do something about my fears of cooking, of making mistakes at work (cries).

   T: You are so full of rage now, but there seems no place for it. Then you quickly worry about making mistakes.

   a. behavior therapy
   b. gestalt therapy
   c. existential therapy
   d. person-centered therapy

4. C: I am so worried about making mistakes. I check and recheck my work at the agency. My boss, Bob, has never been critical, but I am so worried about making mistakes. Sometimes I lose my concentration and daydream. I often daydream of this ugly vampire with an axe killing me and the whole office.

   T: It is possible that this monster, a common symbol, represents the anger inside of you, aggressive impulses that you are not aware of.

   a. gestalt therapy
   b. Jungian therapy
   c. object relations therapy
   d. reality therapy

5. C: Ever since I have been a child, I have dreamed of monsters at night and had daydreams about them. The dreams always frighten me. They were really bad when I was younger. I would hide under my covers and suck my thumb.

   T: Tell me more about how you behaved when you woke up then. (T thinks: I wonder if she regressed to an earlier period of development.)

   a. cognitive therapy
   b. ego psychology
   c. object relations therapy
   d. Jungian therapy
   e. existential therapy

6. C: I remember a time when I cried and Mom came; I felt fine until she left. Then I got scared again, afraid something bad would happen.

   T: Having your mother there provided comfort for you. (T thinks: Her mother was an important holding environment, but she wasn't there often enough, it seems.)

   a. cognitive therapy
   b. ego psychology
   c. object relations therapy
   d. Jungian therapy
   e. existential therapy

7. C: My mother had to work a lot. I can remember standing at the window waiting for her to come home. Sometimes she would be late and I would get scared, wondering if she had been killed in a car accident.

    T: Tell me more about your thoughts about the possibility that your mother could die and thoughts about the possibility of your own eventual death.

    a. cognitive therapy
    b. ego psychology
    c. object relations therapy
    d. Jungian therapy
    e. existential therapy

8. C: When I had thoughts about my mother dying, I would get very frightened and be so scared. I wouldn't know what to do if she died.

    T: Can you feel your neck tightening and your breathing change? Can you finish this sentence? "I'm aware that ..."

    a. behavior therapy
    b. gestalt therapy
    c. existential therapy
    d. person-centered therapy

9. C: I am aware that I feel so frightened now. I am here with you, and I feel safe. But I think I was aware of how scared I was as a child sometimes. That scare comes back to me at times when I'm at home and Desmond starts drinking.

    T: The safety you feel here is in such contrast with the terror you experienced as a child and now with your husband. (The therapist responds in a way that helps Chris think about her own mortality and the threat her husband poses to her own life.)

    a. behavior therapy
    b. gestalt therapy
    c. existential therapy
    d. person-centered therapy

10. C: I think: I must be strong for the children. I'm so weak, such a failure.

    T: It would be nice to be strong for the children, but you don't HAVE TO be strong for them.

    a. Adlerian therapy
    b. behavior therapy
    c. cognitive therapy
    d. reality therapy
    e. REBT

11. C: But I know that they expect me to be with them all the time and take care of them like my mother did sometimes.

    T: You seem to be able to read their minds, but it really isn't possible to know what they are thinking, is it?

    a. Adlerian therapy
    b. behavior therapy
    c. cognitive therapy
    d. reality therapy
    e. REBT

243

12. C: No, I want to be strong for them. I want to be confident with them and not anxious like I am.

   T: I think that it would be helpful for you to act as if you are strong, to pretend that you know how to discipline them, how to encourage them.

   a. Adlerian therapy
   b. behavior therapy
   c. cognitive therapy
   d. reality therapy
   e. REBT

13. C: When my son, Paul, acts up, I get so tense. I'm not sure what to do.

   T: That might be a good time to try the relaxation procedures that I have taught you.

   a. Adlerian therapy
   b. behavior therapy
   c. cognitive therapy
   d. reality therapy
   e. REBT

14. C: I will try them, but I always mess up everything I do.

   T: Perhaps, this thought "I always mess up everything I do" is an overgeneralization. Do you mess up everything that you do at work?

   a. Adlerian therapy
   b. behavior therapy
   c. cognitive therapy
   d. reality therapy
   e. REBT

15. C: I don't mess up everything I do. I do what I need to do at work.

   T: But those are someone else's needs. Let's look at your own needs, such as your needs for belongingness and for fun.

   a. Adlerian therapy
   b. behavior therapy
   c. cognitive therapy
   d. reality therapy
   e. REBT

16. C: I would feel a lot better if I had time to enjoy myself, like going out dancing with my husband. But when we go out, he gets smashed.

   T: Well, it might be helpful for us to consider how best to work with his problems. (T thinks: Desmond seems to have a great deal of difficulty separating his intellectual processes from his emotional ones.)

   a. Bowen's intergenerational approach
   b. Minuchin's structural approach
   c. Haley's strategic approach
   d. solution-focused therapy
   e. narrative therapy

244

17. C: He always gets drunk when we go out, so it would be hard to work with his problems.

    T: Can you think of an exception to this when you go out and he is not drunk?

    a. Bowen's intergenerational approach
    b. Minuchin's structural approach
    c. Haley's strategic approach
    d. solution-focused therapy
    e. narrative therapy

18. C: Yes, I went to Paul's school with Desmond for a teacher's conference. He was fine. He was sober. He asked the teacher good questions. He really cares about Paul. I worry because he isn't close to Amanda.

    T: Perhaps the four of you can come in and we can approach this as a family. (T thinks: If the family comes in together, perhaps I can join with them and help them change their current boundaries.)

    a. Bowen's intergenerational approach
    b. Minuchin's structural approach
    c. Haley's strategic approach
    d. solution-focused therapy
    e. narrative therapy

19. Taking the entire sequence of 18 therapeutic responses, the therapist's approach could best be described as similar to

    a. Prochaska's theoretical integration.
    b. Wachtel's cyclical psychodynamics.
    c. Lazarus's multimodal therapy.
    d. none of these.

20. If this were an actual therapeutic dialogue instead of an exercise, how would you rate the therapist's pattern of responses?

    a. excellent
    b. good
    c. average
    d. terrible

The answer to questions 19 and 20 is "d". The therapist changes his theoretical approach with each statement. There is no rationale for the therapist's switch from one theory to another. Chapter 17 describes appropriate integrative approaches that use more than one theory. These approaches do not present a random, unsystematic approach to combining therapies as this dialogue does. If the current dialogue were to continue, both the therapist and Chris are likely to end up quite confused about the goals and methods used in therapy. Contrast the clarity of theory presented in the other chapters with the lack of direction and purpose of therapy in this exercise.

STRENGTHS AND LIMITATIONS

You may find it helpful to summarize your view of the strengths and limitations of each theory. You may do this by looking at the strength and limitation sections from each chapter in this study guide and by consulting the Critique of theories on pages 606 to 615 of the text.

	STRENGTHS	LIMITATIONS
Psychoanalysis		
Jungian Analysis		
Adlerian Therapy		
Existential Therapy		
Person-Centered Therapy		
Gestalt Therapy		
Behavior Therapy		
Rational Emotive Behavior Therapy		
Cognitive Therapy		
Reality Therapy		
Constructivist Approaches		

Feminist Therapy		
Family Therapy		
Other Psychotherapies (Asian, Body, Interpersonal, Psychodrama, Creative Arts)		
Integrative Approaches		

A QUIZ ON ALL THEORIES OF THERAPY

The following 25 multiple choice questions cover all theories except those described in Chapter 15. Most questions ask you to identify which theory a certain concept or technique is associated with.

_____ Q1. Social interest was a characteristic that _____ believed healthy individuals should possess.

    a. Alfred Adler
    b. Erik Erikson
    c. Sigmund Freud
    d. Carl Jung
    e. Anna Freud

_____ Q2. The shadow is a(n)

    a. alter ego in ego psychology.
    b. former self in self psychology.
    c. archetype in Jungian psychology.
    d. elusive contact boundary in gestalt therapy.
    e. difficult concept in person-centered therapy.

_____ Q3. Analyzing the client's life style is an assessment approach in

    a. Adlerian therapy.
    b. object relations psychology.
    c. Jungian analysis.
    d. existential therapy.
    e. behavior therapy.

_____ Q4. Projective techniques, such as the Rorschach Test, are LEAST likely to be used in

    a. psychoanalysis.
    b. behavior therapy.
    c. Jungian analysis.
    d. existential therapy.
    e. person-centered therapy.

_____ Q5. The therapy that is specifically designed to treat individuals with narcissistic characteristics is

    a. drive theory.
    b. self psychology.
    c. Jungian analysis.
    d. existential therapy.
    e. feminist therapy.

_____ Q6. The therapy that is most likely to ask a client to put words to his tight stomach is

    a. existential therapy.
    b. behavior therapy.
    c. gestalt therapy.
    d. feminist therapy.
    e. person-centered therapy.

_____ Q7. Client: I can't stand the way my mother is always butting into my relationship with my husband.

Therapist: You are so angry at your mother for not respecting you and interfering with your relationship with your husband.

The therapist's response is most consistent with

    a. existential therapy.
    b. behavior therapy.
    c. gestalt therapy.
    d. feminist therapy.
    e. person-centered therapy.

_____ Q8. Introjection, swallowing whole the opinions of others, is a concept that is most consistent with

    a. existential therapy.
    b. drive theory.
    c. gestalt therapy.
    d. feminist therapy.
    e. object relations.

_____ Q9. Stimulus control, a change method in Prochaska's transtheoretical approach, has been taken from

    a. cognitive therapy.
    b. behavior therapy.
    c. rational emotive behavior therapy.
    d. feminist therapy.
    e. reality therapy.

_____ Q10. A goal of _____ is to help clients learn a philosophy that will help them reduce the chances that they will be disturbed by overwhelming irrational thoughts.

    a. cognitive therapy
    b. behavior therapy
    c. rational emotive behavior therapy
    d. feminist therapy
    e. reality therapy

_____ Q11. Power analysis is a technique used most often in

    a.   cognitive therapy.
    b.   behavior therapy.
    c.   rational emotive behavior therapy.
    d.   feminist therapy.
    e.   reality therapy.

_____ Q12. Making plans and following through on them is a characteristic of

    a.   cognitive therapy.
    b.   behavior therapy.
    c.   rational emotive behavior therapy.
    d.   feminist therapy.
    e.   reality therapy.

_____ Q13. The therapy that is LEAST concerned about using techniques is

    a.   existential therapy.
    b.   Jungian therapy.
    c.   gestalt therapy.
    d.   feminist therapy.
    e.   reality therapy.

_____ Q14. Questioning is a technique that is LEAST likely to be used in

    a.   existential therapy.
    b.   behavior therapy.
    c.   gestalt therapy.
    d.   feminist therapy.
    e.   person-centered therapy.

_____ Q15. Guided discovery is an active technique most often associated with

    a.   cognitive therapy.
    b.   behavior therapy.
    c.   gestalt therapy.
    d.   feminist therapy.
    e.   reality therapy.

_____ Q16. A sociological or political approach to understanding the client's problem is most likely to be found in

    a.   cognitive therapy.
    b.   behavior therapy.
    c.   gestalt therapy.
    d.   feminist therapy.
    e.   reality therapy.

_____ Q17. Which of these therapies is LEAST likely to use role playing as a therapeutic technique?

    a.   cognitive therapy
    b.   behavior therapy
    c.   gestalt therapy
    d.   feminist therapy
    e.   person-centered therapy

249

_____ Q18. To become a more authentic individual is the goal of

     a.   existential therapy.
     b.   behavior therapy.
     c.   gestalt therapy.
     d.   feminist therapy.
     e.   person-centered therapy.

_____ Q19. Which of the following is most likely to have a different therapeutic approach depending on the client's psychological diagnosis?

     a.   cognitive therapy
     b.   behavior therapy
     c.   gestalt therapy
     d.   feminist therapy
     e.   reality therapy

_____ Q20. Client: I have to get my boss to like me and appreciate my work.

Therapist: It would be nice to have your boss like you, but you don't HAVE to get him to like you and your work.

The therapist who made this statement is most likely practicing

     a.   cognitive therapy.
     b.   behavior therapy.
     c.   rational emotive behavior therapy.
     d.   feminist therapy.
     e.   reality therapy.

_____ Q21. Taking responsibility for oneself and meeting one's own needs without interfering with the needs of others is most likely to be a goal of

     a.   cognitive therapy.
     b.   behavior therapy.
     c.   rational emotive behavior therapy.
     d.   feminist therapy.
     e.   reality therapy.

_____ Q22. Although disputing is a technique that cognitive therapists might use, it is particularly associated with

     a.   behavior therapy.
     b.   rational emotive behavior therapy.
     c.   feminist therapy.
     d.   reality therapy.

_____ Q23. Many therapies can be used alone. Which of the following cannot be used alone?

     a.   cognitive therapy
     b.   behavior therapy
     c.   gestalt therapy
     d.   feminist therapy
     e.   reality therapy

_____ Q24. The psychoanalytic concept of splitting is most similar to which one of these concepts from cognitive therapy?

    a.   all or none thinking
    b.   labeling
    c.   magnification
    d.   Socratic dialogue

_____ Q25. Which of the following theories is LEAST similar to psychoanalysis?

    a.   Jungian analysis
    b.   Adlerian therapy
    c.   Bowen's intergenerational approach
    d.   reality therapy

ANSWER KEY

1.	a	11.	c
2.	b	12.	a
3.	d	13.	b
4.	b	14.	c
5.	b	15.	d
6.	c	16.	a
7.	e	17.	d
8.	b	18.	b
9.	c	19.	d
10.	e	20.	d

QUIZ

Q1.	a	Q11.	d	Q21.	e
Q2.	c	Q12.	e	Q22.	b
Q3.	a	Q13.	a	Q23.	d
Q4.	b	Q14.	e	Q24.	a
Q5.	b	Q15.	a	Q25.	d
Q6.	c	Q16.	d		
Q7.	e	Q17.	e		
Q8.	c	Q18.	a		
Q9.	b	Q19.	a		
Q10.	c	Q20.	c		

251

CHAPTER 17

INTEGRATIVE THEORIES

Three of the most well known integrative approaches are presented. Each has a very different view of how to integrate theories. In this chapter of the Student Manual, the case of Rose is used to help you better understand three integrative approaches. These are summarized and questions are asked about each of the three integrative theories.

INTEGRATIVE THERAPIES SELF-INVENTORY

Directions: By comparing your beliefs about personality and therapy to those of integrative theories, you should have a clearer idea of how much you will need to suspend your beliefs or change attitudes to understand integrative theories. You may find it helpful to complete this section before and after you read the chapter. In this way you can see if your views have changed. There are no correct answers, only an opportunity to express your views.

Put an "X" on the line so that it indicates how much you agree or disagree with the statement: A=Agree, D=Disagree.

D　　　　　　A

_____ 1. Several theories can be combined together to be used in psychotherapy and counseling.

_____ 2. Theories provide a consistent way to conceptualize client problems.

_____ 3. Using more than one theory can be helpful in understanding the personality of a client.

_____ 4. Concepts from psychoanalysis and behavior therapy can be combined while still presenting a consistent theoretical approach.

_____ 5. Using only one theory can limit a therapist's flexibility.

_____ 6. Concepts from many theories can be combined to make an entirely different theory that is internally consistent.

_____ 7. If I were counseling, I would want to use more than one theory.

_____ 8. Some theories are better than others for certain types of client problems.

_____ 9. Research is important in determining which theories to use with clients.

_____ 10. Counseling or therapy without a grounding in theory tends to make it difficult to develop clear goals and know which techniques should be used with clients.

252

_____ 11. In using several theories, it is helpful to assess the client's readiness for change.

_____ 12. Integrative theories can draw from theories as diverse as Adlerian, psychoanalytic, REBT, behavioral, and cognitive.

_____ 13. Certain theories may only work for certain types of problems.

_____ 14. Using many theories can be helpful so that the therapist can work with feelings, behaviors, thoughts, sensation, and imagination.

_____ 15. Using one theory of personality and different therapeutic techniques from many theories gives many treatment possibilities while retaining a consistent way of treating patients.

TYPES OF THERAPEUTIC INTEGRATION

There are several different approaches to integrating theories of psychotherapy and counseling. In this chapter, three are described: theoretical integration, assimilative, and technical eclecticism.

theoretical integration A psychotherapeutic approach that combines the personality theory concepts and techniques of two or more theories.

assimilative approach A psychotherapeutic approach in which personality theory and the psychotherapeutic techniques of one theory is the major approach, and one or more other theories are used to supplement it.

technical eclecticism A psychotherapeutic approach in which one personality theory is selected and techniques may be used from any theory, but they are used in a way that is consistent with the personality theory that has been selected.

In the next section, I will describe the case of Rose, a 33-year-old woman suffering from depression. Then I will summarize three different theoretical approaches to integration: Prochaska's transtheoretical approach, which also uses theoretical integration, Wachtel's cyclical psychodynamics, which uses the theoretical integration method, and Lazarus's multimodal therapy, which fits the technical eclecticism model. Then I will ask questions so that you can respond from a specific integrative point of view. There are many systematic approaches to integrating theories of therapy. Each approach has several advantages.

CASE EXAMPLE OF ROSE

Rose is a 33-year-old married woman who reports symptoms of anxiety and depression. Four years ago, she was an electrical engineer. She enjoyed the challenging problems on which she worked on a daily basis. However, even at that time, she would worry about getting projects in on time and worry about whether or not they would be well-received. Now that she is at home raising her three-year-old son, Alfred, she finds that she is worrying more, but often about things that she considers trivial. Her husband, Raoul, is a marketing manager who works long days. He feels that Rose's worries and her increasingly depressed behavior is incomprehensible. He sees Rose as having plenty of time and little to worry about, as he does not expect her to be earning an income now.

Raoul's lack of understanding has contributed to Rose's stress level. She often feels tense when she wakes up. Sometimes she can feel her heart beating. At other times, she finds herself breathing quickly, while at the same time feeling tension in her neck and shoulders. When she is tense, she finds that she is irritable with Alfred when he acts the way three-year-olds typically act.

In the last few months, Rose has become increasingly depressed. She sometimes feels that she has no value, that her husband and son would be better off without her. She has less energy to spend time with Alfred. Getting out of bed is difficult. Sometimes she doesn't change out of her nightgown until afternoon.

Rose recognizes that she is more anxious and depressed than she has ever been and wishes to get therapeutic help.

WACHTEL'S CYCLICAL PSYCHODYNAMICS

At its most basic, Wachtel's cyclical psychodynamics takes two theories and combines them. The personality theories are combined to provide an assessment of patients' problems and an understanding of their personalities. The techniques are combined in prescribed ways to bring about change. Sometimes more than two theories are used in this way. Concepts from psychoanalytic theory are combined with those from behavior therapy (and also cognitive and family systems approaches). The cyclical aspect of Wachtel's view refers to the belief that psychological problems create problems in behavior, and problems in behavior create psychological conflicts or problems.

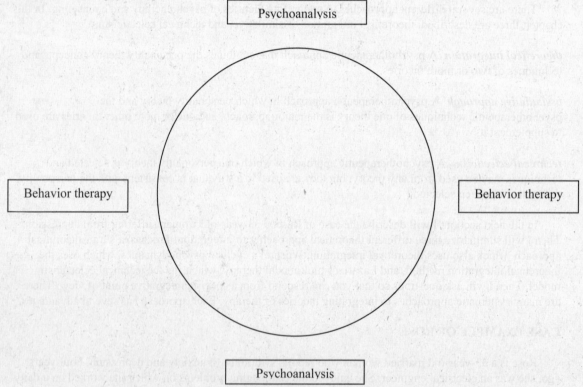

The text presents an overview of Wachtels's cyclical psychodynamic model. That overview should be sufficient to show how a therapist draws concepts from other theories to develop his or her system.

Try to use Wachtel's cyclical psychodynamic model with Rose. Answer the following questions as if you were Rose's therapist.

254

QUESTIONS ABOUT USING WACHTEL'S CYCLICAL PSYCHODYNAMIC APPROACH WITH ROSE

1. When Rose comes into your office, she describes her problems and her concern that dealing with her mother's alcoholism as a child may have contributed to her current problems. Trying to understand the development of her problem, you are likely to take this approach.

    a. behavioral
    b. existential
    c. Jungian
    d. psychoanalytic

2. When Rose develops an understanding of her problems, she then wants to address the problems of her feelings of bodily tension. Which theory of therapy are you most likely to use with her?

    a. behavioral
    b. existential
    c. psychoanalytic
    d. reality

3. Rose starts to see the impact that her anxiety, especially her bodily tension, is having on Raoul and Alfred. What method of therapy are you likely to use to help her develop insight into herself?

    a. behavioral
    b. existential
    c. psychoanalytic
    d. reality

4. Which of these statements best describe your style of doing psychotherapy with Rose using cyclical psychodynamics?

    a. assess Rose's problems using psychoanalysis; use behavior therapy to make changes
    b. assess Rose's problems using psychoanalysis and behavior therapy; make changes using behavior therapy
    c. assess Rose's problems and make changes using behavior therapy; use psychoanalysis only as a way of understanding her background
    d. assess Rose's problems using psychoanalysis and behavior therapy; use them both to make therapeutic change

PROCHASKA'S TRANSTHEORETICAL APPROACH

Perhaps the most well known transtheoretical approach, Prochaska's system, focuses on readiness for change, types of problems, and change processes. The change processes have been adapted from different theories of therapy and are applied only to certain types of problems or stages. For this approach, theories serve as a source of developing therapeutic techniques and are not used directly as they are in theoretical integration and in technical eclecticism. To provide an overview of Prochaska's transtheoretical approach, the five stages of readiness for change, the five levels of problems, and the ten change processes are listed here.

255

READINESS FOR CHANGE	TYPES OF PROBLEMS (and theories that fit them best)	CHANGE PROCESSES
pre-contemplation - considering, but not willing to change	*symptoms/situational*: behavior therapy, solution-focused therapy	*consciousness-raising* - therapist interprets, gentle confrontation
contemplation - seriously considering , but not committed to change	*maladaptive cognitions*: Adlerian therapy, rational emotive behavior therapy, cognitive therapy	*catharsis/dramatic relief* - acing out problems, such as the empty chair
preparation - intending to change and making some changes	*interpersonal conflicts*: family therapy (general), interpersonal therapy, reality therapy, psychodrama	*self-reevaluation* - individual evaluates what must be done to change
action - commitment is clear and shows consistent change		*environmental reevaluation* - looking at the role of others in the problem
	family systems/conflicts: Bowenian, structural, strategic, experiential and humanistic family system therapies	
maintenance - client works to continue change and prevent relapse		*self-liberation* - choosing new ways to address problems
	intrapersonal conflicts: psychoanalytic therapy, Jungian therapy, existential therapy, gestalt therapy, narrative therapy, creative arts therapies	*social liberation* - making social changes
		counter conditioning - learning new ways of responding
		stimulus control - controlling how one deals with stressful situations
		contingency management - reinforcing and shaping behavior
		helping relationships - maintaining a good therapeutic relationship

The text presents just an outline of Prochaska's well-developed transtheoretical model. That overview should be sufficient to show how this integrative theory can be used with clients.

Try to use Prochaska's transtheoretical approach with Rose. Answer the following questions as if you were Rose's therapist.

QUESTIONS ABOUT USING PROCHASKA'S TRANSTHEORETICAL APPROACH WITH ROSE

5. In your first session with Rose, you will try to assess these major issues. Which of these three would be of paramount importance to assess at the beginning of therapy?

    a.   readiness for change
    b.   levels of problems
    c.   change processes

256

6. Although all are important, readiness for change (a) is important to assess early in therapy. Rose says that she has been thinking about changes that she wants to make in her life and is determined to make therapy work. Which of these stages of change is Rose most likely to be in?

   a. pre-contemplation
   b. contemplation
   c. preparation
   d. action
   e. maintenance

7. Rose says that she wants to address her physical symptoms first: her heart palpitations and her bodily tensions. Which level of problems does this physical feeling refer to?

   a. symptoms
   b. maladaptive thoughts
   c. interpersonal conflicts
   d. intrapersonal conflicts
   e. family conflicts

8. Which of these levels of problems does Prochaska's transtheoretical approach prefer to address first??

   a. symptoms
   b. maladaptive thoughts
   c. interpersonal conflicts
   d. intrapersonal conflicts
   e. family conflicts

9. To treat her heart palpitations and bodily tension which one of these four change processes are you most likely to adopt?

   a. consciousness raising
   b. self-liberation
   c. social liberation
   d. stimulus control

10. As you work with Rose on stimulus control (d), she is better able to manage her anxiety. Rose now considers how she wants to change her feelings of depression and wants to take steps to change how she acts with her son, husband, and other family members. Which change process would most likely be appropriate for you to address with Rose?

   a. consciousness-raising
   b. self reevaluation
   c. social liberation
   d. stimulus control

LAZARUS'S MULTIMODAL THERAPY

In multimodal therapy, one personality theory forms the basis for assessing patients' problems and understanding their personalities. Specifically, Arnold Lazarus uses personality theory concepts from social cognitive theory and takes techniques from many other theories which he applies in a manner that is consistent with social cognitive theory. In his theory, Lazarus assesses seven modalities, gathered from many theories, which he also uses in producing therapeutic change. The seven major modalities are represented in the acronym BASIC I.D.

BASIC I.D. An acronym that includes the seven fundamental concepts of multimodal therapy: Behavior, Affect, Sensation, Imagery, Cognition, Interpersonal relationships, and Drugs/biology.

Behavior: Habits, responses, and reactions that can be observed and measured.

Affect: A variety of emotions and moods, such as being depressed, angry, anxious, happy, helpless, tense, and lonely.

Sensation: The basic senses of seeing, hearing, touching, tasting, and smelling, and negative sensations that may include headaches, dizziness, numbness, stomach trouble, hallucinations, or sexual disturbances.

Imagery: Fantasies, mental pictures, images, and dreams. Body image and self-image are given special attention.

Cognition: Thoughts, ideas, values, and opinions. Of importance are negative thoughts about oneself, such as being stupid, crazy, unattractive, or worthless.

Interpersonal relationships: How one interacts with family, friends, colleagues, teachers, or others.

Drugs/biology: The entire area of health and medical concerns. Physiological functioning and drugs (prescribed or unprescribed) are considered when understanding the individual's personality.

In order to assess client problems and to make changes in the seven modalities, Lazarus has developed techniques that help in the observation of modalities and in tracking clients as they switch modalities.

firing order The sequence of modalities that occurs when an individual perceives an event, for example, Interpersonal-Sensation-Imagery.

tracking Observing and responding to the sequence or firing order of the seven modalities (BASIC I.D.) of different clients.

bridging Being aware of and responding to a client's current modality before introducing another modality to the client.

Two other techniques are helpful in multimodal therapy. Time tripping deals with the Imagery modality, and the deserted island technique can be helpful in learning more about all of the modalities.

time tripping A technique in which clients are asked to picture themselves going backward or forward in time to deal with events or issues.

deserted island technique A fantasy experience in which clients are asked what the therapist would learn if he or she were alone with the client on a deserted island. It is designed to help the therapist learn more about the client's seven modalities.

The text presents an overview of Lazarus's multimodal therapy. This description should help to demonstrate the way in which Lazarus uses the seven modalities.

Try to use Lazarus's multimodal therapy model with Rose. Answer the following questions as if you were Rose's therapist.

11. Rose says to you: "Sometimes what happens to me is I snap at Alfred and then feel anxious, as well as angry at myself. Then I think, you really are crazy."

    Please identify the three modes that Rose is using.

    a. imagery, sensation, cognition
    b. behavior, affect, cognition
    c. behavior, sensation, imagery
    d. interpersonal relationships, imagery, affect

12. The sequence in which the modalities occur in the client's speech is referred to as

    a. bridging.
    b. firing order.
    c. time tripping.
    d. tracking.

13. As you follow Rose's shift from one modality to another, you are using

    a. bridging.
    b. firing order.
    c. time tripping.
    d. tracking.

14. When you respond to Rose, you say "When you make an impatient or angry remark to Alfred, you not only get more tense, but you blame yourself in harsh ways."

    In making this response, multimodal therapists would say that you are

    a. listening to Rose's modalities, and responding to each of them in the order that she gives them.
    b. being genuine and empathic with Rose's pain.
    c. initiating a cognitive therapy intervention.
    d. making a behavioral intervention consistent with social cognitive theory.

15. The answer to the preceding question is "a". What term do multimodal therapists use for listening to a client's modalities and using these modalities to influence the therapist's reply?

    a. bridging
    b. firing order
    c. time tripping
    d. tracking

16. You say to Rose: "Imagine yourself going forward in time to talk to Alfred about his tantrums when he is older."

    What multimodal technique are you using?

    a. bridging.
    b. firing order.
    c. time tripping.
    d. tracking

17. What modality does the technique in Question 16 use?

    a. affect
    b. behavior
    c. imagery
    d. sensation

SPECIAL TOPICS

OE1. Why do you think therapists continue to be attracted to the idea of integrating two or more theories into their work? (683)

_____

_____

OE2. How could Wachtel's cyclical psychodynamic approach include a sensitivity to multicultural issues? (685 to 686)

_____

_____

OE3. How does the construct of gender fit into the use of integrative therapies? (685)

_____

_____

OE4. What multicultural issues can complicate the use of integrative therapies? (685 to 686)

_____

_____

_____

OE4. Outline your own integrative theory of therapy: Choose a theoretical integration model, an assimilative model, or a technical eclecticism model. Use Table 16.1 (633 to 634) for assistance in selecting the personality theory and Table 16.4 (638 to 639) for assistance in selecting the therapeutic techniques that you might use. You will probably need more paper for this exercise.

_____

_____

_____

_____

_____

STRENGTHS AND LIMITATIONS

What do you believe are the strengths and limitations of integrative approaches?

STRENGTHS	LIMITATIONS
_____	_____
_____	_____
_____	_____
_____	_____
_____	_____
_____	_____
_____	_____

CONSTRUCTIVIST AND INTEGRATIVE APPROACHES: A QUIZ

True/False Items. Decide if the following statements are "more true" or "more false" as they apply to constructivist and integrative therapies.

T   F   Q1.   Readiness to change is an important aspect of multimodal therapy.

T   F   Q2.   Wachtel's cyclical psychodynamics approach uses ten different processes to move from one therapeutic technique to another.

T   F   Q3.   Lazarus's multimodal therapy uses two or more theories, making use of both therapeutic techniques and theories of personality from different theories.

T   F   Q4.   An assimilative approach is one method for integrating theories.

T   F   Q5.   The basic idea of Lazarus's multimodal therapy is to use seven modalities for understanding the client and for helping to bring about therapeutic change.

T   F   Q6.   Prochaska's transtheoretical approach to integrating theories draws effective techniques from other theories to make a new theory.

T   F   Q7.   Prochaska's transtheoretical model and Wachtel's cyclical psychodynamic model are examples of a theoretical integration approach.

T   F   Q8.   Wachtel's cyclical psychodynamics model is one which combines theories of personality and theories of psychotherapy of two or more therapies.

T   F   Q9.   Using any techniques which seem appropriate for therapeutic change is an example of how to use Wachtel's cyclical psychodynamics approach.

T   F   Q10.   In multimodal therapy, Lazarus uses social cognitive theory as a means for understanding the behavior and personality of his clients.

Multiple choice items: Select the best answer from the alternatives given. Many of the questions ask you to choose the constructivist or integrative therapy that most closely fits the question.

_____ Q11. If you question a client's commitment to changing behavior, you would probably be conceptualizing using

    a. Prochaska's transtheoretical model.
    b. Wachtel's cyclical psychodynamics.
    c. Lazarus's multimodal therapy.

_____ Q12. As a therapist, you observe that your client imagines her husband is angry at her. You notice a switch from Imagery to Behavior. You are probably using this approach:

    a. Prochaska's transtheoretical model.
    b. Wachtel's cyclical psychodynamics.
    c. Lazarus's multimodal therapy.

_____ Q13. Lazarus would describe the technique that you use to observe a client

    a. coping.
    b. firing order.
    c. miracle question.
    d. tracking.

_____ Q14. You decide to make use of psychoanalytic, behavioral, cognitive, and family systems personality theory as a way to understand a client's problems and therapeutic techniques from these theories as a way to help her with her problems. You are using which integrative approach?

    a. assimilative
    b. theoretical integration
    c. technical eclecticism

_____ Q15. Imagine that you were unfamiliar with theories of psychotherapy and wanted to use a theory which is self contained and which would deal with motivation to change. Which approach would you use?

    a. Prochaska's transtheoretical model.
    b. Wachtel's cyclical psychodynamics.
    c. Lazarus's multimodal therapy.

_____ Q16. You decide that you are going to help your client by using specific techniques that you have gathered from several theories. These techniques include catharsis/dramatic relief, stimulus control, and contingency management. You would be using

    a. Prochaska's transtheoretical model.
    b. Wachtel's cyclical psychodynamics.
    c. Lazarus's multimodal therapy.

_____ Q17. Time-tripping is a technique used in

    a. Prochaska's transtheoretical model.
    b. Wachtel's cyclical psychodynamics.
    c. Lazarus's multimodal therapy.

262

_____ Q18. Observing and responding to clients' switching from one type of modality to another is associated with

    a. Prochaska's transtheoretical model.
    b. Wachtel's cyclical psychodynamics.
    c. Lazarus's multimodal therapy

_____ Q19. Combining the personality theory and change techniques of both behavior therapy and psychoanalysis is the basis of

    a. Prochaska's transtheoretical model.
    b. Wachtel's cyclical psychodynamics.
    c. Lazarus's multimodal therapy.

_____ Q20. The use of the BASIC I.D. to establish goals is associated with

    a. Prochaska's transtheoretical model.
    b. Wachtel's cyclical psychodynamics.
    c. Lazarus's multimodal therapy.

_____ Q21. Being aware that a client is changing from Affect to Behavior in multimodal therapy would be called

    a. bridging.
    b. environmental reevaluation.
    c. stimulus control.
    d. time tripping.

_____ Q22. In Prochaska's transtheoretical model, the change process of social liberation is most similar to this theory

    a. psychoanalysis
    b. REBT
    c. feminist therapy
    d. reality therapy

_____ Q23. In Prochaska's transtheoretical model, which of these is least similar to concepts found in behavior therapy?

    a. counter conditioning
    b. contingency management
    c. self-reevaluation
    d. stimulus control

_____ Q24. An approach to integrative therapy that uses one major theory for both personality theory and therapy techniques, and other theories to supplement it is called

    a. biased.
    b. theoretical integration.
    c. technical eclecticism.
    d. assimilative.

_____ Q25. In Lazarus's multimodal therapy, a client's dreams would fit into which of the following modalities?

    a. affect
    b. sensation
    c. imagery
    d. cognitions

263

ANSWER KEY

1.	d	11.	b
2.	a	12.	b
3.	c	13.	d
4.	d	14.	a
5.	a	15.	b
6.	c	16.	c
7.	a	17.	c
8.	a		
9.	d		
10.	b		

QUIZ

Q1.	F	Q11.	a	Q21.	a
Q2.	F	Q12.	c	Q22.	c
Q3.	F	Q13.	d	Q23.	c
Q4.	T	Q14.	b	Q24.	d
Q5.	T	Q15.	a	Q25.	c
Q6.	T	Q16.	a		
Q7.	T	Q17.	c		
Q8.	T	Q18.	c		
Q9.	F	Q19.	b		
Q10.	T	Q20.	c		

Chris Marker

A
Grin
Without
a Cat

Whitechapel Gallery

Foreword

Visionary French filmmaker Chris Marker (1921-2012) created vivid film essays that lace realism with science fiction and lyricism with politics. His influence extends across art, experimental film and mainstream cinema. Yet he remains relatively unknown to a wider audience. This is in part because of his reclusiveness – he rarely gave interviews, did not allow himself to be photographed and worked under multiple pseudonyms of which 'Chris Marker' is the most well known. When asked for a portrait of himself he would often send a photograph of a cat; indeed, animals frequently appear in his films – especially cats and owls – as totemic alter egos. Marker became legendary however, among aficionados, like the leader of an underground resistance movement.

Marker worked as a journalist, essayist and editor before becoming a filmmaker as part of the so-called Nouvelle Vague ('New Wave') in the late 1950s. He is often given credit for renewing cinema, not least for his innovations in the genre of the 'essay-film', a hybrid of documentary and personal reflection and the style in which he became an acknowledged master. Such hybridity and restless crossing between media and forms were emblematic for Marker. His work is poetic and humorous, analytical, political and philosophical, a reflection of the complexity of the world. This exhibition shows him as a multifaceted artist and intellectual, working as an editor, writer, filmmaker, photographer and pioneer of new media and installation art. In many ways it is his way of working – as much as the result of that work – that has been such an inspiration to younger generations of artists.

His restless intellect was also reflected by his compulsion to travel. Marker was a lifelong traveller who documented in his distinctive style the journeys he took, the people he encountered and the cultural and political upheavals of the countries he visited. All of which is evident in his work: from his editorship in the 1950s of the *Petite Planète* series of guidebooks, which included essays and photography of the highest quality, to his many films from places as far apart as Siberia, Guinea-Bissau, Cuba and Finland. In his film *Si j'avais quatre dromadaires* (If I Had Four Camels, 1966), an amateur photographer and two friends reflect in voice-over about photographs taken on voyages to 26 countries. Marker's skill with the travelogue form would later find unforgettable expression in the magisterial essay-film *Sans soleil* (Sunless, 1982).

Marker's camera was his eye. His astonishing range of footage can encompass a temple in Tokyo devoted to cats to frozen flowers in a Siberian science station. Marker pictures our cultural rituals, ancient and modern – visiting a shrine, playing video games, protesting on the streets. He spliced his images with found footage including fragments of movies, cartoons, ads and newsreels. Musical scores are interwoven with the noises of everyday life; haunting commentaries are narrated as if from the future, meditating on history and memory; 'I compare dreaming to cinema and thinking to television'.

Among his most famous works is *La Jetée* (The Pier, 1962), a film made up almost entirely of still images. In the exhibition we show a rare version with an alternative beginning, as well as Marker's workbook for the film, giving a new insight into the creation of this unique work. Unlike most of Marker's films it is a work of pure fiction, science fiction to be more specific. A post Third World War survivor, living in an urban ruin, is the subject of an experiment. A group of scientists / captors, send him into the future. What allows him to travel through time is not a machine but his memory of an image. For Marker, images are the ultimate time machines, vehicles for our travels across not only three but also this fourth dimension.

Marker's use of montage, inspired by early pioneers such as Sergei Eisenstein and Dziga Vertov, puts him in the role of both editor and curator in his 1990 installation, *Zapping Zone*. As curator Bill Horrigan described it, '…the Photo Browse sections… are essentially ordered ransackings of his own photo archives, offering up still images in ever-varied sequences and combinations'.

The exhibition that accompanies this book takes us on a journey through the themes that absorbed him – the museum, travel, film, revolution and war. We also encounter portrayals of his friends including Christo, Roberto Matta and Andrei Tarkovsky. Great classics such as *Les Statues meurent aussi* (Statues Also Die, 1953), *Le Joli Mai* (The Merry Month of May, 1962), *Le Fond de l'air est rouge* (A Grin Without a Cat, 1977), *Zapping Zone* (1990-94) are presented alongside photographs and book works offering a sequence of multimedia environments saturated with sound and image.

Marker's fascination with our planetary cultures, his appetite for new images and technologies, his exuberant use of language – are underscored by darkness; memory and desire are counterbalanced by signs of trauma and disillusionment. We can interpret these as subjective or objective expressions – of surviving a war, of recognising the brutalities of colonialism, of witnessing failed revolutions. Yet like Alice in Wonderland, Marker is unsettled but absorbed by the vision of a grin without the cat.

Enabling new publics to become physically immersed in Marker's unique vision and for readers to take with them a souvenir and an interpretation of the experience, the Chris Marker Estate, and in particular Mabel Nicolaÿ Duflo must be specially thanked for making key works available. This is also the case for the many lenders to the exhibition. We are most grateful to Bernard Blistène and his colleagues, Brigitte Leal, Olga Makhorff, Alain Dubillot, and Sylvie Soulignac at the Centre Pompidou.

A long time champion of Marker as a visual artist, Peter Blum and his colleagues David Blum and Aaron Stempien at the Peter Blum Gallery, New York have been tremendously generous in lending works, expertise and support. We are also most grateful to Nicola Mazzanti and Jean-Paul Dorchain at the Royal Film Archive in Belgium.

For permission to screen and reproduce Marker's films for the exhibition and this book, our thanks to Inger Servolin, Jasmina Sijercic and all at Iskra; Claire Winter and her colleagues at La Sofra; Laurence Braunberger and all at Les Films du Jeudi; Florence Dauman, Anne-France Mournet and the team at Argos Films; and Suzanne Diop and her colleagues at Présence Africaine Editions.

We would also like to thank Tamsin Clark, Richard Bevan and Jason Simon for their loans of key archival materials. Also to Bill Horrigan, at the Wexner Center for the Arts, Ohio and Charlotte Saluard at Ciné Lumière for their invaluable assistance with this project.

At the Whitechapel Gallery a passionate engagement with Marker's legacy informed the translation of his multifaceted oeuvre into a show and a book by a dedicated team including Habda Rashid, Assistant Curator, Christopher Aldgate, Gallery Manager, Richard Johnson, Technical Advisor and Gareth Evans, Adjunct Film Curator.

The curatorial team, Magnus af Petersens, Christine Van Assche, Curator at Large, Centre Pompidou and Chris Darke, writer and film critic, structure and choreograph our journey into the world of Chris Marker.

Our audiences, including the many artists who have hungered to gain first-hand access to this legendary figure, owe them a great debt of gratitude. Their deep engagement with their subject has also informed some important new writing compiled here.

Joining them in offering critical perspectives on Marker's oeuvre are Raymond Bellour and Arnaud Lambert. Their texts are complemented by Marker's own early writings, translated here for the first time. Our thanks to these authors and to the designer Fraser Muggeridge for creating a book that will make an invaluable companion to understanding Marker's work.

Our thanks also to colleagues at the Barbican Centre and the Ciné Lumière at the Institut Français who are presenting parallel film seasons in London to accompany the exhibition at the Whitechapel Gallery.

It is our dream that through this book, as well as the exhibition, Marker's legacy will continue to resonate through the twenty-first century.

Magnus af Petersens, Curator at Large
Iwona Blazwick, Director

Mourning the Dead (Anti-OAS Demo, Paris, 1962), 1962
'Staring Back Series: I Stare 1', 1952-2006

Chris Marker, the Time of the World

Christine Van Assche

To the Happy Many[1]
Chris Marker

'I manage to frame again the top portion of my old photograph', writes Chris Marker in the book *Staring Back*, talking about two photographs of the same view of place de la République taken in 1962 and 2002. 'In between I have been in Japan, Korea, Bolivia, Chile. I have filmed students in Guinea-Bissau, medics in Kosovo, Bosnian refugees, Brazilian activists, animals everywhere. [...] In the middle, on the balcony, the tree has grown just a little. Within these few inches, forty years of my life.'[2]

Place de le République (Paris, 2002), 2002
'Staring Back Series: I Stare 1', 1952-2006

This linking of two photographs taken 40 years apart and the accompanying text encourage us to look at Marker's oeuvre from a similar angle, relating works from different periods. We might consider texts and books from the early period (1947-64), travel films or the celebrated *La Jetée* (1959-62), political films (1967-77) including the equally famous *Le Fond de l'air est rouge* (A Grin Without a Cat, 1977), installations from 1990-97, the pieces Marker made between 1990 and 2012 with or for the internet under the name Sandor Krasna and his last work, the website *Gorgomancy* (2007-2014).

The quotation from Marker reflects an attitude that he often adopted – revisiting a place, a city, a face, an event or a character after some years, recognising that life has continued in the meantime, time has done its work and the political situation in the place or country has evolved.

The structure of the exhibition *Chris Marker: A Grin Without a Cat* has taken its cue from this attitude, suggesting possible correspondences between books, films, installations, archive documents and the photographs that Marker took throughout his life.

I.

The exhibition is divided into four main sections, starting with the section entitled 'Statues Also Die: The Museum', which opens with Marker's conception of the personal museum, the *Ouvroir* (workspace), which he created on *Second Life* with the help of his friend and computer expert Max Moswitzer between 2005-10. We are welcomed into the exhibition by Guillaume-en-Égypte, Marker's famous avatar and intermediary between viewer and author, who invites us to explore the virtual museum before embarking on a visit of the very real exhibition.

A contemporary of French writer André Malraux and his 'Imaginary Museum', Marker was always interested in the idea of a collection of works from different parts of the world, including pieces made by others, pieces he had made himself or works made by others that he had revisited, in the days when artworks were discovered

Ouvroir. The Movie, 2010 (in association with Max Moswitzer)

1. 'A la multitude heureuse', dedication in the credits of *Le Joli Mai* (The Merry Month of May), Chris Marker and Pierre Lhomme, 1962.
2. Chris Marker, *Staring Back*, exhibition catalogue, Wexner Center for the Arts, Columbus, OH, US, 2007, p.43. To accompany the Chris Marker *Staring Back*, exhibition at the Wexner Center for the Arts, Ohio State University, Columbus, OH, US, 12 May - 12 August 2007.

Ouvroir. The Movie, 2010 (in association with Max Moswitzer)

through postcards and other reproductions in colour or black and white.[3]

Les Statues meurent aussi (Statues Also Die), a film co-directed with Alain Resnais in 1953, offers an early reflection of Marker's curiosity about works from very different cultures, including African civilizations, at a time when only a few artists were paying them any attention. The film's commentary (written by Marker) remains pertinent today, adding a vital critical element and an avant-garde vision of the world:

> Classified, labelled, preserved in the ice of glass cases and collections, [masks] become part of the history of art. A paradise of forms in which the most mysterious kinships develop: we recognise Greece in an African head more than two thousand years old, Japan in an Ogowe mask, India, the Sumerian idols, our own Romanesque Christs and our Modern art.[4]

This universal vision, with its hybridization of civilizations and mixing of styles and origins, recurs throughout Marker's work on art and foreshadows the twenty-first century.

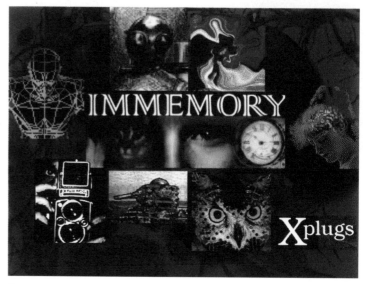

Immemory, 1997

Immemory (1997) is Marker's own imaginary museum, a Proustian cartography that is also his undoubtedly fictional autobiography. It is arranged into broad 'zones': War, Photography, Cinema, Travel, Poetry, Memory and Museum, where we can view Marker's selection of various masterpieces from the history of art, reworked using his graphic palette. This work, which I produced in the years 1990-97 with Les Films de l'Astrophore, foregrounds Marker's personal archives, some images from which first appeared in the books of the *Petite Planète* (Small Planet) series and his book-length critical study *Giraudoux par lui-même* (Giraudoux In His Own Words 1952), or later in *Zapping Zone* (1990-94), edited 'from a very great number of images that were drawn, painted, constructed and reconstructed according to the possibilities of video and computer graphics, or simply using the age-old art of collage, which Marker employed with great pleasure.'[5]

In conceptual terms, each piece presented overflows the section into which we have placed it, because all of Marker's works are laden with different signs that require rhizomatic readings.

3. French writer André Malraux first published *Le Musée imaginaire* in 1947 and was Minister for Cultural Affairs under President Charles de Gaulle from 1958-69.
4. Extract from the commentary of *Les Statues meurent aussi*, Chris Marker and Alain Resnais, 1953.
5. Raymond Bellour, 'Le Livre, aller, retour', in Christine Van Assche, Raymond Bellour and Laurent Roth, *Qu'est-ce qu'une madeleine? À propos du CD-ROM Immemory de Chris Marker*, Yves Gevaert Éditeur / Centre Georges Pompidou, Paris, 1997, p. 92.

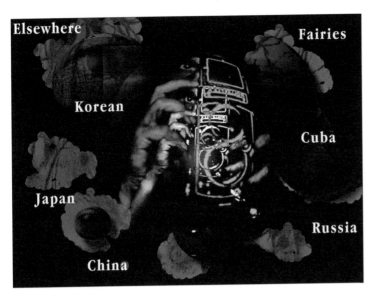

Elsewhere   Fairies

Korean

Cuba

Japan

Russia

China

Immemory, 1997

II.

The second section, 'Petite Planète: Travelogues', starts with a presentation of the *Petite Planète* travel guides, a series edited by Marker for publishers Éditions du Seuil from 1952 until the early 1960s. Though they were clearly travel guides, they were also philosophical and political essays on a range of countries including Germany, Belgium and China. To create them, Marker commissioned great authors, such as Armand Gatti for China, and photographers well known today, including Henri Cartier-Bresson, William Klein and Agnès Varda. He also supervised the very avant-garde layout of the books.

In parallel to this work, Marker made a number of trips with the organisation 'Peuple et culture' to make documentary essays such as *Dimanche à Pékin* (Sunday in Peking, 1956), *Lettre de Sibérie* (Letter From Siberia, 1957) and *Cuba si!* (1961) and the book (described by Marker as a 'short film') *Coréennes* (1959), following a trip to Korea. In some of the countries he visited he also presented films.

Marker's exploration of other cultures reflects his boundless curiosity. Film and stills cameras to hand, he would set off in search of images, of an image, a 'previous image', a 'marking image' or 'an image of happiness'. 'Images in Marker's work are inextricably linked to travel', writes Arnaud Lambert. And gradually a process of substitution takes place: 'If images can

replace or represent journeys, this is because, in Marker's mind, they are equivalent to a space-time and a lived experience.'[6]

The film *Sans soleil* (Sunless, 1982) is one of the works in which Marker creates correspondences between images filmed in Iceland, Japan and Guinea-Bissau, editing them into 'zones' that foreshadow the various 'space-time zones' of the multimedia *Zapping Zone* and the interactive CD-ROM *Immemory*.

In today's globalised world we believe it is important to highlight the tireless research that enabled Marker, ahead of his time, to put together an international body of works. A perfect example of this is the installation *Zapping Zone: Proposals for an Imaginary Television*, created for the *Passages de l'image* exhibition at the Centre Pompidou in 1990. It is a travelogue inviting the viewer to move instantly from Berlin to Paris or from Sarajevo to Tokyo, from a zoo to a bridge wrapped by Christo, from an exhibition by Roberto Matta in Paris to a ballad by Arielle Dombasle in Tokyo. In the 'Sequences' zone, Marker selected extracts from his films (including *Sans soleil*, *Le Joli Mai* and *Le Fond de l'air est rouge*), creating his own mini-retrospective.

This piece, and the rest of his oeuvre, demonstrates that Marker had a universalist conception of the world at a time when such a notion was still comparatively rare. 'It is six o'clock across all the Earth', says Marker in the film *Si j'avais quatre dromadaires* (If I Had Four Camels, 1966). 'Six o'clock over Peking's Forbidden City. Daybreak over Brussels, and over Prague, over Tehran and over Berlin.'

Unlike the linearity of films – although the term is not very appropriate to Marker's films – multimedia installations, interactive CD-ROMs and websites allow us to visit an exhibition in different ways. Editing, a precious tool in the construction of Marker's films, now becomes the work of the viewer / visitor, who is an active participant in the exhibition. This interactive attitude is something Marker welcomed in relation to his CD-ROM *Immemory*. 'My fondest wish', he writes in the accompanying booklet, 'is that there might be enough familiar codes here (the travel picture, the family album, the totem animal) that the reader-visitor could imperceptibly come to replace my images with his, my memory with his, and that my *Immemory* should serve as a springboard for his own pilgrimage through Time Regained.'[7] In *Ouvroir* on *Second Life*, Marker

6. Arnaud Lambert, *Also Known as Chris Marker*, Le Point du Jour, Cherbourg, 2013, p.157 and p.159. See Arnaud Lambert, 'Image (journey)', in this catalogue, pp.76-83.
7. Chris Marker, *Immemory*, Éditions Centre Pompidou, Paris, 1998. English translation *Immemory: A CD-ROM by Chris Marker*, Exact Change, Cambridge, MA, 2008.

also enables visitors and browsers to move freely and interactively through the world he has created.

As in most of these pieces, the paradigm of memory is at work. In *Zapping Zone*, writes Marker, 'the same image will return from one screen to the next in the form of its different avatars, film frame here, video version there, reworked on a computer, as part of a collage, described in writing … To the point where, supposing that they remember them, visitors will no longer know to which "race of image" exactly they should attach the memory. So that, if there is a memory, it will be above all the memory of a 'passage' (transition).'[8]

Marker never travelled without a notebook, stills camera, film camera or, from very early on, a more practical video camera. Some of his photographs are presented in this section. They reflect his close interest in human beings and the expressions of his contemporaries. Often these photographs are in fact film frames from the torrent of moving images that he filmed. In an exchange with Bill Horrigan, who curated the photographic exhibition *Staring Back* at the Wexner Center for the Arts in 2007, Chris Marker wrote that he had extracted meaningful images from the flow of video and television, 'developing the concept of "superliminal" which is a sort of counterpoint to subliminal. Instead of one frame lost in the stream of other, different frames, superliminal is one frame lost in the stream of almost IDENTICAL frames, or so it seems, for when you take them one by one, one happens to be THE real photogram, something nobody then has perceived, not even the guy who shot it (me, in most cases).'[9]

III.

On one of the many occasions that I visited Marker in the years 1986-2012, he had just received yet another thesis on *La Jetée* (The Pier, 1962). In response to my questions about the film, he told me that he could not understand why people were interested in it, or why they wasted so much time analyzing it, and that in any case he did not have time to read what they wrote. When I expressed my amazement, he added that the film had entirely slipped from his grasp as he was making it and that all its elements had been beyond him.

Even as a 'UFO', *La Jetée* deserves a section to itself – entitled 'Memories of Things to Come: The Future-Past of Film' – particularly as the film will be shown here on a loop (the exhibition permits repeat viewings). An exercise

book containing text and images and acting also as a script, given by Marker to Jacques Ledoux, an actor in the film and at the time director of the Belgian Cinematheque, will be displayed while the film is being screened. Portrait photographs of some of those involved, friends and actors, will also be on show. Unlike Marker's other films, which can be categorised as documentary essays, *La Jetée* is closer to science fiction, constructed entirely from photographs, and has had a considerable influence on other filmmakers and artists – too many to be listed here. *La Jetée* has a relationship to the installation *Owls At Noon Prelude: The Hollow Men* (2005), based on the poem *The Hollow Men* (1925) by TS Eliot, which reflects on the devastation of Europe after the First World War and which introduces the final part of the exhibition.

IV.

The fourth section, entitled 'When the Century Took Shape: War and Revolution', contrasts with the preceding section in its return to Marker's unwavering interest in rebellions, revolutions, attempts at regime change and the popular movements by which peoples give public voice to their opinions. He followed such movements in different countries on many continents, including North America, Bolivia, Bosnia-Herzegovina, Brazil, Cuba, Chile, China, Russia, Czechoslovakia and Vietnam, and also much closer to home in Besançon, Saint-Nazaire and Paris.

In 1962 Marker took a photograph on place de la République in Paris, showing people leaning against a barrier watching what we imagine to be a demonstration. In 2002 he returned to place de la République and photographed the same view, framed in the same way, again showing passers-by watching a demonstration, in front of a tree that had grown in the intervening time. Between the two images lie 40 years of experience, travel, filming, people, reading and making.

We reflect the approach adopted by Marker in this photograph through two films: *Le Joli Mai*, shot in Paris and co-directed with Pierre Lhomme, and *Chats perchés* (The Case of the Grinning Cat) filmed by Marker with his small digital video camera in the same city in 2004.

8. Chris Marker, *Projet: Logiciel / Catacombes*, proposal for the installation *Zapping Zone: Proposals for an Imaginary Television*, written in 1987 and preserved in the archives of the Centre Georges Pompidou, MNAM, Nouveaux Médias.
9. Bill Horrigan, 'Some Other Time', in Chris Marker, *Staring Back*, exhibition catalogue, Wexner Center for the Arts, Columbus, OH, US, 2007, p.138.

Le Joli Mai is a documentary on postwar Paris, modern civilization, modernity and its iconic values, such as the city and objects produced by recent industrialisation (cars, household devices), and also on the context of decolonisation and the events leading to the independence of Algeria and the Évian Accords of 18 March 1962, which ended the Algerian War. With this film the two photographer filmmakers give us a 'portrait' of the society of the time, which is sometimes in tune with the onrush of modernity and sometimes lags behind. It has been said that the film's content heralds the concerns underpinning the demands expressed in the demonstrations in May 1968.

Chats perchés, 2004

Le Joli Mai, with Pierre Lhomme, 1962

In 2004 Marker returned to the population of Paris, filming them on political demonstrations. He shows us the inhabitants of a contemporary France, a nation fully aware that it was in its postcolonial period. The portraits show French men and women who are full of life, aware of contemporary social and political issues and responding to the same utopia of shared happiness.

As Bill Horrigan notes in the catalogue of the *Staring Back* exhibition, *Chats perchés* is a kind of 'epilogue-sequel' to *Le Joli Mai*. At any rate, elements recur from one film to the other, as do certain photographs in the 'Staring Back' series.[10]

In 1978, the year after *Le Fond de l'air est rouge*, Chris Marker made an installation in the form of a wall of screens called *Quand le siècle a pris formes: Guerre et Révolution* (When the Century Took Shape: War and Revolution). It was commissioned by the Centre Pompidou for its *Paris-Berlin* exhibition and created in collaboration with François Helt. It shows a montage of archive footage of events from the first 30 years of the twentieth century, 'tangible beacons' as Marker wrote, deliberately portrayed in the cinematic language of the time (newsreels from the First World War, the German and Russian revolutions and the postwar period), intercut with text. Marker describes it as not so much a 'history lesson' as 'an isolation of the elements that made the end of the First World War and the revolutionary period the repertoire of almost everything that has altered the contemporary vision of the world.'[11]

The section 'When the Century Took Shape: War and Revolution' also includes documents that Marker produced from around 2004 and sent to friends across the world, initially by fax and then by email. Under the auspices of his faithful avatar Guillaume-en-Égypte, he portrays and distorts political developments, providing humorous critiques and adopting positions on the events of the day.

His vision of the contemporary world remained constant from his first film, *Olympia 52* (1952) through the books he wrote or edited, the various films he made over 40 years and his multimedia installations, CD-ROMs and websites, to *Stopover in Dubai* of 2010, one of his last pieces: 'Since then, the time of the finite world has begun, we have become heirs to the entire Earth, our future is in the stars...'[12]

Poptronics, 2007-11

10. Bill Horrigan, 'Some Other Time', in Chris Marker, *Staring Back*, exhibition catalogue, Wexner Center for the Arts, Columbus, OH, 2007, p.138.

11. Proposal for *Quand le siècle a pris formes: Guerre et Révolution* preserved in the archives of the Centre Georges Pompidou, MNAM, Nouveaux Médias.

12. Chris Marker, 'Petite Planète', *27 rue Jacob*, no.10, Éditions du Seuil, summer 1954, p.1. (Introduction to the *Petite Planète* series)

Statues Also Die
THE MUSEUM

Les Statues meurent aussi (Statues Also Die), 1950-53
Alain Resnais and Chris Marker
Black and white, 35mm, 30 minutes

Ouvroir. The Movie, 2010
Chris Marker in association with Max Moswitzer
Colour, video, 30 minutes

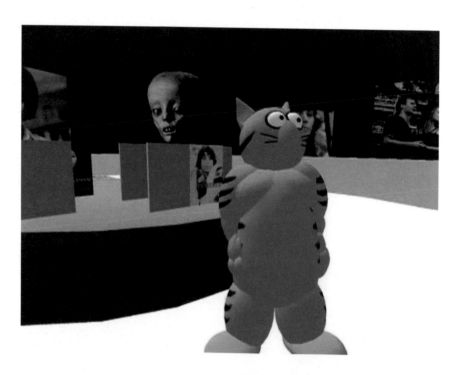

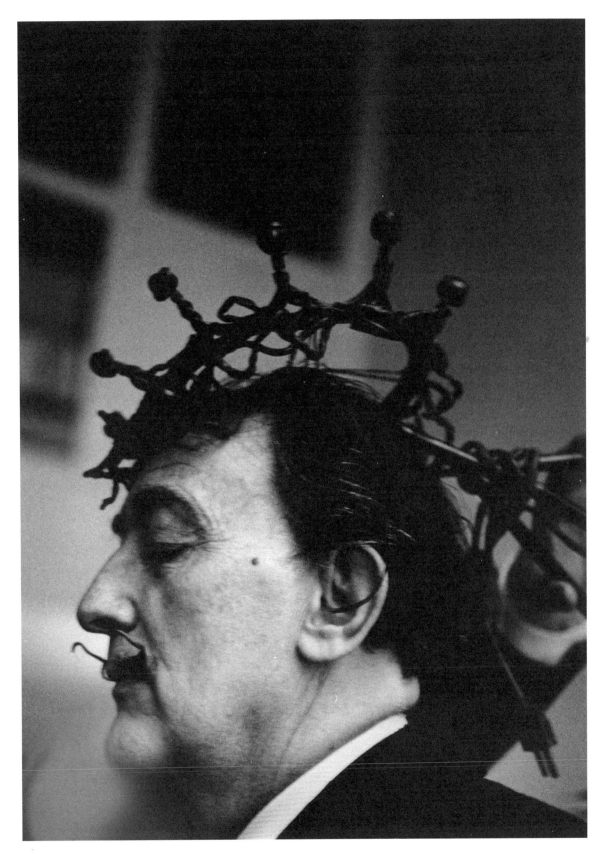

Immemory, 1997
Interactive multimedia installation: 1 hard drive 34 Megabytes,
3 Macintosh computers, 1 painted cat, colour, sound,
French and English language

Les Statues meurent aussi (Statues Also Die), 1950-53
Alain Resnais and Chris Marker
Black and white, 35mm, 30 minutes
(and following four pages)

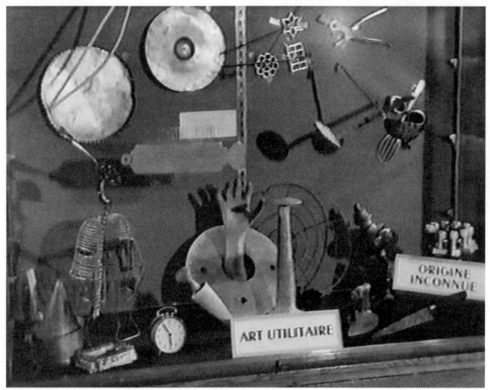

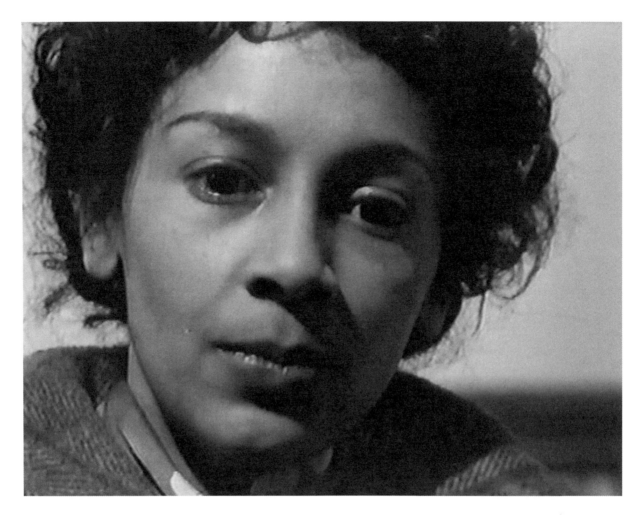

19

20

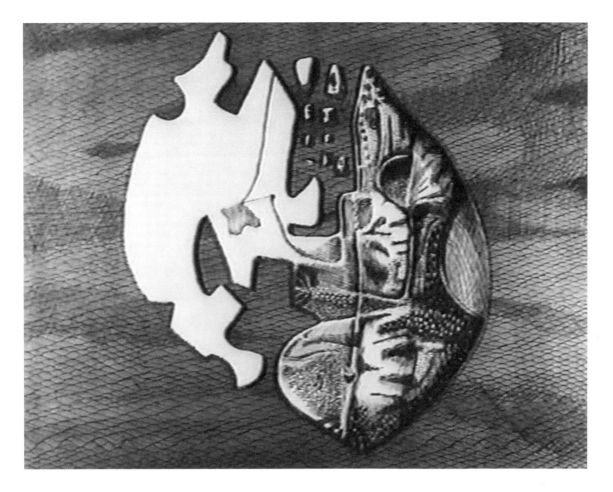

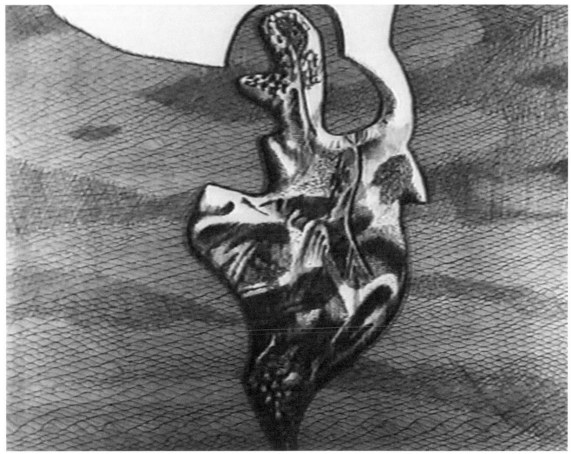

Petite Planète
TRAVELOGUES

Sans soleil (Sunless), 1982
Colour, 16mm blown up to 35mm, 103 minutes

Zapping Zone (Proposals for an Imaginary Television), 1990-94
Mixed media installation: 13 monitors, 13 videos, 7 computers, 7 computer
programmes, 4 lightboxes with 80 slides, 10 photomontages colour /
black and white, 1 maneki neko
Installation view: Centre Pompidou, Paris, 1994-95

24

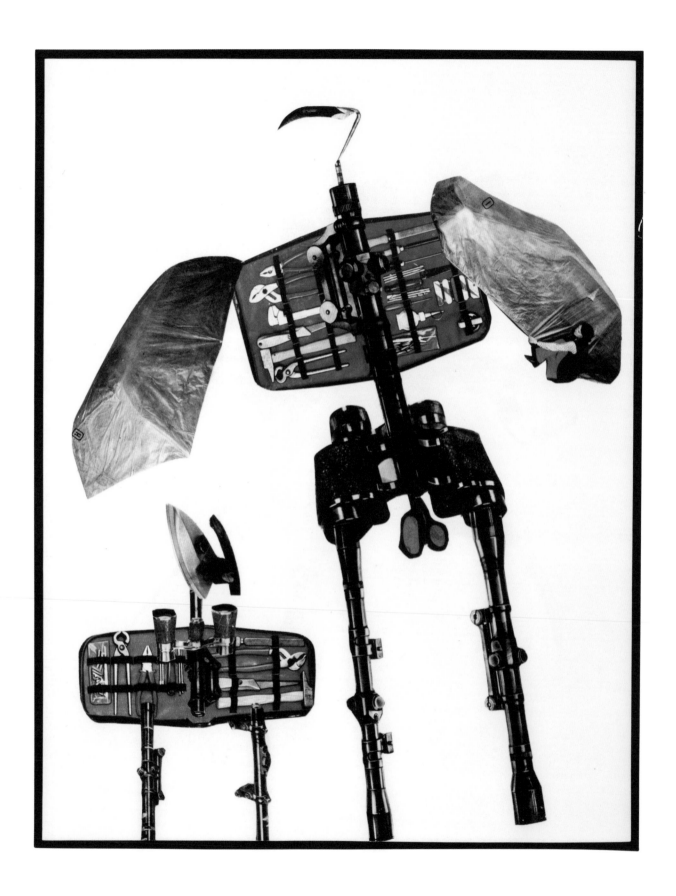

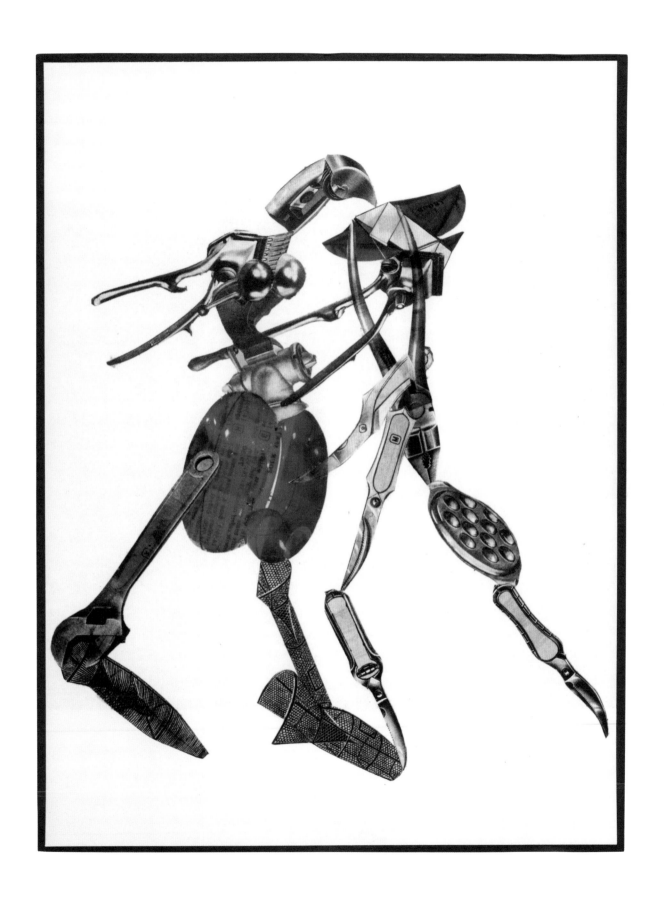

Untitled (Tehran 1960s), 1960s
'Staring Back Series: I Stare 2', 1952-2006
Black and white photograph mounted on aluminium
35.2 × 26.4 cm

Kurosawa (1985), 1985
'Staring Back Series: They Stare', 1952-2006
Black and white photograph mounted on aluminium,
35.2 × 24.1 cm

Listening to Poetry (Moscow 1950s), 1950s
'Staring Back Series: I Stare 2', 1952-2006
Black and white photograph mounted on aluminium
24.8 × 35.2 cm

Sans soleil (Sunless), 1982
Colour, 16mm blown up to 35mm, 103 minutes
(and following five pages)

41

Chris Marker and Jason Simon
Petite Planète Poster, 2006
Offset lithograph

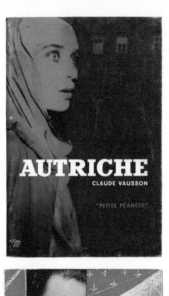

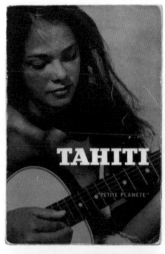

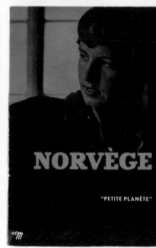

HOLLANDE
"PETITE PLANÈTE"

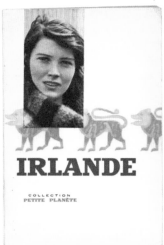

IRLANDE
COLLECTION
PETITE PLANÈTE

GRÈCE
"PETITE PLANÈTE"

ALLEMAGNE
"PETITE PLANÈTE"

TUNISIE
"PETITE PLANÈTE"

CHINE
"PETITE PLANÈTE"

IRAN
"PETITE PLANÈTE"

ISRAËL
"PETITE PLANÈTE"

DANEMARK
"PETITE PLANÈTE"

PORTUGAL
"PETITE PLANÈTE"

BRÉSIL
"PETITE PLANÈTE"

JAPON
YÉHME
PETITE PLANÈTE

SAHARA
"PETITE PLANÈTE"

URSS
"PETITE PLANÈTE"

PETITE PLANÈTE
1954–1964
sous la direction de
Chris Marker

Orchard, New York
Extra City, Antwerp
Poster by Jason Simon
2006

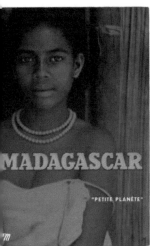

MADAGASCAR

VENEZUELA
"PETITE PLANÈTE"

ÉGYPTE
"PETITE PLANÈTE"

MAROC
"PETITE PLANÈTE"

POLOGNE
"PETITE PLANÈTE"

At the Sign of the Black Cat

Chris Darke

I opened the email and my computer crashed. Then the one next to me crashed and the one next to that until all the monitors in the cyber-café were dark. Then the lights went out. From my chipboard cubicle I watched as people emerged from buildings across the road to gather on the pavement and shrug at the shop fronts. It was November 2003 and I was in Paris to meet Chris Marker. I was convinced it was the email he'd sent containing directions to his address that had blown the fuses along the rue de la Roquette. I wondered if the famously reclusive filmmaker had turned into a Fantômas of the digital age, able to impose his will invisibly on the city. Still, if I ever made it to our rendezvous the incident might serve as an amusing icebreaker, so I passed the time mentally translating the phrase, 'Your email crashed the cyber-café!' into literal French, though I suspected its ugly jostle of Anglo-Saxon risked offending Marker's literary ear and would bring our encounter to an abrupt end. Then the lights came back on and my computer screen blinked into life, like an opening eye.

La Jetée, 1962

Sans soleil, 1982

Directions finally in hand, I entered the subterranean corridors of the métro, my destination the district of Ménilmontant to the east of the city. I wondered why I didn't feel nervous and whether the thought was itself a sign of nerves. I recalled the story of the film critic Serge Daney who became so anxious when driving to meet Jean-Luc Godard for the first time that he had to stop the car to throw up. I observed my fellow passengers, the snoozers and the straphangers. Behind each glazed eye a private film rolled.

Maraîchers. My stop. I was curious to see Marker's neighbourhood. It was evidently at a 45-degree slide across the map and down the social pyramid from Neuilly-sur-Seine where Christian Hippolyte François Georges Bouche-Villeneuve had been born in July 1921. One of the things I admired about Marker was how he had spent his life on the run from the class he had been born into. The name 'Chris Marker' – a radical abbreviation that served as an exit visa from a bourgeois background and a world traveller's pseudonymous flag of convenience – was an emblem of his flight and the freedom that came with it. (But, as someone once said, he could do nothing about the privilege that allowed him to choose).

I was even more curious to reach my destination. Following his directions, I made my way along rue des Pyrénées, turned right at the intersection with rue des Orteaux and passed under a bridge onto rue Courat. I found myself in a deserted residential street. My instructions told me that the house had no number so I was to look out instead for a sign. (An assumed name. An unnumbered building. A secret sign. Had I wandered into a film?) And there it was, on the entrance to a long, municipal-looking, four-storey block that resembled a decommissioned post office – a Craven A cigarette card with its cartoon of a black cat. I knocked at the frosted glass, the door opened, and I stepped into the world of Chris Marker.

In 1999 I was making magazine items for the television channel Film Four when a dream assignment fell into my lap. The channel had bought the TV rights to a number of Marker's films, including *La Jetée* (The Pier, 1962), and a short piece was needed which would introduce the film to British viewers. I leapt at the chance to pay tribute to 'the best-known author of unknown movies', as Marker described himself, so I set about assessing the available material. In 1997, Marker had released *Immemory*, an extraordinary CD-ROM of images, texts and film clips, assembled in a labyrinthine tour of his life's work, which I drew on to explore the links between *La Jetée* and Alfred Hitchcock's *Vertigo* (1958). I knew Marker would not submit to the indignity of self-promotion so there was no point in requesting an interview. However, Film Four supplied me with footage of Terry Gilliam rhapsodising over *La Jetée*, which was the inspiration for his Hollywood 'remake' *Twelve Monkeys* (1995). I supplemented this with contributions from the American producer-director Michael H. Shamberg, a friend and collaborator of Marker, who agreed to talk about the man himself. And by a stroke of good fortune (or was it fate in disguise?) Marker's multimedia installation *Silent Movie* (1995) was about to open in London.

I wanted to highlight the uniqueness of *La Jetée* and place it in the context of his career (a word Marker despised) while avoiding too dry and dutiful a tone. So I decided to play, as best I could, with some of Marker's own techniques and tropes. To approximate the fleet-footed lightness of his commentaries I wrote a voice-over about a time traveller landing in London. The logo of the *Silent Movie* exhibition figured prominently onscreen at times to allude to Marker's own reticence. And in keeping with a motif that runs throughout his work, I cut where I could on looks and gazes, observing what he describes in *Sans soleil* (Sunless, 1982) as 'the magical function of the eye'. But the act of cutting into *La Jetée* itself to select illustrative sequences felt akin to a transgression, like taking a hammer to a piece of jewellery to extract the stones. And there was one moment in particular I knew I couldn't touch.

It was while making the piece that I first met Marker, who was in town for the opening of *Silent Movie*. I'd been invited to have dinner with him along with a group of critics and curators and we assembled at the Institute of Contemporary Arts. I remember walking down a long corridor and seeing a figure at the other end that I knew was Marker. I introduced myself and told him about my short film. He confirmed he wouldn't talk about his work but otherwise would assist me with whatever I needed. During the meal I observed him with interest, while trying not to look like I was gawking. I noticed the fashionable, sandy-coloured combat gear he was wearing and the vigour with which he tucked into the Chinese food. He looked in good shape for a man in his late 70s: spry, alert and happy to talk. His high-domed, shaved head and piercing eyes lent him a somewhat otherworldly aspect, which had no doubt contributed to the image of 'Marker the Martian' that had been in circulation since the 1950s.

In the weeks and months that followed I was in contact to request this or that permission and I gained an insight into how he dealt with the business of filmmaking, which seemed to be entirely on his own terms. While I could consult Argos Films and Les Films du Jeudi, production companies with which he had a long association, it was Marker himself, at the other end of a fax machine or email, who signed off on things – in his own fashion. On one occasion I faxed him a release form to sign, indicating his consent to my use of material from *Immemory*.

In next to no time a tongue of paper was protruding from my fax machine. It was the release form … the dotted line empty. Instead, a handwritten note made it clear he didn't recognise the legal status of the document and that 'We aren't all as Americanized over here as you guys.' I took the point; the initials beneath Marker's scrawled squib would have to do.

When the piece was completed I sent him a VHS copy, went on holiday and forgot about it, more or less. The fact that I got a response – and a positive one, Marker liked the lightness of the piece, which he described as 'witty' – made me reflect on his way of working. Here was a filmmaker (and for the sake of simplicity let's stay with that professional designation, although Marker was much more than 'just' a filmmaker) for whom PR was anathema. The cloak of invisibility he wrapped himself in was a way of deflecting unwanted attention, but when one did actually get through to him, as I was to find out, one discovered a humorous, supportive, though still slightly intimidating personality. If his cultural status in France was uncontested, even while he maintained a low profile, his audience further afield was largely self-selecting. Perhaps this explained Marker's kindly response to my piece, indicating his pleasure at knowing that there was another, younger generation out in the wider world that regarded his work as crucial.

What happened a couple of years later came as a complete surprise. In 2001, I received an email from Argos Films telling me of plans to release a DVD edition of both *La Jetée* and *Sans soleil* and that Marker wanted to include my short film, which he'd entitled *Chris on Chris*, among the extras. (Nor was my surprise in any way diminished when they told me they couldn't pay for it.)[1]

The door closed behind me and I stepped down into… It was an artist's studio, certainly, but one that was something between a cabinet of curiosities and a spaceship. Towards the rear of the large, high-ceilinged interior stood banks of computer terminals, ranks of hard drives and monitors tuned silently to TV broadcasts from around the world. Wooden bookshelves divided up the whitewashed, rectangular space; figurines of cats and owls, Marker's totemic creatures, proliferated. I recognised objects from his films. The model of a human cerebellum made from pipe cleaners that featured in *Sans soleil* hung in a metal cage. Perched at one of the workstations was the talkative toy bird from *Level Five* (1996). Marker

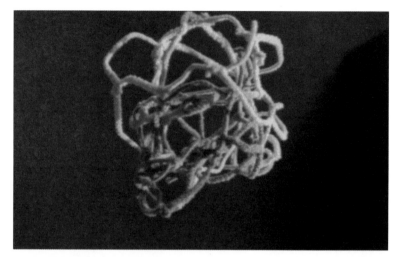

Sans soleil, 1982

Level Five, 1996

1. *Chris on Chris* was uploaded to YouTube in 2010 by somebody other than its author: see www.youtube.com/watch?v=1HrujmaJ5zU

2. Claude Lanzmann, *The Patagonian Hare: A Memoir*, trans. Frank Wynne, Atlantic, London, 2012, p. 278.

invited me to take a seat in an area set aside for visitors where two canvas-backed chairs were arranged, the names 'Kim Novak' and 'Alfred Hitchcock' emblazoned on them. (Was he Hitch that day and I Madeleine? Or was it the other way round?) And all about me, Marker's treasures: photographs, reproductions of paintings, Russian newspapers, Japanese magazines, T-shirts with eye-catching designs, stacked on tabletops, in piles on the floor – a horde of material, graphics, text, to be recombined and juxtaposed. A mother lode of *bricolage*. It was like stepping into Marker's brain.

He folded himself into his seat, a long-limbed man, lean and supple for his advanced years, which showed in his sunken cheeks though not in his eyes. His pale-blue gaze was direct, giving him a frank, no-nonsense demeanour. I had the impression of looking at an old soldier. While his body language was loose and relaxed, there was a sense of sharpness about him, of being absolutely present, which made me think of clandestinity and combat. What had those eyes seen, I wondered, when he served in the Resistance and the American army of liberation during the Second World War? We'd been chatting in French since my arrival and now that we settled down to talk in earnest I asked if he preferred to speak in English, a language I knew he was fluent in. He indicated not. For a moment I had the impression that I was being tested and felt intensely nervous at the thought of conversing with Marker in French. I remembered that one of the first emails I ever received from him (he always wrote in English) had opened with the greeting 'Hi, Man'; my girlfriend at the time had looked over my shoulder and said delightedly, 'Chris Marker's a hippy!'

I asked him what he was working on and he told me about *Immemory 2*. The project sounded no less ambitious than its predecessor, an account of the history of the twentieth century. But this time, he insisted, *not* as a CD-ROM. By now Marker was firmly in the post-filmic phase of his work and occupied himself exclusively with the tools afforded by the ever-evolving world of digital multimedia. And therein lay the problem. When it came to *Immemory 2*, he lamented, 'The format hasn't been invented yet.' Would working with an assistant help, I ventured? The question wasn't entirely innocent. My fantasy had Marker slapping his forehead and exclaiming, 'An assistant? Of course! When can you start?' His actual reply was gently dismissive, 'I'd rather scream and shout at myself.'

He was 'a *bricoleur*', he explained. Nothing more. The technology he'd assembled simply enabled him to pursue this humble activity in the most up-to-date manner possible. It was the means that were sophisticated, not the method. I suggested that in French *bricolage* sounded like an elevated calling, bringing to mind Roland Barthes and Claude Lévi-Strauss, whereas 'tinkering', its English equivalent, made one think of a bloke in a garden shed. Marker observed drily that he didn't have a garden. And with a hint of disbelief at the way his work was received, he added, 'I make these things and people take me for Plato!'

Marker was a courteous conversationalist. Enquiring about my own work he admitted that he found writing the hardest of tasks and it was the best he could do to produce a couple of hundred satisfactory words a day. But he was laconic in expression. As we talked further I noticed that he spoke through gritted teeth, barely moving his mouth, as though his jaws were wired. His observations and responses came in concise asides followed by silence. While this could be disconcerting, I quickly decided not to compensate by babbling through such moments. Years later I read in Claude Lanzmann's account of first meeting Marker in the 1950s that he had a prognathous – or projecting – lower jaw.[2]

After years of travelling, the world came to him now. He proudly itemised what his home production set-up allowed him to do, which was basically everything. He could harvest images from his own vast archive, from global TV and the internet. He could venture out when necessary with his beloved digital video camera. He could arrange and organise the treasures he collected and increasingly disseminate them as he wished. He barely needed to leave the studio, he explained. 'The birds bring me the neighbourhood news', he added. He waved his hand towards a tiny open window set high up in the nearby wall with a gesture of such Franciscan gracefulness that I expected a sparrow to swoop in and settle on his wrist.

La Jetée, 1962

We talked for the best part of two hours and towards the end of the afternoon he asked if I'd like a drink. He rose and disappeared through a door. While he was gone, I looked about me again. I thought of my dead friend, the filmmaker Marc Karlin, who had first worked with Marker in 1968 and collaborated with him over the next two decades, and whose own films were deeply influenced by the man he called '*Le Maître*'. As I took in the studio again and noticed that beneath all the artefacts and equipment the room was actually quite Spartan, and the only other living space was a small mezzanine reached by a short set of wooden steps, it was Marc's other name for him that came to mind – 'The Monk'. Marker returned with a bottle and a couple of glasses, and poured two measures. We spoke a toast in Russian, and fired back the shots of ice-cold, peppered vodka.

He makes films and everyone thinks that they're about serious subjects. In fact, they're all personal messages.[3]

Guillaume-en-Égypte

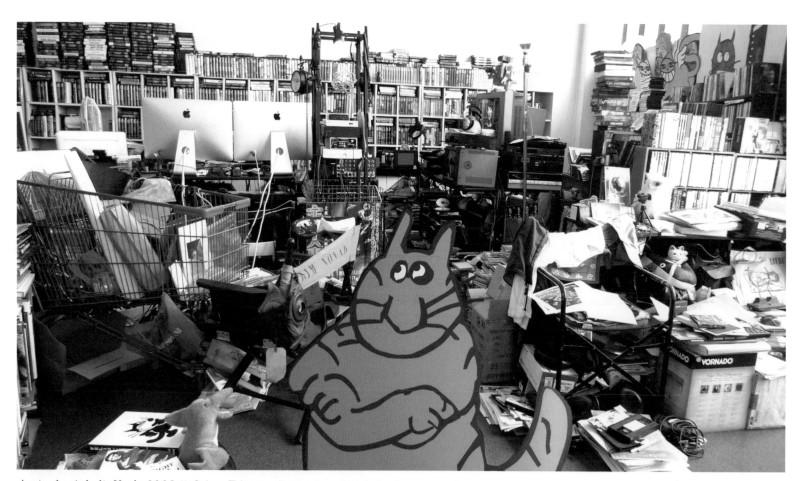

Agnès de ci de là Varda, 2008-11, Colour, TV series, 5 episodes × 45 minutes © agnes varda

3. 'Guillaume-en-Égypte: Mes neufs vies sont très remplies', interview with Chris Marker, *pop'lab: Guillaume-en-Égypte au Brésil*, no.11, October 2009, p.9. See www.poptronics.fr/Sans-Chris-Marker. Trans. CD.

Memories of Things to Come
THE FUTURE-PAST OF FILM

La Jetée (The Pier), 1962
Black and white, 35mm, 29 minutes

Silent Movie, 1995
5 channel video installation, continuous loop, dimensions variable
Installation view: *Chris Maker Silent Movie and Selected Screenings*
Curated by The Pier Trust, Beaconsfield, London, 1999

Silent Movie (photographs), 1995
18 framed black and white photographs
17.8 × 23.5 cm (each)

Ligia Branice, year unknown
'Staring Back Series: They Stare', 1952-2006
Black and white photograph mounted on aluminium
25.1 × 35.2 cm

William Klein and wife Jeanine, year unkown
'Staring Back Series: I Stare 2', 1952-2006
Black and white photograph mounted on aluminium
27.3 × 35.2 cm

Alexandra Stewart, year unkown
'Staring Back Series: They Stare', 1952-2006
Black and white photograph mounted on aluminium
25.1 × 35.2 cm

Chilean Mummy, year unknown
'Staring Back Series: They Stare', 1952-2006
Black and white photograph mounted on aluminium
35.2 × 26.7 cm

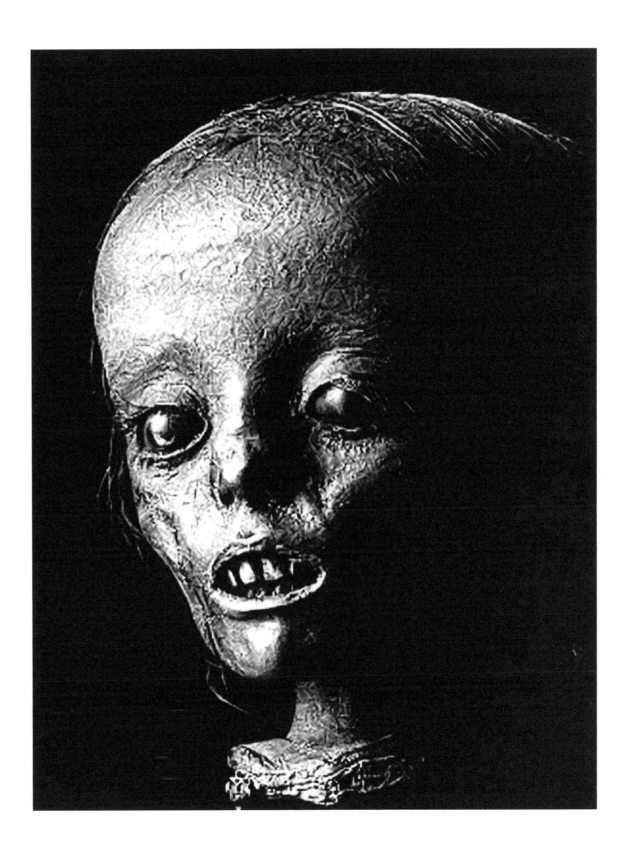

La Jetée

Nicola Mazzanti

From its concept to its realisation, the project of *La Jetée* (1962) was developed by Chris Marker with the support and collaboration of Jacques Ledoux, then the director of the Royal Belgian Cinémathèque. At the time, many French filmmakers regularly visited the Cinémathèque to view the films they needed for their projects, thanks to private screenings organised by Ledoux. This was how Truffaut prepared for his famous interview with Alfred Hitchcock, and how Chris Marker came to watch a long list of science-fiction classics in preparation for *La Jetée*.

But in the case of *La Jetée*, Ledoux's involvement went well beyond a few screenings. He tried, unsuccessfully, to raise funds for the production. He helped Chris Marker in devising the technique used in the film: as proven by the film's credit 'filmed with the Ledoux process' (*procédé Ledoux*). Obviously, such a method never formally existed, but it is evidence that Ledoux's involvement in the creative process went well beyond appearing in the film in the role of the 'Scientist'.

Thanks to this close collaboration two extremely precious and rare collection items came to the Cinémathèque. The first is an exercise book containing an early version of the film's *découpage* or editing list. It consists of five single and 12 double pages with written annotations by Chris Marker and dozens of images – one or more for each shot of the film (they are in fact contact photographs printed off the film negative). The editing order contained in the copybook does not fully correspond to any of the known versions of the film, thus suggesting an early stage of development, somewhere between the shooting and the editing room.

The second is a unique print donated by Chris Marker to the archive. Again, the print witnesses a different stage of the film's development. The editing is completed and it corresponds to the well-known 'definitive' version of the film, with one major difference – the opening credit sequence is in fact in movement. In other words, in this early version the film opens with a man running on the pier ('*la jetée*') at Orly airport. Then the images are frozen, the credits end, and the film starts. Later on, Chris Marker must have changed his mind and produced a different opening credits sequence, in which the images, from the very beginning, are already frozen; the tone and the structure of the film thus changes completely.

In summary, the exercise book and the Cinémathèque's version of the film are unique witnesses allowing a glimpse into the creative process leading to *La Jetée* as we all know it.

LA JETÉE

Séquence A

OF 1

2

3

4

5

6

7

8

9

10

11

12

13

14

FF
4 images

Séquence A _

Séquence B _   Destruction Paris _

Toutes les photos s'enchaînent _

    B. 1 _ s'enchaînera avec le dernier série A en 96×96 _

    B. 1/B2 et ainsi de suite jusqu'à B. 20 s'enchaînent

        48×48 _

    Le n° 21 vous sera fourni Vendredi matin _

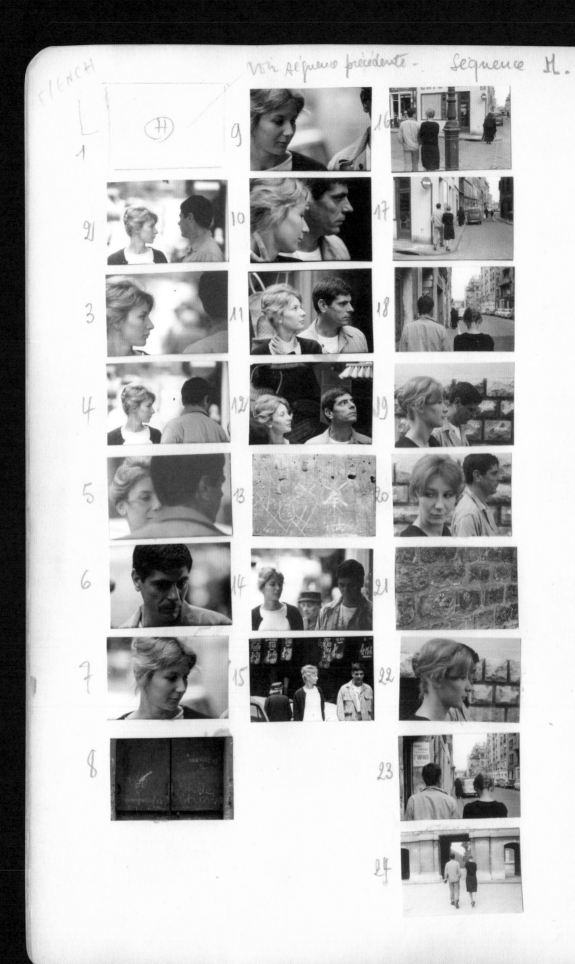

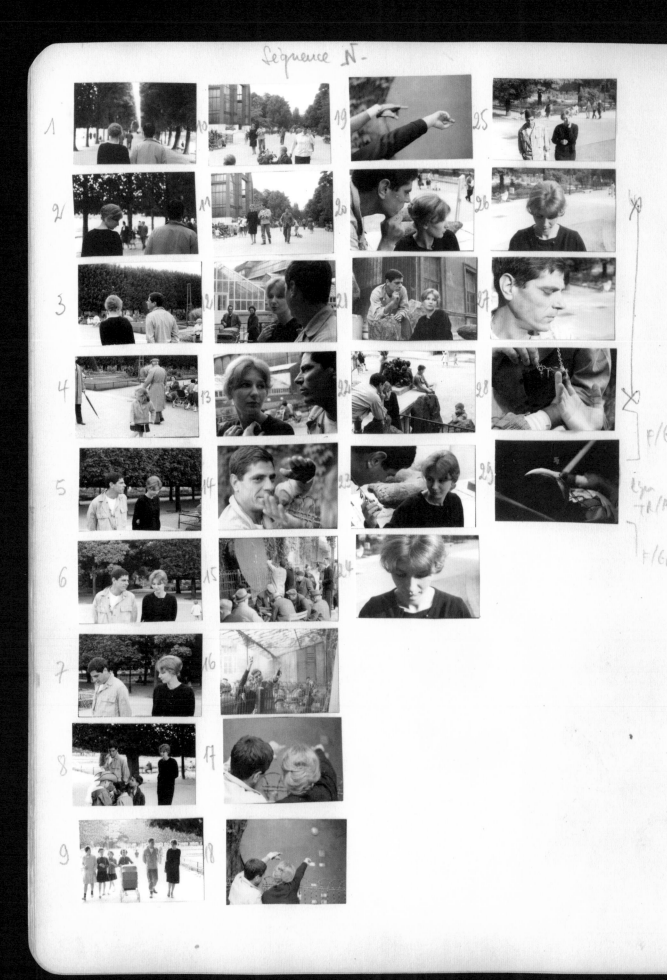

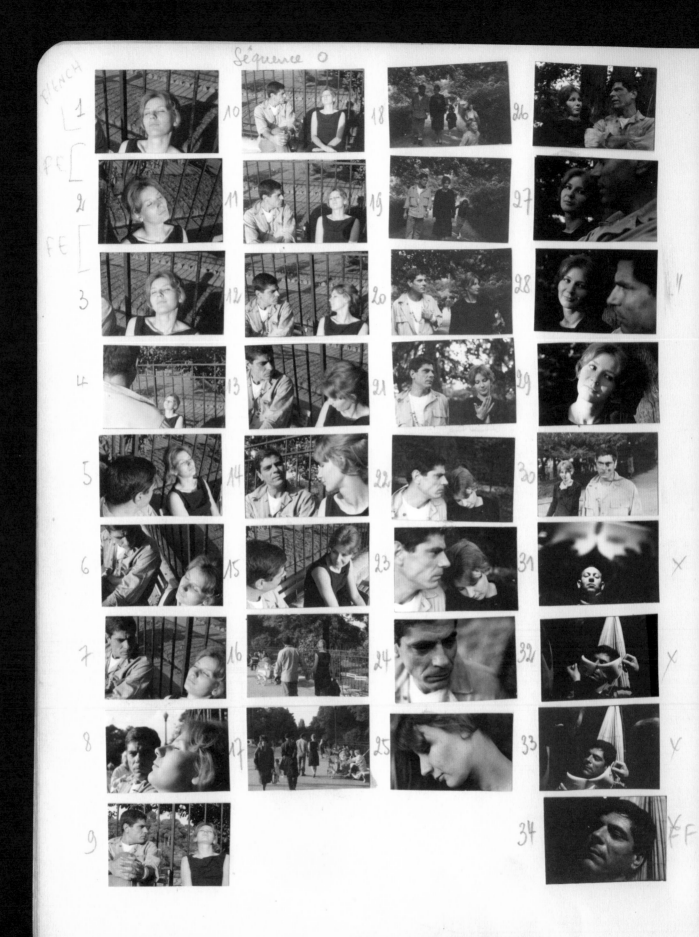

le 0.3 est trop court en clair
succèssen le 7 -
sauter 10 et 12
sauter 16 et 17
sauter 22 -

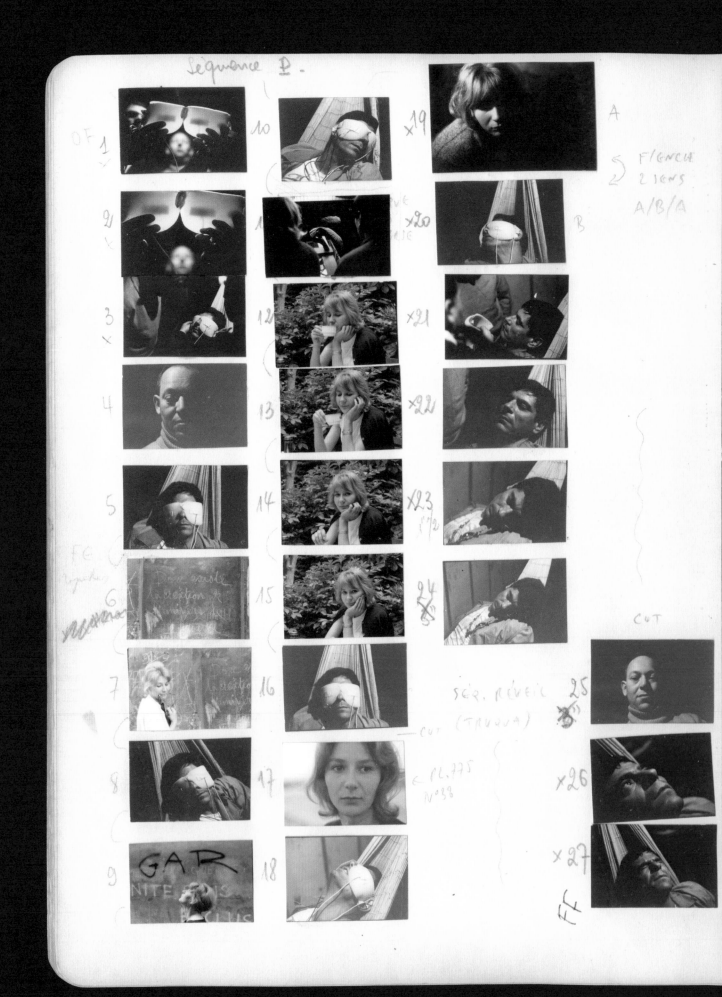

manquent . ④ /8 -   /6 ⑪ /6 - /8 - 24 - 25 -

(6 6 a été donné sous   7 . 21 a.)

↓   ↓

double   mis un
                                          25 a
                                    (plan des 2) -

Fondu 2 - Hélène

~~Ne refaire ? 23~~ tré flou Duffort

retourne sucer le P. 9 - et passer donc .
        de 8 à 15 -

_____

P. 5 /7 /~~8~~ ~~/9/11/12~~ 15 / 16 -

P. 19/ 20 -
P. 24   avec fondu -
P. 27 avec fondu .

67

Séquence complète

6" + F/ENCH

F/ENCH me A: 789-37A-

Marker Forever

Raymond Bellour

Front page of Gorgomancy website, www.gorgomancy.net

Once again I open *Immemory* (1997), as everyone can now do on the Centre Georges Pompidou's *Gorgomancy* site.[1] I enter the CD-ROM that has become unreadable to anyone who has not preserved an old Mac G3 running OS 9, which still gives access to this work dating from the high-tech equivalent of the Middle Ages. I see the homepage with its eight zones. I open the 'Cinema' zone with its '3 cult movies'. I click on *Wings*, William Wellman's war film of 1927, with its three vertical images laid out like film frames. To a musical accompaniment, the moving image in the central frame shows a drama in which two aeroplanes collide in flight, giving the pilot barely enough time to put out a hand for protection before he is killed. A title asks: 'Is it the first film that I SAW?', followed by words superimposed on the poster image of a couple entwined against a sky studded with planes: 'Are you the only one to remember that at its release, the orchestra accompanying *Wings* was playing the scherzo from *A Midsummer Night's Dream* during the dogfights?' Leaving aside the other two options in the 'Cinema' zone, *Aelita* (1924) and *Vertigo* (1958), I plunge deeper into the *Wings* section with repeated clicks of the mouse. First, delicately reframed and lovingly annotated, comes the image of Simone Genevois, the Joan of Arc of 1929 who 'taught a seven-year-old child how a face filling the screen was suddenly the most precious thing in the world'. Then war returns in the shape of more films: *Les Croix de Bois* (The Wooden

Cross, 1932) and *All Quiet on the Western Front* (1930; 'War and tombs, a good beginning for a film buff's life'). After this comes Count Dracula, clue to a metaphorical genealogy. I resist the many temptations to branch off and the women arrive en masse: Garbo in a bouquet, a cascade of first names, an image of Ingrid (Thulin, whom Marker called 'the world's most beautiful actress' in *Si j'avais quatre dromadaires* (If I Had Four Camels, 1966)) and Tatiana (Samoilova, who closes the 'Woman' sequence in five images of poignant idealism, the last with a pose and smile highly reminiscent of the heroine of *La Jetée* (The Pier, 1962)). Then comes a page rich with film titles, signs of a rare and exemplary cinephilia that immediately calls up other friendly filmmakers: Tarkovsky, Kurosawa, Coppola and Costa-Gavras with his *The Confession* (1970). We have now reached the end of this section, marked by the reappearance of the icon signposting the way to the 'Cinema' zone – a hollow CGI bust made of orange threads – and oft-cited, words suddenly rendered dramatic by a mercilessly throbbing sound and given extra weight by Marker's death: 'From *Wings* to *Star Wars* I have seen many things fly over the world's screens. Perhaps cinema has given all it can give, perhaps it must make room for something else. Jean Prévost writes somewhere that death is not so grave, that it consists only in rejoining all that one has loved and lost. The death of cinema would be only that, an immense memory. It is an honourable destiny.'

I watch *Level Five* again. It is Marker's last feature, dated 1996. Official chronology places it between *Silent Movie* of 1995, an installation paying tribute to silent cinema, and *Immemory*. However, the film was long delayed by difficulty in finding the Reverend Shigeaki Kinjo, a crucial witness to the tragedy of Okinawa, while the CD-ROM

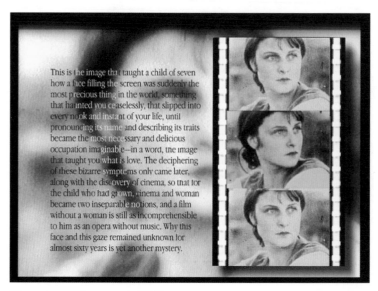

'Cinema' zone, *Immemory*, 1997

project, officially started in 1993, almost certainly spent a long time in the form of dormant fragments in Marker's computer – we might guess at least from *Zapping Zone* (1990-94), his first large installation for the exhibition *Passages de l'Image* at the Centre Pompidou (following the simple wall of screens of *Quand le siècle a pris formes* for the *Paris-Berlin* exhibition in 1978). *Zapping Zone* was subtitled 'Proposals for an Imaginary Television' and initially entitled *Logiciel / Catacombes*. All these pieces form a single, multiform movement, with its own different forces and internal tensions. In the press release, whose every word he weighed, Marker presents *Level Five* as the last element in a quest that had led him, in the course of a few years, 'towards what is rather pompously called the new technologies, to test their interaction with historical or documentary intent'. In the self-interview given to Dolores Walfisch, for which he provided both questions and answers, he states that, alongside video games and computer images, his 'favourite hallucinations' include 'the presence of a lady' as a necessary counterweight to the horror of history apprehended by the senses and intellect. This is what makes his film 'a semi-documentary.'[2] He also says that the ability to make a film with two people, at home, in a room six-foot-by-ten, gives filmmakers 'the wherewithal […] for intimate, solitary film-making. The process of making films in communion with oneself, the way a painter works or a writer.'

I watch *Level Five* again on my computer – I have already seen it in the cinema more than once – straight through, with headphones. I am overwhelmed, and once again convinced that this film, which still, 40 years after Alain Renais's *Night and Fog* (1955) and *Hiroshima mon amour* (1959), obliges us to 'reckon with an extra character: the human race', has a unique position on the very fine line between old and new, the cinema we have known, and which happily has survived, and something else that is hollowing out a space within it.[3] This other thing is linked to solitude, which Maurice Blanchot called 'essential', and also to the computers that people solitude

as no machine has ever peopled human beings before. You can feel this throughout *Level Five*, as Laura struggles with the game of life and death she is constructing. The machine constantly confronts her with reality and virtuality, notably through the types of image that she combines and works with, from the simplest photographic analogy to the most highly drawn abstraction. The real and the virtual are two sides of the same enigma, intertwining and reproducing each other, just as, in Marker's underlying method, described by Resnais 50 years ago now as better than Leonardo da Vinci's, images are beaten from words and words struck from images.[4] But also here – generated by the machine through the fiction that it creates and which *Level Five* embodies and virtualises – is something entirely new: OWL 'Optional World Link', 'the network of networks' that 'gives access to all available networks: radio, television, computerized, existing and non-existing, present and yet to come'.

Level Five, 1996

A film of this kind opens up two perspectives, which interfere with each other in improbable ways. The first reflects the desire for what is still a film, more tentacular, in tune with this new technology, which seems to hold the century in its grip through its wars – notably the First World War, which consummated the destruction of Europe. This is the project of *Owls At Noon*, of which only the prologue was ever made, in the form of an installation described as a 'Prelude' and entitled *The Hollow Men* (2005), based on TS Eliot's famous poem of 1925. The piece comprised eight screens showing a great variety of black-and-white archive stills alternating on a strict a/b/a/b/a/b basis with words from

1. Officially launched in 2013. Following instructions left by Marker the site continues to be developed. It currently includes *La Solitude du chanteur de fond* (The Loneliness of the Long Distance Singer, 1974); *Mémoires pour Simone* (Memories for Simone, 1986); *L'Héritage de la chouette* (The Owl's Legacy, 1989); *Immemory* (1997); *Ouvroir, The Movie* (2010); and *Stopover in Dubai* (2011). The site also contains works by other artists chosen by Marker [Editor's note]. (Produced by Centre Georges Pompidou, Christine Van Assche / Les Films du Jeudi, Laurence Braunberger).
2. According to the adage of Columbia boss Harry Cohn, recalled by Marker: 'A documentary is a film without a woman. If there's a woman it's a semi-documentary.'
3. As Serge Daney, citing Blanchot, said of Resnais being caught up in 'the writing of disaster'. Serge Daney, *Ciné journal, Cahiers du cinéma*, 1986, p.164.
4. See Guy Gauthier, 'Entretien avec Alain Resnais sur Chris Marker, 1963', *Trafic* no.84 winter 2012, pp.55-58.

the poem, also treated as images, and continually moving in a way that governs and alarms perception. *The Hollow Men* is officially the most disturbing of Marker's works since *La Jetée* – with all the difference there is between an installation (a presentation, as he preferred to call it) and a film.[5]

Owls at Noon Prelude: The Hollow Men, 2005

The second perspective involves a surrender to the logics of the internet, to which the singular craftsmanship of *Immemory* opened the way. While seemingly a self-portrait undermining the false antinomies of fiction and documentary, the CD-ROM was based on the assumption that both its subject and its unfolding were infinitely extensible. Ideally it was intended to cover not just Marker's entire oeuvre and associated elements (texts, books, films, photos, archives, etc., freely associated and annotated by their author), but all the possible links generated by a work of culture and memory of this kind. And, rather than remaining a physical object for restricted viewing, *Immemory* was ultimately intended to be screened on the internet, accessing a virtually limitless memory. In this way it would fully become 'immemory' – all the world's memory focused on a single point – even if the real *Immemory*, updated but unchanged, is today simply a not-so-simple component of *Gorgomancy*.

For reasons doubtless related as much to the logics of invention, life and survival as to those of age and fatigue, Marker decided to direct all his efforts down this internet-based path.[6] Of course this did not stop him freely shooting short films intended to be viewed online. He made frequent returns to photography, his lifelong love, that light, everyday art that moves so readily from gallery to book to computer screen.[7] He also found the internet to be an ideal forum for the renewal of intelligence that

was always his strength, and which was illustrated by his humorous collaboration with the Poptronics site (another element of *Gorgomancy*). Lastly and crucially, it seems that in the site *Second Life* (opened in 2003), Marker discovered two priceless advantages: it enabled him to give free rein to the intransigent modesty of unbridled subjectivism (in the booklet for *Level Five* he said, 'All I can offer is myself') and soothed his all-consuming obsession with time and death, for ever set in images in *La Jetée*, by playing at thwarting it. As in *Level Five*, which seems to be a reprise of *La Jetée*, this obsession assumed both the tormented fulfilment of cinema and the obscure promise of its virtualization.

So much has been written about *La Jetée* in the last 50 years. But perhaps there are still things to be said. What happens to the viewer of *La Jetée*, this film made entirely of still images, apart from one brief moment that highlights the paradox? It seems obvious that simply devising a narrative using images apparently devoid of movement – which was new at the time – is not enough to deny movement to them, since their succession, reinforced by optical devices (dissolves and fades to black), a spoken commentary and music, is enough to give back to time what appears to have been taken from it. To be persuaded of this we need only watch the other film of still images (photos and paintings) made four years later, *Si j'avais quatre dromadaires*, which has the delightful, digressive charm of a free-form essay, given consistency by a three-way dialogue in voice-over; it informs, criticises and moves viewers, but does not really disturb them beyond brief points of fascination, made more apparent by the use of still images. The profound sense of unease generated by *La Jetée* must therefore have its origins elsewhere, in what the images show and what the voice says of them, giving their stillness an extreme power to disturb.

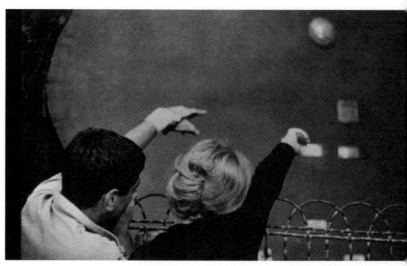

La Jetée, 1962

The long first section accumulates data that seems objective despite its slide towards fantasy: the manifestation of trauma in the imprint of images from childhood, oscillating between a glimpse of a woman's face and a man's death; the Third World War and the destruction of Paris; in underground passages spared by radioactivity, the victors' experiment on prisoners in order to transmute space into 'another time'; the man whose story the film tells has been chosen for his fixation on an image from the past. With the masked face of the supine man, the film changes direction and images begin to well up. After this point, apart from close-ups returning to the hero and his invisible eyes, we see only what he is apparently seeing, including all the shots in which he appears with the woman he meets (and beyond, right up to his meeting with the people of the future), all characterised by a temporal and psychological uncertainty that hovers between perception and the imagery of dreams and imagination. It is here that the still images take on their full importance. For, while the more or less immediate memory of any film, as seen through the variable intermittences of its projection, proceeds by the interposing of still or barely moving images in the jerking succession of stillnesses that characterises mental images, here the accumulation of images that are all still causes us to become mentally alarmed, until the end when, running towards the woman on the pier, the hero understands 'that this haunted moment, given him to see as a child, was the moment of his own death'.

The consequence of the film's much discussed return to its beginning is to multiply for the viewer the accumulated effects of images that are already caught between memory and forgetting. In this it resembles 'the impossible memory, the insane memory' with which Marker always credited *Vertigo*, saying that *La Jetée* was the 'remake in Paris' of this 'film seen nineteen times', and also that this obliges the viewer of *La Jetée* to see the film twice in order to 'reread the first part in the light of the second'.[8] 'A double viewing' was needed, with the inevitable effect of 'double vision' involved in every repeat viewing of *Vertigo* and also produced by *La Jetée*.[9] However, there are two major differences between the original and its remake. The first is the stillness of the images, which call up a different mental economy, truly 'another time', as though the brain were seeking to observe itself in order to escape an anxiety. The second is the source of the images, which inevitably binds the idealised image of the woman to war, the nuclear threat and mass extermination. We need only read *Le Coeur net* (The Forthright Spirit, 1949), the novel Marker wrote in his youth, in which he borrows from André Malraux, Antoine de Saint-Exupéry, and Howard Hawks's 1939 film *Only Angels Have Wings* (high on *Immemory's* list of films), to see the full extent of this continual superimposition of images of love and death caught in the disasters of the century's history, a century that Marker often said should be erased, so that the nineteenth would lead directly to the twenty-first – if the new century were not already heading for the worst. It is not for the pleasure of words alone that Marker makes Laura say – as she continues the history game started with her dead lover, whose memory she maintains through the computer – 'Okinawa mon amour'. It is a tribute to Resnais, a return of *La Jetée* via *Sans soleil* (Sunless, 1982) that heralded *Level Five*. At the same time it is closing a loop nonetheless later developed by *The Hollow Men*, with the invention of forms to match the hopelessness of the images supporting Eliot's funerary poem, and the idea of a new, tragic network of networks, *Owls At Noon* – the century, again, from one world war to another.

But the bird of Minerva – to whom Marker had devoted a television series in the late 1980s (13 episodes × 26 minutes) that should be on the syllabus in every French school (*L'héritage de la chouette* – The Owl's Legacy – is also present in *Gorgomancy*) – felt out of place. It preferred to join forces with the funny, sensual cat that first appeared in *Immemory* and served its master so well, seeking elsewhere how to keep doing the same things, but differently, following the path of optimal curiosity that has been Marker's rule of life. Hence *Second Life*, the unreal reality of another life and the development of a death-defying game in order to survive the inhumanity of the times while remaining fully aware of it. At the same time Marker was honouring a passion for animated film that had remained intact since the days when the young Christian Marker wrote in praise of Jiří Trnka and his *Prince Bayaya* (1950) and noting 'one of the fundamental powers of cinema, the gift of time that it alone can give at will to drawing, painting and imagery'.[10]

5. 'I've decided to stop using the word 'installation', which has been applied to too much rubbish'. Chris Marker, 'The rest is silent', *Trafic*, no. 46, summer 2003, p. 57.
6. On the production of *The Hollow Men* and the abandonment of *Owls At Noon*, see Colin MacCabe, 'Visites rue Courat', *Trafic*, no. 84, winter 2012, pp. 22–28.
7. See Chris Marker, *Staring Back*, exhibition catalogue, Wexner Center for the Arts, Columbus, OH, 2007, and his series 'Passengers', photographs stolen in the métro, exhibited in New York in 2011 at Peter Blum Gallery and at Rencontres d'Arles.
8. Chris Marker, 'Sans soleil', *Trafic*, no. 6, spring 1993, pp. 91–92.
9. Chris Marker, 'A free replay', *Positif*, 'Le cinéma vu par les cinéastes', June 1994, pp. 79–84, and in *Immemory*. English translation in John Boorman and Walter Donohue (eds), *Projections 4½*, Faber, London, 1995.
10. Christian Marker, 'Une forme d'ornement', *Cahiers du cinéma*, no. 8, January 1952, pp. 66–68.

Here's how Guillaume-en-Égypte explains it, while lifting the veil on the mystery of his origins in an interview given to Poptronics: 'What do you like about this parallel universe? – The world of Bioy,[11] a world of phantoms, people of whom we know nothing, whose appearance is necessarily a lie, but where it's precisely so easy to lie that some perverse souls, I'm sure, get a cunning pleasure from telling the truth, just so as not to be believed. Now I have my island in *SL*. I arrange to meet people there from all over the world. And it's a fact that something is being done there that's absolutely new in the history of communication. It's not quite reality and yet… Telephone and emails, even videoconferencing, don't abolish distance so much as emphasize our effort to overcome it. In *SL* it's abolished. You're there and you're not there at the same time, like my other cousin, Schrödinger's cat. No one has ever experienced this before.'[12]

As soon as we enter the *Ouvroir* (2010), which is at once an archipelago and a film – one of the possible films of *Second Life*, prepared for Marker by Max Moswitzer, his computer expert, animator and friend – we are in a world where everything is shifting. Weightlessness characterises the walk – or maybe it's a run – at any rate the somersaulting steps of the delightful new version of Guillaume, with his compact body, wild moustache and big round eyes, as he leads us from the cinema to the large central room and the gallery of transformed images, the X-Plugs. In virtual terms, everything is here: photographs, books, films, installations, all the past and present of the oeuvre, with its weight of history and thought, its continual capacity for invention. But at the same time it is all lite, transmuted, Marker's cat-being fearlessly holds the gaze of Gorgo the Medusa, thanks to the hand that holds the mouse. When the X-Plugs have run out and the cycle of wars is exhausted, Guillaume stands facing the sea and conjures up Chateaubriand saying he had seen the end of the world at Waterloo. 'What are you watching?' Guillaume asks us.

If, as legend already has it, Chris Marker died at his computer, we hope that he found himself in this second world, invented so that he could go on tolerating the first, through the inventive gentleness of his cat-of-all-trades and the juvenile elegance of his Russo-Japanese avatar Sergei Murasaki, in white T-shirt and tight trousers – forever.

*

I was 22 when my friend Jean Michaud and I imprudently imagined an 'Apology for Chris Marker' on the model offered by Plato.[13] I was 24 when, on the spiral staircase leading to, among other things, the 'Petite Planète' office at Éditions du Seuil, Marker pleaded with me – the word that comes is too strong but I can find no other – or asked me not to write a little book on his films, which already constituted an oeuvre, for the 'Cinéastes d'aujourd'hui' series, in its early days at the time. I had been asked to do so by Pierre Lherminier, following one I had written on Alexandre Astruc. It was just after *La Jetée* (hailed in the last issue of *Artsept*, our Lyon-based journal, where Marker had been a permanent guest). Of course I have not written the book, nor any other on Marker. May these few pages stand in their stead, following so many writings over the years, written for a living man, with respect, admiration and friendship across distance.

(Many thanks to Christine Van Assche and Étienne Sandrin for telling me about *Gorgomancy* and *Second Life*; to Laurence Braunberger for lending me her avatar so I could take a wander around, and to Agnès Varda who, in the first episode of her television series *Agnès de ci de là Varda*, preserved a living image of the improbable studio on rue Courat, in which, with her old friend's complicity, she showed if not a face, at least his hands manipulating books and images, and allowed us to hear his inimitable voice.)

11. This is of course the novel, *The Invention of Morel* by Adolfo Bioy Casares which was published in 1940.
12. www.poptronics.fr/Sans-Chris-Marker (accessed 22 October 2012).
13. Raymond Bellour and Jean Michaud, 'Apologie de Chris Marker: Signes', *Cinéma 61*, no. 57, January 1961.

Ouvroir. The Movie, 2010
(in association with Max Moswitzer)

Image (journey)

Arnaud Lambert

Images in Chris Marker's work are inextricably linked to travel and journeys. The principle is established at the start of his second personal film, *Dimanche à Pékin* (Sunday in Peking, 1956). The journey has its origins in an earlier image, which is then verified in situ (following Gérard de Nerval's principle) in order to be sure (*en avoir le coeur net*, to borrow the title of Marker's novel published in 1949), to see 'for oneself':[1]

> In my mind's eye was an engraving from a children's book, not knowing where it was exactly, and it was at the gates of Peking: the avenue leading to the Ming tombs. And one fine day I was there. It's quite unusual to be able to walk around an image from childhood.
> *Dimanche à Pékin*, 1st minute

Dimanche à Pékin, 1956

Later Marker devoted a sequence in the 'Memory' zone of his CD-ROM *Immemory* (1997) to the famous engraving, transferred from the montage of *Dimanche à Pékin*. This gave him the opportunity to add a few biographical details. Slotted in between the original engraving by Riou and the images of *Dimanche à Pékin* is a photograph dated 1911 of 'uncle Anton Krasna', a focus of fantasy for Marker. So here was not one childhood image, but two, one acting as a booster: layers, already.

The explanation that opens *Dimanche à Pékin* underpins more or less the entire filmography of the 1950s, Marker's so-called 'travel film' period (Peking, Siberia, Cuba, Israel). So, at the start – or rather the starting point – there were images, usually images from childhood.[2] Early comic strip author Christophe's *La Famille Fenouillard* has a special place here: 'The aim of most of my journeys has been to go and check in situ the information provided by this seminal book.'[3] It is this action, emphasised by fiction, that we find embodied in the central character of *La Jetée* (The Pier, 1962). An opening explanation indicates his distinctive nature: he is 'marked by an image from his childhood'; his whole life is governed by the desire to return to the reality of that image. The problem is displaced slightly in *Sans soleil* (Sunless, 1982), where the 'marking' image, the one that it must become possible to 'edit' (one of the film's journeys is to edit in

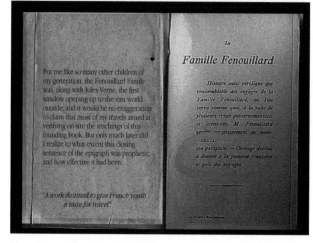

'Travel' zone, *Immemory*, 1997

this image successfully: the power of this isolated image), is an 'image of happiness'. What does it show? Children at the end of a path. An *image of children*. It is moreover impossible not to link these blond Icelandic children to the 'real children' of the 11th minute of *La Jetée*.[4]

This first moment has been perceived fairly clearly. The link between image and travel then undergoes a kind of reversal, which is less discussed. The aim is no longer to qualify images through an experience of reality (going to experience them in situ: travelling for the image), but through them to conduct an experiment (travelling through the image). Images become independent and ultimately give travel its own specific value. This reversal is the underlying principle of *Si j'avais quatre dromadaires* (If I Had Four Camels, 1966). Here the film is no longer the outcome of the journey; it is the editing that creates a journey, through a fictional conversation around photographs 'taken in twenty-six countries between 1955 and 1965': a peregrination in and through images.[5]

This conception is ultimately confirmed as a *topos* of Marker's work, almost a reflex of thought, perceptible in certain metonymic slippages. For example, in the 94th minute of *Sans soleil:* 'And then in its turn the journey entered the "zone"': behind 'journey' we must understand 'film' (on screen, a digest of *Sans soleil* passes through Hayao Yamaneko's electronic machine). The 'Travel' zone of *Immemory* is also structured around this willing belief in the equivalence of images and journeys. It is moreover, and very clearly, a remake of *Si j'avais quatre dromadaires*, imitating the film's tone and citing a few passages: 'Sidewalk in Paris… Sidewalk in Tehran'; later on, 'Daybreak on the Berlin wall'. And, as in the film, the 'journey' is made through photographs, presented without any geographical or temporal order. This apparent lack of rigour is sometimes a little unsettling, particularly since the CD-ROM's 'Photography' zone is geographically structured by country. The forms are so close that it is sometimes hard to tell which zone one is in. This intricate relationship between image and journey is important primarily because it is a good indicator of Marker's relationship to images, and of the conceptions of his imagination in general.

Now we can begin to grasp the extent of the reversal that has occurred: if images can replace or represent journeys, this is because, in Marker's mind, they are equivalent to a space-time and a lived experience. Two models spring to mind to describe this conception of the imagination. The first, never mentioned by Marker as such, is structured around the notion of 'document', the documentary image

La Jetée, 1962

Sans soleil, 1982

1. The etymological source of the word 'autopsy', as Jean-Pierre Vernant notes in episode 5 of *L'héritage de la chouette* (The Owl's Legacy, 1989).
2. See Guy Gauthier, *Chris Marker, écrivain multimedia ou Voyage à travers les medias*, L'Harmattan, Paris, 2001, pp.13-33, or his article 'Images d'enfance', *Théorème*, 'Recherches sur Chris Marker', no.6, 2002, pp.46-59.
3. Chris Marker, *Immemory*, 1997, 'Travel' zone.
4. The photograph of a single, entirely androgynous child looking into the distance.
5. Chris Marker, *Commentaires* vol.2 Éditions du Seuil, Paris, 1967, p.86 (note).

(product of a real, recorded experience). The second is recollection, a paragon discussed by Marker in *Sans soleil* through the principle of possible 'links between memories'. Of course what is interesting is that Marker skilfully confuses these two types of image, for example when, in *Sans soleil*, he suggests that: 'They [these images that I filmed] are my memory.'

> Brooding at the end of the world on my island of Sal in the company of my prancing dogs I remember that month of January in Tokyo, or rather I remember the images I filmed of the month of January in Tokyo. They have substituted themselves for my memory. They are my memory.
> *Sans soleil*, 85th minute

And this confusion is legitimate because every time what is at stake is a particular relationship to the past, which has returned through the (mental or recorded) image with the appearance of a present. The definitions of memory and document are not fundamentally different. While Marker prefers to give primacy to the memory-image, which is particularly evocative, we cannot ignore the document-images, which he uses to show us his imaginary conceptions and share them with us. The 'document' is assumed to have a special relationship with the real past, and so is not quite like any other kind of image. Before being a piece of evidence, it is a temporal complex; rather than a double or reflection, it is a relic or trace[6] (the statutory ambiguity of reproduction), in other words, very quickly, it becomes the reality itself carried by the image. The document reinforces its own transmutation from image to reality with all kinds of reality effects, including connotations of 'rawness'. Marker adopts presuppositions around mechanical images in order to use them to support his fictions. Seen in this light, his documentary practice becomes much richer. Ultimately all these sequences, zones and journeys rely on an overflowing (or accepted) faith in the powers of the image.

Along the way, the question of time travel – so beloved of science fiction and raised many times by Marker – finds an answer. Since each image represents a space-time, the journey through time becomes the product of an interplay of images. The aim is to re-establish contact with a moment in the past, which images permit. What makes it possible to pass from one time to another is having an image of each moment at one's disposal. Marker had just such an archive in the form of the images

he had shot himself in different countries over the course of nearly 60 years.

'[The images] were already inside him and projected themselves.'[7] The fable of the man from 4001, mentioned above and related in the 70-73rd minutes of *Sans soleil*, provides a synthesis of these ideas, combining memory, image, journey and projection in time. The entwining of strands of thought is moreover a component of Marker's definition of the imagination. Let us return to the description. A man is walking on 'those volcanic soils that stick to the soles of your shoes'.

> All of a sudden he stumbles, and the next step it's a year later. He's walking on a small path near the Dutch border along a sea bird sanctuary.
> *Sans soleil*

In the sequence of the man from 4001, who has total recall, 'documents' and 'memories' are images shot on an Icelandic volcano, followed by a shot of the Dutch shoreline – both from a subjective viewpoint. Clearly these images carry a present that is past, something of Holland and Iceland in the early 1980s.

The entire fable and its effectiveness (that is, the effectiveness of 'linked memories', in other words of time travel) rely on the belief fostered by the filmmaker that these images make a 'reality'. But nothing could be less clear: in principle, however perfect, the memory of the year 4001 remains a memory, namely imaginary. The comparisons made in the mind of the man whose story we are told, the famous 'memory links', come with mental images attached. But, in the fable, these images are sufficiently tangible to make the remembered reality 'practicable'. The man from the future travels in time; he moves instantly from Iceland to the Dutch shoreline. His memory becomes reified, the memory takes on concrete form; images have consistency, they make reality.

Described as a film to come ('In Iceland I laid the first stone of an imaginary film'), this fiction of the future is in reality the remake of a film Marker had made before.[8]

6. See Yves Michaud, 'Formes du regard. Philosophie et Photographie', in Michel Frizot (ed), *Nouvelle Histoire de la Photographie*, Adam Biro / Bordas, Paris, 1994, p.736.
7. Chris Marker, 'Phénomène (n.m.)', *Trafic*, no.30, summer 1999, pp.26-33.
8. See Raymond Bellour, 'Le Livre, aller, retour', in Laurent Roth and Raymond Bellour, *Qu'est-ce qu'une madeleine? À propos du CD-ROM Immemory de Chris Marker*, Yves Gevaert Éditeur / Centre Georges Pompidou, Paris, 1997, p.70.
9. Chris Marker, *La Jetée*, 1962, 14th minute.
10. Chris Marker, 'Orphée', *Esprit*, no.173, November 1950, pp.694-701. See also this catalogue, pp.107-115.

The problem of the consistency of images was already present in *La Jetée*. The prisoner manages to tolerate the experiments and slot into other times (the past and then the future) only because his imaginary life is particularly strong ('this man was chosen because of his obsession with an image from the past.')[9] In *La Jetée* as in *Sans soleil*, it is because images have a powerful – it is tempting to say 'palpable' – effect in that they make time travel possible. In a way the fable of 1982 illuminates that of 1962 by emphasising the imagination: the projection mechanisms are no longer a matter of technology (injections, experimental procedures), but are portrayed as mental attributes – perfect memory and full use of the brain.

This understanding of images as instances of space-time (belief or fantasised projection, for now it does not matter which) leads to an original conception of time. Marker's time can be understood only as an imaginary entity. It is images that define time, giving it reality and rhythm. Here again, the fable of 4001 offers a springboard.

A man walks over volcanic ground, he stumbles, and the next step it is a year later, he is walking along the Dutch border. The logical consequence of the total recall with which this man from the future is endowed, the 'full employment' of the brain, is the instant passage from volcanic soils to a coastal path. The transition is a cut: it is instant, but it is a year later. The fable of the man from 4001 describes a situation that is temporally and spatially complex and paratactic: Marker uses the pretext of perfect memory to bring unrelatable moments together by restoring to them full ownership of their presence. The image of a sea bird sanctuary follows that of a volcano, just as before Berlin followed Tehran. It is 'the never absent eternity' that Marker predicted in 1950.[10] And he was far-sightedly speaking the truth. The perfect memory described in the *Sans soleil* sequence is nothing other than a secularised version of the Eden-like temporality of the postwar decades.

> Day breaks in this narrow land. In the beaches to the west, the mountains to the north, in Manara (...) Day breaks in Haifa, day breaks in Tel-Aviv, built on sand, in Jerusalem in the no man's land (...) in Beer-Sheva, where Zazie passes in the Negev, and in Eilat, the little port on the Red Sea.
> *Description d'un combat* (Description of a Struggle) 1960, 13th minute

Peking

Brussels

'Six o'clock across all the Earth' sequence from *Si j'avais quatre dromadaires* (If I Had Four Camels), 1966 (and overleaf)

Prague

Tehran

Berlin

The list of Israeli dawns is only one of many others we could mention in Marker's early films, in which the real disparity between times and spaces is swept away in a ubiquitising, fervent and poetic montage. At the time, this simultaneist reflex expressed itself in different ways. Sometimes the aim was to indicate a need to pull back, step aside or look from afar, so that the singularity of a situation could be seen objectively, in context and at a distance. This panoramic vision, intended to recall the historical continuity and expanse of the world, was expressed, for example, in a long list in the 46th minute of *Cuba sí!* (1961):

> Such was Havana in 1961: machine guns on the rooftops and conga in the streets. In the rest of the world, life went on as normal. What was being talked about in the world at that time? People, countries, fabulous beasts, Algeria, France, America, space, time, the Congo, Laos, Africa, and the forms that violence and prayer would take there in the second half of the century. It was then that people in the world began also talking about Cuba.

At other times it is more directly a matter of singing the Unity of life, the great communion of beings and the world, the principle of a universally shared Identity – Humanity. 'We realize that this creativity is boundless, that everything communicates.'[11] Always, the linking of different situations to the single time of the present acts to transform instants into icons: one dawn in Eilat stands for all dawns in Eilat, past or future. Linking presents gives them eternity. Jean-Paul Sartre described something similar in *À propos de Jean Giraudoux* (1940): 'This evening of all evenings is a "Paris evening"; this little street, of all the streets going up to the Sacré-Coeur, is "rue de Montmartre"; time has stopped, we are living a moment of happiness, an eternity of happiness.'[12]

In *Si j'avais quatre dromadaires* it is said: 'It is six o'clock across all the Earth.' The same time everywhere. 'Six o'clock over Peking's Forbidden City. Daybreak over Brussels, and over Prague, over Tehran and over Berlin.' The dawns photographed by Marker over years of travel are gathered together in a unanimist song. Integral presents, logically unrelatable, are nevertheless linked and brought together by editing. Marker explains:

11. Chris Marker, *Les Statues meurent aussi* (Statues Also Die), 1953, 13th minute.
12. Cited by Marker in *Giraudoux par lui-même* (Giraudoux in His Own Words), Éditions du Seuil, Paris, 1952, p. 21.
13. Chris Marker, *Description d'un combat*, 1960, 6th minute.

'Nostalgia for Eden' sequence from *Si j'avais quatre dromadaires*
(If I Had Four Camels), 1966

And then I don't know, the feeling of
bringing the world together, of reconciling
it, of making all the time zones the same …
it must be part of the nostalgia for Eden,
that it should be the same time everywhere.
Pierre, *Si j'avais quatre dromadaires*,
2nd minute

In *Description d'un combat, Si j'avais quatre
dromadaires* and frequently elsewhere, Marker was
creating a monologue of desire, a film of ubiquity, of
Omniscience – like the 'eye of God', as would be said
in his *Le Souvenir d'un avenir* (Remembrance of
Things to Come) in 2001. These are films in which
time always appears in the present, with the innocence
of birth (at dawn) and lists.

In *Sans soleil* eschatological expressions have been
replaced by 'memory' (boosted to perfection). But memory
is fundamentally a figure of hope and re-enchantment
to which they have bequeathed their missions and
characteristics. We need to examine this temptation
towards Unity, which is recurrent in Marker's work.
'Communicating – establishing order, a relationship
between hostile or incomprehensible things' soon
becomes a matter of editing (in this light it is logical
that Marker uses particularly tolerant shot transitions:
correspondences, analogies, memory).[13] The filmmaker
seems haunted by the idea of gathering together,
a great transversal community uniting all beings and
things, in the four dimensions of space and time. All
of creation! Even the 'most humble things'. And here
Marker places himself within the long time of modernity:

Junkopia, 1981

Since the beginning of the century, through the conversation-poems of Apollinaire, the newspaper collages of Picasso and Braque and the tracings of Max Ernst, to Calder's mobiles and the tick tock shocks of McLaren via others that were less foreseen, a plot unfolds (...) which consists of raising the most humble things from the disdain to which they were abandoned by the art of the egotistical, humanist and megalomaniacal periods. (...) Redemption extends to the whole of creation; gold and lead are guests at the same supper (with a preference for lead).
Giraudoux par lui-même, pp. 25-26

Ultimately Marker did not depart from this declaration of principle, which was even ratified by a short film around 30 years later. *Junkopia* (1981), the utopia of waste, shows sculptures assembled from recycled materials, piled up on waste ground and undoubtedly designed by a disciple of Heath Robinson or Facteur Cheval; at first we seem to be on an island – 'at a latitude of 37°45′ north and a longitude of 122°27′ west' – before discovering the close proximity of a major arterial road and a city – 'filmed in San Francisco, July 1981'.

This temporality of fable relies on an elective relationship to the present. The time of lists and free juxtapositions (freed from causality) is a time apart, liable now and then – for example here – to evade the rigorous, structuring logic of grammatical tenses: the present is the time that reigns in Eden (of Carl Dreyer's *The Passion of Joan of Arc* (1928) Marker speaks of the 'present of eternity'[14]). Like the time of Eden before, the 'memory of the future', the perfect memory of 4001 has revolutionary virtues: it refutes the passing (the direction) of traditional western temporality, asserting that two moments that are separate in space and time can be linked. Concretely, we can imagine the simultaneist temporality imagined by Marker as a plane on which all instants – in other words all memory-images – would lie and be available, similar to a map or 'plate' (in the photographic sense). Stripped of depth, time would be understood as an expanse of possibilities, the unitary assemblage of moments. They would all be there, face up (towards us), all conjoined and ready to be imagined.

In relation to *La Jetée*, Philippe Dubois uses a metaphor: 'Life (the past lived as present from the future) [appears] as a strip of time in which all instants are arranged side-by-side, like film frames.'[15] Indeed the 'film strip' is suggested by a particular extract from the French voice-over: 'Those conducting the experiment tighten their control. Time is rolled back up, the moment passes by again.'[16] It is a filmmaker's, or more precisely an editor's metaphor: the failed strip of film that is rolled up and passes through the viewer again; the manipulation of rolls of film is equivalent to the manipulation of time – the work of the editor rather than the projectionist (the metaphor is 'convenient' but unfortunately a little confused: each film frame, each image, is equivalent to a 'living time', a particular *duration* and the strip of film represents the expanse of time. But to express the temporality that underlies all these fictions of Marker's, we need to understand that this strip does not 'pass by' like a film positive – that is the big problem with this idea: it ultimately leads to a linear temporality. We would do better to understand it as a cataloguing mechanism – indeed Dubois talks about 'lists' and tabular forms – in which presents are somehow preserved and addressed, in other words made available.)

The time-based machinery that is cinema (notably its concrete manipulations in editing and projection) is undoubtedly an operational model. It was cinema which, as both practice and paragon, enabled Marker to refine his singular perception of the image, and thus of space and time. Editing is the correlate of this perception: space-time images must be linked to each other in order to manufacture a journey, in other words an experience of time, a substitute temporality. There is an almost perfect congruence between these ideas, their exploration (in the form of fictions) and the medium used to expound and stage them. The result is a metonymic slippage that reveals Marker's imaginary, characterised by ubiquity of an Edenic type, mnemonic analogism and the cinematographic montage of documents. Three models that conjugate experience in the present; three models that are really only one and which cinema, a 'system of integral ubiquity' as Edgar Morin put it, ultimately subsumes.[17]

---

14. 'The use of close-ups, absence of make-up, neutral sets and costumes all tend towards the same goal, which is to write a film, dare I say, in the present of eternity.' Chris Marker, *'La Passion de Jeanne d'Arc', Esprit*, no.190, May 1952, pp.841-842. This idea is modulated in 'Le film d'un auteur: *La Passion de Jeanne d'Arc*' in Jacques Chevalier (ed), *Regards neufs sur le cinéma*, 'Peuple et Culture' series, no.8, Éditions du Seuil, Paris, 1953, p.259.
15. Philippe Dubois, 'La Jetée de Chris Marker ou le cinématogramme de la conscience', *Théorème*, 'Recherches sur Chris Marker', no.6, 2002, p.41. See also Francis Massart, 'La Science et *La Jetée*', *Trafic*, no.46, summer 2003, p.69.
16. *La Jetée*, 14th minute. The English script loses the metaphor: 'The experimenters tighten their controls and send him back on the trail. Time flows by again, the moment returns.'
17. Edgar Morin, *Le Cinéma ou l'Homme imaginaire. Essai d'anthropologie* (1956), Gonthier, Paris, 1958, p.55.

When the Century Took Shape
WAR AND REVOLUTION

Gay-Lussac Nite(Paris, May 1968), 1968
'Staring Back Series: I Stare 1', 1952-2006
Black and white photograph mounted on aluminium,
27.9 × 39.2 cm

Barr (Paris, May 1968), 1968
'Staring Back Series: I Stare 1', 1952-2006
Black and white photograph mounted on aluminium
24.5 × 35.2 cm

Demo 4 (Paris, May 1968), 1968
'Staring Back Series: I Stare 1', 1952-2006
Black and white photograph mounted on aluminium
35.2 × 25.4 cm

Le Joli Mai (The Merry Month of May), 1962
Chris Marker & Pierre Lhomme
Black and white, 35mm, original version 165 minutes,
restored 2013 version 146 minutes (and following three pages)

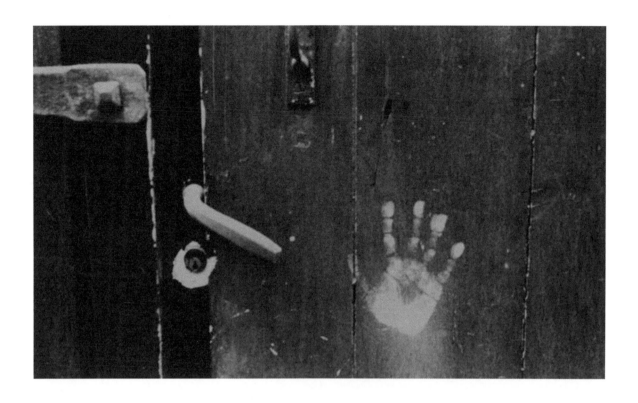

Chats perchés (The Case of the Grinning Cat), 2004
Colour, video, 59 minutes

Owls at Noon Prelude: The Hollow Men, 2005
CD-ROM video for 8 screens, 19 minute loop with sound,
dimensions variable

Owls at Noon Prelude: The Hollow Men (detail)

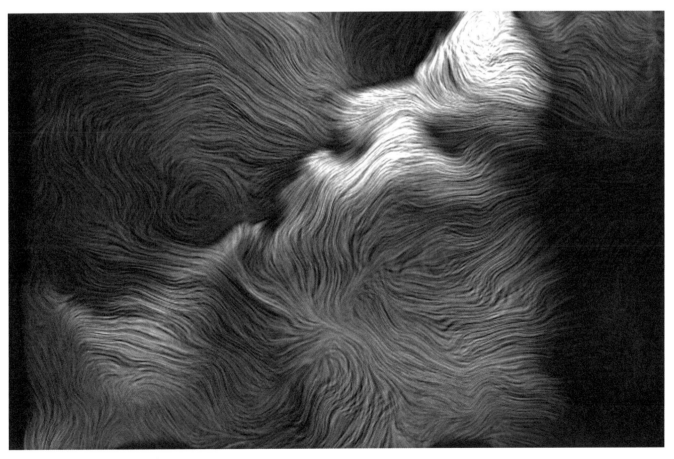

Untitled (from *The Hollow Men*), 2005
Photogravure, 53.3 × 71.7 cm

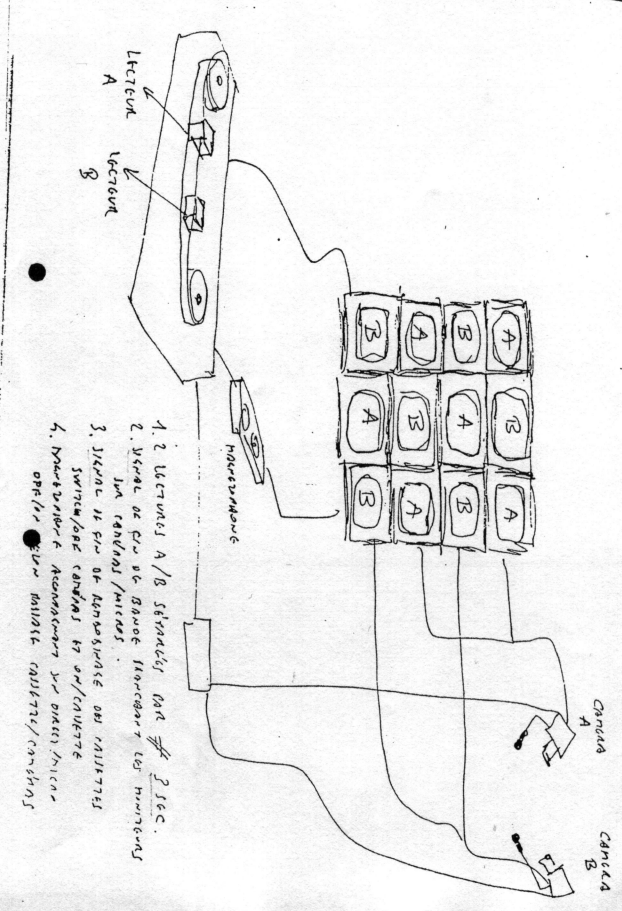

Quand le siècle
a pris formes

Christine Van Assche

Quand le siècle a pris formes (When the Century Took Shape) is a montage of events from the first 30 years of the twentieth century, that Marker described as 'tangible beacons', and which are deliberately treated in the cinematic language of the period (newsreel, 'kino-eye', silent cinema, documents and elements of fiction film). Archive film sequences from the First World War, the Russian and German revolutions, and the postwar period are intercut with text captions.

The sequences are colourised shot-by-shot by a Spectron video synthesiser corresponding to the countries they refer to: brown for Germany, red for Russia and clear blue for the French frontline. The entire work is set to a period composition by Hanns Eisler.

Initially entitled *Guerre et Révolution* (War and Revolution), the installation was first produced for the major interdisciplinary show *Paris-Berlin* at the Centre Pompidou in 1978. Its original configuration consisted of 12 monitors arranged in four rows of three screens, with a three-second delay between the video output of every two monitors thus creating 'a division of rhythm and perception'.

According to Marker, the work is not so much 'a history lesson', but one which 'isolates the elements that made the end of the First World War and the revolutionary period the repertoire of almost everything that has altered the contemporary vision of the world.'

Quand le Siècle a pris formes (Guerre et Révolution)
(When the Century Took Shape (War and Revolution)), 1978
Chris Marker in association with François Helt, music: Hanns Eisler
Multi-media installation: monitor, video, soundtrack, colour, 15:39 minutes

Opposite page: plan of original installation by Chris Marker

97

Le Fond de' l'air est rouge (A Grin Without a Cat), 1977
Black and white / colour, 16mm blown up to 35mm
240 minutes / 180 minutes (and following five pages)

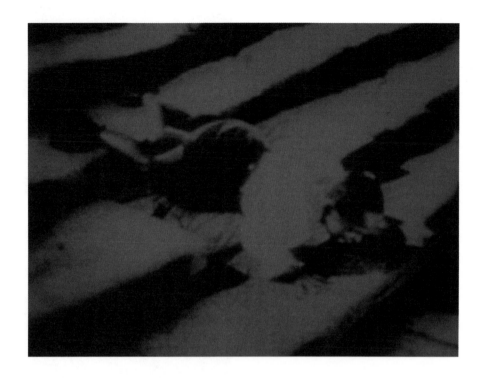

Poptronics, 2007–11
Cartoon commentaries on current affairs created in Photoshop
and featuring Marker's feline avatar Guillaume-en-Égypte. Many were
made for the French website Poptronics and were sent out as faxes
and emails to correspondents and friends.

GEE jesse VE

GEE limbaugh

GEE saddam

GEE amoeba

peppercop GEE eggs

occupy zencat

Gay-Lussac (Paris, May 1968), 1968
'Staring Back Series: I Stare 1', 1952-2006
Black and white photograph mounted on aluminium
24.5 × 35.2 cm

Orphée, 1950, directed by Jean Cocteau

Orphée

Chris Marker

I had the privilege of presenting *Orphée*[1] to a group of young French and foreign filmmakers, towards the end of the holidays. The silence that followed the last image was of the same order as the silence that follows *Parsifal* in Bayreuth: a level of feeling that ought not to be thrown back in its author's face in the small change of a few cheers, so as to be free of it, but that we carry away with us, inside ourselves. There was someone there who'd been sent by the producer. He could have misinterpreted our silence. So we applauded. But this was true acclaim: apart from a progressive Swiss, a post-revolution nouveau-riche type desperately attempting to chain himself to the toilets, to the very carriage of Death, there to denounce the mythology of a decaying society,[2] and apart from an Englishman congenitally immune to all poetry, everyone was already in-thrall to the film. Admiration in fact took second place, for the incredible formal beauties of *Orphée* would only emerge upon reflection. The crucial thing was that the film was beginning its work: we had penetrated the radioactive zone, we were affected, it was no longer in our power to choose to give way or to resist it. And some among us *were afraid*.

The cool reception that, it appears, *Orphée* received upon its world premiere is no doubt due to other factors. Certainly the ranks of Republican guardsmen, the '4m80-wide' carpets,[3] the boxes of sugared almonds covered with Jean Cocteau's drawings, did not, perhaps, make an ideal introduction to this 'meditation on death'. But above all, how could the film not chill the audience that attends these premieres, this Parisian Everyman to whom this is not done and who freezes in horror at the notion that it could be done to him, when he is presented with a work of art that denies him. For *Orphée* can be unlocked by several different keys, and its doors open on to several levels. Its true, sensitive audience, which penetrates the film simply by means of the identification which is cinema's speciality, may grow fearful of itself, as were my young foreigners. An audience of initiates, already in possession of the first key, which, in this Orpheus-Cocteau, as earlier in *Le Sang d'un poète*,[4] reads its own most explicit condemnation, may no longer identify with what they see. The extensions, the harmonics are not for this audience. Naivety, the innocent viewer's primary condition, is denied to our initiate. He will see in the spectacle only what concerns him, that is: his responsibility. If there is in this world a Cocteau legend, a Cocteau caricature that turns this labourer into a man of society, this monk into an acrobat and his brilliance into 'polish', it is the effect of the audiences that attend these premieres. *The gestures of a man who treads upon death must be very funny*, wrote Cocteau in 1923.[5] Since that moment, if he reveals his game, if this contrary magician unveils his props, opens his cupboards, reveals that his white magic is black magic, his pigeons are alive, his women really are chopped into pieces and he really is walking upon death, his audience will drop him. Loftily excluded from the debate between Orpheus and his Death, incapable of the humility and the detachment by which an ordinary viewer may nevertheless play his part in the sacrifice, he loses interest in a dream that ceases to be his.[6]

*

Doubting the power of cinema to 'pose problems', as we say, is to cast doubt on a technique of revelation that is as old as the mind, even to forget the role of myth, which is to refract, to reduce: using a model appropriate to his needs, the patient takes the measure of the mystery. This is the function of the fable, of the apparition, of the miracle. From Mount Sinai to Paramount, the only difference lies in the audience. In order to have us take the measure of death, in his first *Orphée*, the stage play, Cocteau went straight for that most *serious* of templates: the music hall. The sets had that toughness and fragility shared by fairground stalls; the objects came into play as do the accessories of a tightrope walker, of a trapeze artist; the characters themselves drew on the metaphors of tightrope and safety net. For this undertaking, our well-worn 'theatre', made comfortable by luxury and idleness, would not do. Actors were no longer appropriate, those sleek men who disguise themselves inside upholstered dressing rooms. What Cocteau needed were acrobats, thin men who put on their make-up in the corridors and risk their lives every evening in a single, endlessly perfected exercise. But this was to unsettle both theatregoers, who understood not an instant of it, and those who frequented the circus, who would not set foot in Cocteau's theatre. Only the cinema could make the miracle possible, with its borderless audience; its actors, animals on their hind legs that are simultaneously gods, its Indians, its undeniable corpses. In his 1926 dedication, Cocteau said of *Orphée* that admiration left him cold and his only concern was to be direct. It does indeed seem that the only credibility with which an artist can work these days is that of film – and that Saint Thomas requires no more than a Technicolor projection to be persuaded.

I haven't got that fine passage in *La Difficulté d'être*[7] to hand, the one in which Cocteau talks about those who struggle to believe in the truth of the mind's adventures. In it he says, roughly, that the battle, the risk, the fear, the flight are not solely the realm of the body. Some of these take place in the soul, without thereby becoming any less real or less dangerous. This passage should clarify the method by which *Orphée* was assembled – a method that proceeds not by means of 'symbols', which is to say by substitution, but by elaboration. We watch *Orphée* as we read Kafka: not worrying about what the characters 'represent', staying instead at the level of the story. Yet in this story, each word resounds from the other side of the wall and, without sacrificing any of its own architecture, it simultaneously builds an invisible path where what we find are indeed the soul's adventures. So much so that the fable is no longer that game of characters familiar from the moral tale, in which each image can be peeled away to reveal the meaning printed beneath it – but rather the imitation and the prefiguring of a truth of which the fable permits us only to feel the depth and estimate our distance. We may, however, imagine that in this, more than ever, the poet has kept to a strict law, that of a two-fold realism. His microcosm must be precise, must possess a crystalline accuracy – moreover, Cocteau has been at pains to point out that the supernatural too has its laws. Hence the excess of verisimilitude and of attention to detail that we find in *Orphée*. The horse in the play and its messages have been replaced by a car equipped with a wireless radio. A real car, real wireless. The formulae that the author uttered while hidden behind the image in *Le Sang d'un poète* now come in the form of the personalised messages to which radio has accustomed us. Everywhere this search for solidity, for the fact, for that narrow reality which is not substantially different from the reality of souls, of death, which is both similar to it and foreign, like the front and back of a tapestry. Even the reality that is closest to us: that of the war, of messages transmitted by radio, of ruins, of purge trials. Which is not to suggest that Cocteau cynically 'uses' features of our times to make the myth meaningful to us (it demands all the thoughtlessness of a new-style critic at *Combat*[8] to make that mistake). For if he does employ these things, it's the era itself that did so first. The notorious messages, so similar in form to those transmitted by the BBC's Radio Londres, appear in the *Orphée* of 1926. The radar-like instrument that François Périer uses, the existence of which seems quite normal in this era of cybernetics, was used by the angels Raphaël and Azrael in the theatre play and doubtless it appeared baroque at the time. It is understood these days that one of the attributes of dreaming is a peculiar freedom with respect to time. Hardly surprising then that the poet snatch shapes as yet impossible to identify out of the future, things that will remain the object of mystery or mockery until their formal advent delivers them to us. By transplanting his messages into shortwave signals, by finding the other side of the mirror in bombed-out Saint-Cyr, by making SS motorcyclists be his angels of death, Cocteau is only picking up on the epoch's own properties. Nature does not imitate art, but moves to fulfil her prophesies.

It is doubtless due to the same concern for greater rigour that the decisive role of the objects in *Orphée* arises. All kinds of things can be done with characters and feelings, yet not be at all convincing. An object, with its weight, its materiality, its ambiguous status as both servant and enemy, makes its presence felt. The most sensational example to date of an object *in play* in cinema seems to me to be Orson Welles's revolving door in *The Lady From Shanghai*: one of those revolving doors that looks like an upright portcullis, as they have inside Concorde métro station, which allow people through *in one direction only*. When Welles as the sailor goes through that door, leaving Rita Hayworth dying, it is not he but the door that guarantees he will not return, cannot return, that the story has played out and that what he is leaving behind – a wife and cheap thrills – he is leaving forever. But in *Orphée* there is the rear-view mirror. While in the play Orpheus is induced to look at Eurydice and so to lose her again by a playwright's sleight of hand (Orpheus has slipped and only turns so as to steady himself), in the film he sees her in the rear-view mirror. No more tricks; no more subterfuge allowed. This rear view is a deathtrap. We have been warned that mirrors are doors and what is our rear-view if not yet another mirror? Above all it partakes in the power that objects have over us, of stopping us from retracing our steps and of forcing us to see what is behind us. Only a moment earlier, Orpheus has managed to avoid a photograph of Eurydice, caught in the alternative disconcerting trap of likenesses. Finally, how could we forget that epitome of realism and disorientation: Heurtebise (a real chauffeur) entering Eurydice's home (a real young woman, inside a real house) to the sound of Gluck's

Orpheus and Eurydice (real music, playing on a real radio). A scene in which everything is normal, solid, reasonable, in which nevertheless the secret architecture of adventure is revealed; in which a flesh and blood Heurtebise enters, glowing with the admission of his true intentions, in which everything is bathed in a different light, which we might for fun call supernatural, without resorting to any magic other than that born of the most natural associations between living things and objects. This moment is both one of the most moving in the film and one in which Cocteau's purpose is clearest – which would appear to demonstrate the excellence of his method. One thinks of those small heartbreaks in a poem by TS Eliot that a line from Dante combined with some mere everyday detail can provoke. We are at the crossroads of time and eternity, in a most palpable present. Eternity, never absent, becomes, for a moment, perceptible. What's funny is that those who are most impervious to this realist alchemy will admit without demur the crassest of miracles, complete with invisible violins suddenly blooming, like chickens, from beneath the pillows in a love scene in any Hollywood film.

*

I can think of only one film in the history of cinema that can be compared to *Orphée*: Carl Dreyer's *Vampyr*, with its metaphysics of incarnation. But where Dreyer ambitiously tackled the general problem of death, Cocteau tells his own story.

Orpheus's Death insists on this point: she is *his* death, not death in general. Everyone carries his own death inside him. His Guardian Death, like a Guardian Angel. This is a familiar theme among Jean Cocteau's works. If, like Welles (this is doubtless a factor in their friendship), Cocteau is incapable of making a work that does not incidentally reveal his deepest obsession, or that does not relate to his life – where Welles, through his incarnations of Kane, Macbeth, and even in the dialogues in *The Lady From Shanghai*, poses both to us and himself the problem of Evil (up to what point can we live with Evil?), Cocteau reveals his long familiarity with death. He unmasks himself from the start. In the fifth minute of play (as they say on the sports channels), Diaghilev's 'Astonish me!' betrays him. So we discover, grown up and made flesh and blood, a fair few familiar motifs. Death's assistants are announced in *Plain-chant*:[9]

For it is not Death herself who kills
She has her assassins.

And from image to image, from one scene to the next, echoes from all his previous works reverberate in this film and merge with it just as an object laid upon a mirror rejoins its reflection and with it forms a single object. All we need to understand this whole delicate mechanism of the poet's relationship with his work and with his Death is some memory of what has gone before, whether it's a question of Death's power over love ('More than Venus, Oh Death, you inhabit our beds'[10]) or of the poet's power over his Death and the paradox of immortality ('Death shall not have me alive'; 'To write is to kill … death.'[11] etc.) And as usual, this precautionary exegesis exceeds the work and extends into its context. Just as the viewer who laughs at *Le Sang d'un poète* is obliged to recognise himself within the film cheering along at a torture – and consequently to judge himself, here every criticism is already forestalled. When RS in the *Observateur* writes: 'In no film … are mirrors so often stepped through. But this time, no one believes it' – he is only picking up the very words of the statue in *Le Sang*: 'I congratulate you. You wrote that we would be walking through mirrors *and you didn't believe it*.' This is the nub of the drama, and Cocteau is perfectly aware of the tension. But this too is the poet's function: a constant, exhausting effort to reduce the two opposing faces of reality. It is from this disjunct between the two worlds that, like a stereoscope, poetry can create its landscape. And it is in this way too that the cinematograph becomes our best vehicle for poetic exploration. We do not pass through the mirror. We do not pass through the screen. And yet we do travel through the screen, we live the lives of the screen's characters, we inhabit the world of the screen. The film becomes the end point, the most advanced realm of the demiurge. It is natural that it should seem crude, laughable even, seen from the angle of our nostalgia for poetic intervention in the 'real' world. But you might as well reproach man for not being God. A wholly triumphant poetry would be silence; it is in its failure, in its unfulfilled efforts towards an impossible reconciliation that it covers the distance between us and those handsome cadavers in which we recognise ourselves.

This may be why cinema has such a unique place in Jean Cocteau's work, why it isn't at all thanks to the glamour of a brand-new technique or toy (Welles's 'electric train set') that it finds such a key place in his oeuvre, but due to the ambiguous nature of this world that is the closest to our own, the last lie before the truth. In his poetic experiments with all the arts, Cocteau followed the reverse order to that of Hegel's spirit, a pathway to disincarnation that ran from architecture to poetry. Jean Cocteau's entire oeuvre is, in contrast, a striving for weightiness, for the most precise apprehension of the world. Dependent at first on orders, on messages from the ether, connected to his receiver like a radio operator, rendering the minutes of his interviews in his poems like Orpheus in his car, he has never stopped seeking, in novels, theatre, drawing, travel, by means of language and of colour, the 'snowy wire of the pipe-cleaner' and 'light's Indian ink',[12] ways of weighing down the invisible, of catching Death in his trap, an ink that betrays the presence of angels and shows us *ghosts turned suddenly into blue trees*.[13] The cinematograph is the last and the richest of these tools for exploration. We know the importance Cocteau attaches to waves and signals, to all the media of mechanical revelation. The poet often appears in his work as a kind of recording instrument. And certainly he considers the camera a machine for multiplying, for sharpening the senses, an X-ray generator that reveals more than we set before it, a tool for disclosing secrets. 'The surprises of photography' is one of the subtitles of *Le Sang d'un poète*, in which, 'caught in the trap of his own film', Cocteau blamed his discerning camera for the revelation of his own face instead of his hero's. This recalls the photographer in *The Wedding Party on the Eiffel Tower*.[14] A miracle, the reverse of the wonder-climber seen by all but never recorded on film, Cocteau dreams of a film that is sufficiently sensitive to preserve accurate forms where the human eye would see only confusion. Meanwhile, he collaborates with the mysterious, feeds his ravening camera dishes prepared in advance, it is true, but of which he ultimately expects a prodigious metamorphosis. So he is able to write, as for *Le Sang d'un poète*: *How can I reproach anyone for misunderstanding a film that I understand so little myself*,[15] and distance himself from his film, far away as sleep, unrecountable as a dream, transmissible only by that second miracle of which only the cinematograph is capable: by making others dream it too.

*

All of this, of course, does not go to show that *Orphée* is either a good or a bad film. On this point too, the question has long been settled by Cocteau himself.

It is neither beautiful nor ugly, it has other merits,[16] was the conclusion of one of his poems. It is upon these other merits that the debate necessarily hinges, I feel, that we might ask the critic to envisage, instead of declaring his helplessness.[17] Not that it should be necessary to go back through Cocteau's oeuvre in order to judge, nor is it a question of a film accessible only to a certain coterie. I have seen a young German, completely ignorant of Cocteau's work, comment on *Le Sang d'un poète*, substituting his own experience as a prisoner in Russia for the snowball fight, in which the blood of one side and the cheers of the other made him feel a kinship of 'shock'. He had understood that this is the crux of the film and, starting with that substitution, he reconstructed the whole, naturally misreading the significance of certain details (sometimes childishly so: he turned the famous five-pointed star into the Soviet star) but this mattered little: he was no longer recounting Cocteau's film to us but his own, for which Cocteau had provided his material. And in the end, with all his errors, he may have come closer to the true intention of the poem, which is not to be read but to be rewritten, silently, by the reader, in his own name.

Such is the gift I will to all who see *Orphée*. Nevertheless, if the film's principal merit is to push into the background the formal beauty which is generally cinema's sole priority, it would be quite unjust to say nothing at all about it. Especially as its beauty is not gratuitous but coincides profoundly with Cocteau's method and aims. That independence, that lucidity peculiar to the camera that I discussed above, find their expression in, for example, Nicolas Hayer's extraordinary framing: each image is composed like a tableau yet without ever restricting the characters' freedom of movement, as if, allowing the actors to gather as they pleased, his camera would instinctively find the position that would extract the maximum significance from their gathering. (Of course, this is neither more nor less than the definition of good composition that I present here. Naturally…) And what text could be more appropriate alongside the image of Maria Casarès in that famous photograph at the car door than this passage from a story told by Jean Cocteau on the eve of the first Christmas of the war: *She had a fearful beauty. She was so beautiful that our eyes could not admit it and we would have thought her ugly if we had managed to catch a glimpse of her.*[18] And as Jean Marais was never more handsome nor did he ever act so well, and as François Périer, that nice demon, was skinned like a rabbit so as to give us an unforgettable angel-face, and as Juliette Gréco, her mien both lioness and marble statue, torn from her dives and her taboos, is a revelation, as is Edouard Dhermitte, well directed for once – all this is not negligible either. I admire people who are sufficiently jaded as to be unmoved by the unending spectacle of this soul of Cocteau's, ill at ease in its only body, that lavishes its genius on all that comes near, that lifts creatures and objects to their highest realisation – and, what's more, with the supreme politeness of thanking them for it.

La Jetée, 1962

1. Directed by Jean Cocteau and first released in 1950 (editor's note).
2. Franz Thomassin countered with the unanswerable contention that 'death is the poor man's only luxury'.
3. See *Le Film Français* of 6 October, to whom top marks for *froideur*.
4. *Le Sang d'un poète* (The Blood of a Poet), a film directed by Jean Cocteau, 1930 (translator's note).
5. Trans.[SL].
6. I don't think it necessary to identify my many quotations from Cocteau in this article. Curious readers will do better to look for themselves and then to find others.
7. Jean Cocteau, *La Difficulté d'être* (The Difficulty of Being), Éditions Paul Morihien, Paris, 1947 (editor's note).
8. The French left-wing newspaper begun as part of the Resistance and openly published for a few years after the war (translator's note).
9. Jean Cocteau, *Plain-chant*, Éditions Stock, Paris, 1923 (editor's note).

10. Jean Cocteau, 'Mieux que Vénus, Ô Mort, vous habitez nos couches' (editor's note).
11. Jean Cocteau, 'La Mort ne m'aura pas vivant'; 'Ecrire c'est tuer du vide, tuer de la mort' (editor's note).
12. Jean Cocteau, 'le laiton neigeux des débourre-pipe'; 'l'encre de la lumière'(editor's note).
13. Jean Cocteau, 'les fantômes soudain devenus arbres bleus' (editor's note).
14. Jean Cocteau, *Les Mariés de la Tour Eiffel*, 1921, a ballet with libretto (translator's note).
15. 'Puis-je reprocher à qui que ce soit de mal comprendre un film que je comprends si mal moi-même' (Trans. SL).
16. Jean Cocteau 'Il n'est ni beau ni laid, il a d'autres mérites' (editor's note).
17. See for example the staggering 'survey' of the film in the newspaper *L'Aurore*.
18. Jean Cocteau, 'Elle était d'une beauté effrayante, si belle que les yeux n'auraient pu l'admettre et l'eussent trouvée laide s'il leur avait été possible de l'entrevoir.' (editor's note).

Metro 2 (Paris 2004), 2004
'Staring Back Series: I Stare 2', 1952-2006

Chris Marker

Pat Cormon used to sell all kinds of cold things in his shop that was itself rather like a fridge. The day after VJ Day, when that rain began that would not stop before the following day, he went to stand in his doorway to watch the show.

People were starting to run or ducking into houses. The sky had emptied all at once, like a playing field. Somewhere above Pat's head, an illuminated advert was spinning and bathing the façades with great lickings of blue, endlessly sweeping round, making him feel seasick. At pavement level, a burst water pipe was sculpting ferocious plumes of water. Little by little, the ghost of an upside-down town appeared beneath the street, and little doubled men, like paper cut-outs folded in two, fluttered along in mid-air.

Jerry appeared in the shop like the world created out of chaos. The seven days of Creation all bundled up in his sheepskin jacket darted across the chaos-room, through the chaos-light stippled with chaos-rain, leaving Jerry-as-Adam in Marines uniform, the colour of Heaven on Earth. The Lord Himself – by which I mean Pat – greeted him rather begrudgingly, but Jerry did not seem in the least bit concerned.

'After all, we have put an end to it, this good old war', he announced, with satisfaction.

'We had Right on our side', Pat said, gravely.

'Certainly', said Jerry. 'It's a good thing; Right. And the Bomb is another good thing. Two good things going for us, eh, Pat? We're a great country.'

'A soldier shouldn't joke about these things', said Pat.

'Sorry', said Jerry. 'I haven't had time to learn how a soldier should behave around civvies. Living in so many foxholes, one becomes quite the fox oneself. I shall have to learn the hens' lingo. Then I'll be able to make conversation without scandalising you.'

'Hey, you sonofa…'

'Don't be crude, Pat. If the angels hear you, they'll go parroting it to all the right-thinking people in this town, and *they*'ll take their business elsewhere.'

'I'm sorry you're a lunatic', said Pat.

'I'm delighted', Jerry retorted.

Night was falling. The neon washing machine churned on, choppy and ever more nauseating.

'Lousy weather', said Jerry. 'I had a date at the Park but it's flooded. Think I'll go to the Flit Flat instead. Won't you come?'

'Certainly', said Pat. 'Certainly I'll come running about in this weather to hear a cursed dirty nigger slobbering into his trumpet.'

'I see', said Jerry. 'You still have ideas about negroes. It's a prejudice, if you know what that means. I met some on the other side of the ocean that knew how to drink for all the world like regular men.'

'If you want to know what I think, you've had it, Jerry my boy', Pat said. 'You're starting to crack jokes and ramble on about things. You're not good for much any more, if you want my opinion.'

'You're awfully fine like that, Pat', said Jerry. 'You gesticulating there in the window and the rain lighting you up on all sides, just like the monkey in that good old rhyme by Carl Sandburg. You know...'

Jerry went and stood by the door, in the midst of the revolving wash of light, and gaily declaimed:

There was a tree of stars sprang up on a vertical panel of the south
And a monkey of stars climbed up and down in this tree of stars...[1]

'There you go now with your damned poetry', grumbled Pat, and turned his back to Jerry.

Night had now fallen altogether. A bunch of paper streamers thrown from a window the day before had got tangled up around the arm of a streetlamp above the shop, and this luminous arm, scribbled through by the rain, looked somehow powdered like the phosphorescent snow that people put on the trees over Christmas.

'It was only a dream, o-ho, ya-ya, loo-loo, only a dream, five, six, seven, five, six seven', Jerry concluded with an energetic flourish.

'There's not a drop of sense in anything you say', commented Pat, amiably.

'You'll never understand that some words out there can unscrew the world', said Jerry, very excited. 'Nothing holds still any more, just as if this dump we're in were all of a sudden to get on the road – yes! – and go for a wander across the whole town.'

'I've got my feet on the ground', said Pat, irascibly. 'And you can talk like that for weeks without either me or you stopping having our feet on the ground, and the same street in the same place, and this old shack around us, till the end of time.'

'Till the end of time', said Jerry. 'But as you say, it'll have to end one day, huh? And if the old shack gave up the ghost, huh, Pat?'

Pat shrugged, exasperated. He hated Jerry, who always came and told him stories that were half dreamt-up; you never knew if he was being serious or if he was teasing. I wonder if he gets all this out of books; and now the worst of it is you can't tell a soldier who's been decorated, wounded and everything to go and get lost. And that feeling of uneasiness that followed Jerry's visits, as if somewhere in his ravings he had touched on some old wound of Pat's, something hidden, shameful, a dormant pain, the source of which had been lost, yet it endured, kept enduring like remorse. Then merely through being thought of, the pain would waken again, a kind of oppression, disgust, as if the world had suddenly lost all meaning, as if without warning a woman at your side were to dissolve right away. Just then, Pat saw a woman coming out of the rain, and her deathly face in the blue and violet whirl of the light. Now at the door, now inside the shop, and asking permission to take shelter from the downpour. Pat grumbled a vague assent, caught up in the queasy lurch of the violet light and the world's end. The water gargoyles in a fit of hiccoughs. The Christmas tree branch bedecked with moving light, vibrating beneath that dead, undulating glow, that obscene caress, spiritless, persistent.

'You know what I thought', Jerry went on, in a lower tone. 'It's something you shouldn't put about too much, but you, it doesn't matter, you won't believe it. You know what so many of us have come to thinking, in our foxholes and other spots? The only thing we've taken with us?'

'I'm not listening to you', said Pat. He was focusing all his willpower on not putting his hands up to his mouth, on keeping them clenched in his pockets.

'That's just it, Pat. Exactly. The end of the old shack. Don't take me for one of those nutcases yelling that the world will blow up because we have offended our Lord. It's nothing like an explosion or a celestial fury. Something like, if you will… going rotten. The town's fallen to ashes, your legs and your hands and the table and the stones all mixing together, joining up, like the chains and the prisoners' feet. And a shop like yours, Pat, which comes apart and goes off along the streets, all the way to the sea.'

The woman looked at him in surprise. She had a beautiful face like a Northern warrior, and a violent, swollen mouth, shining in the rain. The top half of her face was hidden in the door's shadow. The mouth remained fully lit, strangely yielding and exposed. Since seeing her, Pat felt his breath coming more quickly.

Jerry appeared completely to have forgotten about the end of the world and his prophesies. Perched on a corner of the counter, he was doing an impression of 'Frankie Boy' Sinatra. Outside, the lights' spinning seemed faster, more pitiless, dragging the façades into its merry-go-round, drawing tight around the town as if to make it burst. Pat watched the woman's mouth, gleaming like a beacon. 'My Nancy', sang Jerry, hands outstretched in a gesture of adoration. The gargoyles spewing in stained-glass colours. The light poured its unclean, purple embrace over the woman's lips. Pat was trembling. Jerry jumped to his feet, put on his fur-trim jacket, still singing.

'...You can't resist her, sorry for you, she has no sister! No angel...[2] I'm heading off to the Flit Flat, it's too gloomy at your place, Pat. Bye now, try to be good with the girl. So long, little sister. I'll be seeing you, Pat.'

He dived away into the rain, the dead light, the dancing façades. Pat and the woman stood still by the window for a long while, in the silence. And the shadows brushing over the woman's mouth, in the light of sin.

Now a strange thing happened. Pat Cormon thought he knew his street and his daily surroundings like the back of his hand. In this grid-planned town everything joined up, everything fit together. If you stood in the middle of his doorway, the door opposite would slot perfectly into the smallest of his glass panes. Pat had tested this more than once in his idle hours, closing one eye then the other so as to see it jump to one side. Had he always been mistaken, or was this yet another effect of these cursed lights? He could have sworn that the door across the road now distinctly overlapped the window's edge. Pat began to look with one eye then the other, then realised he must be making quite an idiot of himself and stopped. Cursed lights.

'Your friend looked a bit worked up', the woman said. Pat watched her mouth in a daze, as if only now discovering that it could *also* talk. She had a lovely smooth voice, dark and alive, like her lips.

'I think he was drunk', said Pat. 'He was talking about the end of the world.'

'It's interesting', said the woman, with a little laugh. 'And it particularly interests me.' She pressed her forehead against the glass. The light rose up her face. The flesh around her eyes was slightly paler. When she lowered her eyelids, it was like two tombs freshly buried. 'I had a friend who arranged to meet me at the end of the world. I've been waiting ever since.'

'Here we go', thought Pat venomously. 'Here come the confessions.' At the same time he looked over to the other side of the street. He squinted. Cursed lights. The other door still looked as though it had moved.

'You have a lovely voice', said Pat. And was shocked that he had said so.

'Yes… He also used to talk about my voice. He said… that it existed beyond words, like music. And also that the Angel of Death would call him with my voice.'

'Is he dead?' asked Pat, for something to say.

'Not even', replied the woman. She looked up again. The shadow dropped back to her mouth, encroaching a little on the upper lip. Pat looked sideways at her, his breath rapid, and realised at the same time, in fright, that he no longer dared look at the other door.

'He used to write to me: "Your voice stays in me like an open wound. Like a wound that would call me with living lips, from your lips." Do you write things like that, yourself?'

Hearing her talk about her lips, Pat began to shiver like an animal in pain.

'No, I don't write things like that. I don't think – I don't say things like that. It's just more nonsense', he burst out, 'like him with his end of the world.'

'Yes', she said, 'and you don't believe in it. And yet…' Her voice was still very calm. 'And yet the other side of the road is no longer quite where it should be. And you know it.'

Pat spun round in horror.

'What did you say?'

'And you don't dare look at it any more.'

She looked down. And once again the lights rise up to her pale hair, again her closed eyes, fresh tombs, again mauve and blue bites like shadows of fatigue on her mouth.

Pat sensed that something in his mind was hardening and huddling away, while everything else was moving horribly. He dared to look outside. The door opposite was now level with his right-hand window. It was still distinctly drifting. The two sides of the road were slowly sliding out, like ships passing sidelong to each other. Pat was choking with fear. He vaguely heard the woman pronounce a name, the name of a cinema, a cinema that was a little further along

on the left, on the other side of the road. He repeated it mechanically –
and then said it again, almost stammering, when he saw the cinema itself,
a glittering, glacial square mass, projecting a great sheet of white light
into the rustling disintegration of the street.

'Are you afraid?' asked the woman.

Now Pat begins to tremble properly. From the depths of the night, the
houses line up and loom like panels of a film set. They have the stiffness and
menace of great winged Assyrian lions. Something moves within the town.
Demons load the façades on to their backs in order to prepare the spectacle.
The sickening merry-go-round of lights, violet, mauve, blue, draws everything
in and leads the parade. Like a heavy turntable set in motion, the road turns
faster and faster. The mad windows halloo after foxes around the bright beacon
of the woman's mouth. The fascination of that mouth grips Pat. The gargoyle
spouts hiccough towards her, warriors dying at the feet of a desired woman.
The lights draw in the houses, mislay and abandon the houses like lost children,
and escape from the houses to blot out that mouth with a great lick of its raging,
unclean tongue, before disappearing altogether. The Angel of Death calls with
Her voice. And from the depths of the foxholes, Jerry and all the dead signal
to the towns passing by. Thumbing lifts from houses, but no one stops. Pat
guesses at everything that will happen, the shop reaching the end of the town
and then the sea. And in the windows, as steady, as inert as ever, like pedestrians
or cars, the lighthouses straining into the night, the blurred images of radio
broadcasts seeking help from the stars, and the ships gliding on in silence
beneath the windows, in the spray, branded by their headlights. And that
mouth. The cruise ships calling SOS.

'The cruise ships are calling SOS...', says the woman.

'Listen...', says Pat. 'I don't know what you've come here for...'

He was shivering. The woman stood near him, her mouth hot and defenceless
like a dead bird. He realised that he hadn't even been able to make out her body,
lost in the shadows and obscured by the muddled lights, yet from it rose something
that was both a promise and a threat. He dared not look her in the eyes, but on
the breath approaching closer and closer he smelled the scents of a body wet with
rain, of bitten fruit, and of something like the taste of annihilation.

All at once, he leapt backwards.

'Get out of here', he said furiously. 'I don't know what you came here for
but get out, before... before...'

She stood there quite still for a moment, facing him, not even attempting to look surprised. His hands flapped at the counter, unable to settle on it. Outside, only the streetlamp's arm remained visible, like the branch of a Christmas tree, sparkling in the night beneath the scrawl of the rain. Somewhere above their heads, a neon advert spun and spun, bathing the world in great licks of its blue tongue, a slow, obstinate, defiling sweep. And the unmoving mouth, now in shadow, like an animal readying to pounce.

'Get out', Pat repeated.

She turned, pulled up her hood, laid one hand on the door. Pat closed his eyes, heard the door click. Then he stepped outside in his turn, watched her move away. The street was in its rightful place, the doors all aligned. He watched her for a long while. Little by little she advanced in the rain with a regular step, clearly distinguishable, her head a little bent inside the hood. A passer-by like the others.

Pat went back inside, wet through. The rain was falling more calmly, straight to the ground. The ghost of an upside-down town lived in the street. The light revolved. At pavement level, a burst water pipe sculpted gargoyle spouts of water. Pat shook his head, as if to chase away, along with the rainwater, the dead ghosts and the residue of those strange, strange times.

October 1945

1. Carl Sandburg, *Monkey of Stars* in *The Complete Poems of Carl Sandburg*, Harcourt Brace Jovanovich, New York, NY, 1969, p.401 (editor's note).
2. From the lyrics to 'Nancy' by Harrington, Leo Arthur / Minehan, David James Jr. (editor's note).

List of works

*Indicates excerpt

Films and videos

Les Statues meurent aussi (Statues Also Die),
1950-53
Directors: Alain Resnais, Chris Marker
Black and white, 35mm, 30 minutes
Production: Tadié-Cinéma / Présence Africaine
Editions
© PRÉSENCE AFRICAINE EDITIONS

La Jetée, (The Pier), 1962
Black and white, 35mm, 29 minutes
Unique print: an early cut of the film with a different
version of the opening scene.
© 1963 Argos Films
Collection: Royal Film Archive, Belgium

* *Le Joli Mai* (The Merry Month of May), 1962
Directors: Chris Marker, Pierre Lhomme
Black and white, 35mm, original version
165 minutes, restored 2013 version 146 minutes
Production: Sofracima
Courtesy La Sofra, Paris

Le Fond de l'air est rouge
(A Grin Without a Cat), 1977
Black and white / colour, 16mm blown
up to 35mm, restored version 180 minutes
Production: Iskra / Institut National
de l'Audiovisuel (INA) / Dovidis
© Iskra, Paris

* *Sans soleil* (Sunless), 1982
Colour, 16mm blown up to 36mm, 103 minutes
Production: Argos Films
© 1983 Argos Films

* *Chats perchés* (The Case of the Grinning Cat),
2004
Colour, video, 59 minutes
Production: Les Films du Jeudi / Arte
© Chris Marker, Les Films du Jeudi, Paris

Ouvroir. The Movie, 2010
Chris Marker in association with Max Moswitzer
Colour, video, sound, 30 minutes
Production: Les Films du Jeudi
Collection: Centre Pompidou, MNAM,
Nouveaux Médias
© Chris Marker, Les Films du Jeudi, Paris
Courtesy Centre Pompidou

Multimedia installations

*Quand le Siècle a pris formes (Guerre
et Révolution)* (When the Century Took Shape
(War and Revolution)), 1978
Chris Marker in association with François Helt
Music: Hanns Eisler
Multimedia installation: monitor, video,
soundtrack, colour, 15:39 minutes
Limited edition 1/1 (exhibition copy)
Production and collection: Centre Pompidou,
MNAM, Nouveau Médias
Courtesy Centre Pompidou

*Zapping Zone (Proposals for an
Imaginary Television)*, 1990-94
Mixed media installation: 13 monitors,
13 videos, 7 computers, 7 computer
programs, 4 light boxes with 80 slides,
10 photomontages colour / black and white,
1 maneki neko
Limited edition 1/1
Production and collection: Centre Pompidou,
MNAM, Nouveaux Médias
Courtesy Centre Pompidou

Silent Movie, 1995
5 channel video installation, continuous loop,
dimensions variable
Edition of 3
Chris Marker Estate
Courtesy Peter Blum Gallery, New York

Immemory, 1997
Interactive multimedia installation: 1 hard drive
34 Megabytes, 3 Macintosh computers, 1 painted
cat, colour, sound, French and English language
Limited edition 1/1
Production: Centre Pompidou, MNAM,
Nouveaux Médias and Les Films de l'Astrophore
Collection: Centre Pompidou, MNAM,
Nouveaux Médias
Courtesy Centre Pompidou

*Owls at Noon Prelude:
The Hollow Men*, 2005
CD-ROM video for 8 screens,
19 minute loop, dimensions variable
Edition of 6
Chris Marker Estate
Courtesy Peter Blum Gallery, New York

Prints

Breathless, 1995
Digital print, 100.3 × 66 cm
Edition of 20
Chris Marker Estate
Courtesy Peter Blum Gallery, New York

Hiroshima Mon Amour, 1995
Digital print, 100.3 × 74.9 cm
Edition of 20
Chris Marker Estate
Courtesy Peter Blum Gallery, New York

Owl People, 1995
Digital print, 100.3 × 68.6 cm
Edition of 20
Chris Marker Estate
Courtesy Peter Blum Gallery, New York

Rin Tin Tin, 1995
Digital print, 100.3 × 74.9 cm
Edition of 20
Chris Marker Estate
Courtesy Peter Blum Gallery, New York

*Untitled (*from *The Hollow Men)*, 2005
Photogravure, 53.3 × 71.7 cm
Edition of 15
Chris Marker Estate
Courtesy Peter Blum Gallery, New York

Mural based on the *Petite Planète* poster
by Chris Marker and Jason Simon, 2006
Digital print, 206 × 150 cm (printed 2014)
Courtesy Centre Pompidou and Jason Simon

Photography

Silent Movie, 1995
18 framed black and white photographs
Each image: 17.8 × 23.5 cm
Edition of 3
Chris Marker Estate
Courtesy Peter Blum Gallery, New York

'Staring Back Series: Beast of...', 1952-2006
Edition of 3
Chris Marker Estate
Courtesy Peter Blum Gallery, New York

Selected works from the series:

Norway (1950s), 1950s
Black and white photograph mounted
on aluminium, 35.2 × 25.4 cm

Untitled (Rome, 1955), 1955
Black and white photograph mounted
on aluminium, 55.3 × 36.8 cm

Jerusalem Street (1960), 1960
Black and white photograph mounted
on aluminium, 35.2 × 25.1 cm

'Staring Back Series: I Stare 1', 1952-2006
Edition of 3
Chris Marker Estate
Courtesy Peter Blum Gallery, New York

Selected works from the series:

*Mourning the Dead (anti-OAS demo,
Paris, 1962)*, 1962
Black and white photograph mounted
on aluminium, 55.6 × 40.3 cm

Anti-OAS demo 1 (Paris, 1962), 1962
Black and white photograph mounted
on aluminium, 25.4 × 35.2 cm

Anti-OAS demo 3 (Paris, 1962), 1962
Black and white photograph mounted
on aluminium, 25.7 × 35.2 cm

Vietnam demo 2 (Paris, 1966), 1966
Black and white photograph mounted
on aluminium, 26.4 × 35.2 cm

March 1 (Pentagon, 1967), 21 October 1967
Black and white photograph mounted
on aluminium, 23.5 × 35.2 cm

March 2 (Pentagon, 1967), 21 October 1967
Black and white photograph mounted
on aluminium, 26.7 × 35.2 cm

March 3 (Pentagon, 1967), 21 October 1967
Black and white photograph mounted
on aluminium, 26.7 × 35.2 cm

March 4 (Pentagon, 1967), 21 October 1967
Black and white photograph mounted
on aluminium, 25.4 × 35.2 cm

March 5 (Pentagon, 1967), 21 October 1967
Black and white photograph mounted
on aluminium, 27.6 × 35.2 cm

March 6 (Pentagon, 1967), 21 October 1967
Black and white photograph mounted
on aluminium, 25.7 × 35.2 cm

March 7 (Pentagon, 1967), 21 October 1967
Black and white photograph mounted
on aluminium, 26.4 × 35.2 cm

Nazi (Pentagon, 1967), 21 October 1967
Black and white photograph mounted
on aluminium, 23.5 × 35.2 cm

Barr (Paris, May 1968), 1968
Black and white photograph mounted
on aluminium, 24.5 × 35.2 cm

Demo 1 (Paris, May 1968), 1968
Black and white photograph mounted
on aluminium, 35.2 × 26.7 cm

Demo 3 (Paris, May 1968), 1968
Black and white photograph mounted
on aluminium, 35.2 × 26.6 cm

Demo 4 (Paris, May 1968), 1968
Black and white photograph mounted
on aluminium, 35.2 × 25.4 cm

Demo 5 (Paris, May 1968), 1968
Black and white photograph mounted
on aluminium, 23.5 × 35.2 cm

Demo (Paris, May 1968), 1968
Black and white photograph mounted
on aluminium, 35.2 × 23.5 cm

Gay-Lussac (Paris, May 1968), 1968
Black and white photograph mounted
on aluminium, 24.5 × 35.2 cm

Gay-Lussac Nite (Paris, May 1968), 1968
Black and white photograph mounted
on aluminium, 27.9 × 35.2 cm

Place de la République (Paris, 2002), 2002
Black and white photograph mounted
on aluminium, 27.3 × 35.2 cm

*Immigrants burying L. Schwartzenberg 2
(Paris, 2003)*, 2003
Black and white photograph mounted
on aluminium, 26 × 35.2 cm

Demo anti Le Pen 2 (Paris, 2004), 2004
Black and white photograph mounted
on aluminium, 26.4 × 35.2 cm

Demo antiwar 1 (Paris, 2004), 2004
Black and white photograph mounted
on aluminium, 24.1 × 35.2 cm

Mayday (Paris, 2004), 2004
Black and white photograph mounted
on aluminium, 26 × 35.2 cm

Demo 1 (Paris, 2006), 2006
Black and white photograph mounted
on aluminium, 35.2 × 31.1 cm

Demo CPE 2 (Paris, 2006), 2006
Black and white photograph mounted
on aluminium, 35.2 × 27 cm

Demo 5 (Paris, 2006), 2006
Black and white photograph mounted
on aluminium, 26.7 × 35.2 cm

Demo 6 (Paris, 2006), 2006
Black and white photograph mounted
on aluminium, 26.7 × 35.2 cm

Demo 9 (Paris, 2006), 2006
Black and white photograph mounted
on aluminium, 24.1 × 35.2 cm

Demo 10 (Paris, 2006), 2006
Black and white photograph mounted
on aluminium, 26 × 35.2 cm

Demo 12 (Paris, 2006), 2006
Black and white photograph mounted
on aluminium, 26.7 × 35.2 cm

Demo 16 (Paris, 2006), 2006
Black and white photograph mounted
on aluminium, 26 × 35.2 cm

Demo 17 (Paris, 2006), 2006
Black and white photograph mounted
on aluminium, 24.8 × 35.2 cm

Demo 19 (Paris, 2006), 2006
Black and white photograph mounted
on aluminium, 25.7 × 35.2 cm

Lie-in AIDS 2 (Paris 2006), 2006
Black and white photograph mounted
on aluminium, 25.1 × 35.2 cm

'Staring Back Series: I Stare 2', 1952-2006
Edition of 3
Chris Marker Estate
Courtesy Peter Blum Gallery, New York

Selected works from the series:

Pushkin Museum 2 (Moscow, 1957), 1957
Black and white photograph mounted
on aluminium, 35.2 × 25.1 cm

Listening to Poetry (Moscow, 1950s), 1950s
Black and white photograph mounted
on aluminium, 24.8 × 35.2 cm

Untitled (Leningrad, 1963), 1963
Black and white photograph mounted
on aluminium, 35.2 × 27.9 cm

Untitled (Tehran, 1960s), 1960s
Black and white photograph mounted
on aluminium, 35.2 × 26.4 cm

Untitled (Santiago de Cuba, 1960s), 1960s
Black and white photograph mounted
on aluminium, 35.2 × 16 cm

Bitplayers Imamura (Tokyo, 1980), 1980
Black and white photograph mounted
on aluminium, 35.2 × 23.3 cm

Untitled 3 (Cape Verde, 1982), 1982
Black and white photograph mounted
on aluminium, 25.4 × 35.2 cm

Métro 2 (Paris, 2004), 2004
Black and white photograph mounted
on aluminium, 26.4 × 35.2 cm

Salvador Dalí, year unknown
Black and white photograph mounted
on aluminium, 35.6 × 24.8 cm

William Klein and wife Jeanine,
year unknown
Black and white photograph mounted
on aluminium, 27.3 × 35.2 cm

'Staring Back Series: They Stare', 1952-2006
Edition of 3
Chris Marker Estate
Courtesy Peter Blum Gallery, New York

Selected works from the series:

Siberian Driver (1957), 1957
Black and white photograph mounted
on aluminium, 35.2 × 27.6 cm

Untitled (Paris, 1950s), 1950s
Black and white photograph mounted
on aluminium, 35.2 × 23.5 cm

Young Girl (Bissau, 1980), 1980
Black and white photograph mounted
on aluminium, 26 × 35.2 cm

Untitled (Bissau, 1982), 1982
Black and white photograph mounted
on aluminium, 35.2 × 35.2 cm

Demonstrator (Narita, 1982), 1982
Black and white photograph mounted
on aluminium, 35.2 × 27 cm

Kurosawa (1985), 1985
Black and white photograph mounted
on aluminium, 35.2 × 24.1 cm

Ligia Branice, year unknown
Black and white photograph mounted
on aluminium, 25.1 × 35.2 cm

Chilean Mummy, year unknown
Black and white photograph mounted
on aluminium, 35.2 × 26.7 cm

Alexandra Stewart, year unknown
Black and white photograph mounted
on aluminium, 25.1 × 35.2 cm

Maroussia Vossen, year unknown
Black and white photograph mounted
on aluminium, 25.7 × 35.6 cm

Untitled (Cape Verde), year unknown
Black and white photograph mounted
on aluminium, 24.8 × 35.2 cm

Documents

Books presented from the *Petite Planète* series.
Chris Marker was the series editor from 1954
to 1958:

Autriche, Claude Vausson, Éditions du Seuil,
Paris, 1954

Suède, F. Règis Bastide, Éditions du Seuil,
Paris, 1954

Italie, Paul Lechat, Éditions du Seuil,
Paris, 1955

Hollande, Bernard Pingaud, Éditions du Seuil,
Paris, reprint 1959 (original 1954)

Irlande, Camille Bourniquel, Éditions du Seuil,
Paris, 1955

Grèce, Mimica Cranaki, Éditions du Seuil,
Paris, 1955

Allemagne, Joseph Rovan, Éditions du Seuil,
Paris, 1957

Tunisie, Michel Zeraffa, Éditions du Seuil,
Paris, 1955

Suisse, Dominique Fabre, Éditions du Seuil, Paris, 1955

Espagne, Dominique Aubier et Manuel Tuñon de Lara, Éditions du Seuil, Paris, reprint 1962 (original 1956)

Turquie, André Falk, Éditions du Seuil, Paris, 1956

Chine, Armand Gatti, Éditions du Seuil, Paris, reprint 1961 (original 1957)

Iran, Vincent Monteil, Éditions du Seuil, Paris, 1957

Israël, David Catarivas, Éditions du Seuil, Paris, reprint 1960 (original 1957)

Danemark, Jean Bailhache, Éditions du Seuil, Paris, reprint 1965 (original 1957)

Portugal, Franz Villier, Éditions du Seuil, Paris, 1957

Tahiti, Jean-Marie Loursin, Éditions du Seuil, Paris, reprint 1967 (original 1957)

Belgique, Thérèse Henrot, Éditions du Seuil, Paris, 1958

Inde, Madeleine Biardeau, Éditions du Seuil, Paris, 1958

Brésil, Pierre Joffroy, Éditions du Seuil, Paris, 1958

Chris Marker's continuing contribution until 1964:

Sahara, François Vergnaud, photography by Chris Marker, Éditions du Seuil, Paris, reprint 1960 (original 1959)

URSS, Jean Marabini, photography and cover photograph by Chris Marker, Éditions du Seuil, Paris, 1959

Yougoslavie, Jean-Marie Domenach et Alain Pontault, photography and cover photograph by Chris Marker, Éditions du Seuil, Paris, reprint 1968 (original 1960)

Finlande, Georges Desneiges, photography and cover photograph by Chris Marker, Éditions du Seuil, Paris, 1960

Norvège, Sylvain Pivot, photography by Chris Marker, Éditions du Seuil, Paris, 1960

Venezuela, Jean Ulric, photography and cover photograph by Chris Marker, Éditions du Seuil, Paris, reprint 1966 (original 1961)

Maroc, Vincent Monteil, Chris Marker contribution not listed, Éditions du Seuil, Paris, 1962

Égypte, Simonne Lacouture, photography by Chris Marker, Éditions du Seuil, Paris, 1962

Pologne, Éva Fournier, cover photograph by Chris Marker, Éditions du Seuil, Paris, 1963

All courtesy Richard Bevan and Tamsin Clark

Chris Marker
La Jetée Workbook, undated
Exercise book, 27 × 21 cm
Collection Royal Film Archive, Belgium

Chris Marker, *Coréennes*
Éditions du Seuil, Paris, 1959
Collection Raymond Bellour

Raymond Bellour (ed.),
Artsept 1 / 2 / 3
UFOLEIS, Rhône, 1963
Collection Raymond Bellour

Chris Marker and L'Avant-Scène Cinéma,
'La Jetée', *L'Avant-Scène Cinéma*,
June, 1964
Courtesy Chris Darke

Chris Marker, *Commentaires*
Éditions du Seuil, Paris, 1961
Collection Christine Van Assche

Chris Marker, *Commentaires 2*
Éditions du Seuil, Paris, 1967
Collection Christine Van Assche

Chris Marker, *Immemory*
Centre Georges Pompidou, Paris, 1998
Collection Christine Van Assche

Christine Van Assche, Raymond Bellour and Laurent Roth, *Qu'est-ce qu'une madeleine? A propos du CD-ROM Immemory de Chris Marker*
Yves Gevaert Editeur / Centre Pompidou, Brussels / Paris, 1997
Collection Christine Van Assche

Chris Marker, *La Jetée: Ciné-Roman*
Zone Books / MIT Press, New York / Cambridge, MA, 2008, designed by Bruce Mau
Courtesy Chris Darke

Chris Marker
Poptronics, 2007-11
A selection from a series of cartoon-commentaries on current affairs created in Photoshop and featuring Marker's feline avatar Guillaume-en-Égypte (GEE). Many were made for the French website Poptronics between 2007 and 2011 and were also sent out as faxes and emails to Marker's correspondents and friends.

Filename	Date
GEE amoeba	07/10/2007
GEE Barack	05/04/2007
GEE Jesse VE	05/11/2008
GEE limbaugh	09/08/2009
GEE McGoohan	15/01/2009
GEE saddam	30/12/2006
Occupy zencat	12/10/2011
Peppercop GEE eggs	23/11/2011
Peppercop rope	23/11/2011

Courtesy Chris Darke

Filmography

Chris Marker
Born 29 July 1921, Neuilly-sur-Seine, France.
Died 29 July 2012, Paris, France.

Film & Video

La Fin du monde vue par l'ange Gabriel
(The End of the World as seen by the Angel
Gabriel), c.1950
Lost

Olympia 52, 1952
Black and white, 16mm blown up to 35mm,
82 minutes.
Production: Peuple et Culture.

Un fichu métier (A Lousy Job), c.1955
Lost

Dimanche à Pékin (Sunday in Peking), 1956
Colour, 16mm blown up to 35mm, 22 minutes.
Production: Pavox Films / Argos Films.

Lettre de Sibérie (Letter From Siberia), 1957
Colour, 16mm blown up to 35mm, 61 minutes.
Production: Argos Films / Procinex.

Description d'un combat
(Description of a Struggle), 1960
Colour, 35mm, 60 minutes;
Production: Wim van Leer / SOFAC.

Cuba sí!, 1961
Black and white, 16mm blown
up to 35mm, 52 minutes.
Production: Films de la Pléiade.

La Jetée (The Pier), 1962
Black and white, 35mm, 29 minutes.
Production: Argos Films.

Le Mystère Koumiko
(The Koumiko Mystery), 1965
Colour, 16mm blown up to 35mm, 54 minutes.
Production: Sofracima / Apec /
Service de la Recherche de l'ORTF.

Si j'avais quatre dromadaires
(If I Had Four Camels), 1966
Black and white, 35mm, 49 minutes.
Production: Norddeutscher Rundfunk / APEC.

Jour de tournage (Filming Day), 1969
Black and white, 16mm, 11 minutes.
Production: Société pour le Lancement
des Oeuvres Nouvelles (SLON).

On vous parle de Brèsil: Tortures
(Report on Brazil: Torture), 1969
Black and white, 16mm, 20 minutes.
Production: SLON.

On vous parle du Brèsil: Carlos Marighela
(Report on Brazil: Carlos Marighela), 1970
Black and white, 16mm, 17 minutes.
Production: SLON.

*On vous parle de Paris: Les Mots
ont un sens* (Report on Paris:
Words have a Meaning), 1970
Black and white, 16mm, 20 minutes.
Production: SLON.

La Bataille des dix millions
(The Battle of the Ten Million), 1970
Black and white, 16mm, 58 minutes.
Production: KG Production / SLON /
RTB / ICAIC.

*On vous parle de Prague: Le Deuxième
procès d'Artur London* (Report on Prague:
The Second Trial of Artur London), 1971
Black and white, 16mm, 28 minutes.
Production: SLON.

Le Train en marche (The Train Rolls On), 1971
Black and white, 16mm, 32 minutes.
Production: SLON.

L'Ambassade (The Embassy), 1973
Colour, Super 8, 22 minutes.
Production: EKF.

La Solitude du chanteur de fond (The
Loneliness of the Long Distance Singer), 1974
Colour, 16mm blown up to 35mm, 60 minutes.
Production: Le Seuil audiovisuel.
Available at: www.gorgomancy.net

Le Fond de l'air est rouge
(A Grin Without a Cat), 1977
Colour, black and white, 16mm blown up
to 35mm, 240 minutes / 180 minutes.
Production: Iskra / Institut National
de l'Audiovisuel (INA) / Dovidis.

Junkopia, 1981
Colour, 16mm blown up to 35mm, 6 minutes.
Production: Argos Films.

Sans soleil (Sunless), 1982
Colour, 16mm blown up to 36mm, 103 minutes.
Production: Argos Films.

AK, 1985
Colour, 35mm, 71 minutes.
Production: Serge Silberman / Greenwich Films /
Herald Ace Inc. / Herald Nippon Inc.

Mémoires pour Simone,
(Memories for Simone), 1986
Colour, 35mm, 61 minutes.
Production: Festival International
du Film de Cannes.
Available at: www.gorgomancy.net

L'Héritage de la chouette
(The Owl's Legacy), 1989
Television series
Colour, video, 13 episodes × 26 minutes.
Production: Attica Art Productions /
FIT Productions / La Sept.
Available at: www.gorgomancy.net

Berliner ballade, (Berlin Ballad), 1990
Television report
Colour, video, 22 minutes.
Production: Antenne 2 / Les Films du Jeudi.

Bestiaire (Bestiary), 1985-90
Colour, video, total 9:04 minutes
Chat écoutant la musique
2:47 minutes.
An Owl is an Owl is an Owl
3:18 minutes.
Zoo Piece
2:42 minutes.

Getting Away With It, 1990
Music video for the group Electronic
Colour, video, 4:27 minutes.
Production: Michael H. Shamberg.

Le Tombeau d'Alexandre
(The Last Bolshevik), 1993
Colour, black and white, video, 118 minutes.
Production: Les Films de l'Astrophore / Michael
Kustow / La Sept / Epi Dem Oy / Channel 4.

Le 20 heures dans les camps
(Primetime in the Camps), 1993
Colour, video, 27 minutes.
Production: Les Films de l'Astrophore.

Casque bleu (Blue Helmet), 1995
Colour, video, 27 minutes.
Production: Les Films de l'Astrophore.

Level Five, 1996
Colour, video blown up to 35mm, 106 minutes.
Production: Argos Films / Les Films de l'Astrophore.

Une journée d'Andrei Arsenevitch
(One Day in the Life of Andrei Arsenevich), 1999
Colour, video, 55 minutes.
Production: AMIP / La Sept-Arte / INA /
Arkéïon Films.

Un maire au Kosovo (A Mayor in Kosovo), 2000
Colour, video, 28 minutes.

Avril inquiet (Restless April), 2001 [unfinished]
Colour, video, 52 minutes.

Chats perchés (The Case of the Grinning Cat),
2004
Colour, video, 59 minutes.
Production: Les Films du Jeudi / Arte.

Un an de télé vu par Guillaume
(One Year of TV as seen by Guillaume), 2007
Colour, video, 75 minutes.

Stopover in Dubai, 2010
Colour, video, 30 minutes.
Available at: www.gorgomancy.net

Ouvroir. The Movie, 2010
Chris Marker in association with Max Moswitzer
Colour, video, 29 minutes.
Production: Les Films du Jeudi / Arte.
Collection: Centre Pompidou, MNAM, Nouveaux
Médias.

And You Are There, 2011
Music video for the group Damon and Naomi
Colour, video, 4:44 minutes.

Selected Co-Directed Films

Les Statues meurent aussi
(Statues Also Die), with Alain Resnais, 1953
Black and white, 35mm, 30 minutes.
Production: Tadié-Cinéma / Présence Africaine.

Le Joli Mai (The Merry Month of May),
with Pierre Lhomme, 1962
Black and white, 35mm, original version
165 minutes, restored 2013 version 146 minutes.
Production: Sofracima.

Loin du Vietnam (Far from Vietnam),
with William Klein, Joris Ivens, Claude Lelouch,
Agnès Varda, Jean-Luc Godard, 1967
Colour, 35mm and 16mm, 115 minutes.
Production: SLON.

La Sixième face du pentagon
(The Sixth Side of the Pentagon),
with François Reichenbach, 1968
Colour, 16mm, 28 minutes.
Production: Les Films du Jeudi /
Les Films de la Pléiade.

À bientôt, j'espère (Be Seeing You),
with Mario Marret, 1968
Black and white, 16mm, 45 minutes.
Production: SLON.

Classe de lutte (Class Struggle), directed
by Groupe Medvedkine de Besançon, 1969
Black and white, 16mm, 37 minutes.
Production: SLON.

Die Kamera in der Fabrik (The Camera
in the Factory), with Groupe Medvedkine
de Besançon, 1970
Black and white, 16mm, 88 minutes.
Production: SLON.

Vive la baleine (Long Live the Whale),
with Mario Ruspoli, 1972
Colour, 35mm, 17 minutes.
Production: Prodix / Argos Films.

*On vous parle de Chili: Ce que
disait Allende* (Report on Chile:
What Allende Said), with Miguel Littin, 1973
Black and white, 16mm, 16 minutes.
Production: SLON.

*2084: Video clip pour une réflexion
syndicale et pour le plasir* (2084: Video Clip
for the Trade Unions' Reflection and Pleasure),
with Groupe Confédéral Audiovisual CFDT, 1984
Colour, video, 10 minutes.
Production: La Lanterne / Groupe Audiovisuel
de la CFDT.

Le Souvenir d'un avenir (Remembrance
of Things to Come), with Yannick Bellon, 2001
Black and white, 35mm, 42 minutes.
Production: Arte France / Les Films de l'Equinoxe.

Selected Film Collaborations

Nuit et brouillard (Night and Fog),
Alain Resnais, 1955
Colour, black and white, 35mm, 32 minutes.
Production: Argos Films.
Chris Marker: assistant director and collaboration
on commentary.

Toute la mémoire du monde
(All the World's Memory), Alain Resnais, 1956
Black and white, 35mm, 22 minutes.
Production: Films de la Pléiade.
Chris Marker: collaboration on production
and commentary.

Les Hommes de la baleine
(The Men of the Whale), Mario Ruspoli, 1956
Colour, 16mm blown up to 35mm, 26 minutes.
Production: Argos Films / Les Films Armorial.
Chris Marker: commentary (under the name
Jacopo Berenizi).

Le Mystère de l'atelier 15
(The Mystery of Studio 15), André Heinrich
and Alain Resnais, 1957
Black and white, 35mm, 18 minutes.
Production: Les Film Jacqueline Jacoupy.
Chris Marker: commentary.

Les Astronautes (The Astronauts),
Walerian Borowczyk, 1959
Colour, 35mm, 12 minutes.
Production: Argos Films / Les Films Armorial.
Chris Marker: unspecified collaboration.

Django Reinhardt, Paul Paviot, 1959
Black and white, 35mm, 22 minutes.
Production: Pavox Films.
Chris Marker: commentary.

À Valparaiso (Valparaiso), Joris Ivens, 1963
Colour, black and white, 35mm, 29 minutes.
Production: Argos Films / University of Chile.
Chris Marker: commentary.

La Douceur du village (The Village Pleasure),
François Reichenbach, 1964
Black and white, 35mm, 47 minutes.
Production: Les Films de la Pléiade.
Chris Marker: editing.

La Brûlure de mille soleils (The Heat
of a Thousand Suns), Pierre Kast, 1964
Colour, 35mm, 25 minutes.
Production: Argos Films /
Service de la Recherche de l'ORTF.
Chris Marker: editing.

Europort: Rotterdam, Joris Ivens, 1966
Colour, 35mm, 20 minutes.
Production: Argos Films /
Service de la Recherche de l'ORTF.
Chris Marker: French commentary.

El primo año (La Première Année / Year 1),
Patricio Guzmán, 1972
Colour, 35mm, 90 minutes.
French distribution: SLON.
Chris Marker: re-editing, prologue and dubbing.

Puisqu'on vous dit que c'est possible
(We Maintain it is Possible), Collective
Direction, 1973
Colour, 16mm, 43 minutes.
Production: Crepac-Scopcolor.
Chris Marker: organisation and editing.

Kashima Paradise, Yann Le Masson
and Bénie Deswarte, 1974
Black and white, 16mm blown
up to 35mm, 106 minutes.
Production: Coferc.
Chris Marker: collaboration on commentary.

La Spirale (The Spiral), Armand Mattelart,
Jacqueline Meppiel and Valérie Mayoux, 1975
Colour, 35mm, 155 minutes;
Production: Les Films Molière / Reggane Films /
Seuil Audiovisuel.
Chris Marker: coordination and commentary.

Le Labyrinthe d'herbes (The Grass
Labyrinth), Shuji Terayama, 1979
Colour, 35mm, 40 minutes.
Production: Pierre Braunberger.
Chris Marker: French adaptation.

Souvenir, Michael H. Shamberg, 1997
Colour, 35mm, 78 minutes.
Production: Cascando Studios.
Chris Marker: electronic images.

Multimedia
and Installations

*Quand le Siècle a pris formes
(Guerre et Révolution)* [When the Century
Took Shape (War and Revolution)], 1978
Chris Marker in association with François Helt
Music: Hanns Eisler
Limited edtion 1/1
Multi-media Installation: monitor, video,
sound track, colour, 15:39 minutes.
Production and Collection Centre Pompidou,
MNAM, Nouveau Médias.

Dialector, c.1985
Computer programme on discs that allows
for an automatic dialogue with a computer.

*Zapping Zone (Proposals for
an Imaginary Television)*, 1990-94
Mixed media installation : 13 monitors, 13 videos,
7 computers, 7 computer programs, 4 light
boxes with 80 slides, 10 photomontages colour /
black and white, 1 maneki neko.
Limited edition 1/1
Production and Collection the Centre Pompidou,
MNAM, Nouveaux Médias.

Silent Movie, 1995
5 channel video installation,
continuous loop, dimensions variable.
Edition of 3
Commissioned by the Wexner Center
for the Arts, Columbus, OH, US.
Chris Marker Estate
Collection: Peter Blum Gallery, New York.

Immemory, 1997
Interactive multimedia installation: 1 hard drive
34 megabytes, 3 Macintosh computers, 1 painted
cat, colour, sound, French and English language.
Limited edition 1/1
Production by the Centre Pompidou, MNAM,
Nouveaux Médias and Les Films de l'Astrophore.
Collection Centre Pompidou, MNAM, Nouveaux
Médias.

Immemory, 1997
CD-ROM
Production and publishing: Centre Georges
Pompidou, MNAM, Nouveaux Médias; Films
de l'Astrophore. English language editions
published in 2002 and 2009 by Exact
Change, Cambridge, MA, US.

Roseware, 1999 (with Laurence Rassel)
Multimedia installation: Iomega Jaz Disk, 2 PC Apple
G3 AV Power Mac, 1 PC Apple 200 MHz Power
Mac, 2 AV monitors, 1 scanner, I video camera,
1 Jaz player, 1 slide projector and screen, tables,
chairs, drawing material.
Commissioned for the Tapiès Foundation,
Barcelona, Spain, 11-24 January 1999.
Production: Constant, Brussels in association
with the Atelier des Jeunes Cinéastes.

*Owls at Noon Prelude:
The Hollow Men*, 2005
CD-ROM video for 8 screens,
19 minute loop, dimensions variable.
Edition of 6
Commissioned by Museum of Modern Art,
New York, NY, US.
Chris Marker Estate
Collection: Peter Blum Gallery, New York.

Online Projects

Poptronics, 2007-10
Website Poptronics: www.poptronics.fr/Sans-
ChrisMarker?var_recherche=chris%20marker
In the guise of his feline avatar Guillaume-en-Égypte,
Marker regularly created a large number of
Photoshop cartoon-collages about current affairs
for the French design and digital culture website.

Kosinski's Channel, 2007-11
YouTube, colour, sound. www.youtube.com/user/
Kosinki/videos
Under the pseudonym Kosinski, Marker posted
several short videos and slideshows, generally
commenting on current affairs.
Leila Attacks (2007, 1 minute), *Guillaume
Movie* (2008, 3 minutes), *Pictures at an
Exhibition* (2008, 8:57 minutes), *Metrotopia*
(2008, 4 minutes), *The Morning After*
(2008, 6 minutes), *Tempo Risoluto* (2011,
6 minutes), *Royal Polka* (2011, 1:23 minutes),
Overnight (2011, 2:42 minutes), *Imagine* (2011,
31 seconds), *Kino* (2011, 1:45 minutes), *iDead*
(2011, 2:27 minutes).

Ouvroir, 2008-12
Second Life, colour, sound. http://secondlife.com/
destination/ouvroir-chris-marker
A virtual archipelago created by Marker in Second
Life in collaboration with Max Moswitzer on the
occasion of the exhibition *Chris Marker: Farewell
to Movies*, Museum of Design, Zurich, Switzerland,
12 March - 29 June 2008.

Gorgomancy, 2007-13
Internet site, colour, sound. www.gorgomancy.net
Production: Centre Georges Pompidou /
Film du Jeudi, with the support of the Centre
Nationale de la Cinématographie, and the Luma
and Liedts-Meesen Foundations.
Following Marker's instructions the site continues
to be developed. It currently includes: *La Solitude
du chanteur du fond* (1974), *Mémoires pour
Simone* (1986), *l'Héritage de la chouette* (1989),
Immemory (1997), *Ouvroir. The Movie* (2010),
Stopover in Dubai (2010), plus a selection from
Marker's collages for Poptronics and works by other
artists chosen by Marker.

Bibliography

Books by Chris Marker

Le Coeur net, Éditions du Seuil, Paris, 1949; published as *The Forthright Spirit*, trans. Robert Kee and Terence Kilmartin, Allan Wingate, London, 1951. Novel.

L'homme et sa Liberté: Jeu pour la veillée utilisant des textes recueillis par Chris Marker, Éditions du Seuil, Paris, 1949. Montage text.

Regards sur le mouvement ouvrier, Éditions du Seuil, Paris, 1951. Montage text.

Giraudoux par lui-même, Éditions du Seuil, Paris, 1952. Critical essay.

La Strada: Un film de Federico Fellini, Éditions du Seuil, Paris, 1955, with Juliette Caputo and François-Régis Bastide.

Coréennes, Éditions du Seuil, Paris, 1959. Text and photography travelogue.

Commentaires I, Éditions du Seuil, Paris, 1961. Collected commentaries and images from Marker's films: *Les Statues meurent aussi; Dimanche à Pékin; Lettre de Sibérie; L'Amerique rêve; Description d'un combat; Cuba si!*.

Commentaires II, Éditions du Seuil, Paris, 1967. Collected commentaries and images from Marker's films: *Le Mystère Koumiko; Soy Mexico; Si j'avais quatre dromadaires*.

Le Fond de l'air est rouge. Scènes de la troisième guerre mondiale 1967–1977. Textes et description d'un film de Chris Marker, Éditions François Maspero and ISKRA, Paris, 1978.

Le Dépays, Éditions Herscher, Paris, 1982. Text and photography travelogue.

Immemory, coproduction Centre Pompidou, Les Films de l'Astrophore, Paris, 1998.

Staring Back, Wexner Center for the Arts, Ohio, OH, 2007.

La Jetée Ciné-roman, 2nd edition, Zone Books, New York, NY, 2008.

Immemory: a cd-rom by Chris Marker, 2nd edition, Exact Change, Cambridge, MA, 2008.

Passengers, Peter Blum Gallery, New York, NY, 2011.

Selected articles and essays by Chris Marker

'Pensée et mouvement. Manifeste des *Cahiers de la Table ronde*', *La Revue française. Cahiers de la Table ronde*, no.1, July-August 1941, under the pseudonym Marc Dornier.

'Parabole de Jerry', *La Revue française. Cahiers de la Table ronde*, no.1, July-August 1941, under the pseudonym Marc Dornier.

'Notes sur la création', *La Revue française. Cahiers de la Table ronde*, no.2, November-December 1941, under the pseudonym Marc Dornier.

'Les vivants et les morts', *Esprit*, no.122, May 1946, under the pseudonym Chris Mayor. Short Story.

Chant de l'endormition, *Mercure de France*, no.1007, July 1947. Poem.

'Till the End of Time', *Esprit*, no.129, January 1947. Short story dated 'October 1945'.

'À propos de paradis terrestre', *Esprit*, no.129, January 1947.

'En attendant la société sans classes?' *Esprit*, no.130, February 1947.

'La mort de *Scarface*, ou les infortunes de la vertu', *Esprit*, no.131, March 1947.

'Actualités imaginaires', *Esprit*, no.132, April 1947.

'L'apolitique du mois', *Esprit*, no.133, May 1947.

'Newsreel', *Esprit*, no.134, June 1947.

Romancero de la montagne, *Esprit*, no.135, July 1947. Poem.

'Grognements indistincts', *Esprit*, no.138, October 1947.

'*Les Enfants Terribles*', *Esprit*, no.142, February 1948.

'La Civilization du digeste: Sauvages blancs seulement confondre', *Esprit*, no.146, July 1948.

'Du Jazz considéré comme une prophétie', *Esprit*, no.146, July 1948.

'La Dame à la Licorne', *Mercure de France*, no.1024, December 1948.

'L'Aube noir', *DOC*, no.49, 1949.

'Les Cents chefs-d'oeuvres du cinéma', *Esprit*, no.156, June 1949.

Les Séparés, *Esprit*, no.162, December 1949. Poem.

'Orphée', *Esprit*, no.173, November 1950.

'Croix de bois et chemin de fer', *Esprit*, no.175, January 1951.

'L'Esthétique du dessin animé', *Esprit*, no.182, September 1951.

'Gérald McBoing-Boing', *Esprit*, no.185, December 1951.

'Le Chat est aussi une personne', *Esprit*, no.186, January 1952.

'Une forme d'ornement (sur *Prince Bayaya* de Jiří Trnka)', *Cahiers du cinéma*, no.8, January 1952, under the pseudonym Christian Marker.

'*La Passion de Jeanne d'Arc*', *Esprit*, no.190, May 1952.

'La Pathétique et réelle aventure du manuscript genial…' *27, rue Jacob*, Éditions du Seuil, no.1, spring 1952, no.2, summer 1952 and no.3, autumn 1952. Strip cartoon.

'Carte veritable des tems que nous voyons', *27, rue Jacob*, Éditions du Seuil, no.4, winter 1952-53. Cartoon.

'Lettre de Mexico', *Cahiers du cinéma*, no.22, April 1953.

'Lettre de Hollywood', *Cahiers du cinéma*, no.25, July 1953.

'L'avant-garde française: *Entr'acte, Un Chien andalou, Le Sang d'un poète*'; 'Le film d'un auteur: *La Passion de Jeanne d'Arc*'; 'Cinéma, Art du XXIe siècle?'. Jacques Chevalier (ed), *Regards neufs sur le cinéma*, Éditions du Seuil, Paris, 1953.

'This Is Cinerama'; 'Hollywood: sur place'; 'Cinéma d'animation: UPA'. André Bazin et al (ed), *Cinéma 53 à travers le monde*, Éditions du Cerf, Paris, 1953.

'Adieu au cinéma allemand?' *Positif*, no.12, November-December 1954.

'*On the Waterfront*', *Esprit*, no.224, March 1955.

'Clair de Chine, en guise de carte de voeux, un film de C. Marker', *Esprit*, no.234, January 1956. Insert booklet of text and photography.

'Réponse à une enquete', *Image et Son*, no.150-151, April-May 1962.

'Les Révoltés de la Rhodia', *Le Nouvel Observateur*, no.123, 22-29 March 1967.

'Cinéma cubain: Che Guevara à 24 images / seconde', *Cinémonde*, no.1832, 21 April 1970.

'William Klein', *Graphis*, no.33, May-June 1978.

'Ran', *Avant-scène cinéma*, no.403-404, June-July 1991.

'Le Tombeau d'Alexandre', *Images documentaires*, no.15, 1993.

'*A free replay* (notes sur *Vertigo*)', *Positif*, no. 400, June 1994. English translation in John Boorman and Walter Donohue (eds), *Projections 4½*, Faber, London, 1995.

'Loin du Vietnam', *Télérama*, no. 2486, September 1997.

Untitled introductory text to the retrospective film programme *Marker mémoire*, Cinémathèque Française, Paris, January-February 1998.

'*Immemory*'. Text in CD-ROM booklet, Centre Georges Pompidou, Films de l'Astrophore, Paris, 1998.

'Filmic Memories', *Film Quarterly*, vol. 52, no. 1, autumn 1998.

'Phénomène (n.m)', *Trafic*, no. 30, summer 1999. English translation in the *Los Angeles Times Book Review*, 29 April 2001. Short story.

'La question: Autour de la musique gravitent des images, quelle est celle qui vous a le plus marqué?' *Les Allumés du jazz*, no. 5, 2001.

'Chris Marker et M. Chat mettent leur patte sur Libé', *Libération*, 4-5 December 2004.

'The Revenge of the Eye: A portfolio for *Artforum*', *Artforum*, vol. 44, no. 10, summer 2006.

'Sixties', booklet for DVD *Le Fond de l'air est rouge*, Arte, ISKRA, INA, Paris, 2008.

'The Last Bolshevik: Reminiscences of A. Ivanovich', *Cineaste*, vol. 33, no. 4, September-November 2008.

'Ben Laden était le héros de ma jeunesse et je ne le savais pas', *Arrets sur image*, 9 May 2011, www.arretsurimages.net/contenu.php?id=3998.

Selected articles and publications about Chris Marker

Francis Gendron, 'Le Socialisme dans la rue', interview with Chris Marker, *Miroir du cinéma*, no. 2, May 1962.

Jean-Louis Pays, 'Chris Marker et Armand Gatti: Des Humanistes Agisssants', *Miroir du cinéma*, no. 2, May 1962.

'Spécial Chris Marker', *Image et Son*, no. 161-162, April-May 1963.

Jean Perret (ed), 'Chris Marker: film, photographie, voyage, écrit et aime les chats', retrospective brochure for *20 ans de cinema offensif, 20 ans de fictions documentairées / de documentaires fictionés*, Geneva, 1982.

O Bestàrio de Chris Marker, Collecção Horizonte de Cinema, no. 14, 1986, Livros Horizonte-Festival Internacional de Cinema de Tróia, Lisbon, 1986.

Raymond Bellour, Catherine David and Christine Van Assche (eds), *Passages de l'image*, exhibition catalogue, Musée nationale d'art moderne, Centre Georges Pompidou, Paris, 1990.

Bill Horrigan (ed) *Chris Marker: Silent Movie*, exhibition catalogue, Wexner Center for the Arts, Ohio, OH, 1995.

Video Spaces: Eight installations, exhibition catalogue, Museum of Modern Art, New York, NY, 1995.

Bernard Eisenschitz (ed) *Chris Marker*, catalogue for the 32nd Pesaro Film Festival, Dino Audino Editore, Rome, 1996.

Birgit Kämper and Thomas Tode, (eds), *Chris Marker filmessayist*, Institut Français de Munich, CICIM, Munich, 1997.

'Dossier Marker', *Positif*, no. 433, March 1997.

Raymond Bellour and Laurent Roth, *Chris Marker – A Propos du CD-ROM Immemory, Qu'est-ce qu'une madeleine?*, Éditions Yves Gevaert / Centre Georges Pompidou, Brussels and Paris, 1998.

Daniel Potter (ed) *Chris Marker: Notes from the era of Imperfect Memory* (website about Marker), www.chrismarker.org.

Guy Gauthier, *Chris Marker, écrivain multimedia ou Voyage à travers les médias*, L'Harmattan, Paris, 2001.

Philippe Dubois (ed) 'Recherches sur Chris Marker', *Théorème* no. 6, Presses Sorbonne Nouvelle, Paris, 2002.

Bamchade Pourvali, *Chris Marker*, Cahiers du cinéma, Paris, 2003.

'Around the World with Chris Marker', Part I, 'Lost Horizons', *Film Comment*, May-June 2003; Part II, 'Time Regained', *Film Comment*, July-August 2003.

Catherine Lupton, *Chris Marker: Memories of the Future*, Reaktion, London, 2004.

'Dossier on Chris Marker: The Art of Memory', *Film Studies*, no. 6, summer 2005.

Nora M. Alter, *Chris Marker*, University of Illinois Press, Urbana and Chicago, IL, 2006.

Roger Tailleur, 'Markeriana: A Scarcely Critical Description of the Work of Chris Marker', *Rouge*, no. 11, 2007; trans. Adrian Martin with Grant McDonald, first published in *Artsept*, no. 1, January-March 1963, www.rouge.com.au/11/marker.html.

Chris Darke, 'Once More, into the Zone... Chris Marker Looks Back, in Wonder', *Vertigo*, vol. 3, no. 6, summer 2007.

Thierry Cormier and Youri Deschamps (eds), 'Chris Marker, Voyages en [immemoire]', *Éclipses*, no. 40, February 2007.

André Habib and Viva Paci (eds), *Chris Marker et l'imprimerie du regard*, L'Harmattan, Paris, 2008.

Janet Harbord, *La Jetée*, Afterall, London, 2009.

'Chris Marker (I)', *Image [&] Narrative*, vol. 10, no. 3, 2009.

'Chris Marker (II)', *Image [&] Narrative*, vol. 11, no. 1, 2010.

Janet Harbord, 'The Skein of the Archive: Denise Bellon and *Remembrance of Things to Come*', Afterall online, 23 March 2010, http://afterall.org/online/the.skein.of.the.archivedenise.bellon.and.remembrance.of.things.to.come/2#.Ut6KnVtFCP8.

Sarah Cooper, *Chris Marker*, Manchester University Press, Manchester, 2010.

Christophe Chazalon (ed), *Chris Marker.ch – On a Quest from Switzerland* (website about Marker), www.chrismarker.ch/topic/index.html.

David Brancaleone, 'The Interventions of Jean-Luc Godard and Chris Marker into Contemporary Visual Art', *Vertigo*, no. 30, spring 2012.

'The Owl's Legacy: In Memory of Chris Marker (1921-2012)', *Sight and Sound*, vol. 22, no. 10, October 2012.

Patricio Guzmán, 'What I Owe to Chris Marker', *Sight and Sound*, November 2012, www.bfi.org.uk/news/what-i-owe-chris-marker, trans. Mar Diestro-Dópido.

Trevor Stark, 'Cinema in the Hands of the People: Chris Marker, the Medvedkin Group and the Potential of Militant Film', *October*, no. 139, winter 2012.

Marker Dossier, *Trafic*, no. 84, winter 2012.

'Spécial Chris Marker', *Avant-scène cinéma*, no. 606, October 2013.

'Dossier Chris Marker', *Positif*, no. 632, October 2013.

Catherine Ermakoff and Bamchade Pourvali (eds), 'Chris Marker', *Vertigo revue du cinéma*, no. 46, autumn 2013.

Arnaud Lambert, *Also Known as Chris Marker*, Le Point du Jour, Cherbourg, 2013.

Mariam Fortes and Lorena Gómez Mostajo (eds), *Chris Marker Immemoria*, Ambulante Ediciones, Mexico, 2013.

Johanne Villeneuve, *Chris Marker. La Compagnie des images*, Les Presses du Réel, Dijon, 2013.

Exhibitions

Selected Solo Exhibitions

2013
Planète Marker, Centre Pompidou, Paris, France
Chris Marker: Guillaume-en-Égypte, The
MIT List Visual Arts Center / Harvard University,
Cambridge, MA, US

2012
Chris Marker: Films and Photos, Moscow
Photobiennale, Moscow, Russia

2011
Passengers, Peter Blum Gallery Chelsea /
Peter Blum Gallery Soho, New York, NY, US /
Thinking Hands, Beijing, China

2009
Quelle heure est-elle?, Peter Blum Gallery
Chelsea, New York, NY, US
Chris Marker: Par Quatre Chemins,
Beirut Art Center, Beirut, Lebanon

2008
Abschied vom Kino / Farewell to Movies,
Museum fur Gegenwartkunst, Zurich, Switzerland

2007
Owls at Noon Prelude: The Hollow Men,
Institute of Modern Art, Brisbane, Australia
Chris Marker: Staring Back, Wexner Center
for the Arts, Ohio State University, Columbus,
OH, US

2005
The Hollow Men, Prefix Institute of Contemporary
Art, Toronto, Canada
Through the Eyes of Chris Marker, Hong Kong
Arts Centre, Hong Kong, China

2003
Rare Videos by Chris Marker, Anthology Film
Archives, New York, NY, US

1999
Chris Marker and Selected Screenings, curated
by The Pier Trust and presented at Beaconsfield,
London, UK

1997
Immemory One, Centre Georges Pompidou,
Paris, France

1995
Silent Movie, Wexner Center for the Arts,
Ohio State University, Columbus, OH, US
Silent Movie, The Museum of Modern Art,
New York, NY, US

Selected Group Exhibitions

2010
Les Rencontres Arles photographie Festival,
Arles, France

2008
Bergamo Film Meeting, Bergamo, Italy

2007
Documenta XII – Film Programme, Kassel,
Germany
Equal, that is, to the real itself, Marian
Goodman Gallery, New York, NY, US
Anachronism & The Otolith Group, Argos –
Center for Art and Media, Brussels, Belgium
*The Unhomely: Phantom Scenes in Global
Society*, Bienal Internacional de Arte
Contemporáneo de Sevilla, Seville, Spain
American Video Art, Laznia Center
for Contemporary Art, Danzig, Poland
*System Error: War Is A Force That
Gives Us Meaning*, Palazzo delle Papesse –
Centro Arte Contemporanea, Siena, Italy

2006
Video: An Art, A History, 1965–2005,
Miami Art Central, Miami, FL, US
Animal Series, Madison Museum of Contemporary
Art, Madison, WI, US

2005
Concerning War, BAK – Basis vor
Actuele Kunst, Utrecht, The Netherlands
Vidéo, un art, une histoire, 1965–2005,
Caixaforum, Barcelona, Spain

2003
*Attack! Kunst und Krieg in den Zeiten
der Medien*, Kunsthalle Wien, Vienna, Austria
*Future Cinema: The Cinematic Imaginary
After Film*, Zentrum für Kunst und
Medientechnologie, Karlsruhe, Germany

2001
*Revolving Doors: Public Sphere / Private
Domain*, Apexart, New York, NY, US

2000
Berlinale 2000, 50th Berlin International
Film Festival, Berlin, Germany
Left Bank Revisited, Harvard Film Archive,
Cambridge, MA, US

1997
L'Autre, 4th Biennale d'art contemporain
de Lyon, Lyon, France
Documenta X, Museum Fridericianum, Kassel,
Germany
Immemory, Chris Marker with *Dial
H-I-S-T-O-R-Y*, Johann Grimonprez,
Centre Pompidou, Paris, France

1993
Time and Tide, The Tyne International Exhibition
of Contemporary Art, Newcastle, England

1978
Paris-Berlin, Centre Georges Pompidou,
Paris, France

Contributors

Raymond Bellour

Raymond Bellour is a researcher, writer and Emeritus Director of Research at the Centre National de la Recherche Scientifique (CNRS), Paris. One aspect of his work relates to literature, including studies of key Romantic writers: *The Brontes: Ecrits de jeunesse* (1972) and *Alexandre Dumas, Mademoiselle Guillotine* (1990), and of contemporary authors, particularly Henri Michaux, on whom he has published *Henri Michaux* (1965) and *Lire Michaux* (2011), as well as editing the complete works for the 'Pléiade' edition (three volumes, 1998-2004).

Another aspect of Bellour's work relates to cinema, about which he has written extensively, including *Le Western* (1966), *L'Analyse du film* (1979) and *Le Corps du cinéma. Hypnoses, émotions, animalités* (2009). Long interested in the relationship between words and images, he has also explored the passages, or mixing, between various states of images: painting, photography, cinema, video and virtual images. This aspect of his work has seen him organise a number of exhibitions including the landmark *Passages de l'image* (1989) and *States of Images: Instants and Intervals* (2005); *Thierry Kuntzel: Lumières du temps* (2006); and *Thierry Kuntzel-Bill Viola: Deux éternités proches* (2010). He has also written some of the key studies of the field, including *L'Entre-images. Photo, cinéma, vidéo* (1990); (published in English as *Between-the-Images* (2012)), *Jean-Luc Godard: Son + Image* (1992); *L'Entre-images 2. Mots, images* (1999); and *La Querelle des dispositifs. Cinéma – installations, expositions* (2012).

In 1991 he founded the renowned film review *Trafic* with Serge Daney.

Chris Darke

Chris Darke is a writer and film critic. For over 20 years his work has been published internationally in publications including *Sight and Sound, Film Comment, Cahiers du cinéma, Trafic, Frieze, Mute, Vertigo* and *The Independent*. He is the author of three books: *Light Readings: Film Criticism and Screen Arts* (2000), a monograph on Jean-Luc Godard's *Alphaville* (2005) and *Cannes: Inside the World's Premier Film Festival* (with Kieron Corless, 2007). He has contributed numerous essays to catalogues and edited collections, as well as translating essays by Raymond Bellour, Jean-Pierre Oudart, Pascal Bonitzer and Marc Augé, among others.

He has also co-written two feature-length screenplays, and made short arts documentaries for British television; his film about Chris Marker's *La Jetée* was included on French, UK, and US DVD releases of *La Jetée* and *Sans soleil*. He was creative consultant on Grant Gee's *Patience (After Sebald)* (2012), a feature-length film essay about WG Sebald's novel *The Rings of Saturn*.

He is currently writing a study of *La Jetée* for the BFI Film Classics series. He is Senior Lecturer in Film at Roehampton University.

Arnaud Lambert

Arnaud Lambert is a critic and filmmaker. He is the author of a study of Marker's work entitled *Also Known as Chris Marker*, first published in 2008 and re-issued in an updated edition in 2013 on the occasion of the 'Planète Marker' retrospective at Centre Pompidou, Paris. He is currently co-directing a film about Marker with Jean-Marie Barbe for the documentary film series 'Lumière de notre temps'.

Nicola Mazzanti

Nicola Mazzanti's text was written specifically for the first public presentation of the unique *La Jetée* print and workbook in the exhibition *Chris Marker: A Grin Without a Cat*, Whitechapel Gallery, London, 2014. Nicola Mazzanti is Director of the Royal Film Archive, Belgium.

Christine Van Assche

Christine Van Assche is a contemporary art historian, specialising in its audio-visual developments. She curated the video and new media collection at the Centre Pompidou between 1982 and 2013, including works by James Coleman, Valie Export, Esther Ferrer, Jean-Luc Godard, Douglas Gordon, Mona Hatoum, Pierre Huyghe, Isaac Julien, Mike Kelley, Chris Marker, Tony Oursler and Pipilotti Rist.

Among the thematic exhibitions she has curated are: *Passages de l'image* (1990); *Sonic Process* (2000); *Video: An Art, A History* (2005-12: international tour); *A Vision of the World: The Lemaître Collection* (2006); *Vidéo Vintage* (2012-13). She has also curated solo exhibitions dedicated to: Nam June Paik, Tony Oursler, Stan Douglas, Mona Hatoum, Johan Grimonprez, Chris Marker, Bruce Nauman, Zineb Sedira, Ugo Rondinone and David Claerbout.

As well as catalogues for solo exhibitions, edited monographs and group catalogues, her publications include *Vidéo et après* (1992); *L'Encyclopédie Nouveaux Médias* (1998-2012); *La Collection Nouveaux Médias du Centre Pompidou (Installations)* (2006) and *Vidéo Vintage* (2012).

Van Assche has produced more than 30 works by artists including the following by Chris Marker: *Zapping Zone: Proposals for an Imaginary Television* (1990-94); *Immemory* (1997) and *Gorgomancy* (2007-13).

Translations

Christine Van Assche, *Chris Marker, The Time of the World*. Translation by Trista Selous © 2014.

Raymond Bellour, *Marker Forever*, originally published in *Trafic*, no.84, winter 2012. Translation by Trista Selous © 2014.

Arnaud Lambert, *Image (journey)*, originally published in Arnaud Lambert, *Also Known as Chris Marker*, 2nd edition, Le Point du Jour, Cherbourg, 2013. Translated by Trista Selous © 2014.

Chris Marker, *Orphée*, originally published in *Esprit*, no.173, November 1950. Translation by Sophie Lewis © 2014.

Chris Marker, *Till the End of Time*, originally published in *Esprit*, no.129, January 1947. Translation by Sophie Lewis © 2014.

Credits

Acknowledgements

The Whitechapel Gallery would like to thank the following organisations and individuals who have generously supported the exhibition:

The Chris Marker Estate, in particular Mabel Nicolaÿ Duflo; Raymond Bellour; Arnaud Lambert; Bernard Blistène, Brigitte Léal, Olga Makhroff, Sylvie Douala-Bell and Alain Dubillot at Centre Georges Pompidou, Paris, France; Peter Blum, David Blum and Aaron Stempien at Peter Blum Gallery, New York, US; Nicola Mazzanti and Jean-Paul Dorchain at the Royal Film Archive, Belgium; Laurence Braunberger and all at Les Films du Jeudi, Paris, France; Suzanne Diop and all at Présence Africaine Editions, Paris, France; Anne-France Mournet and Florence Dauman and all at Argos Films, Paris, France; Jasmina Sijercic and all at Iskra, Paris France; Claire Winter and all at La Sofra, Paris, France; Marc Karlin Archive; Sebastien Groes and Corin Depper from the Memory Network; Sarah Auld; Richard Bevan; Christophe Chazalon; Tamsin Clark; Luke Hall; Bill Horrigan; Tom Meakins; Alex O'Neil; Charlotte Saluard; Jason Simon; Ingrid Swenson; Candy Stobbs and Jonathan Weston

Transport Partner
Martinspeed

Additional support provided by
Institut Français

The Whitechapel Gallery thanks its supporters, whose generosity enables the Gallery to realise its pioneering programmes.

Whitechapel Gallery Director's Circle
The Ampersand Foundation, Ivor & Sarah Braka, Aud & Paolo Cuniberti, D. Daskalopoulos Collection, Greece, Joseph & Marie Donnelly, Maryam & Edward Eisler, Peter & Maria Kellner, Marian Goodman Gallery, Yana & Stephen Peel, Catherine & Franck Petitgas, SAHA, Istanbul, Muriel & Freddy Salem and those who wish to remain anonymous

Whitechapel Gallery Exhibition Patrons
Erin Bell & Michael Cohen, Ida Levine, The Loveday Family, Adrian & Jennifer O'Carroll, Jonathan Tyler and those who wish to remain anonymous

Whitechapel Gallery Patrons
Malgosia Alterman, Vanessa Arelle, Charlotte & Alan Artus, Hugo Brown, Sadie Coles HQ, Swantje Conrad, Alastair Cookson, Donall Curtin, Miel de Botton, Maria de Madariaga, Dunnett Craven Ltd, Jeff & Jennifer Eldredge, Alan & Joanna Gemes, Isabelle Hotimsky, Amrita Jhaveri, Sigrid Kirk, Anna Lapshina, Victor & Anne Lewis, Scott Mead, Jon & Amanda Moore, Bozena Nelhams, Maureen Paley, Dominic Palfreyman, The Porter Foundation, Jasmin Pelham, Mariela Pissioti, The Porter Foundation, Lauren Prakke, Alice Rawsthorn, Jon Ridgway, Alex Sainsbury & Elinor Jansz, Kaveh & Cora Sheibani, Bina & Philippe von Stauffenberg, Hugh & Catherine Stevenson, Tom Symes, Helen Thorpe (The Helen Randag Charitable Foundation), Christoph & Marion Trestler, Emily Tsingou & Henry Bond, Ursula & Ray van Almsick, Audrey Wallrock, Kevin Walters, Susan Whiteley, Roberta S Wolens, Anita & Poju Zabludowicz and those who wish to remain anonymous

The American Friends of the Whitechapel Gallery
Dick and Betsy DeVos Family Foundation, Ambassador and Mrs Louis B Susman and those who wish to remain anonymous

Whitechapel Gallery First Futures
Jam Acuzar, Sharifa Alsudairi, Abdullah Al Turki, Katharine Arnold, Maria Arones, John Auerbach, Edouard Benveniste-Schuler, Fiorina Benveniste-Schuler, Natalia Blaskovicova, Bianca Chu, Nathaniel Clark, Tom Cole, Jonathan Crockett, Celia Davidson, Stéphanie de Preux Dominicé, Alessandro Diotallevi, Michelle D'Souza, Christopher Fields and Brendan Olley, Geraldine Guyot, Asli Hatipoglu, Constantin Hemmerle, Carolyn Hodler, Katherine Holmgren, Zoe Karafylakis Sperling, Deborah Kattan, Tamila Kerimova, Benjamin Khalili, Rasha Khawaja, Frank Krikhaar, Aliki Lampropoulos, Alexandra Lefort, Arianne Levene Piper, Georgina Lewis, Alex Logsdail, Julia Magee, Nina Mahdavi, Kristina McLean, Paul Miliotis, Janna Miller, Gloria Monfrini, Indi Oliver, Yuki Oshima Wilpon, Katharina Ottmann, Juan Pepa, Josephine von Perfall, Alexander V. Petalas, Hannah Philp, Patricia Pratas, Maria Cruz Rashidan, Louisa Robertson, Daniela Sanchez, Eugenio Sandretto Re Rebaudengo, Paola Saracino Fendi, Marie-Anya Shriro, Max Silver, Yassi Sohrabi, Alexander Stamatiadis, Roxana Sursock Karam, Gerald Tan, Edward Tang, Julia Tarasyuk Nayrouz Tatanaki, Giacomo Vigliar, Rosanna Widen, Andrea Wild Botero and those who wish to remain anonymous

Whitechapel Gallery Associates
Ariane Braillard & Francesco Cincotta, Beverley Buckingham, Salima Chebbah, Christian Erlandson & Reagan Kiser, Lyn Fuss, David Killick, Laetitia Lina, John Newbigin, Noble Savage Property, Chandrakant Patel, Fozia Rizvi, Fabio Rossi & Elaine W. Ng, David Ryder Cherrill & Ian Scheer, Karsten Schubert, Henrietta Shields and all those who wish to remain anonymous

We remain grateful for the ongoing support of Whitechapel Gallery Members and Arts Council England.

Published in 2014 by Whitechapel Gallery
on the occasion of the exhibition:

Chris Marker: A Grin Without a Cat

16 April – 22 June 2014
Whitechapel Gallery
77-82 Whitechapel High Street
London E1 7QX
United Kingdom
whitechapelgallery.org

6 February – 29 March 2015
Lunds Konsthall
Mårtenstorget 3
223 51 Lund
Sweden
www.lundskonsthall.se

Organised by the Whitechapel Gallery, London
Co-curators: Christine Van Assche,
Chris Darke and Magnus af Petersens
Assistant Curator: Habda Rashid
Scenography and Production: Christopher Aldgate
Installation: Patrick Lears and Nathaniel Cary
AV Coordination: Richard Johnson,
Thomas Ogden and Stuart Bannister
Screening Programme Curators: Gareth Evans
and Chris Darke

Publication

Edited by Chris Darke and Habda Rashid
In consultation with Christine Van Assche
and Magnus af Petersens
Copy editing by Eileen Daly
Designed by Fraser Muggeridge studio

Published by Whitechapel Gallery, London
First published 2014
© the authors, the artists, the photographers,
the translators, Whitechapel Gallery
Ventures Limited

Whitechapel Gallery is the imprint
of Whitechapel Gallery Ventures Limited

 Whitechapel Gallery

A catalogue record of this book
is available from the British Library

ISBN: 978-0-85488-228-1

To order (UK and Europe)
call +44 (0)202 7522 7888 or
mailorder@whitechapelgallery.org

Distributed to the book trade
(UK & Europe) by Central Books
www.centralbooks.com

Represented in Europe
by Durnell Marketing
orders@durnell.co.uk

Distributed to the book trade
(US & worldwide) by D.A.P.
Distributed Art Publishers
www.artbook.com

Front cover:
Digitally manipulated image taken
from *La Jetée*, 1962

The cover image was a gift from the digital
gods. Or better still, a technological malfunction
which yielded up a found object. We discovered
that when we attempted to 'solarize' a specific
image extracted from Chris Marker's *La Jetée*
(1962), it contained all manner of residual
glitches. Happily so, as it turned out. For,
with some judicious tweaking of the 'hue'
and 'saturation' levels in the colour settings,
a magically inevitable image was delivered.
We leave its interpretation to the reader. As for
how it was arrived at, we cite the words of Jean
Cocteau (themselves quoted in Marker's film
Si j'avais quatre dromadaires (If I Had Four
Camels, 1966)) – 'Since these mysteries are
beyond us, let us pretend to have devised them'.
Chris Darke & Fraser Muggeridge

Opposite contents page:
Guilluaume-en-Égypte taken
from *Immemory*, 1997

Back cover:
Le Joli Mai (detail), 1962